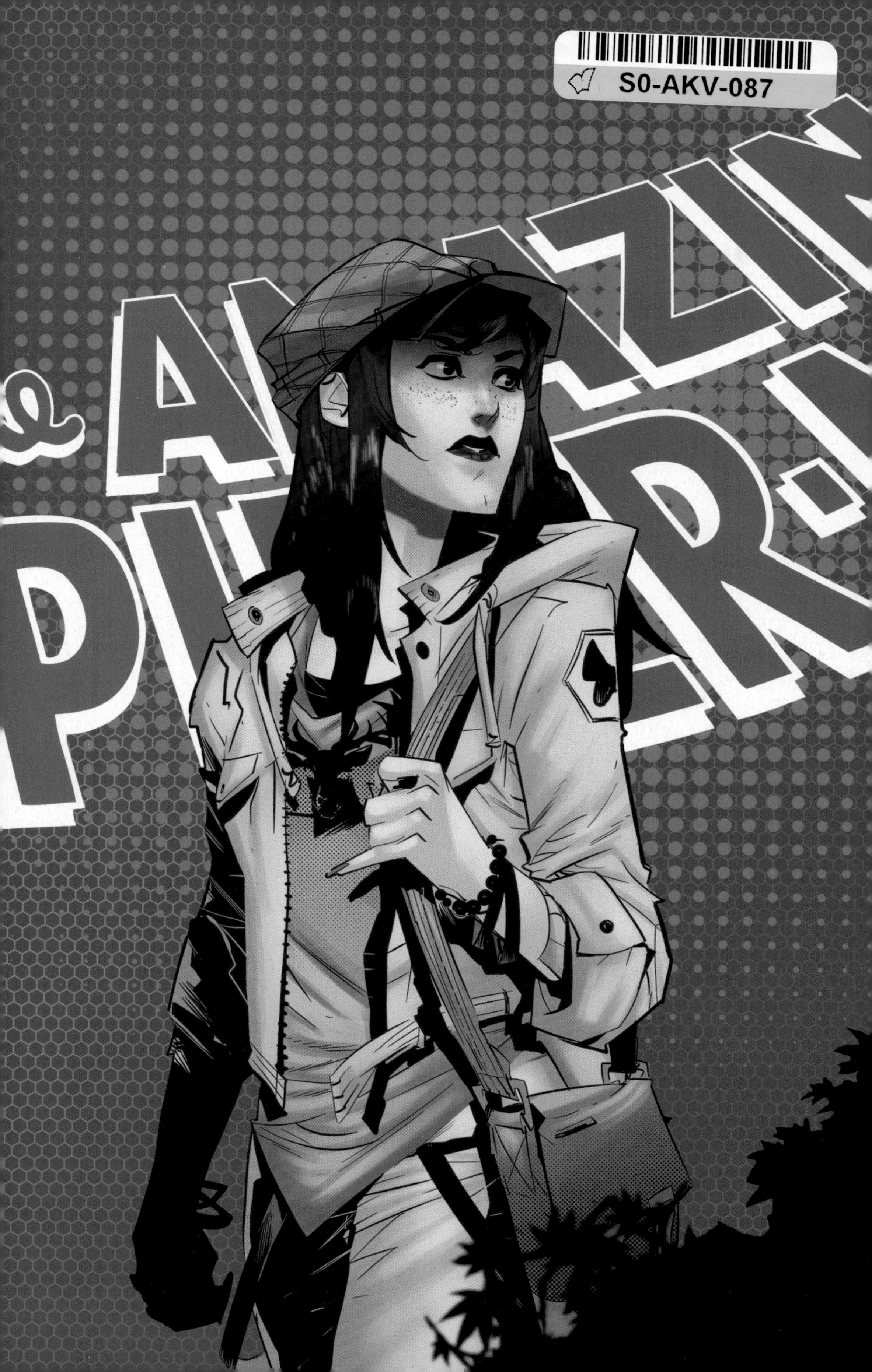

Grad school was always a challenge for Peter, but it pales in comparison with the mysterious and powerful villain named Kindred who could have easily killed Spider-Man. Kindred exhumed the bodies of everyone Spider-Man lost to teach Peter a lesson, and it was only through an extraordinary intervention by Norman Osborn that Peter and his girlfriend Mary Jane were saved. Why did Norman help? He had just figured out that Kindred was actually his son Harry and hoped to save Harry from himself. NYPD CSI Carlie Cooper examined the exhumed bodies and made a startling discovery. Before she could alert Spider-Man, she was kidnapped by Kindred and thrown into a prison cell with none other than...Harry Osborn?!

Meanwhile, many of Spider-Man's other foes have been gathering in the wings...which never bodes well for Spider-Man. Sure would be nice to just be a normal grad student...

SPIDER-MAN CREATED BY STAN LEE & STEVE DITKO

COLLECTION EDITOR JENNIFER GRÜNWALD
ASSISTANT EDITOR DANIEL KIRCHHOFFER ❖ ASSISTANT MANAGING EDITOR MAIA LOY
ASSISTANT MANAGING EDITOR LISA MONTALBANO ❖ VP PRODUCTION & SPECIAL PROJECTS JEFF YOUNGQUIST
BOOK DESIGNER ADAM DEL RE
SVP PRINT, SALES & MARKETING DAVID GABRIEL ❖ EDITOR IN CHIEF C.B. CEBULSKI

AMAZING SPIDER-MAN BY NICK SPENCER VOL. 15: WHAT COST VICTORY? Contains material originally published in magazine form as AMAZING SPIDER-MAN (2018) #70-74. First printing 2021. ISBN 978-1-302-92608-3. Published by MARVEL WORLDWIDE, INC., a subsidiary of MARVEL ENTERTAINMENT, LLC. OFFICE OF PUBLICATION: 1290 Avenue of the Americas, New York, NY 10104. © 2021 MARVEL. No similarity between any of the names, characters, persons, and/or institutions in this magazine with those of any living or dead person or institution is intended, and any such similarity which may exist is purely coincidental. Printed in Canada. KEVIN FEIGE, Chief Creative Officer; DAN BUCKLEY, President, Marvel Entertainment; JOE QUESADA, EVP & Creative Director; DAVID BOGART, Associate Publisher & SVP of Talent Affairs; TOM BREVOORT, VP, Executive Editor; NICK LOWE, Executive Editor, VP of Content, Digital Publishing; DAVID GABRIEL, VP of Print & Digital Publishing; JEFF YOUNGQUIST, VP of Production & Special Projects; ALEX MORALES, Director of Publishing Operations; DAN EDINGTON, Managing Editor; RICKEY PURDIN, Director of Talent Relations; JENNIFER GRÜNWALD, Senior Editor, Special Projects; SUSAN CRESPI, Production Manager; STAN LEE, Chairman Emeritus. For information regarding advertising in Marvel Comics or on Marvel.com, please contact Vit DeBellis, Custom Solutions & Integrated Advertising Manager, at vdebellis@marvel.com. For Marvel subscription inquiries, please call 888-511-5480. Manufactured between 9/3/2021 and 10/5/2021 by SOLISCO PRINTERS, SCOTT, QC, CANADA.

10 9 8 7 6 5 4 3 2 1

the AMAZING SPIDER-MAN

WHAT COST VICTORY?

WRITERS   **NICK SPENCER** WITH **CHRISTOS GAGE** (#74)

AMAZING SPIDER-MAN #70-73

ARTISTS   **FEDERICO VICENTINI** (#70-71),
FEDERICO SABBATINI (#71-72), **ZÉ CARLOS** (#72-73),
MARCELO FERREIRA (#72-73) & **CARLOS GÓMEZ** (#72-73)

COLOR ARTIST   **ALEX SINCLAIR**

COVER ART   **MARK BAGLEY, JOHN DELL** & **BRIAN REBER**

AMAZING SPIDER-MAN #74

PENCILERS   **MARCELO FERREIRA, MARK BAGLEY,**
ZÉ CARLOS, DIO NEVES, CARLOS GÓMEZ,
IVAN FIORELLI & **HUMBERTO RAMOS**

INKERS   **WAYNE FAUCHER, MARCELO FERREIRA,**
ANDREW HENNESSY, ANDY OWENS, ZÉ CARLOS,
DIO NEVES, CARLOS GÓMEZ, IVAN FIORELLI
& **VICTOR OLAZABA**

COLOR ARTISTS   **ANDREW CROSSLEY, EDGAR DELGADO**
& **ALEX SINCLAIR**

SPEC #200 PAGE   **J.M. DeMATTEIS, SAL BUSCEMA** & **BOB SHAREN**

COVER ART   **PATRICK GLEASON** & **ALEJANDRO SÁNCHEZ**

LETTERER   **VC's JOE CARAMAGNA**

ASSISTANT EDITORS   **LINDSEY COHICK** WITH **TOM GRONEMAN**
EDITOR   **NICK LOWE**

#70 VARIANT BY
ROGÊ ANTÔNIO & ALEX SINCLAIR

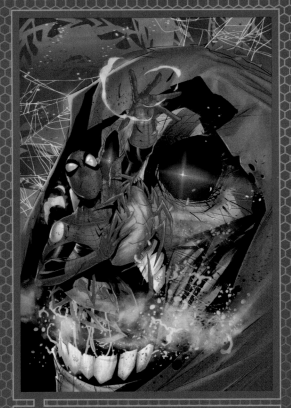

#71 VARIANT BY
FEDERICO VICENTINI & ALEX SINCLAIR

#72 VARIANT BY
CARLOS GÓMEZ & MORRY HOLLOWELL

#73 VARIANT BY
FEDERICO VICENTINI & ALEX SINCLAIR

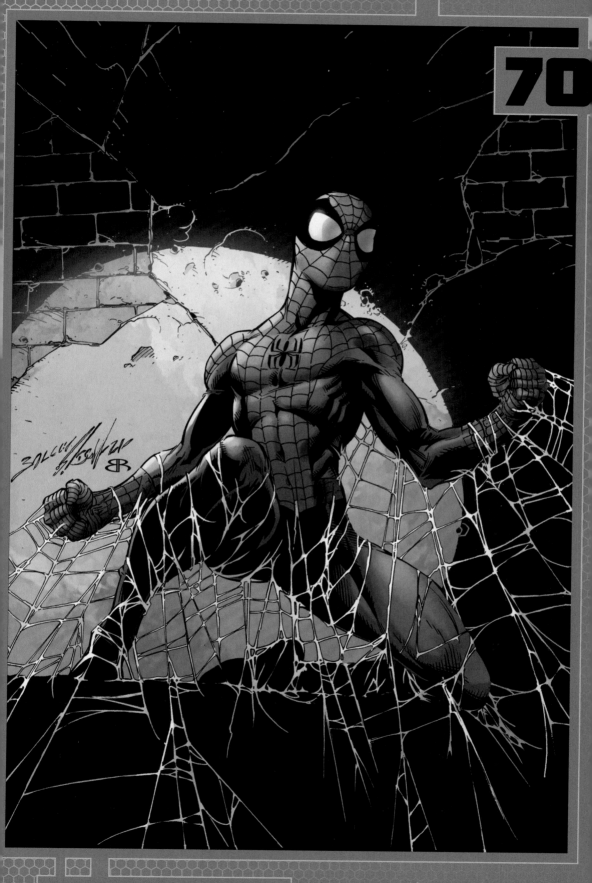

PRELUDE TO SINISTER WAR

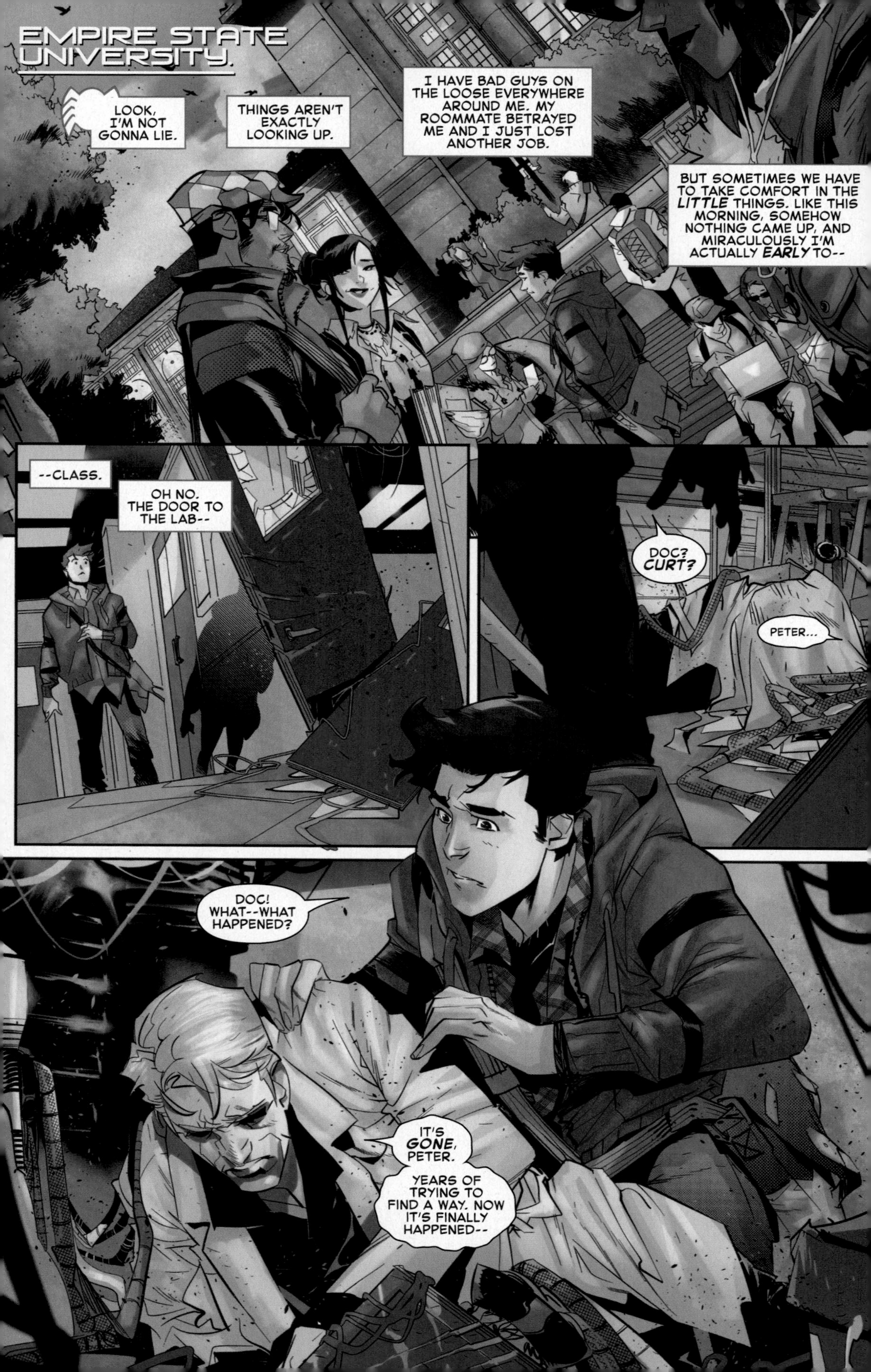
EMPIRE STATE UNIVERSITY.
LOOK, I'M NOT GONNA LIE.
THINGS AREN'T EXACTLY LOOKING UP.
I HAVE BAD GUYS ON THE LOOSE EVERYWHERE AROUND ME. MY ROOMMATE BETRAYED ME AND I JUST LOST ANOTHER JOB.
BUT SOMETIMES WE HAVE TO TAKE COMFORT IN THE LITTLE THINGS. LIKE THIS MORNING, SOMEHOW NOTHING CAME UP, AND MIRACULOUSLY I'M ACTUALLY EARLY TO--
--CLASS.
OH NO. THE DOOR TO THE LAB--
DOC? CURT?
PETER...
DOC! WHAT--WHAT HAPPENED?
IT'S GONE, PETER.
YEARS OF TRYING TO FIND A WAY. NOW IT'S FINALLY HAPPENED--

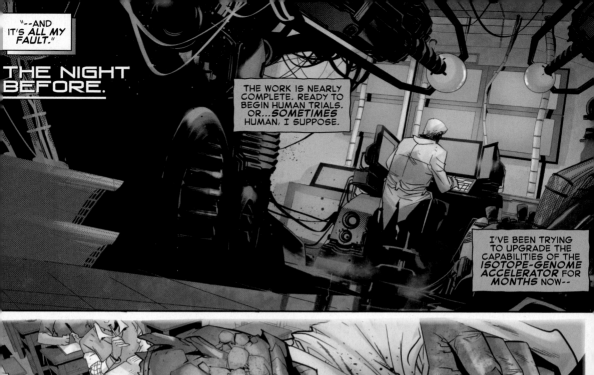

"--AND IT'S ALL MY FAULT."

THE NIGHT BEFORE.

THE WORK IS NEARLY COMPLETE. READY TO BEGIN HUMAN TRIALS. OR...*SOMETIMES* HUMAN, I SUPPOSE.

I'VE BEEN TRYING TO UPGRADE THE CAPABILITIES OF THE *ISOTOPE-GENOME ACCELERATOR* FOR *MONTHS* NOW--

--EVER SINCE I FIRST RETURNED TO *EMPIRE STATE UNIVERSITY.*

THE ACCELERATOR HOLDS ENORMOUS PROMISE AS A MEANS TO ISOLATE AND SEPARATE, FROM A HOST, UNWANTED...*ILLNESSES* OF ALL TYPES. BUT SO FAR, ITS RESULTS HAVE BEEN MIXED.

AT LEAST SO FAR AS I CAN TELL.

BUT RECENT BREAKTHROUGHS LEAVE ME ON THE CUSP OF SOMETHING GREAT.

SOMETHING THAT CAN *CHANGE* LIVES.

OF COURSE, I HAVE *OBLIGATIONS* HERE. TO THE UNIVERSITY, TO THE SCIENTIFIC COMMUNITY. BUT I CAN'T HELP THINKING ABOUT WHAT THIS WILL MEAN FOR MY FAMILY.

AND FOR *ME.*

CURT CONNORS. IF YOU NEVER HAD MY FRIENDSHIP...

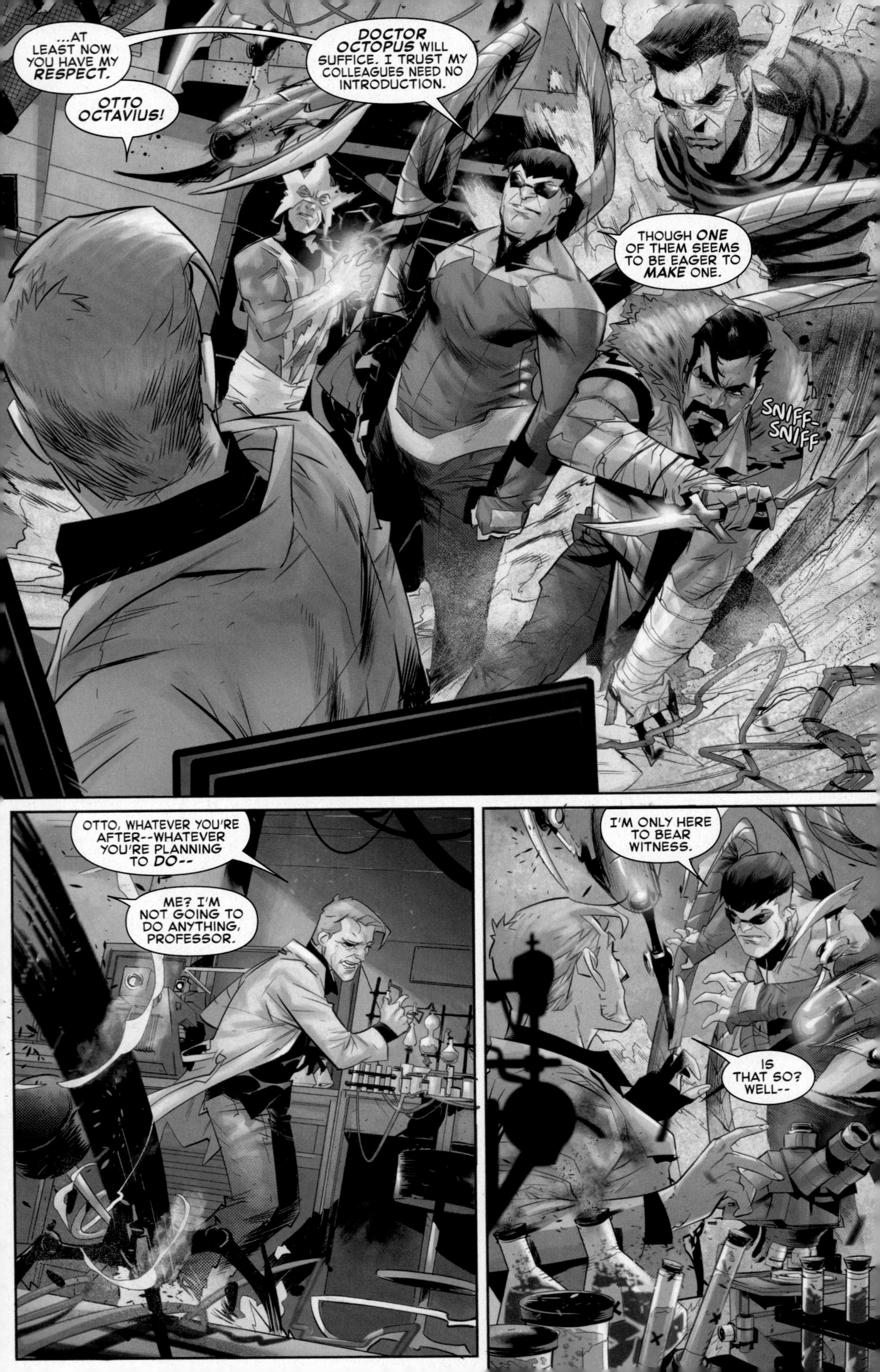

OTTO OCTAVIUS!
DOCTOR OCTOPUS WILL SUFFICE. I TRUST MY COLLEAGUES NEED NO INTRODUCTION.
...AT LEAST NOW YOU HAVE MY RESPECT.
THOUGH ONE OF THEM SEEMS TO BE EAGER TO MAKE ONE.
SNIFF-SNIFF
OTTO, WHATEVER YOU'RE AFTER--WHATEVER YOU'RE PLANNING TO DO--
ME? I'M NOT GOING TO DO ANYTHING, PROFESSOR.
I'M ONLY HERE TO BEAR WITNESS.
IS THAT SO? WELL--

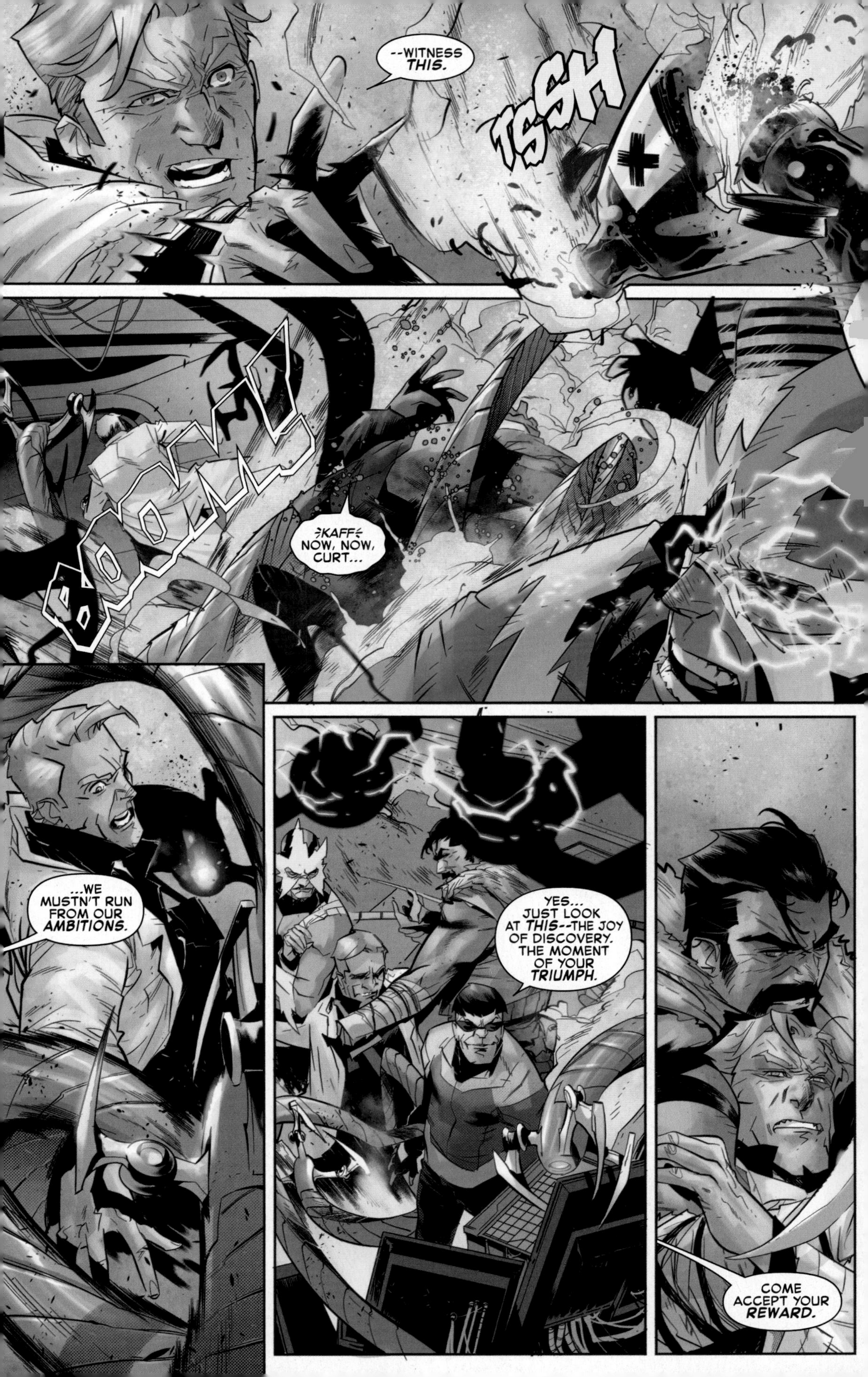
--WITNESS THIS.
TSSH
=KAFF= NOW, NOW, CURT...
...WE MUSTN'T RUN FROM OUR AMBITIONS.
YES... JUST LOOK AT THIS--THE JOY OF DISCOVERY. THE MOMENT OF YOUR TRIUMPH.
COME ACCEPT YOUR REWARD.

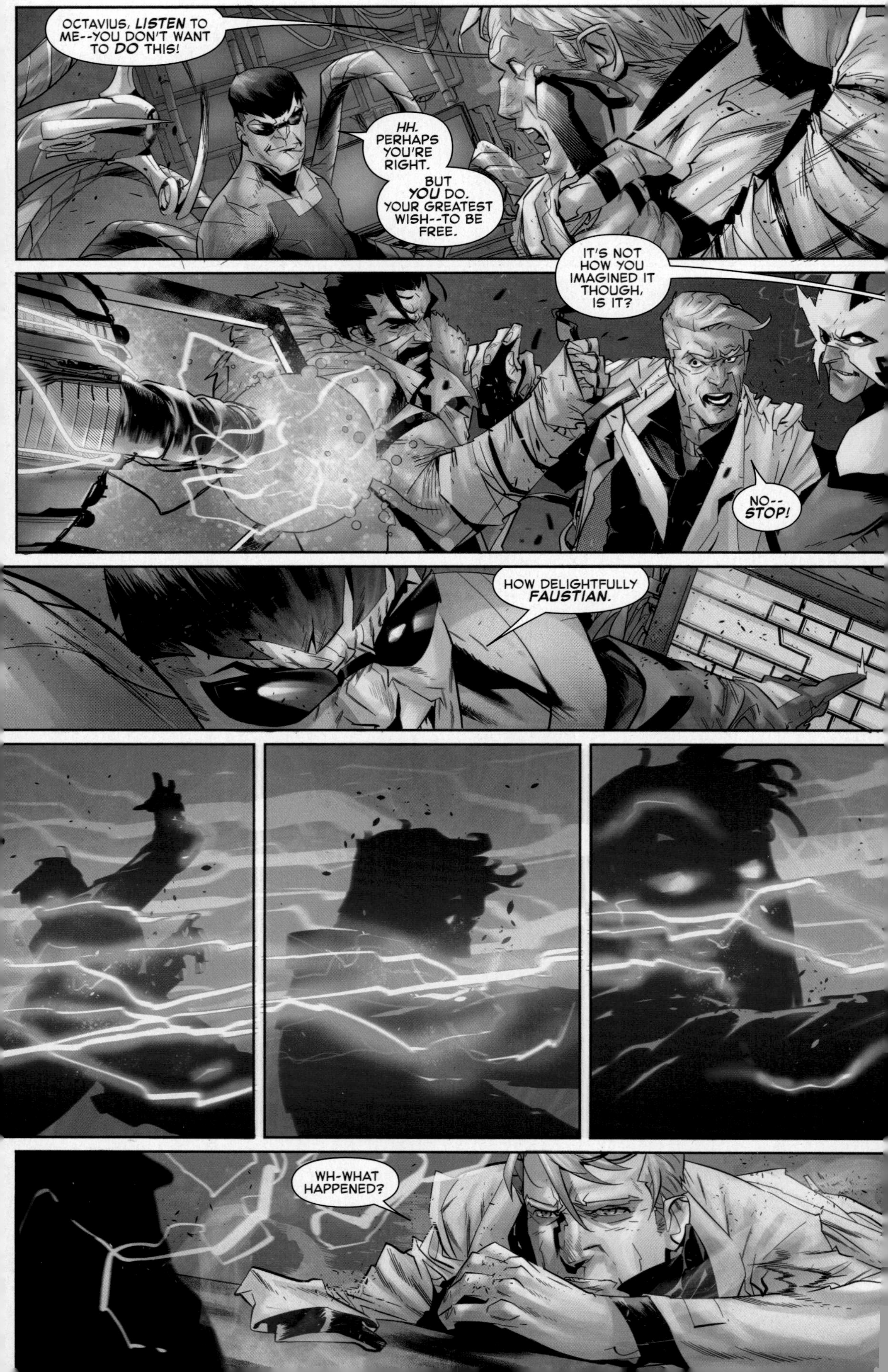
OCTAVIUS, LISTEN TO ME--YOU DON'T WANT TO DO THIS!
HH. PERHAPS YOU'RE RIGHT.
BUT YOU DO. YOUR GREATEST WISH--TO BE FREE.
IT'S NOT HOW YOU IMAGINED IT THOUGH, IS IT?
NO-- STOP!
HOW DELIGHTFULLY FAUSTIAN.
WH-WHAT HAPPENED?

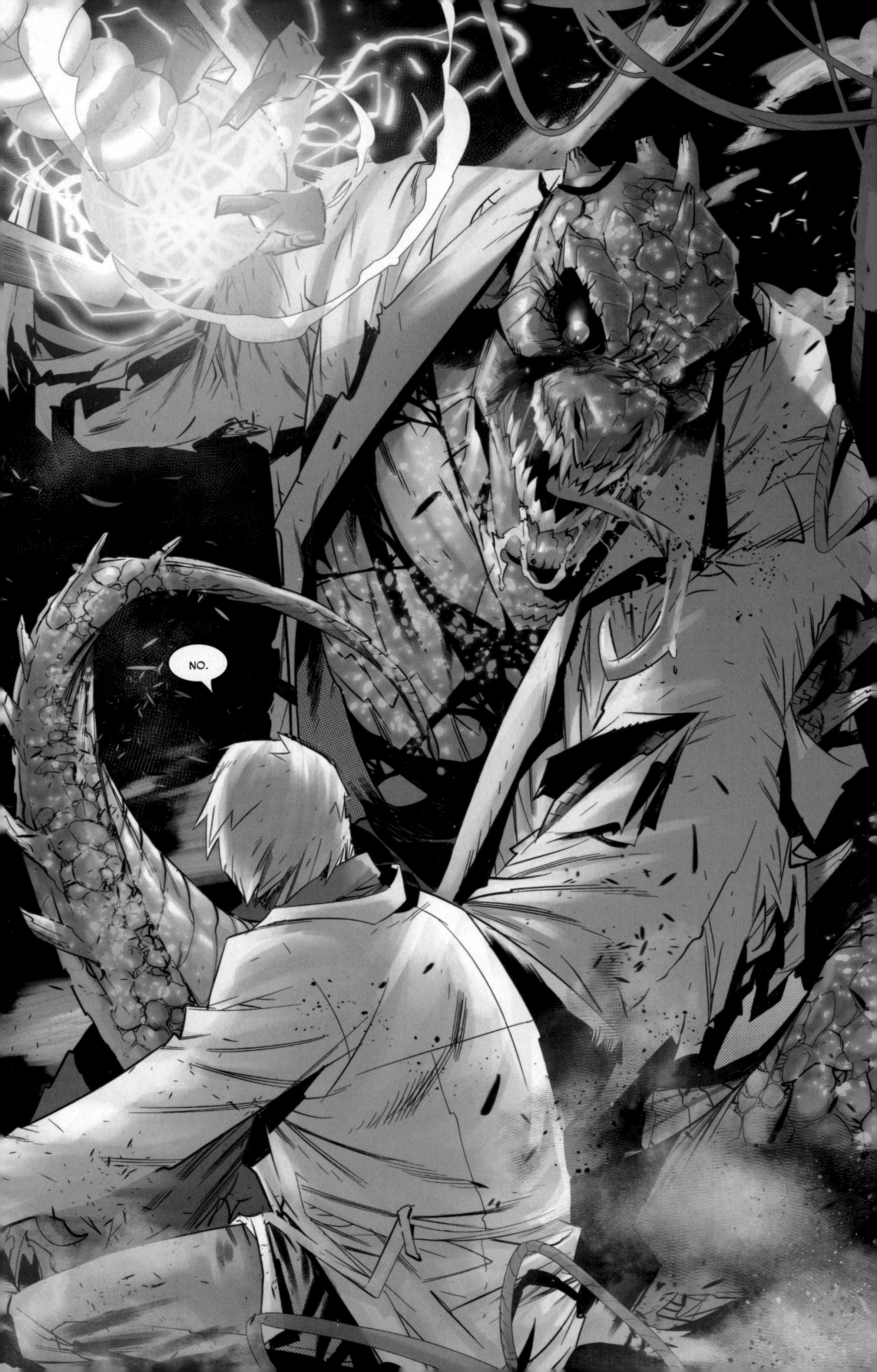
NO.

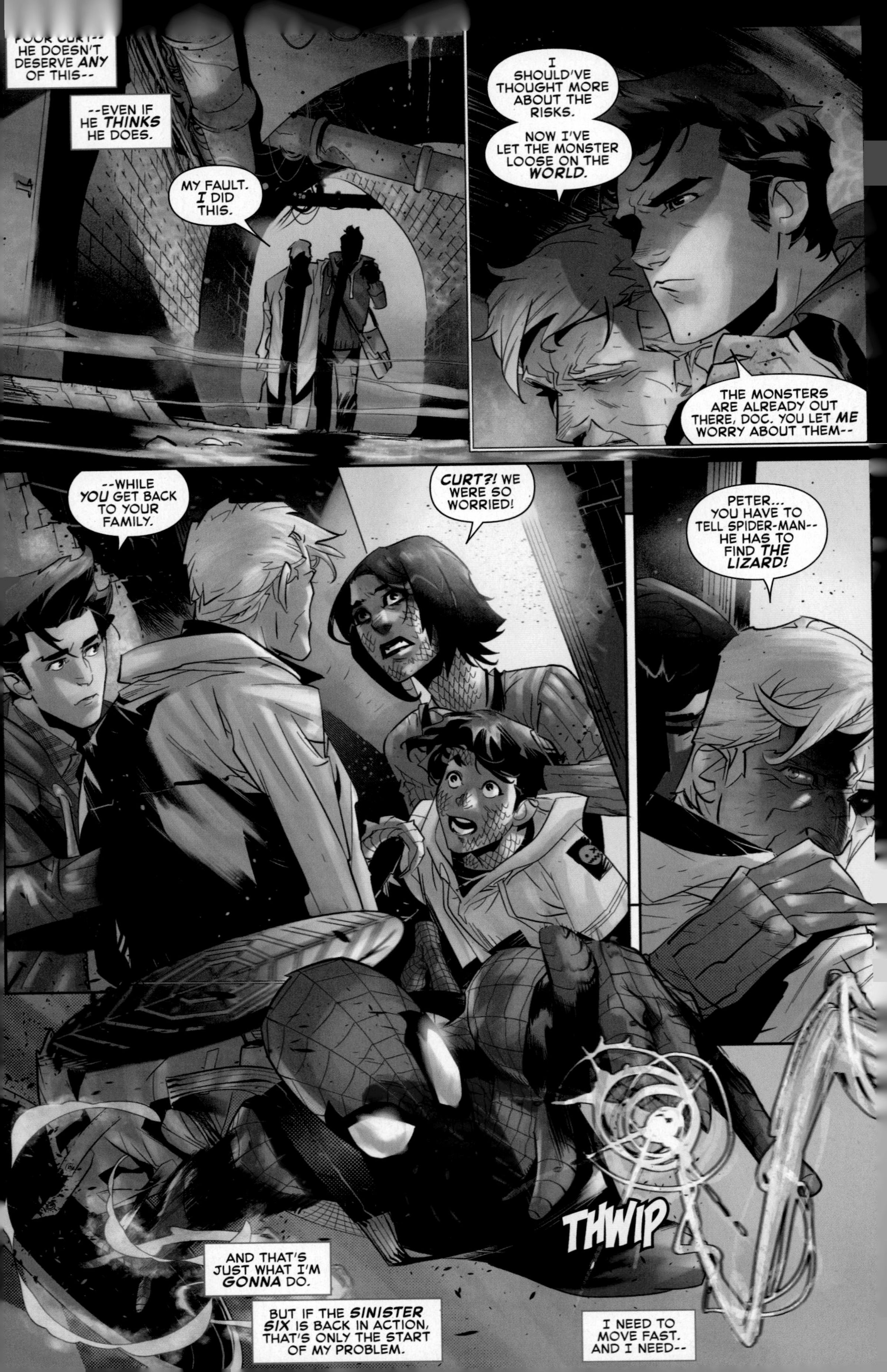
POOR CURT-- HE DOESN'T DESERVE ANY OF THIS--
--EVEN IF HE THINKS HE DOES.
MY FAULT. I DID THIS.
I SHOULD'VE THOUGHT MORE ABOUT THE RISKS.
NOW I'VE LET THE MONSTER LOOSE ON THE WORLD.
THE MONSTERS ARE ALREADY OUT THERE, DOC. YOU LET ME WORRY ABOUT THEM--
--WHILE YOU GET BACK TO YOUR FAMILY.
CURT?! WE WERE SO WORRIED!
PETER... YOU HAVE TO TELL SPIDER-MAN-- HE HAS TO FIND THE LIZARD!
THWIP
AND THAT'S JUST WHAT I'M GONNA DO.
BUT IF THE SINISTER SIX IS BACK IN ACTION, THAT'S ONLY THE START OF MY PROBLEM.
I NEED TO MOVE FAST. AND I NEED--

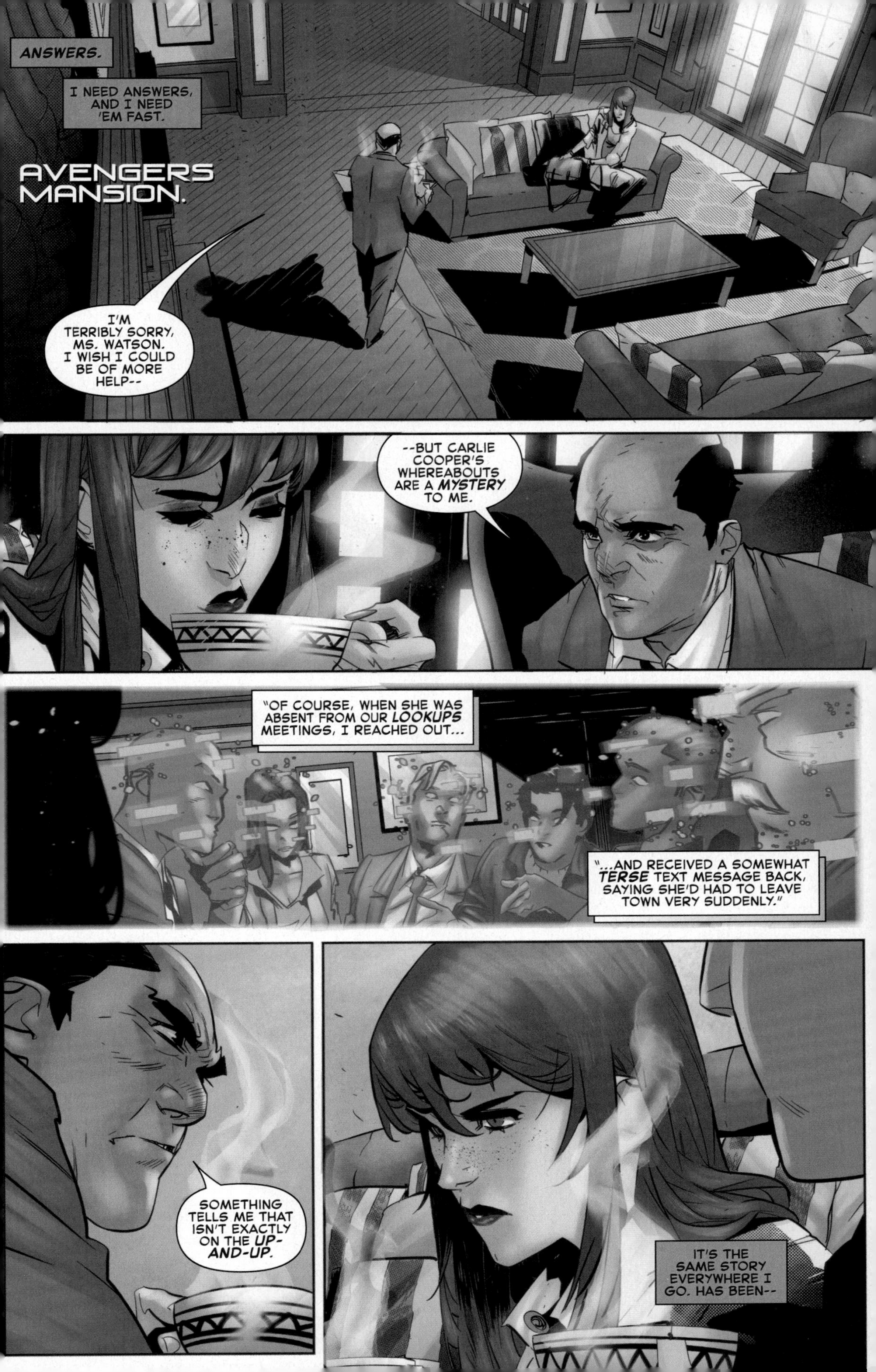
ANSWERS.
I NEED ANSWERS, AND I NEED 'EM FAST.
AVENGERS MANSION.
I'M TERRIBLY SORRY, MS. WATSON. I WISH I COULD BE OF MORE HELP--
--BUT CARLIE COOPER'S WHEREABOUTS ARE A *MYSTERY* TO ME.
"OF COURSE, WHEN SHE WAS ABSENT FROM OUR *LOOKUPS* MEETINGS, I REACHED OUT...
"...AND RECEIVED A SOMEWHAT *TERSE* TEXT MESSAGE BACK, SAYING SHE'D HAD TO LEAVE TOWN VERY SUDDENLY."
SOMETHING TELLS ME THAT ISN'T EXACTLY ON THE *UP-AND-UP.*
IT'S THE SAME STORY EVERYWHERE I GO. HAS BEEN--

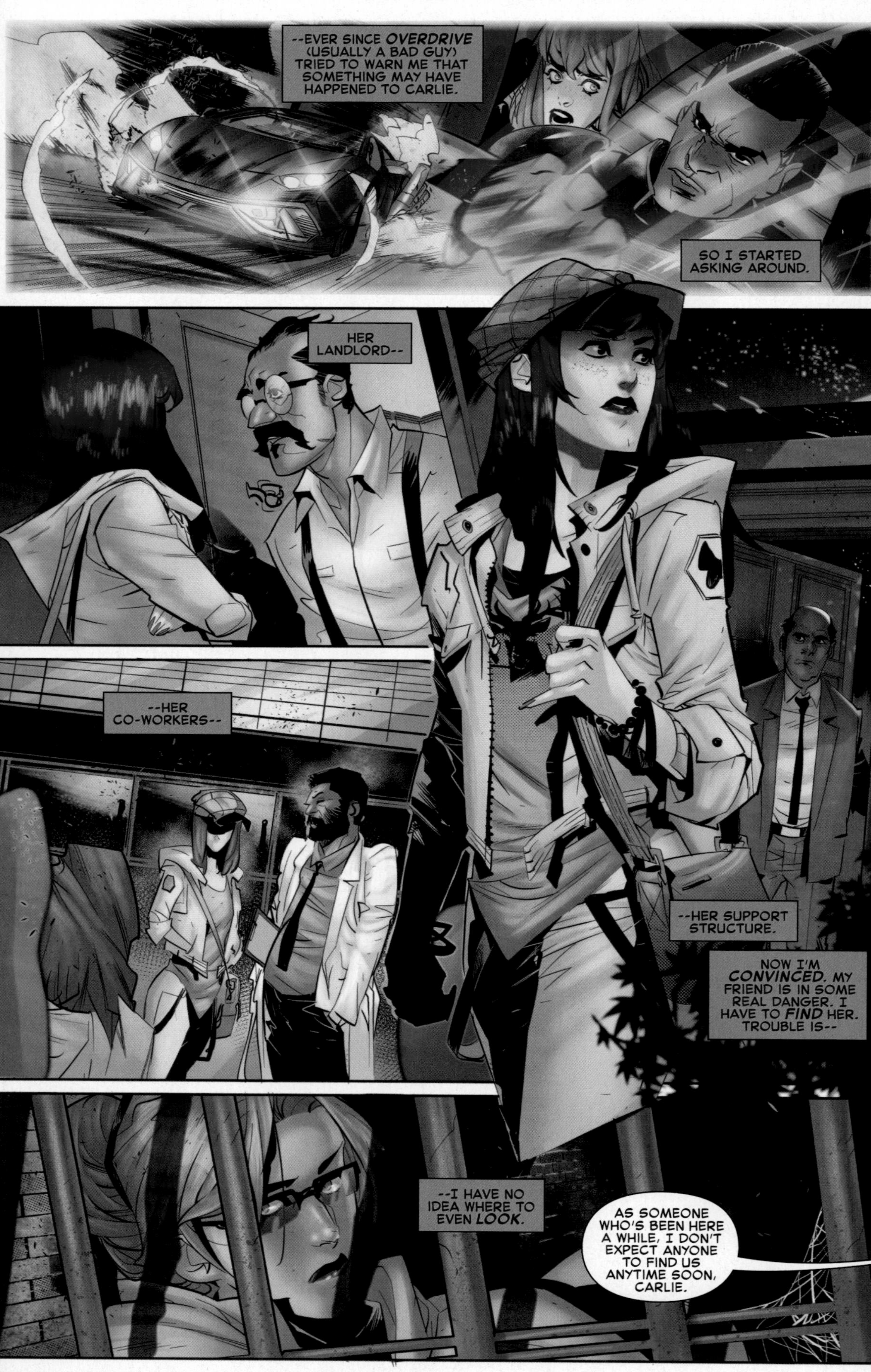
--EVER SINCE OVERDRIVE (USUALLY A BAD GUY) TRIED TO WARN ME THAT SOMETHING MAY HAVE HAPPENED TO CARLIE.
SO I STARTED ASKING AROUND.
HER LANDLORD--
--HER CO-WORKERS--
--HER SUPPORT STRUCTURE.
NOW I'M CONVINCED. MY FRIEND IS IN SOME REAL DANGER. I HAVE TO FIND HER. TROUBLE IS--
--I HAVE NO IDEA WHERE TO EVEN LOOK.
AS SOMEONE WHO'S BEEN HERE A WHILE, I DON'T EXPECT ANYONE TO FIND US ANYTIME SOON, CARLIE.

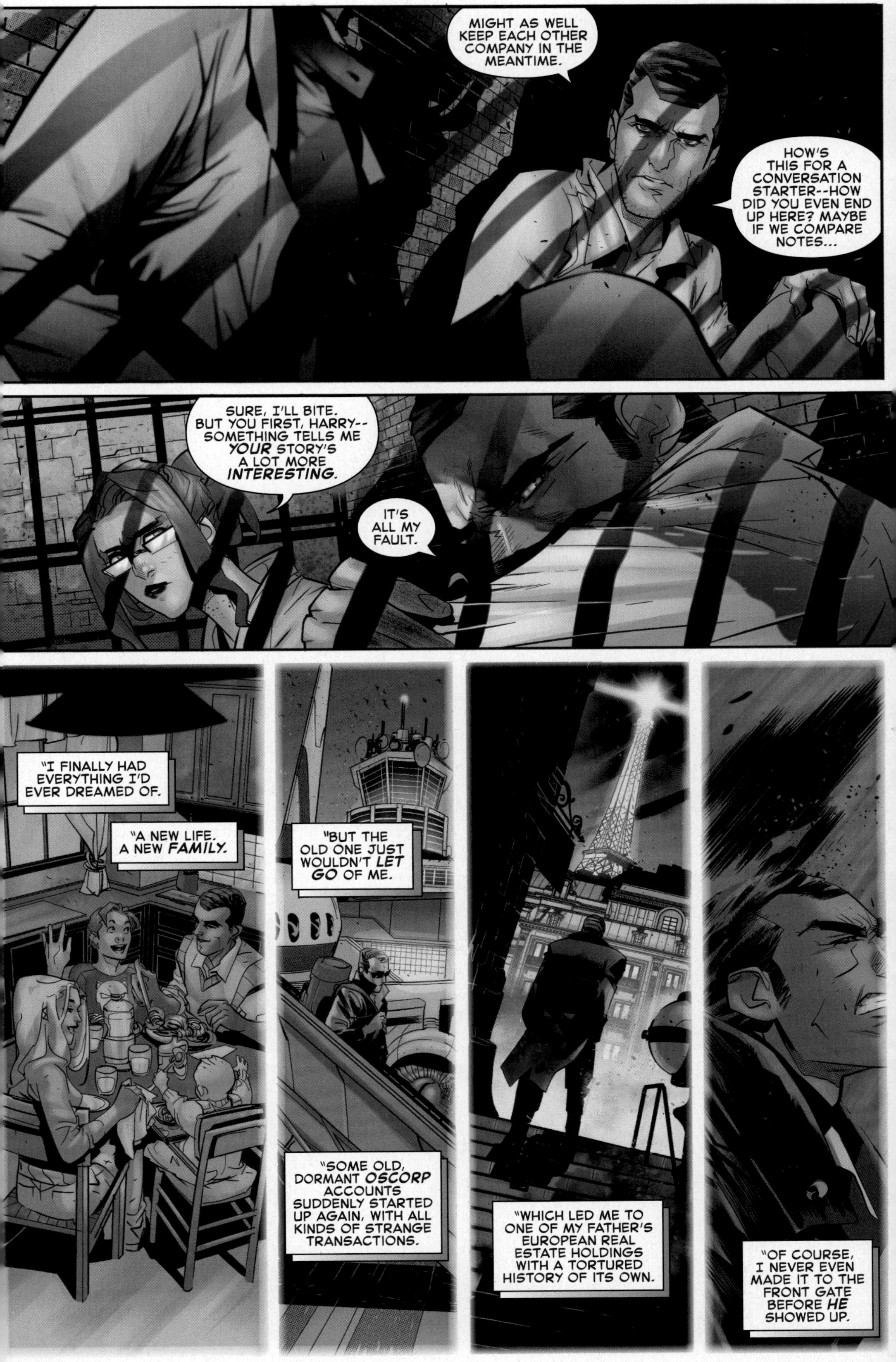
MIGHT AS WELL KEEP EACH OTHER COMPANY IN THE MEANTIME.
HOW'S THIS FOR A CONVERSATION STARTER--HOW DID YOU EVEN END UP HERE? MAYBE IF WE COMPARE NOTES...
SURE, I'LL BITE. BUT YOU FIRST, HARRY-- SOMETHING TELLS ME YOUR STORY'S A LOT MORE INTERESTING.
IT'S ALL MY FAULT.
"I FINALLY HAD EVERYTHING I'D EVER DREAMED OF.
"A NEW LIFE. A NEW FAMILY.
"BUT THE OLD ONE JUST WOULDN'T LET GO OF ME.
"SOME OLD, DORMANT OSCORP ACCOUNTS SUDDENLY STARTED UP AGAIN, WITH ALL KINDS OF STRANGE TRANSACTIONS.
"WHICH LED ME TO ONE OF MY FATHER'S EUROPEAN REAL ESTATE HOLDINGS WITH A TORTURED HISTORY OF ITS OWN.
"OF COURSE, I NEVER EVEN MADE IT TO THE FRONT GATE BEFORE HE SHOWED UP.

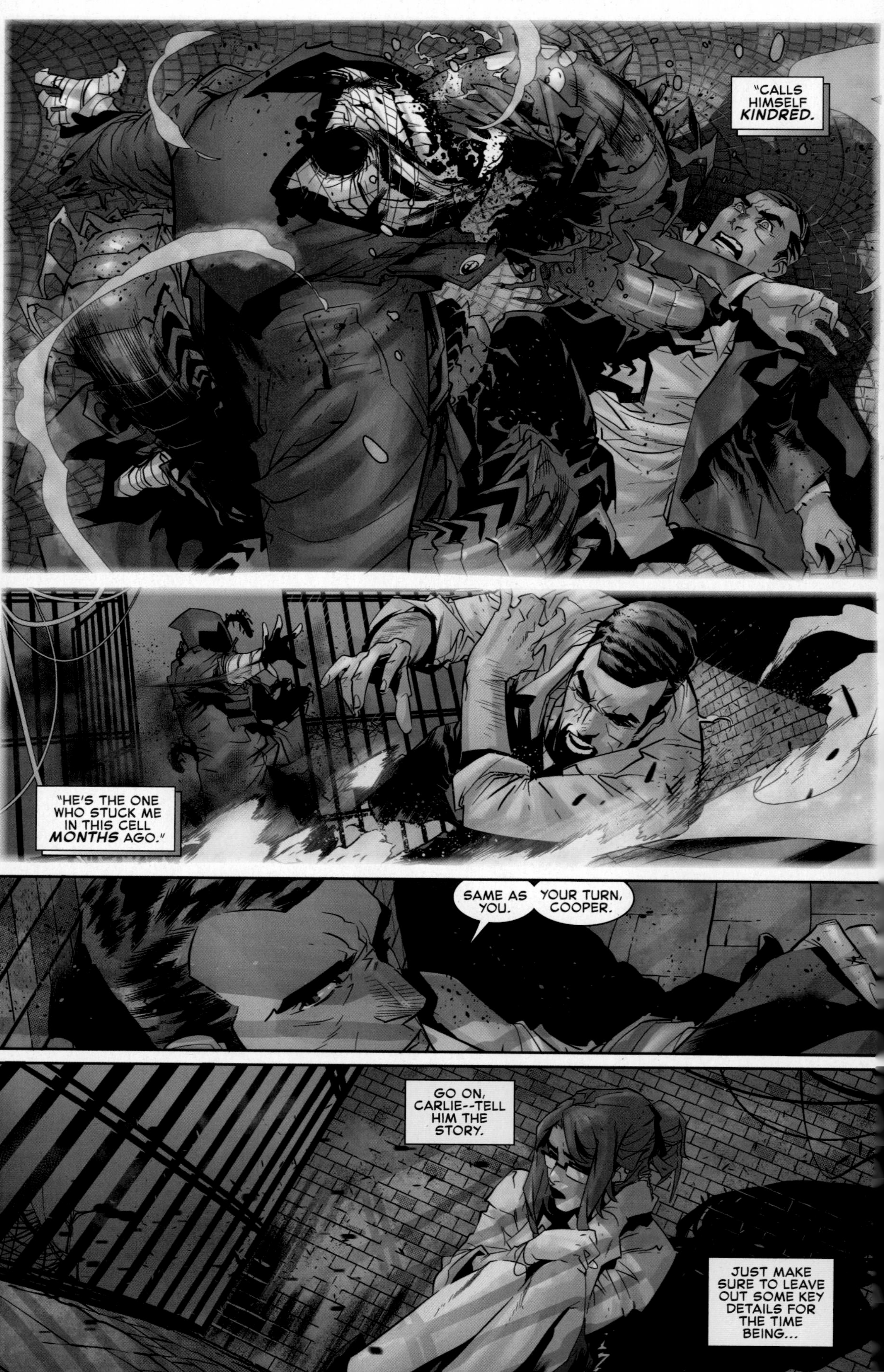
"CALLS HIMSELF KINDRED.
"HE'S THE ONE WHO STUCK ME IN THIS CELL MONTHS AGO."
SAME AS YOU.
YOUR TURN, COOPER.
GO ON, CARLIE--TELL HIM THE STORY.
JUST MAKE SURE TO LEAVE OUT SOME KEY DETAILS FOR THE TIME BEING...

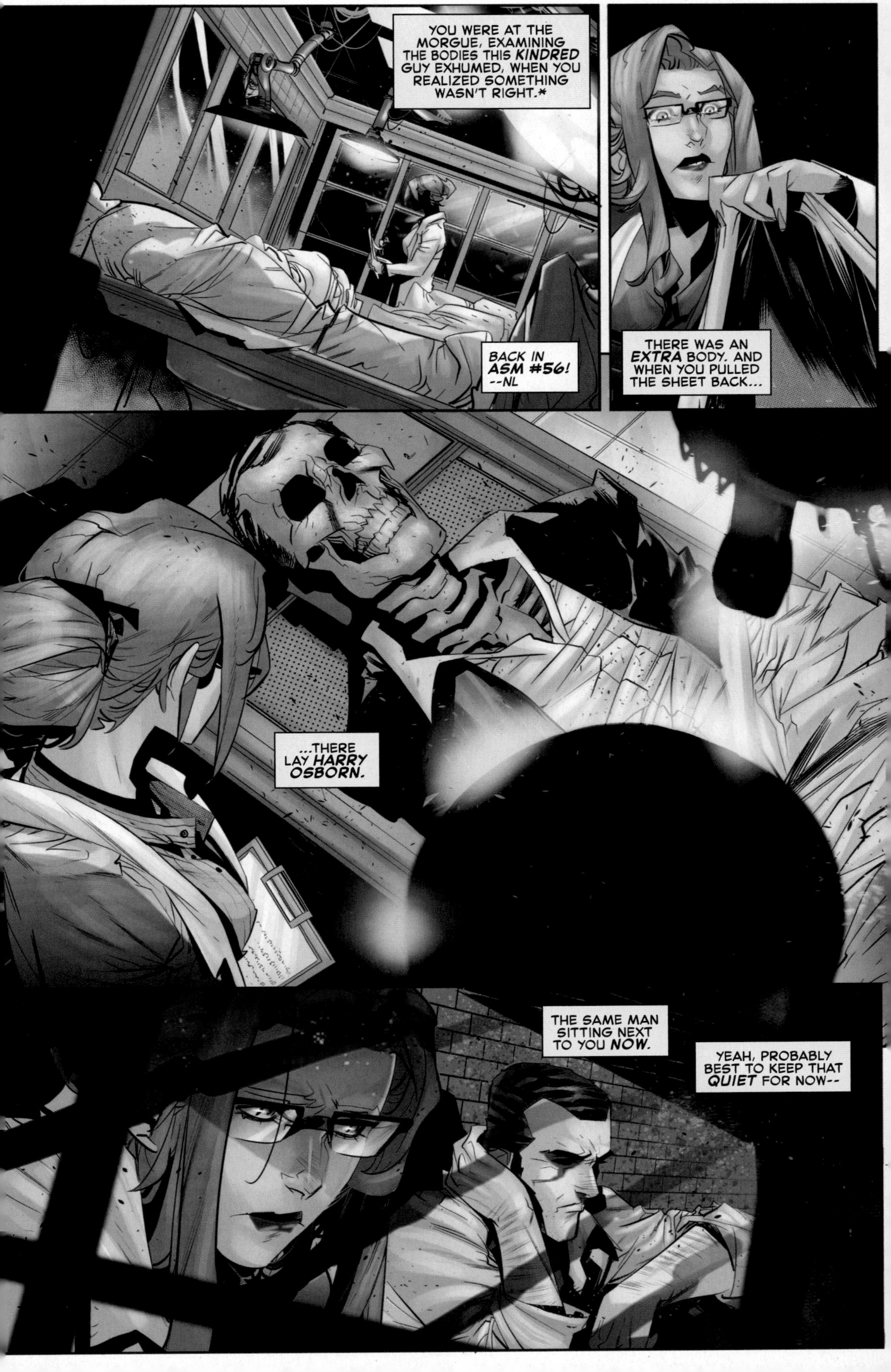
YOU WERE AT THE MORGUE, EXAMINING THE BODIES THIS KINDRED GUY EXHUMED, WHEN YOU REALIZED SOMETHING WASN'T RIGHT.*
BACK IN ASM #56! --NL
THERE WAS AN EXTRA BODY. AND WHEN YOU PULLED THE SHEET BACK...
...THERE LAY HARRY OSBORN.
THE SAME MAN SITTING NEXT TO YOU NOW.
YEAH, PROBABLY BEST TO KEEP THAT QUIET FOR NOW--

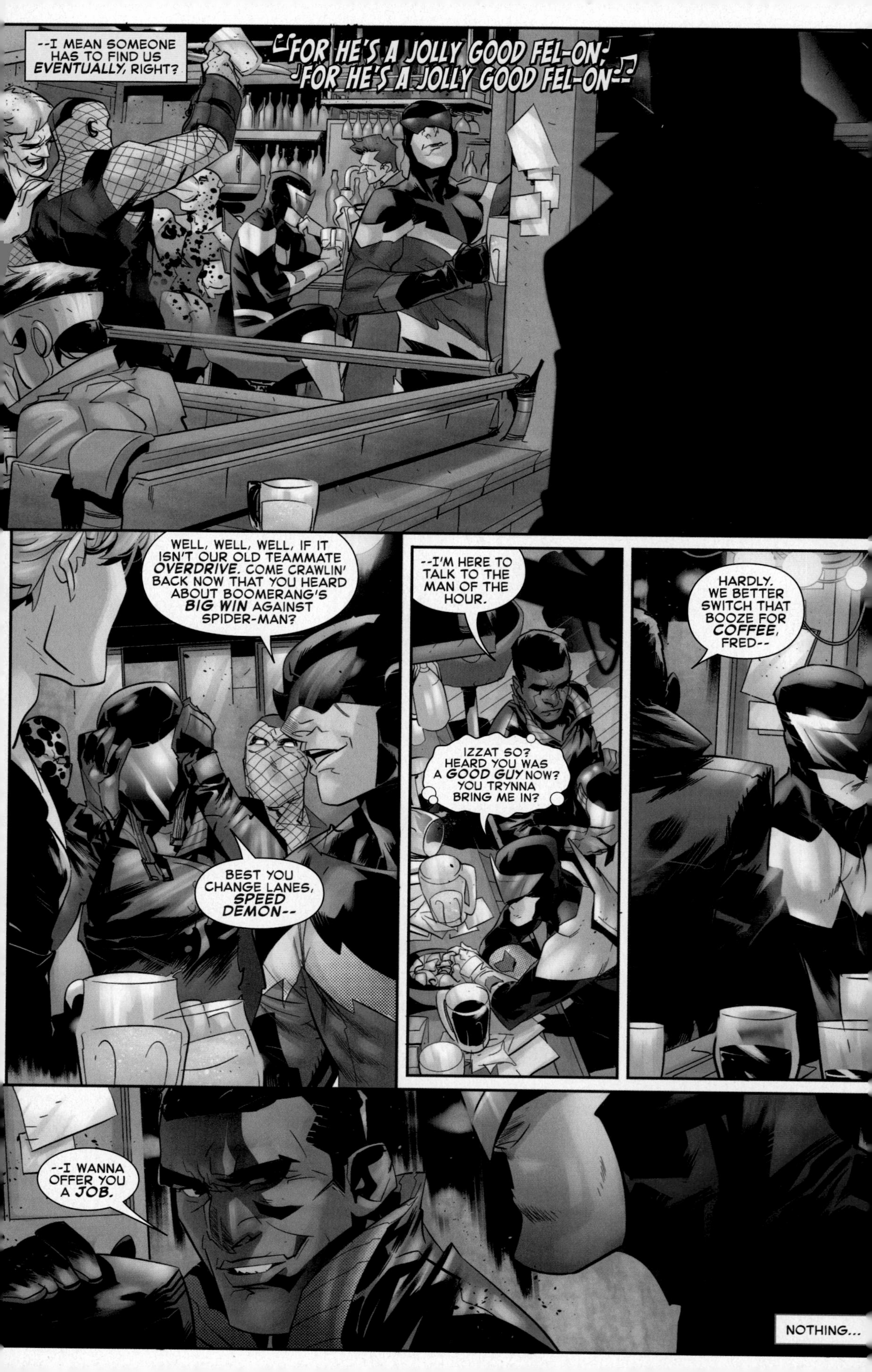
--I MEAN SOMEONE HAS TO FIND US EVENTUALLY, RIGHT?
♪FOR HE'S A JOLLY GOOD FEL-ON;
♪FOR HE'S A JOLLY GOOD FEL-ON--♪
WELL, WELL, WELL, IF IT ISN'T OUR OLD TEAMMATE OVERDRIVE. COME CRAWLIN' BACK NOW THAT YOU HEARD ABOUT BOOMERANG'S BIG WIN AGAINST SPIDER-MAN?
BEST YOU CHANGE LANES, SPEED DEMON--
--I'M HERE TO TALK TO THE MAN OF THE HOUR.
IZZAT SO? HEARD YOU WAS A GOOD GUY NOW? YOU TRYNNA BRING ME IN?
HARDLY. WE BETTER SWITCH THAT BOOZE FOR COFFEE, FRED--
--I WANNA OFFER YOU A JOB.
NOTHING...

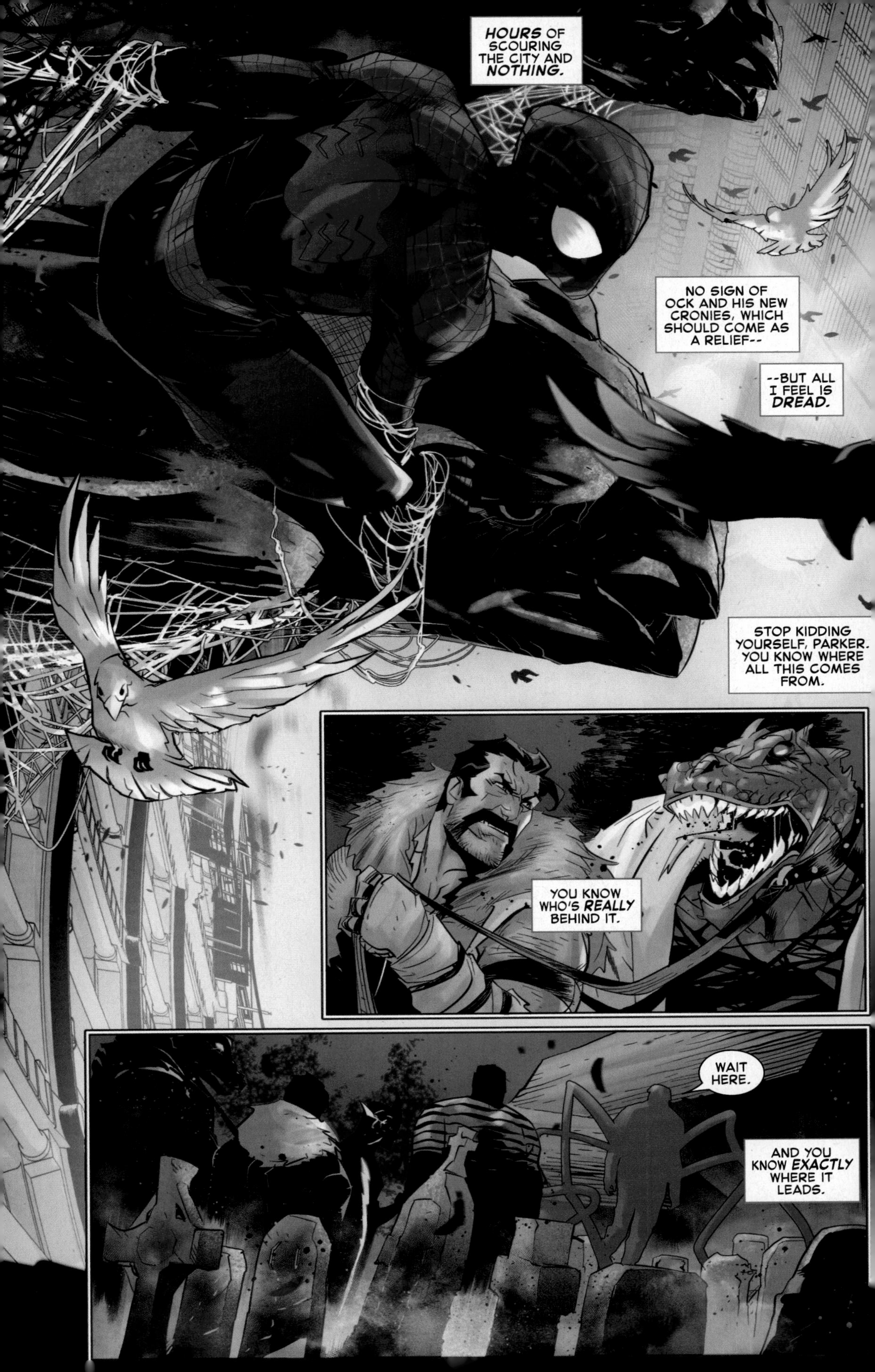
HOURS OF SCOURING THE CITY AND NOTHING.
NO SIGN OF OCK AND HIS NEW CRONIES, WHICH SHOULD COME AS A RELIEF--
--BUT ALL I FEEL IS DREAD.
STOP KIDDING YOURSELF, PARKER. YOU KNOW WHERE ALL THIS COMES FROM.
YOU KNOW WHO'S REALLY BEHIND IT.
WAIT HERE.
AND YOU KNOW EXACTLY WHERE IT LEADS.

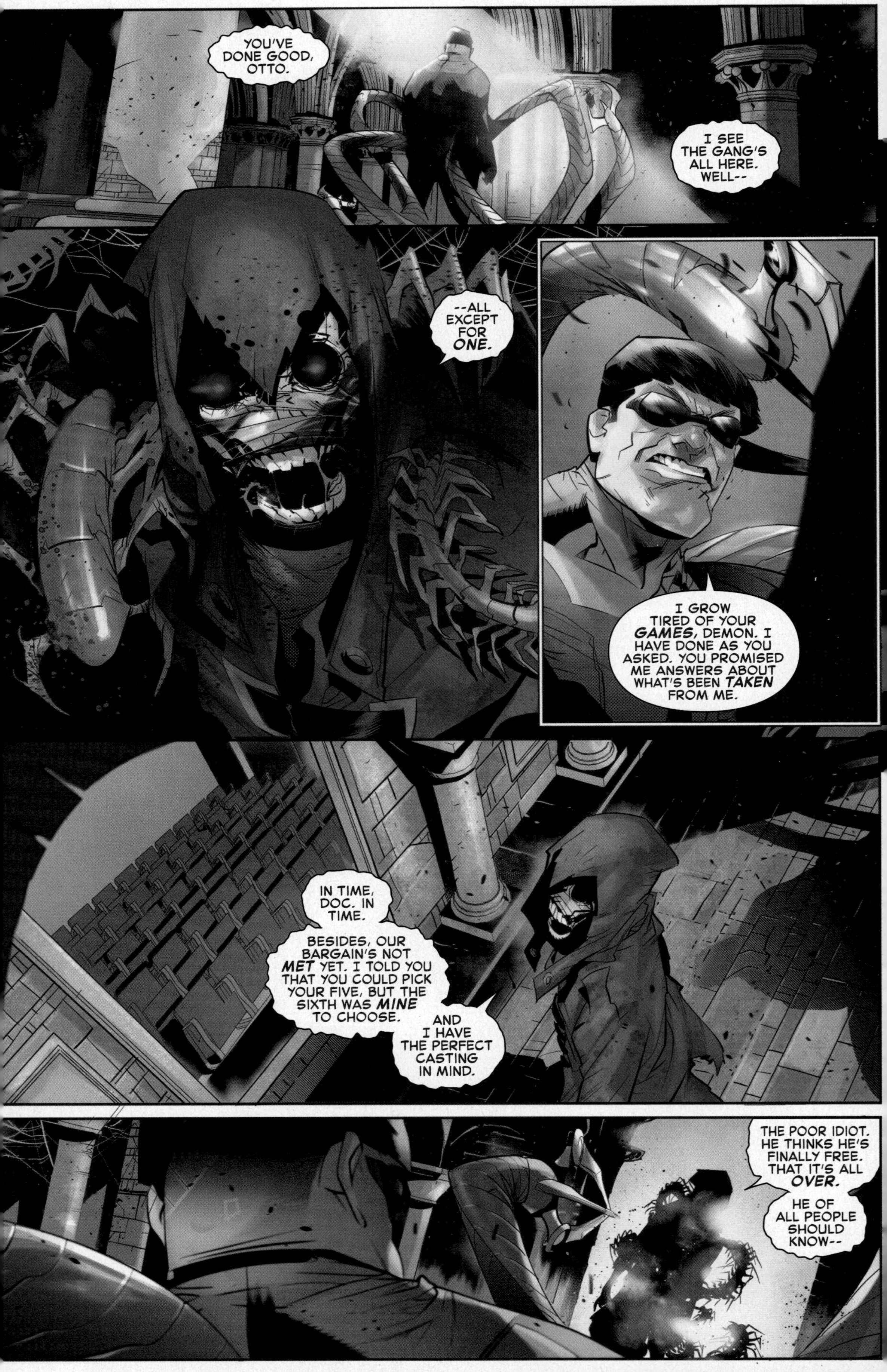
YOU'VE DONE GOOD, OTTO.
I SEE THE GANG'S ALL HERE. WELL--
--ALL EXCEPT FOR ONE.
I GROW TIRED OF YOUR GAMES, DEMON. I HAVE DONE AS YOU ASKED. YOU PROMISED ME ANSWERS ABOUT WHAT'S BEEN TAKEN FROM ME.
IN TIME, DOC. IN TIME.
BESIDES, OUR BARGAIN'S NOT MET YET. I TOLD YOU THAT YOU COULD PICK YOUR FIVE, BUT THE SIXTH WAS MINE TO CHOOSE.
AND I HAVE THE PERFECT CASTING IN MIND.
THE POOR IDIOT. HE THINKS HE'S FINALLY FREE. THAT IT'S ALL OVER.
HE OF ALL PEOPLE SHOULD KNOW--

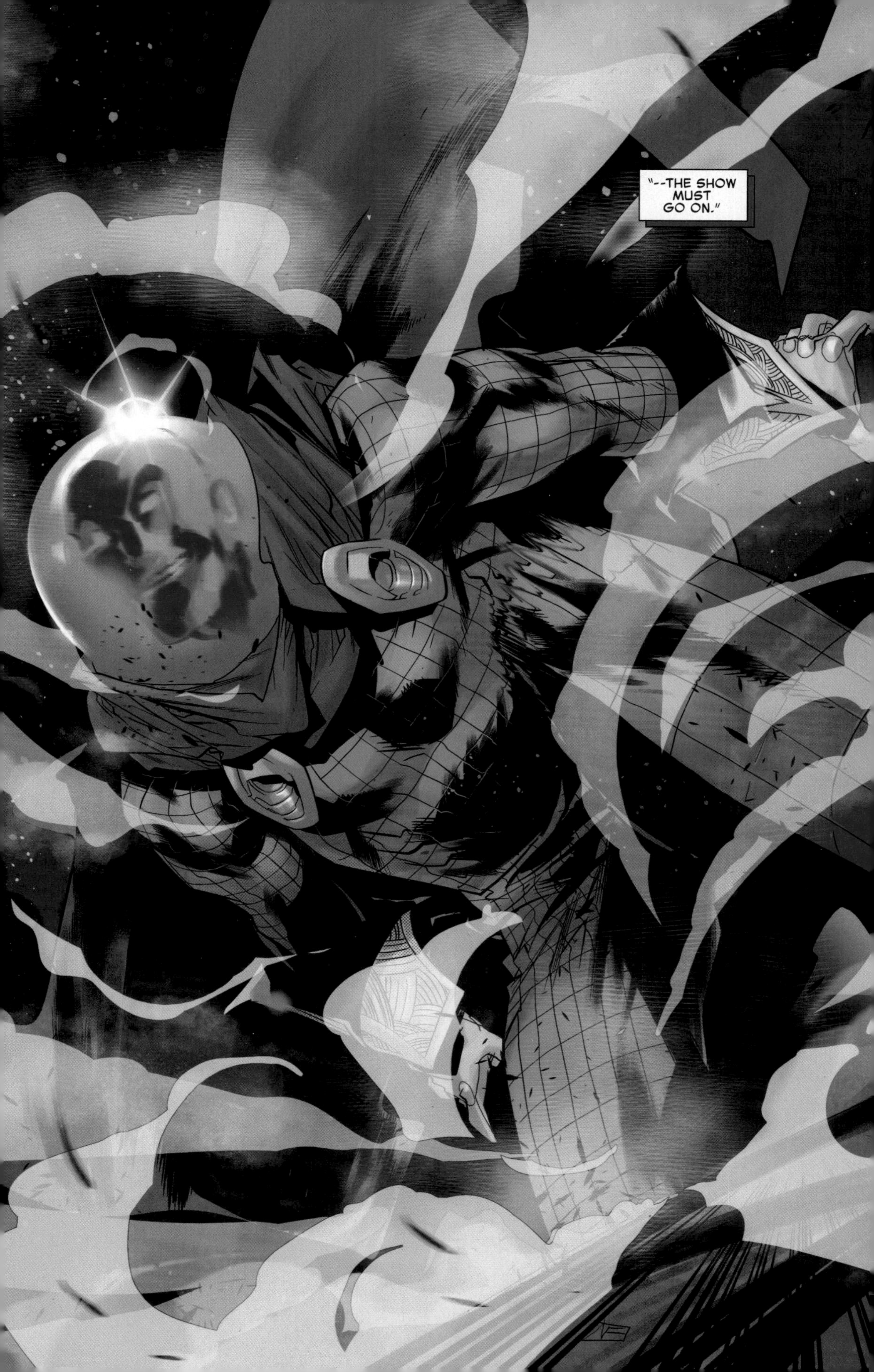
"--THE SHOW MUST GO ON."

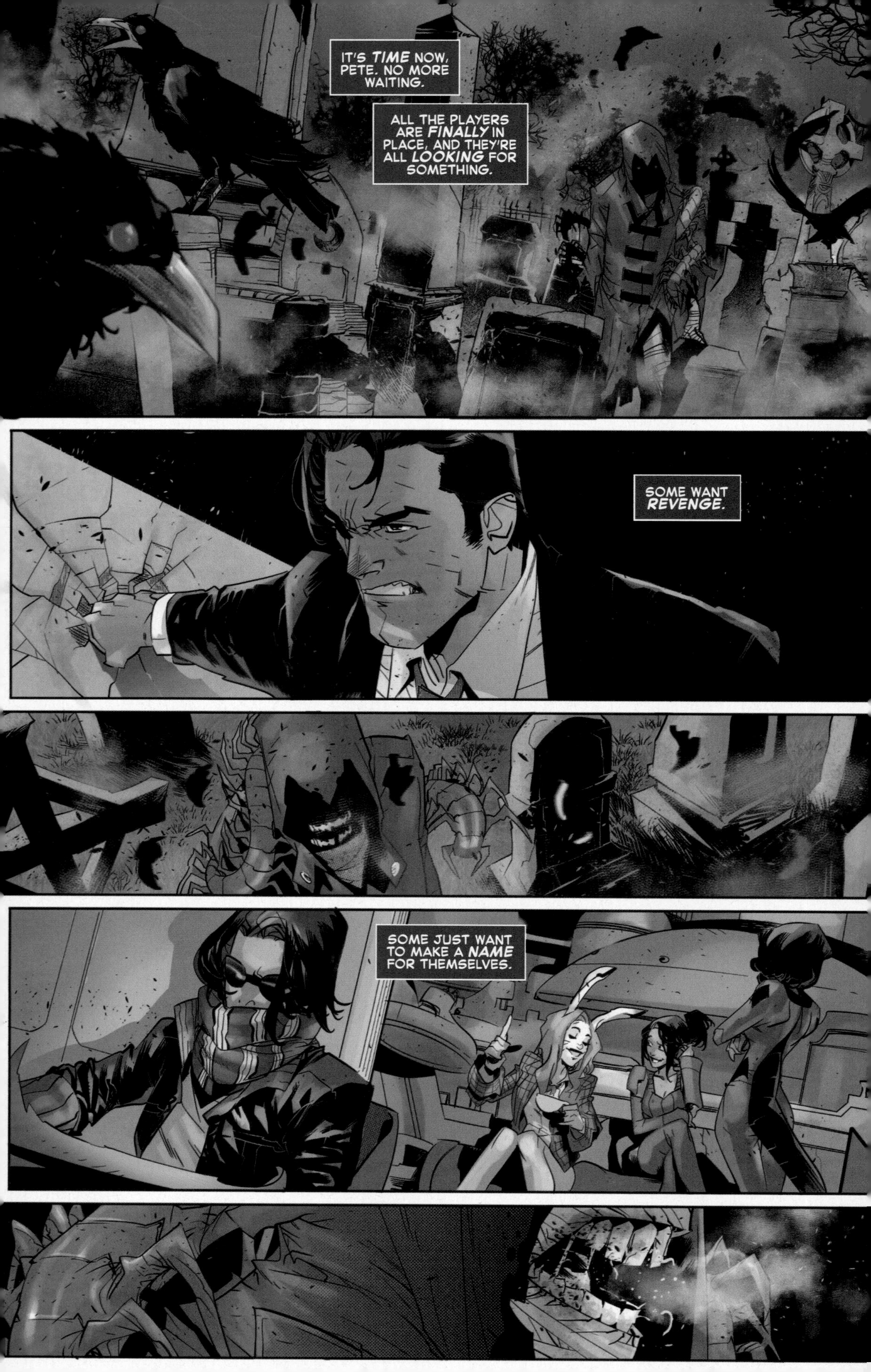
IT'S TIME NOW, PETE. NO MORE WAITING.
ALL THE PLAYERS ARE FINALLY IN PLACE, AND THEY'RE ALL LOOKING FOR SOMETHING.
SOME WANT REVENGE.
SOME JUST WANT TO MAKE A NAME FOR THEMSELVES.

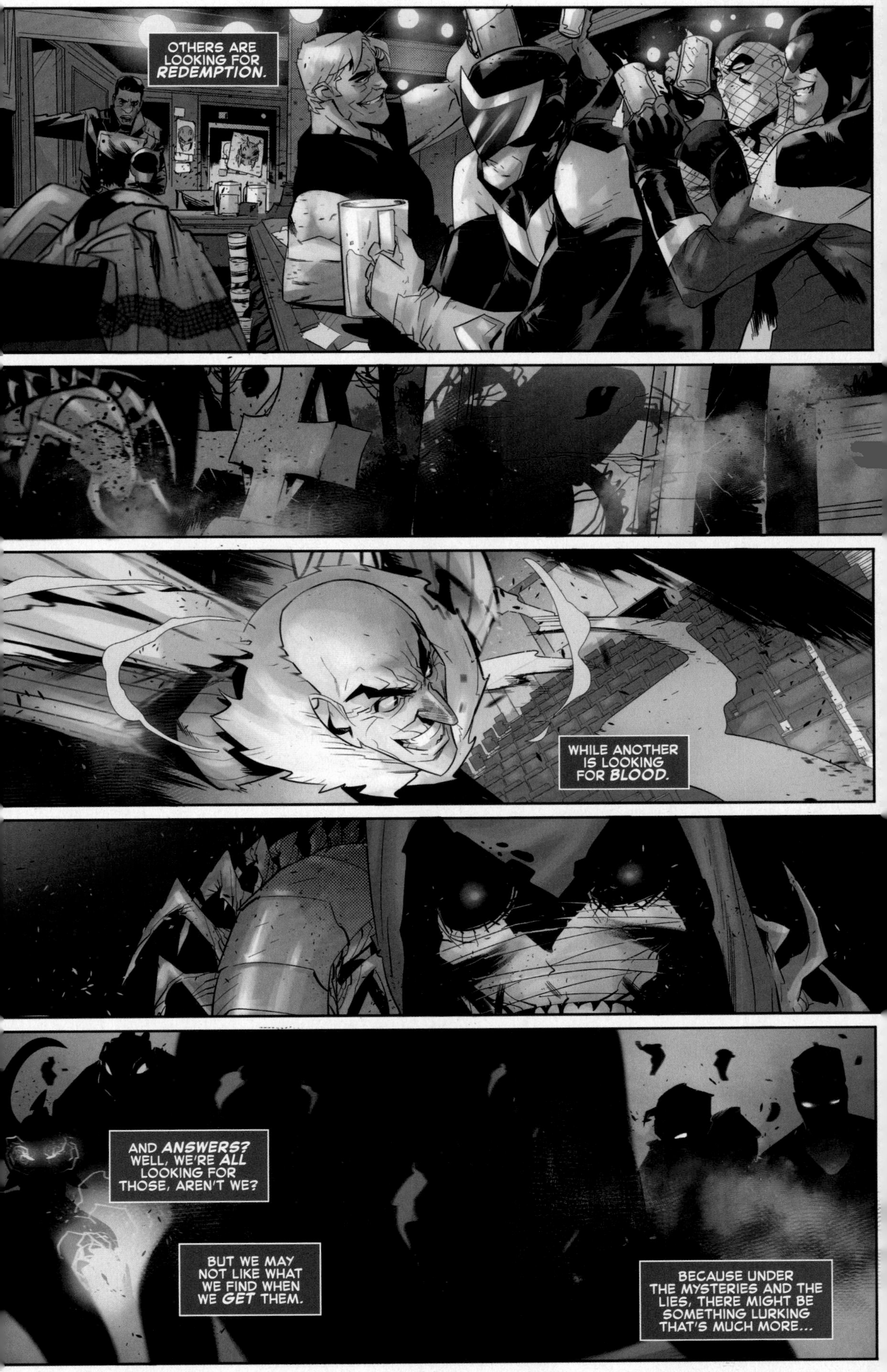
OTHERS ARE LOOKING FOR REDEMPTION.
WHILE ANOTHER IS LOOKING FOR BLOOD.
AND ANSWERS? WELL, WE'RE ALL LOOKING FOR THOSE, AREN'T WE?
BUT WE MAY NOT LIKE WHAT WE FIND WHEN WE GET THEM.
BECAUSE UNDER THE MYSTERIES AND THE LIES, THERE MIGHT BE SOMETHING LURKING THAT'S MUCH MORE...

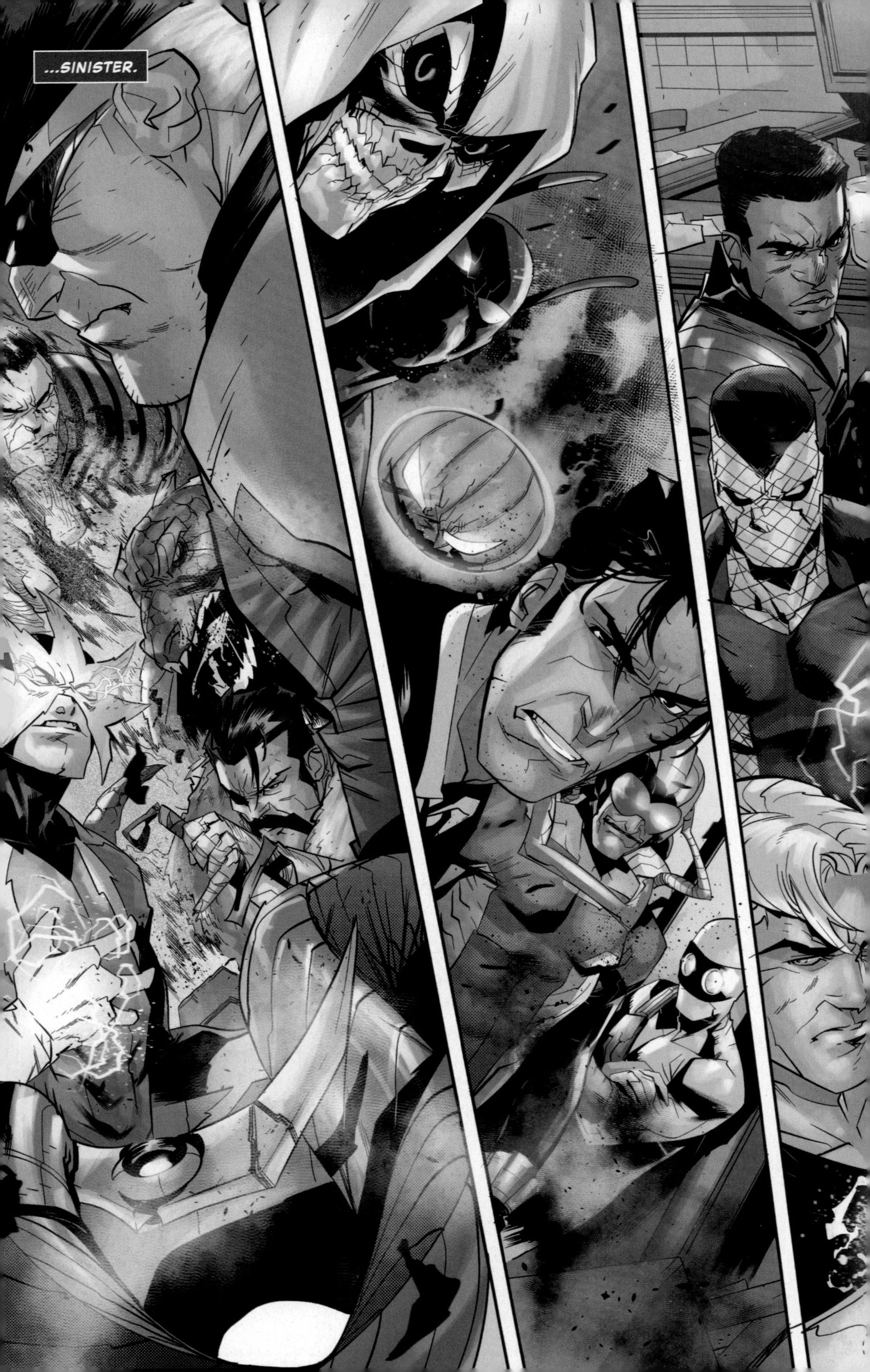
...SINISTER.

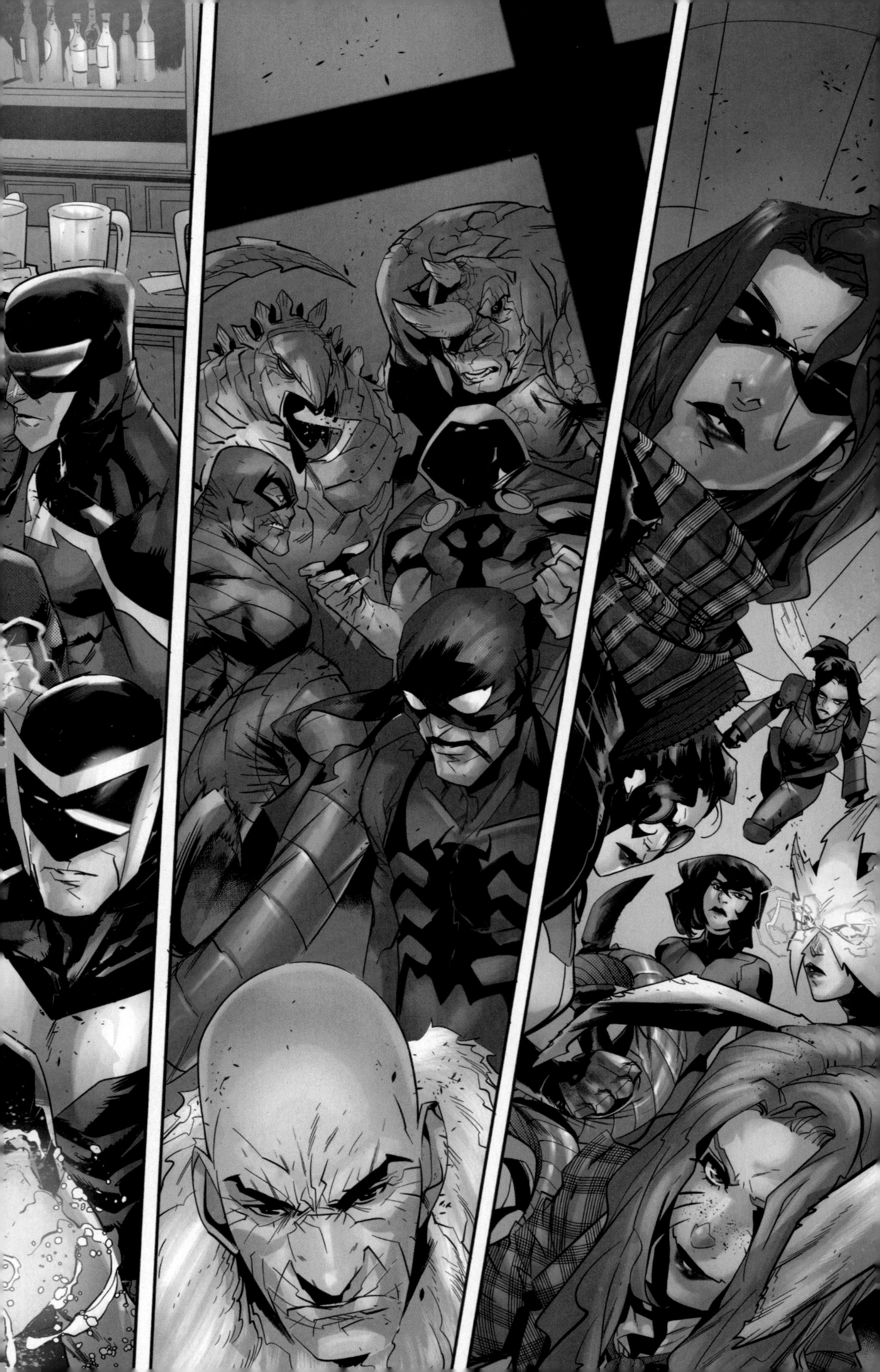

71

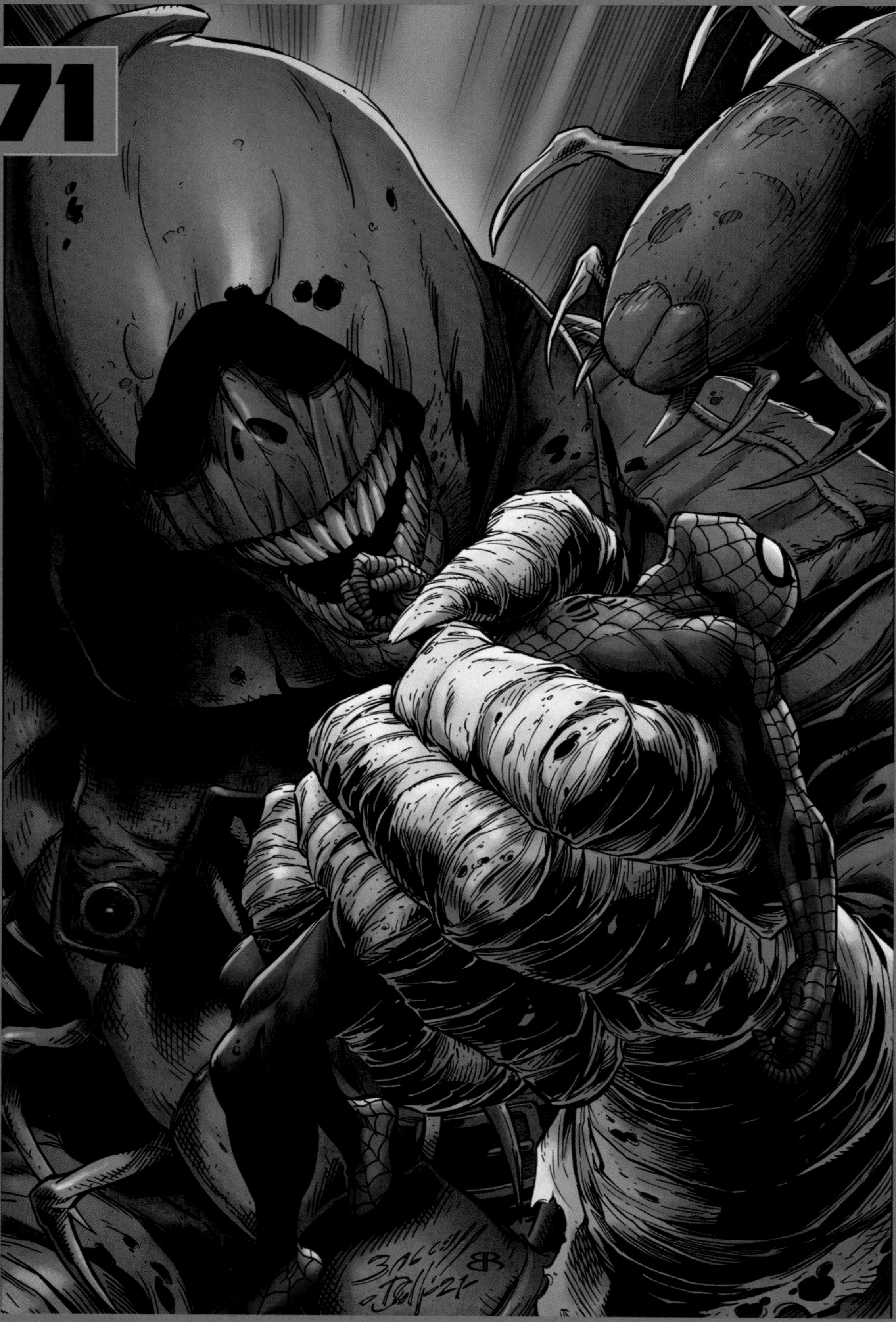

SINISTER WAR PART 1

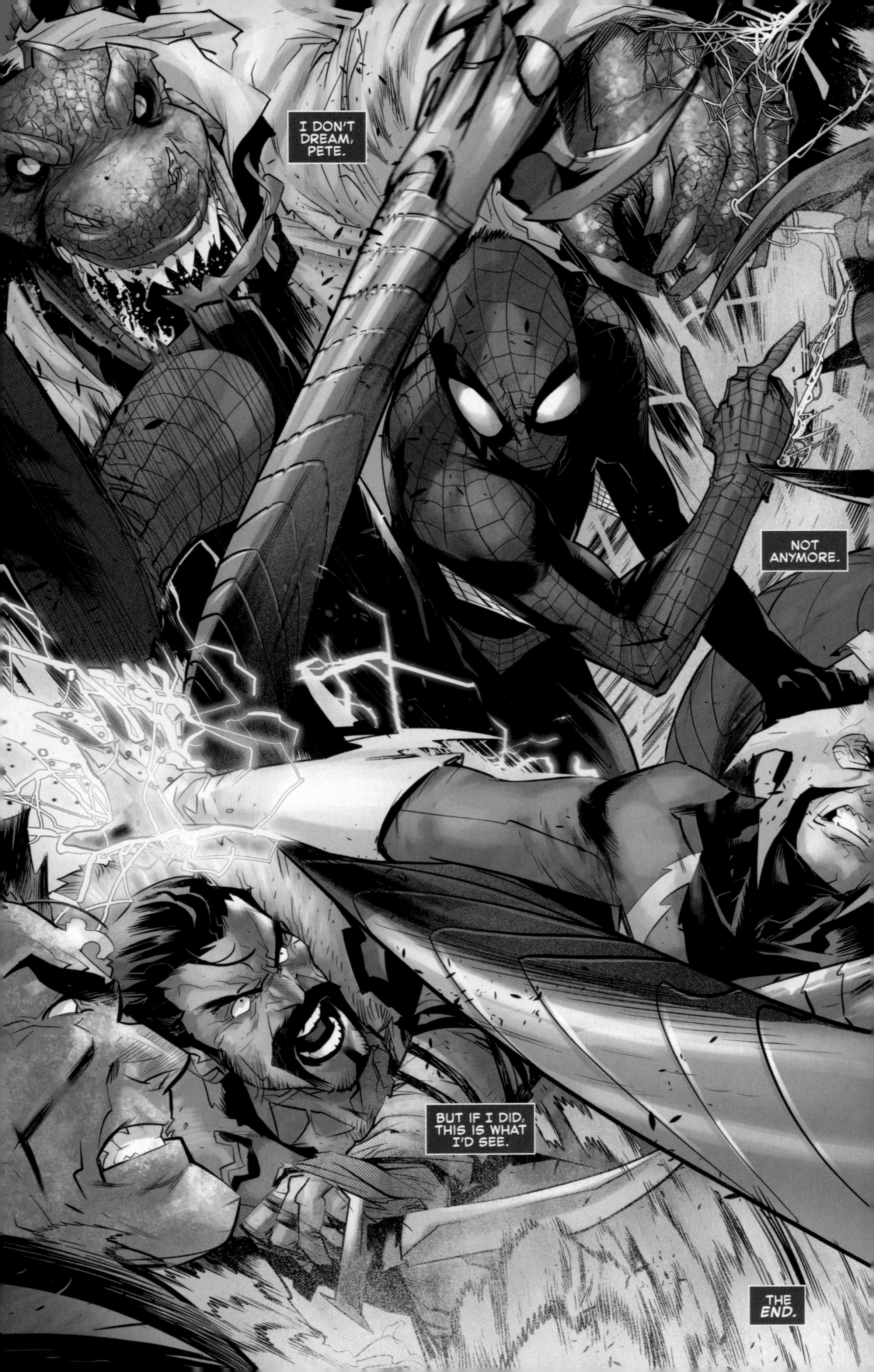
I DON'T DREAM, PETE.
NOT ANYMORE.
BUT IF I DID, THIS IS WHAT I'D SEE.
THE END.

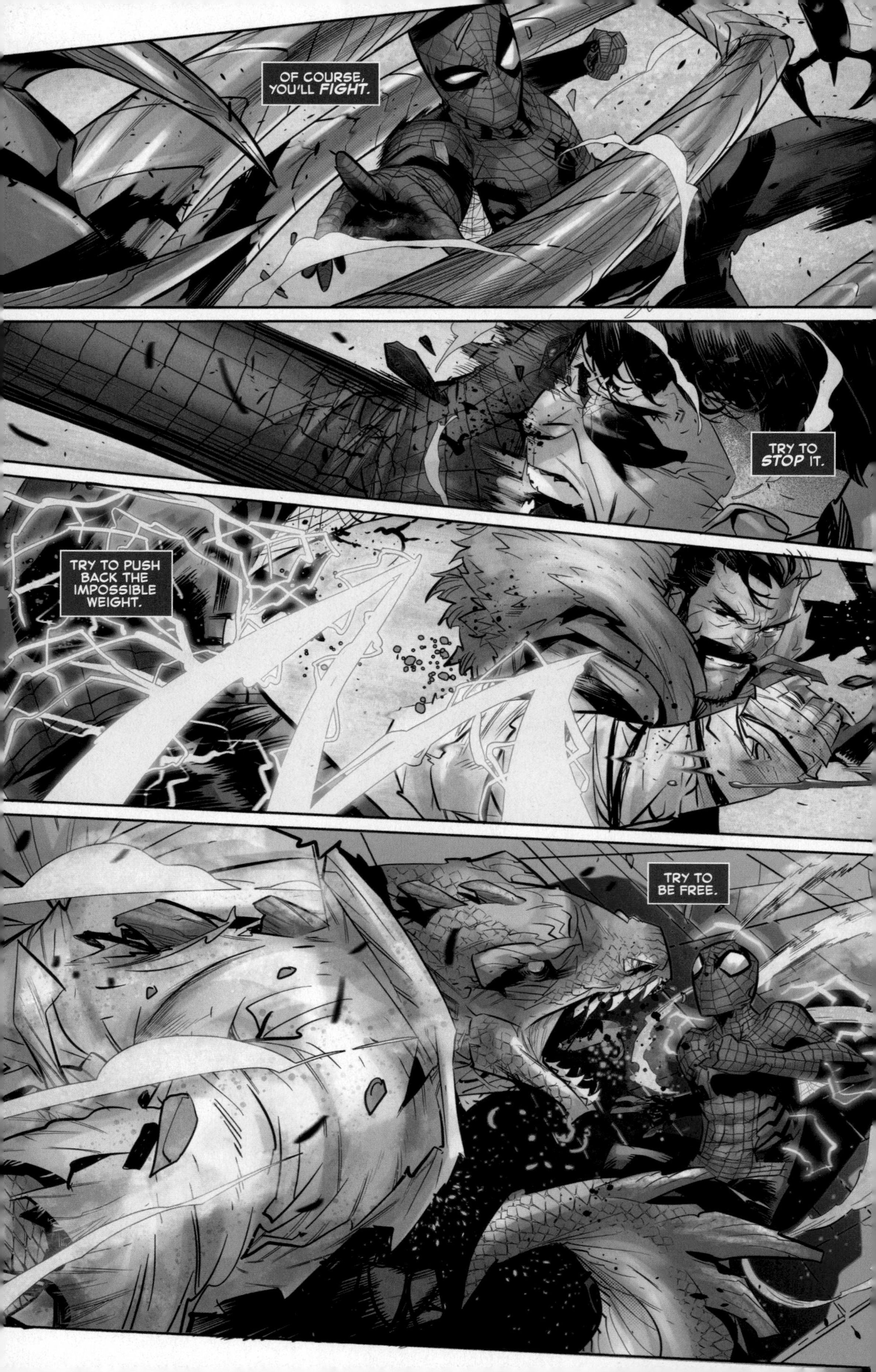
OF COURSE, YOU'LL FIGHT.
TRY TO STOP IT.
TRY TO PUSH BACK THE IMPOSSIBLE WEIGHT.
TRY TO BE FREE.

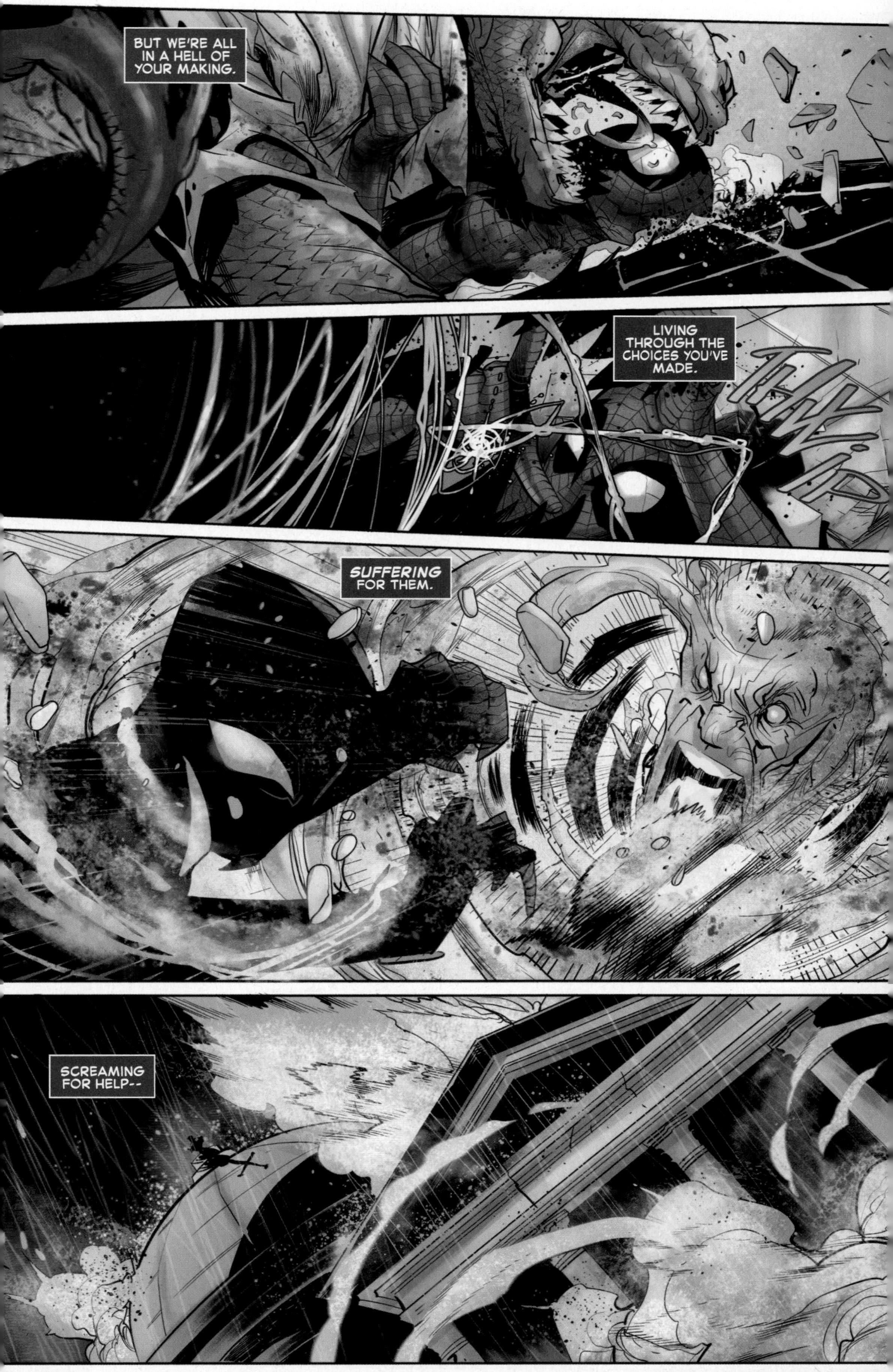
BUT WE'RE ALL IN A HELL OF YOUR MAKING.
LIVING THROUGH THE CHOICES YOU'VE MADE.
THWIP
SUFFERING FOR THEM.
SCREAMING FOR HELP--

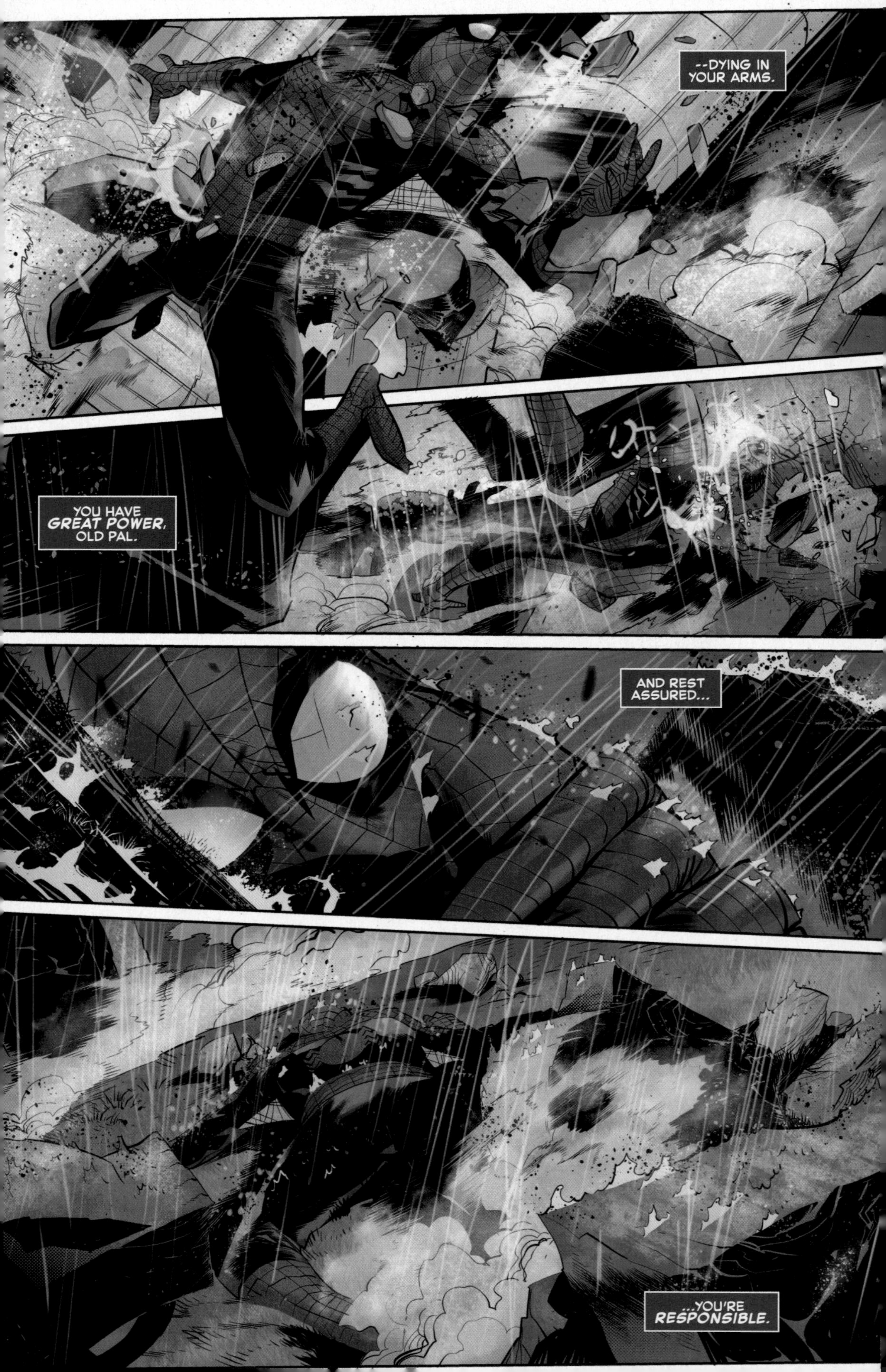
--DYING IN YOUR ARMS.
YOU HAVE GREAT POWER, OLD PAL.
AND REST ASSURED...
...YOU'RE RESPONSIBLE.

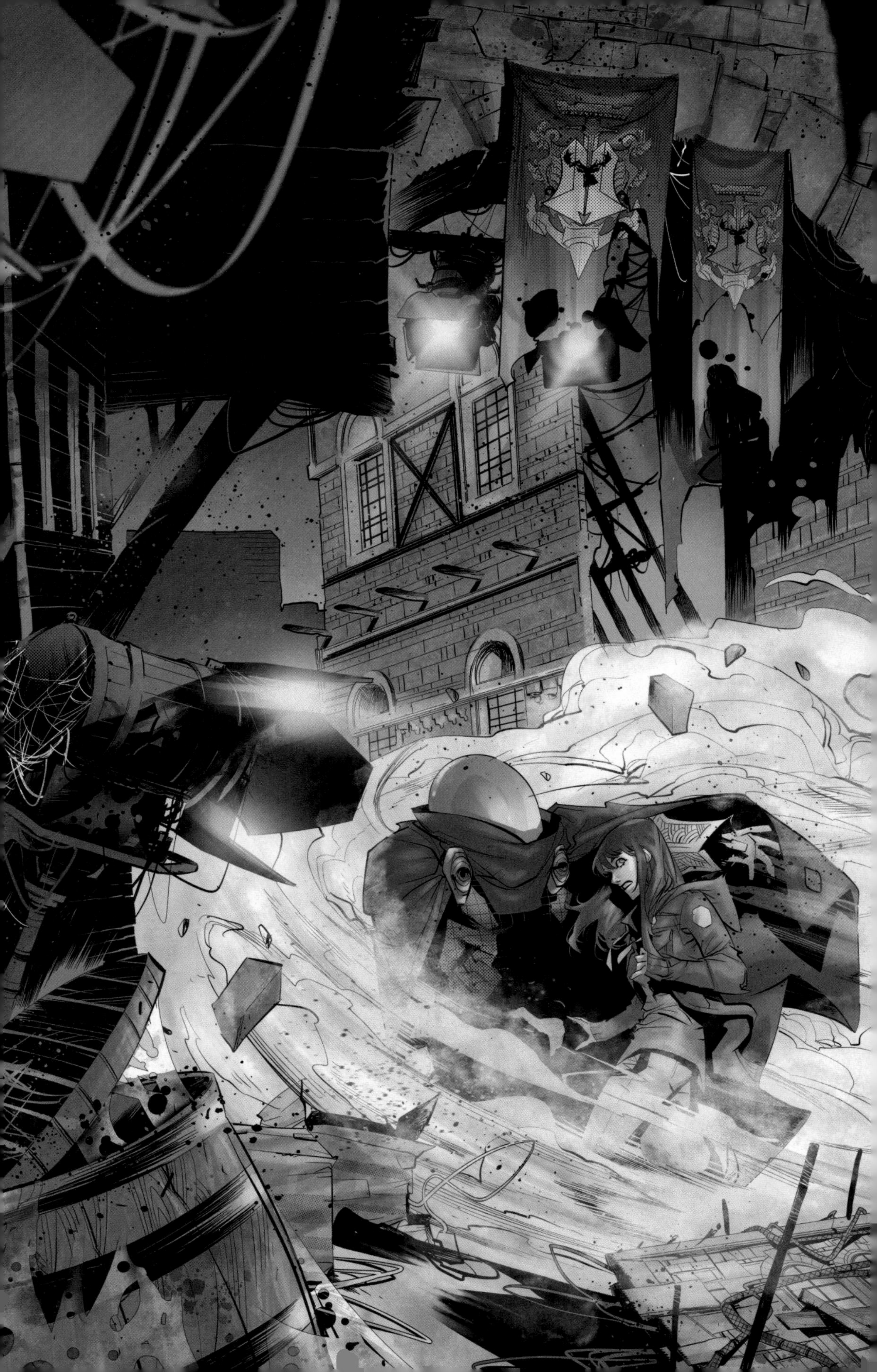

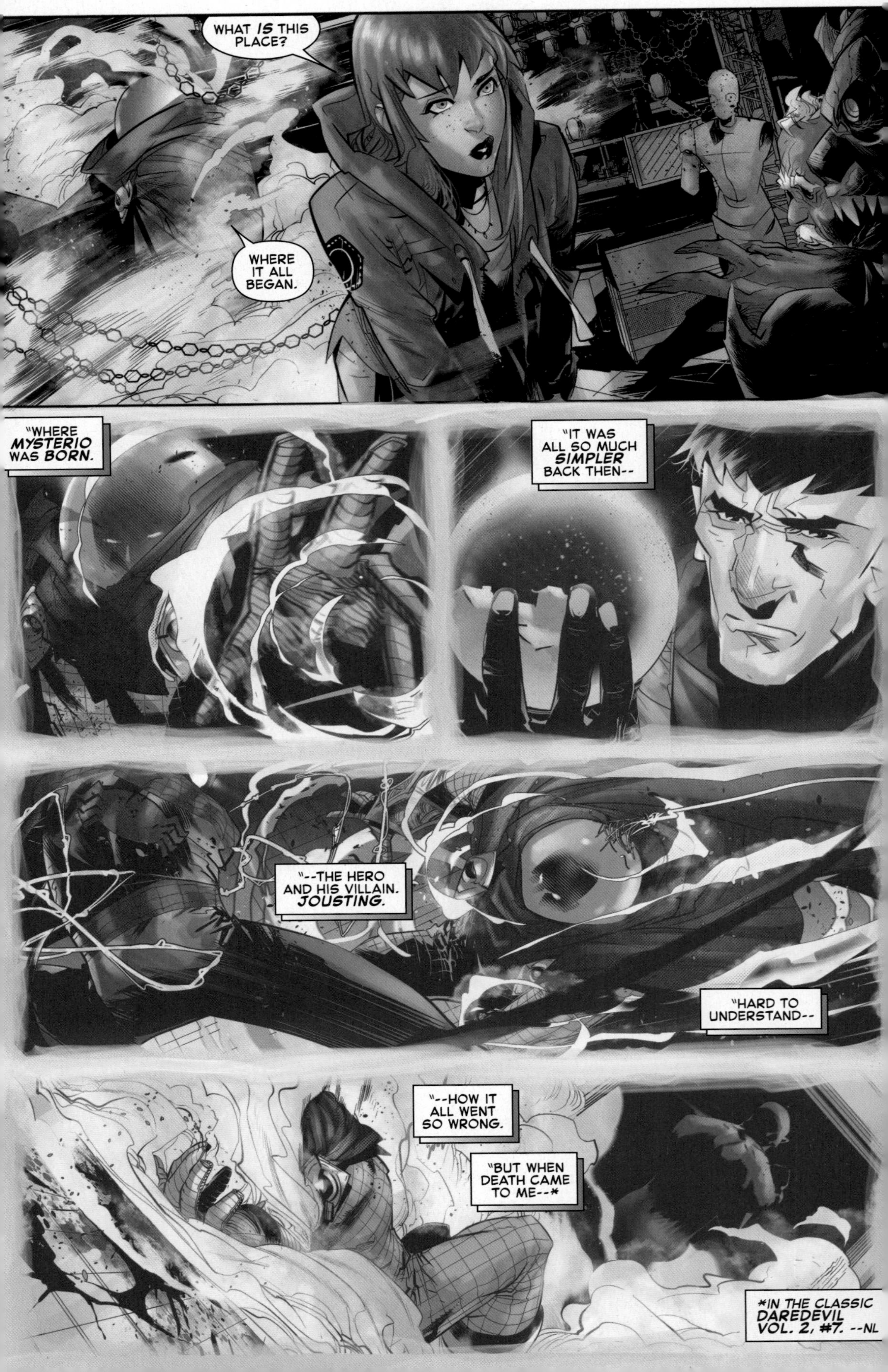
WHAT IS THIS PLACE?
WHERE IT ALL BEGAN.
"WHERE MYSTERIO WAS BORN.
"IT WAS ALL SO MUCH SIMPLER BACK THEN--
"--THE HERO AND HIS VILLAIN. JOUSTING.
"HARD TO UNDERSTAND--
"--HOW IT ALL WENT SO WRONG.
"BUT WHEN DEATH CAME TO ME--*
*IN THE CLASSIC DAREDEVIL VOL. 2, #7. --NL

"--IT DID NOT COME EASY.

"I FACED THE PUNISHMENT FOR MY SINS.

"I SUFFERED FOR WHAT FELT LIKE AN ETERNITY.

"UNTIL *HE* FOUND ME.

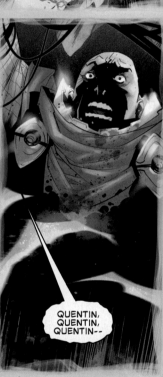

QUENTIN, QUENTIN, QUENTIN--

HAVE I GOT A DEAL FOR YOU...

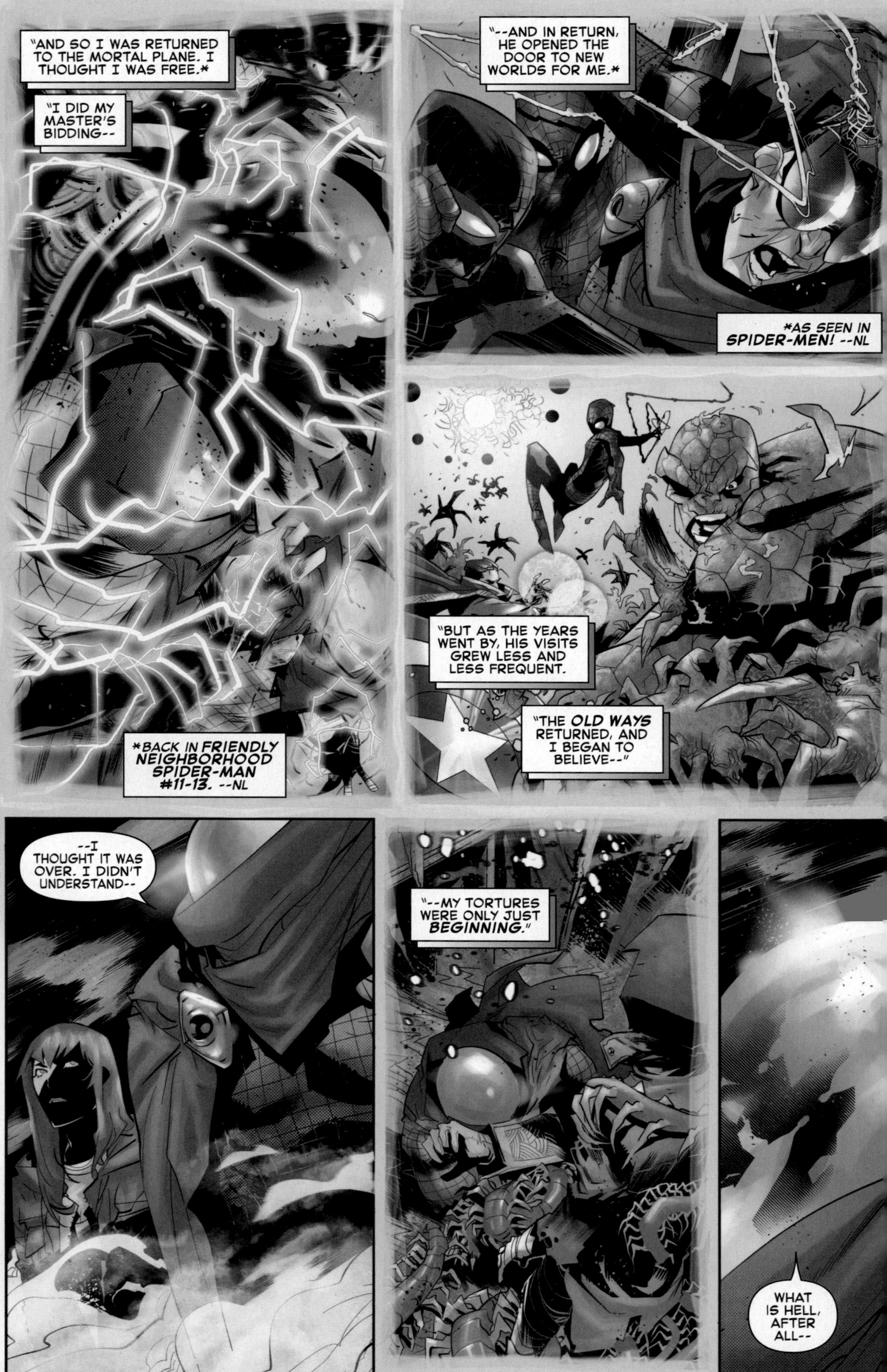
"AND SO I WAS RETURNED TO THE MORTAL PLANE. I THOUGHT I WAS FREE.*
"I DID MY MASTER'S BIDDING--
*BACK IN FRIENDLY NEIGHBORHOOD SPIDER-MAN #11-13. --NL
"--AND IN RETURN, HE OPENED THE DOOR TO NEW WORLDS FOR ME.*
*AS SEEN IN SPIDER-MEN! --NL
"BUT AS THE YEARS WENT BY, HIS VISITS GREW LESS AND LESS FREQUENT.
"THE OLD WAYS RETURNED, AND I BEGAN TO BELIEVE--"
--I THOUGHT IT WAS OVER. I DIDN'T UNDERSTAND--
"--MY TORTURES WERE ONLY JUST BEGINNING."
WHAT IS HELL, AFTER ALL--

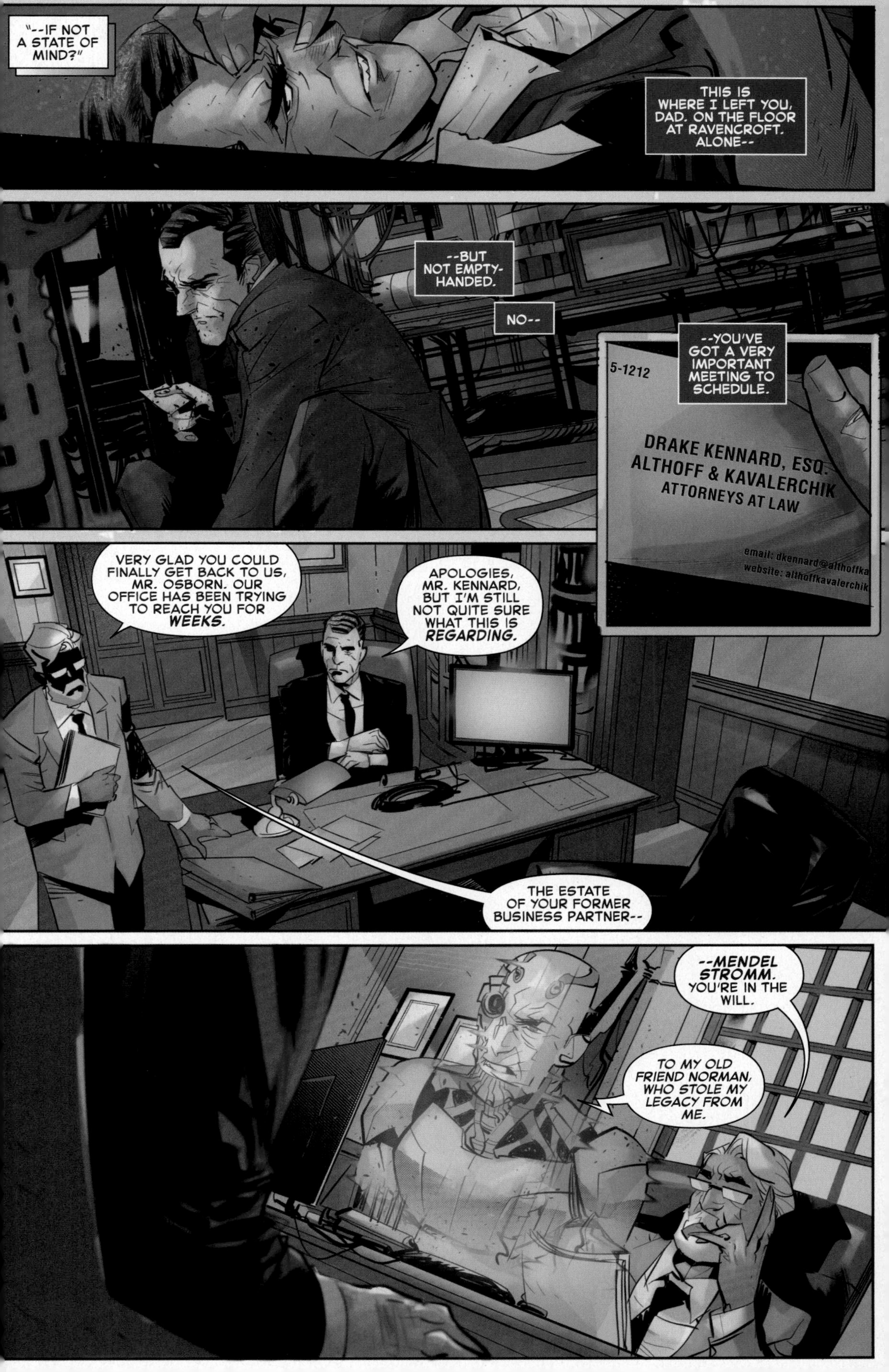
"--IF NOT A STATE OF MIND?"
THIS IS WHERE I LEFT YOU, DAD. ON THE FLOOR AT RAVENCROFT. ALONE--
--BUT NOT EMPTY-HANDED.
NO--
--YOU'VE GOT A VERY IMPORTANT MEETING TO SCHEDULE.
5-1212
DRAKE KENNARD, ESQ.
ALTHOFF & KAVALERCHIK
ATTORNEYS AT LAW
email: dkennard@althoffka
website: althoffkavalerchik
VERY GLAD YOU COULD FINALLY GET BACK TO US, MR. OSBORN. OUR OFFICE HAS BEEN TRYING TO REACH YOU FOR WEEKS.
APOLOGIES, MR. KENNARD, BUT I'M STILL NOT QUITE SURE WHAT THIS IS REGARDING.
THE ESTATE OF YOUR FORMER BUSINESS PARTNER--
--MENDEL STROMM. YOU'RE IN THE WILL.
TO MY OLD FRIEND NORMAN, WHO STOLE MY LEGACY FROM ME.

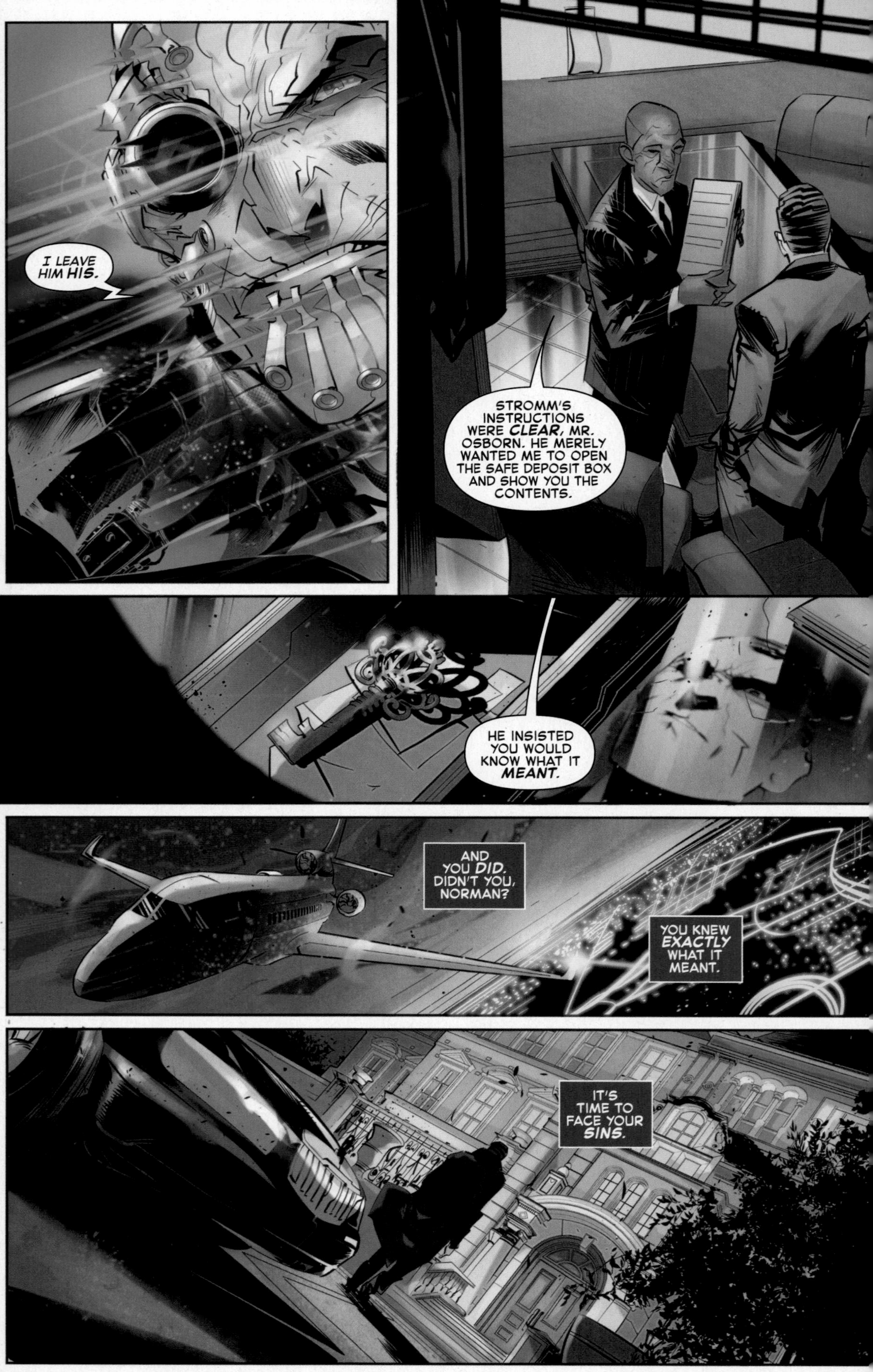
I LEAVE HIM HIS.
STROMM'S INSTRUCTIONS WERE CLEAR, MR. OSBORN. HE MERELY WANTED ME TO OPEN THE SAFE DEPOSIT BOX AND SHOW YOU THE CONTENTS.
HE INSISTED YOU WOULD KNOW WHAT IT MEANT.
AND YOU DID, DIDN'T YOU, NORMAN?
YOU KNEW EXACTLY WHAT IT MEANT.
IT'S TIME TO FACE YOUR SINS.

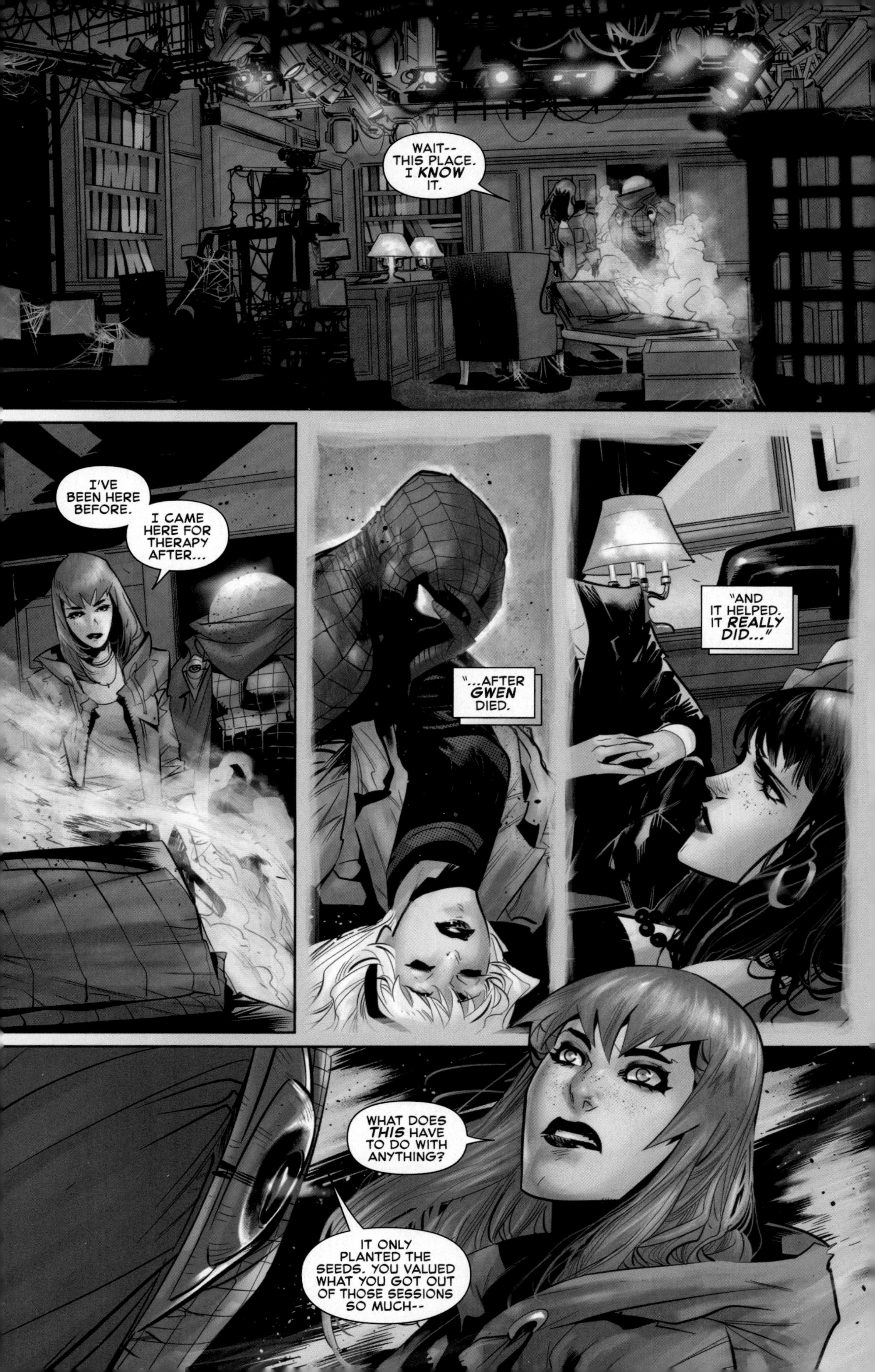
WAIT-- THIS PLACE. I KNOW IT.
I'VE BEEN HERE BEFORE.
I CAME HERE FOR THERAPY AFTER...
"...AFTER GWEN DIED.
"AND IT HELPED. IT REALLY DID..."
WHAT DOES THIS HAVE TO DO WITH ANYTHING?
IT ONLY PLANTED THE SEEDS. YOU VALUED WHAT YOU GOT OUT OF THOSE SESSIONS SO MUCH--

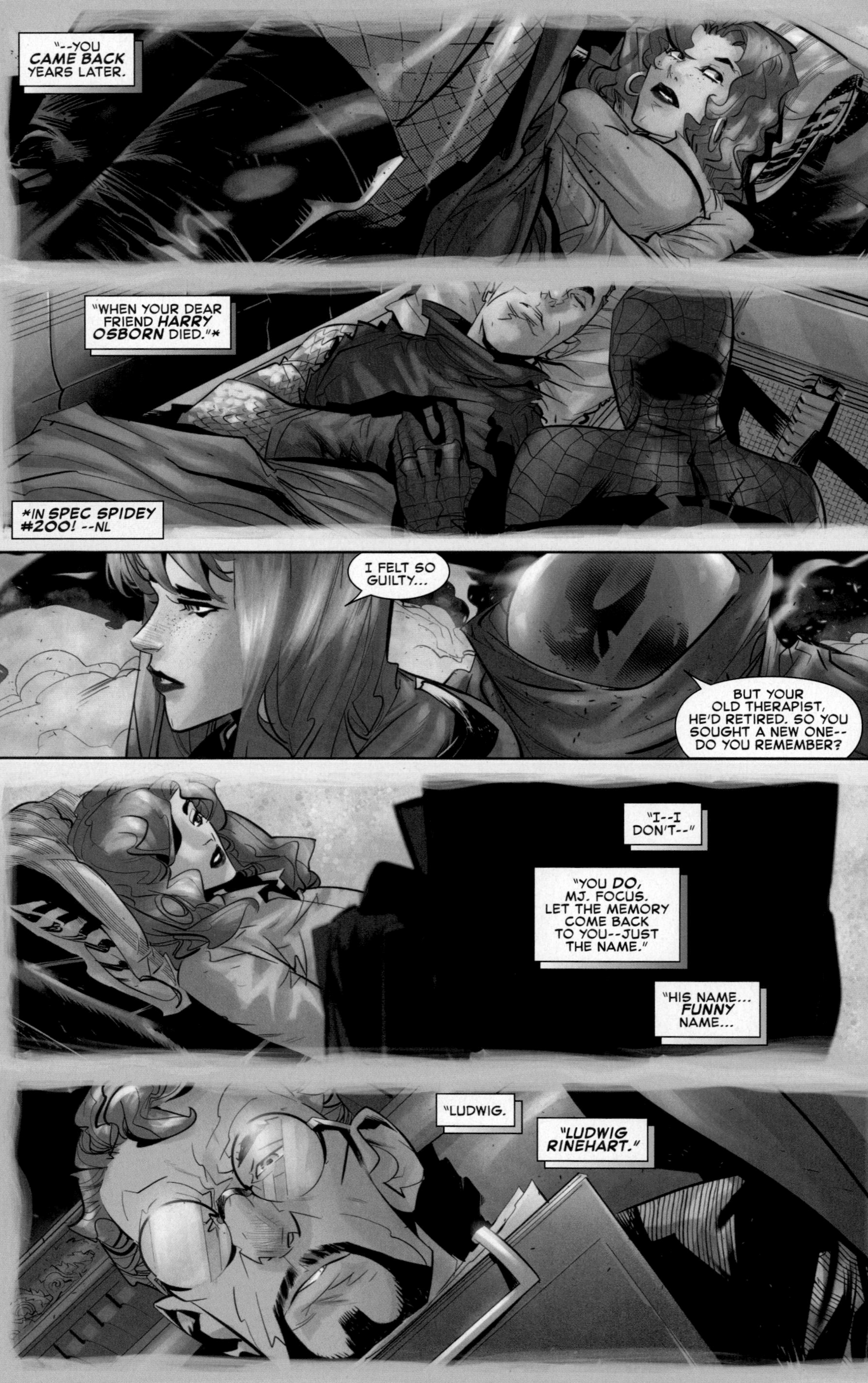
"--YOU CAME BACK YEARS LATER.
"WHEN YOUR DEAR FRIEND HARRY OSBORN DIED."*
*IN SPEC SPIDEY #200! --NL
I FELT SO GUILTY...
BUT YOUR OLD THERAPIST, HE'D RETIRED. SO YOU SOUGHT A NEW ONE-- DO YOU REMEMBER?
"I--I DON'T--"
"YOU DO, MJ. FOCUS. LET THE MEMORY COME BACK TO YOU--JUST THE NAME."
"HIS NAME... FUNNY NAME...
"LUDWIG.
"LUDWIG RINEHART."

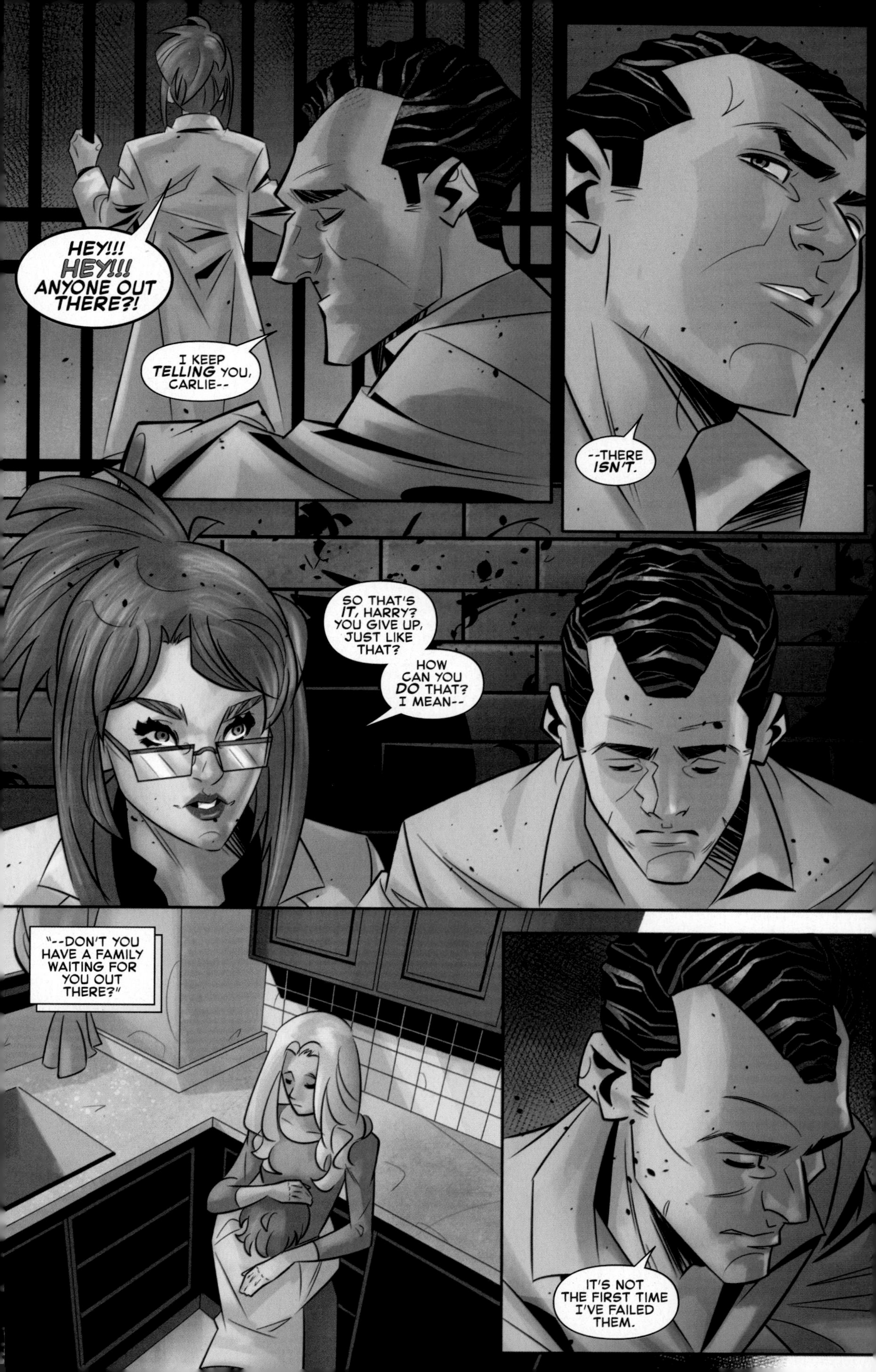
HEY!!! HEY!!! ANYONE OUT THERE?!
I KEEP TELLING YOU, CARLIE--
--THERE ISN'T.
SO THAT'S IT, HARRY? YOU GIVE UP, JUST LIKE THAT?
HOW CAN YOU DO THAT? I MEAN--
"--DON'T YOU HAVE A FAMILY WAITING FOR YOU OUT THERE?"
IT'S NOT THE FIRST TIME I'VE FAILED THEM.

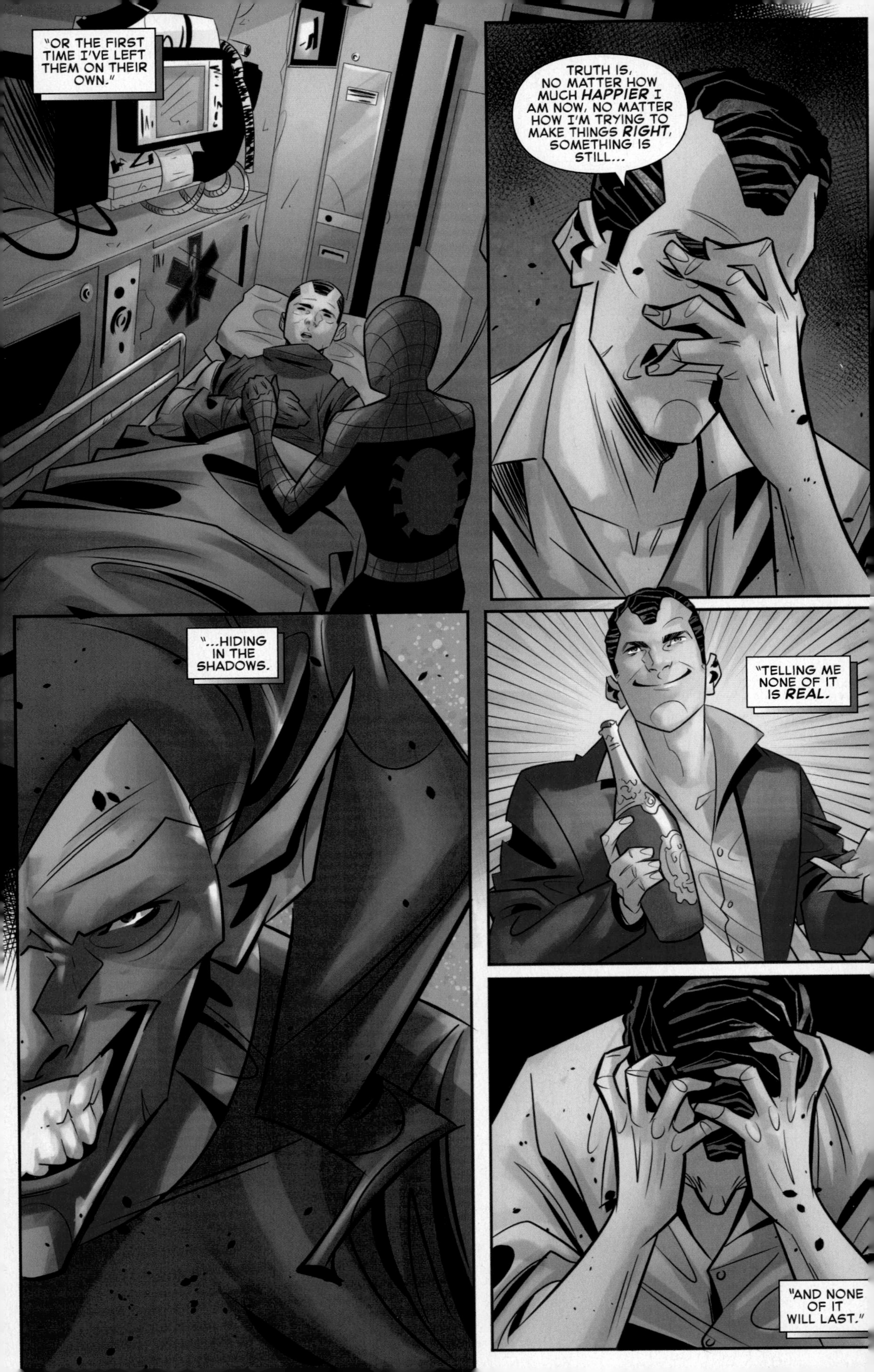
"OR THE FIRST TIME I'VE LEFT THEM ON THEIR OWN."
TRUTH IS, NO MATTER HOW MUCH HAPPIER I AM NOW, NO MATTER HOW I'M TRYING TO MAKE THINGS RIGHT, SOMETHING IS STILL...
"...HIDING IN THE SHADOWS.
"TELLING ME NONE OF IT IS REAL.
"AND NONE OF IT WILL LAST."

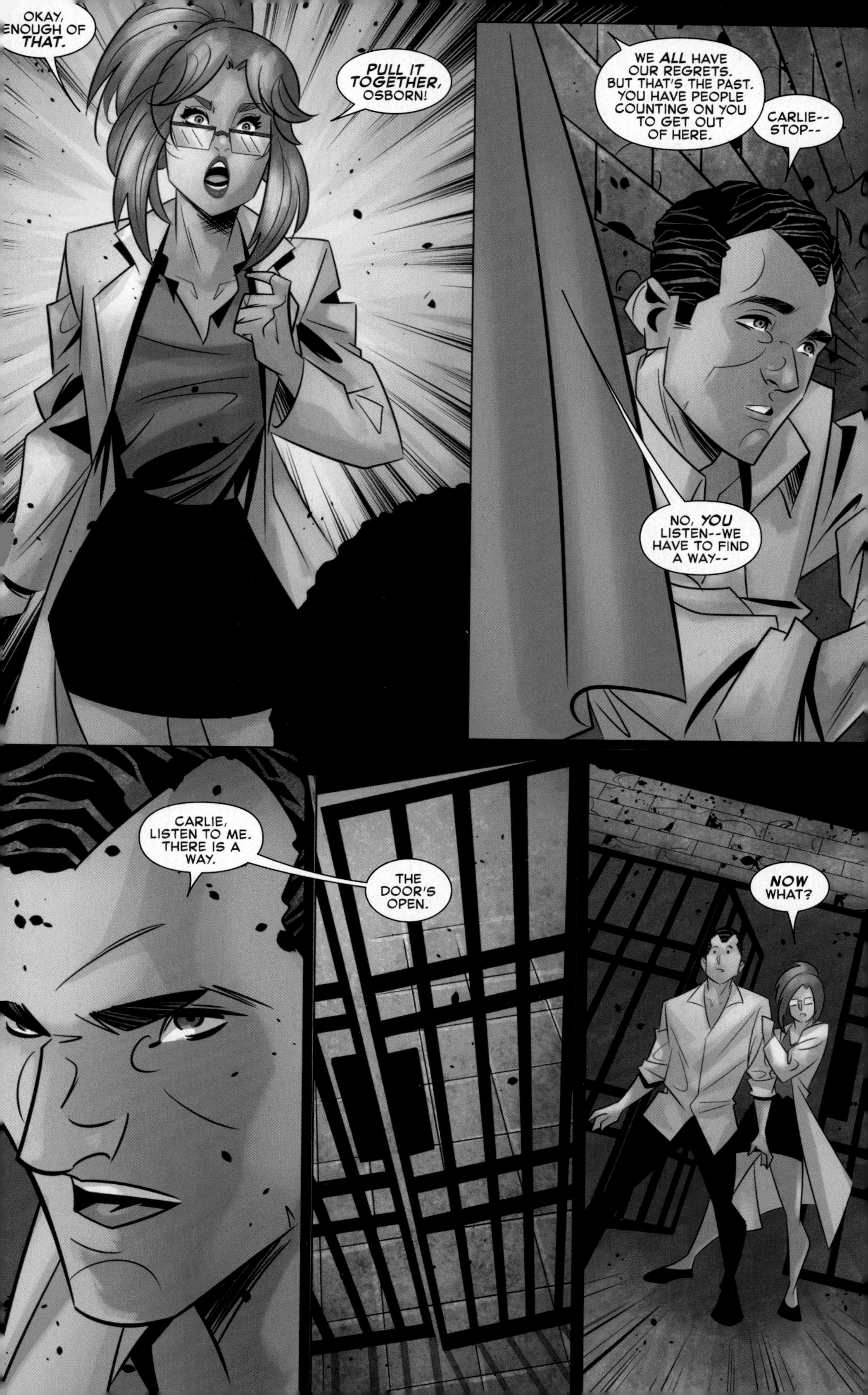
OKAY, ENOUGH OF THAT.
PULL IT TOGETHER, OSBORN!
WE ALL HAVE OUR REGRETS. BUT THAT'S THE PAST. YOU HAVE PEOPLE COUNTING ON YOU TO GET OUT OF HERE.
CARLIE-- STOP--
NO, YOU LISTEN--WE HAVE TO FIND A WAY--
CARLIE, LISTEN TO ME. THERE IS A WAY.
THE DOOR'S OPEN.
NOW WHAT?

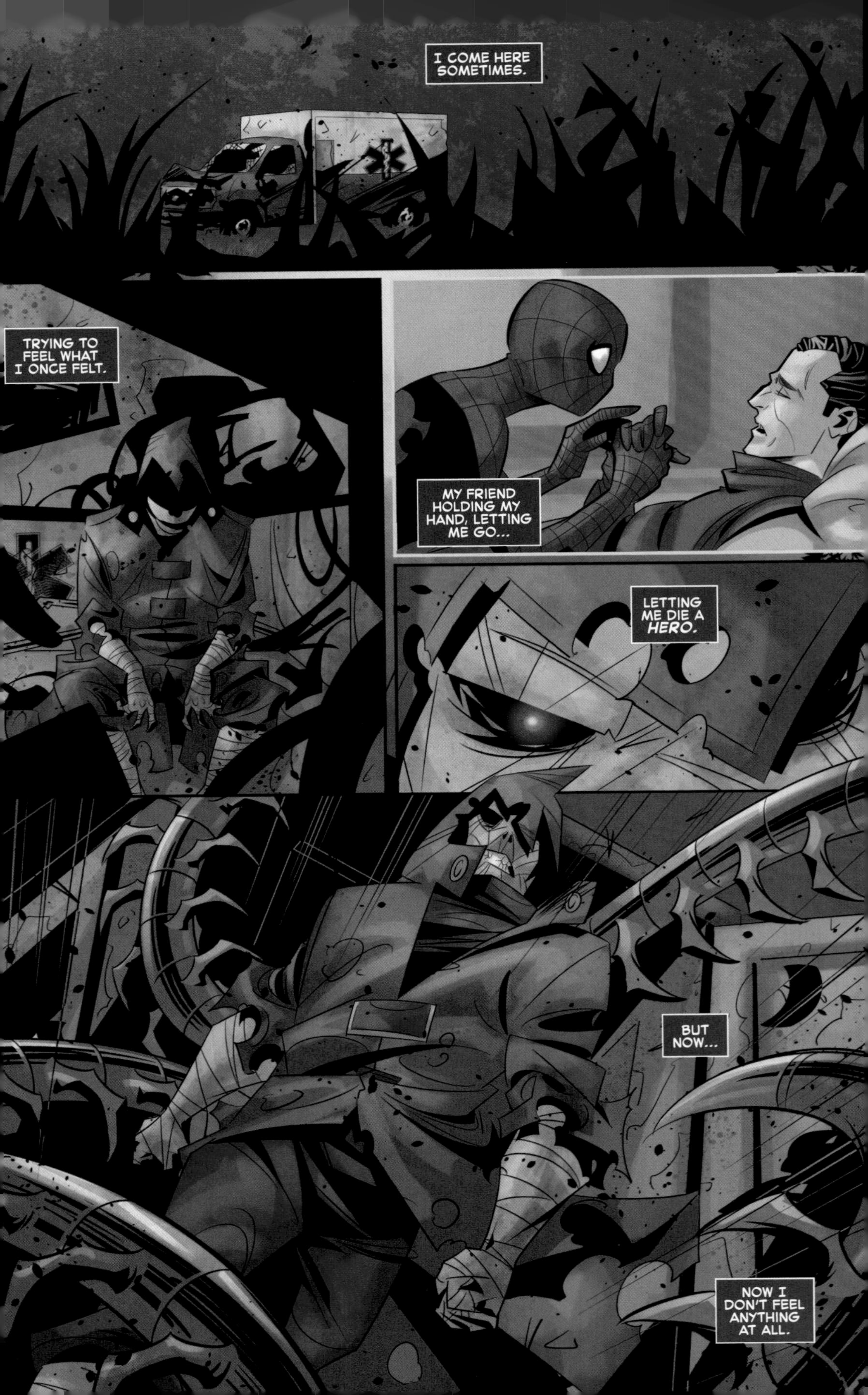
I COME HERE SOMETIMES.
TRYING TO FEEL WHAT I ONCE FELT.
MY FRIEND HOLDING MY HAND, LETTING ME GO...
LETTING ME DIE A *HERO.*
BUT NOW...
NOW I DON'T FEEL ANYTHING AT ALL.

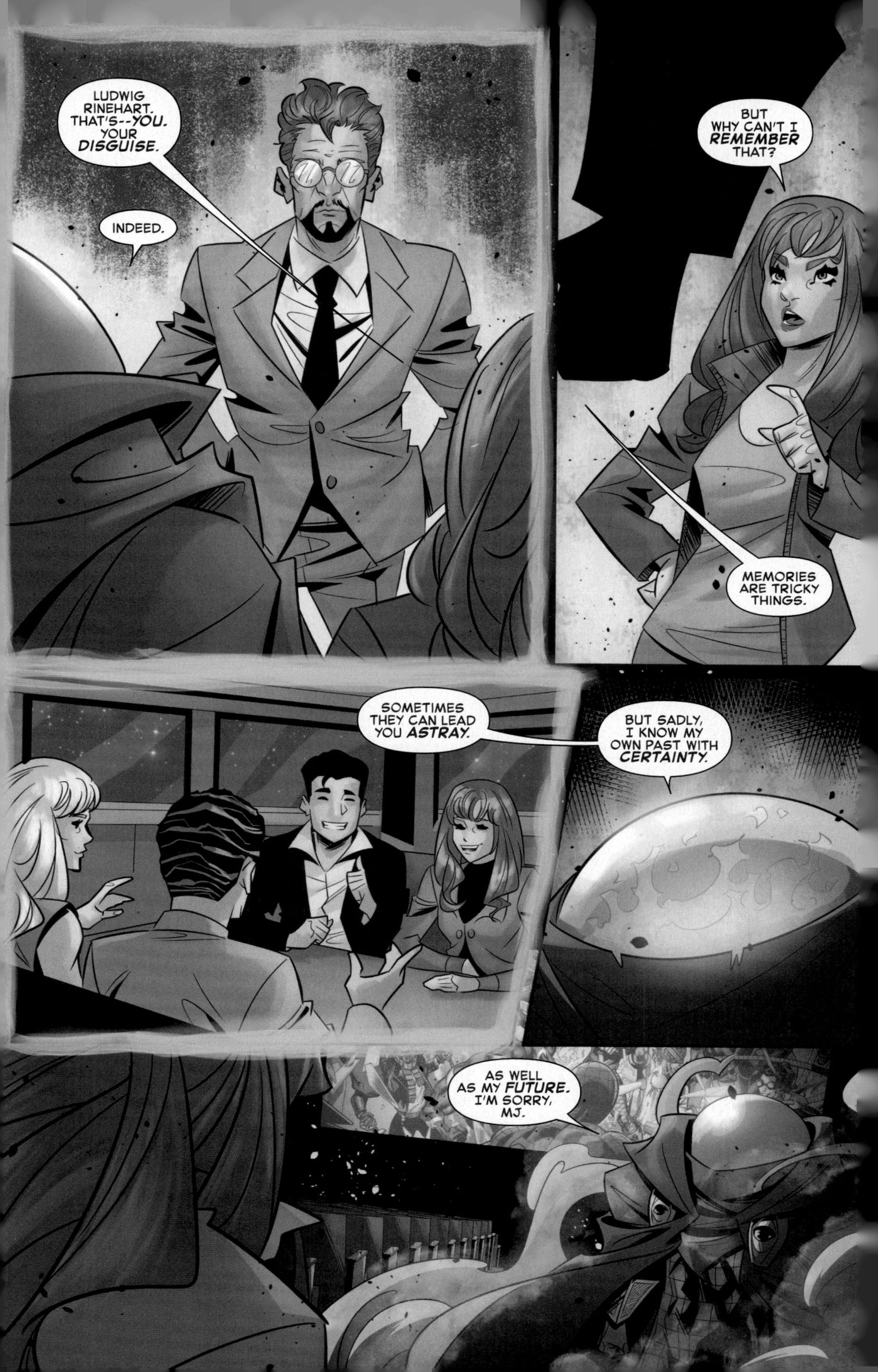
LUDWIG RINEHART. THAT'S--YOU. YOUR DISGUISE.
INDEED.
BUT WHY CAN'T I REMEMBER THAT?
MEMORIES ARE TRICKY THINGS.
SOMETIMES THEY CAN LEAD YOU ASTRAY.
BUT SADLY, I KNOW MY OWN PAST WITH CERTAINTY.
AS WELL AS MY FUTURE. I'M SORRY, MJ.

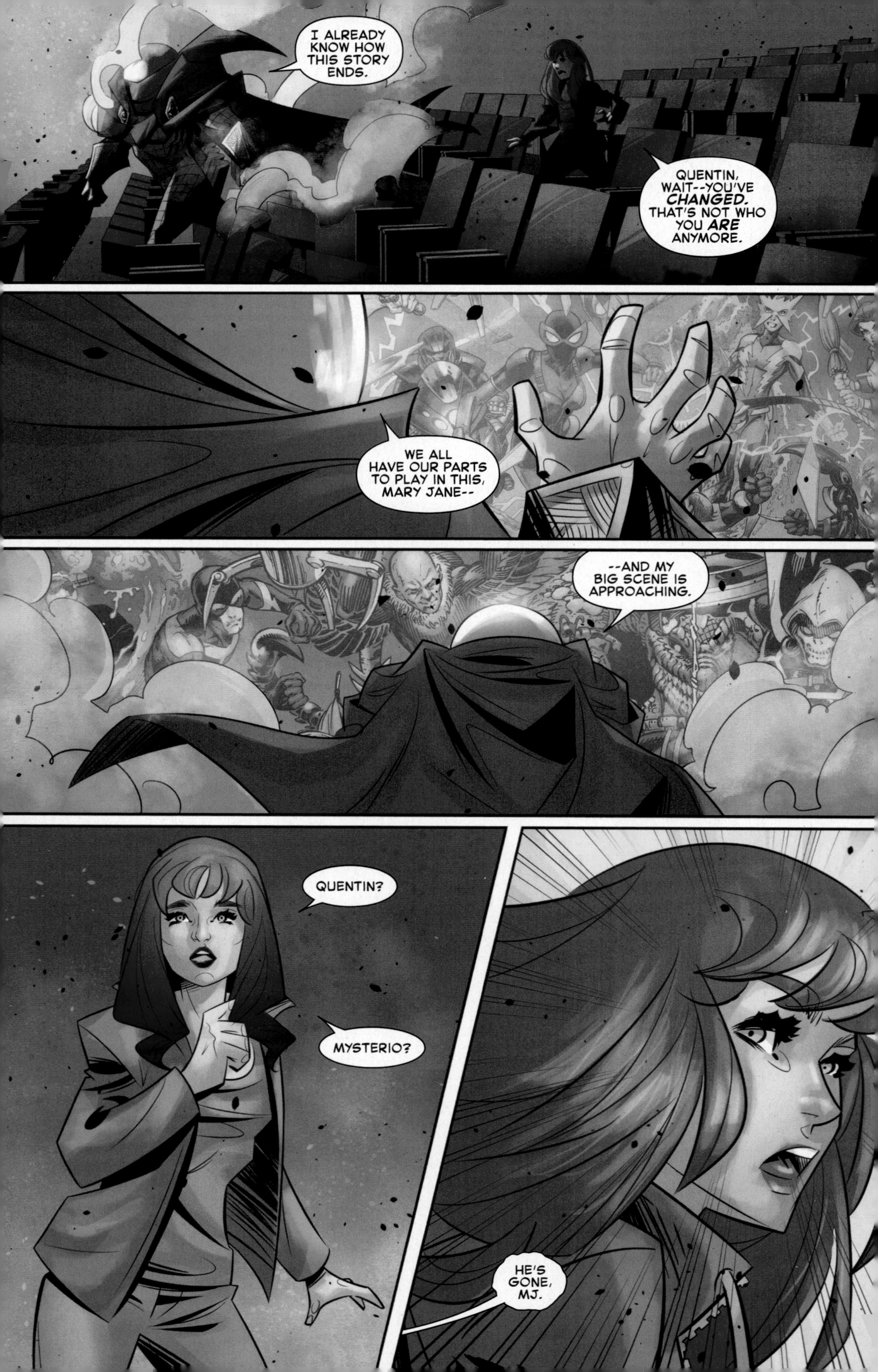

I ALREADY KNOW HOW THIS STORY ENDS.
QUENTIN, WAIT--YOU'VE CHANGED. THAT'S NOT WHO YOU ARE ANYMORE.
WE ALL HAVE OUR PARTS TO PLAY IN THIS, MARY JANE--
--AND MY BIG SCENE IS APPROACHING.
QUENTIN?
MYSTERIO?
HE'S GONE, MJ.

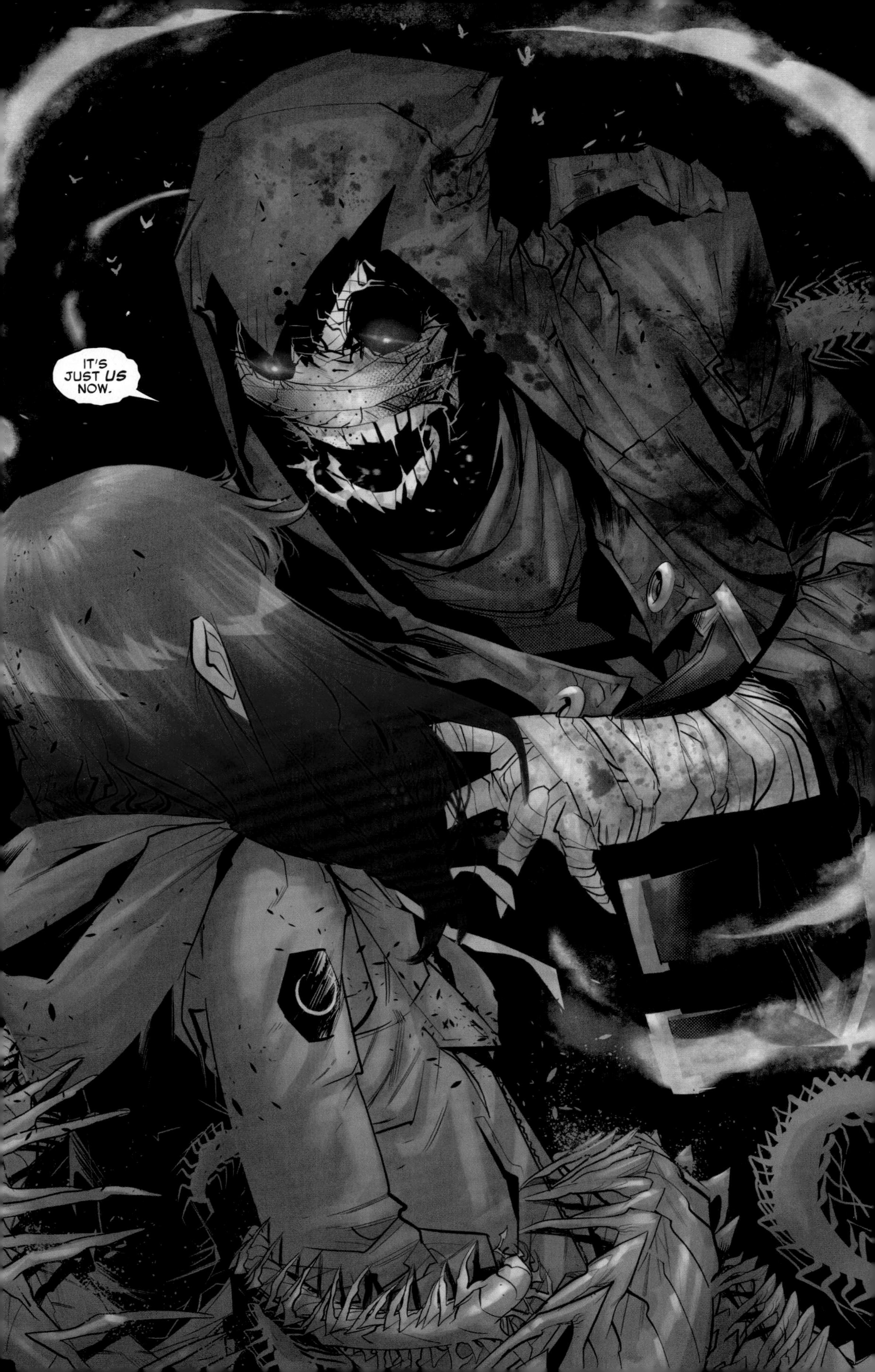
IT'S JUST US NOW.

72

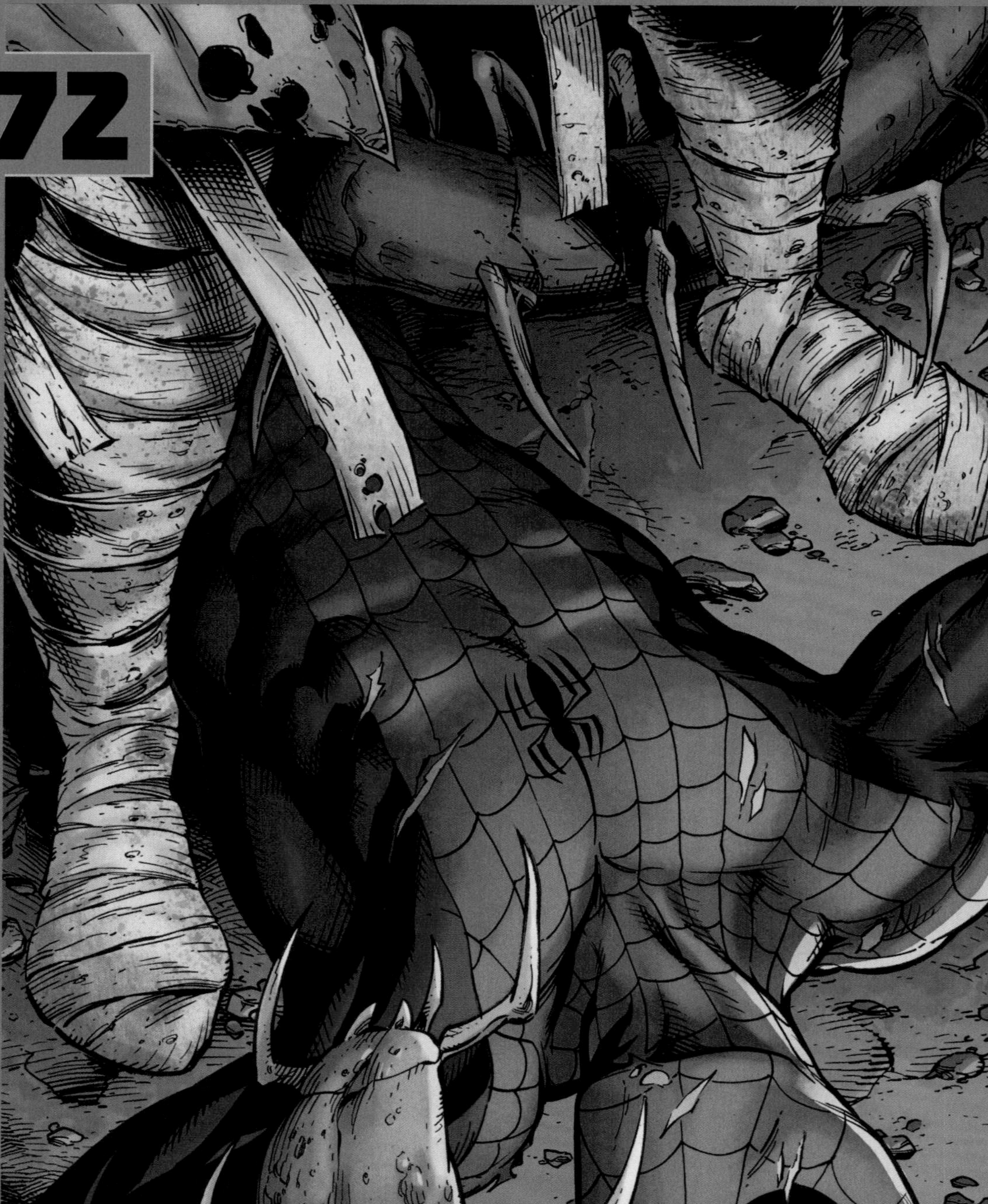

SINISTER WAR PART 2

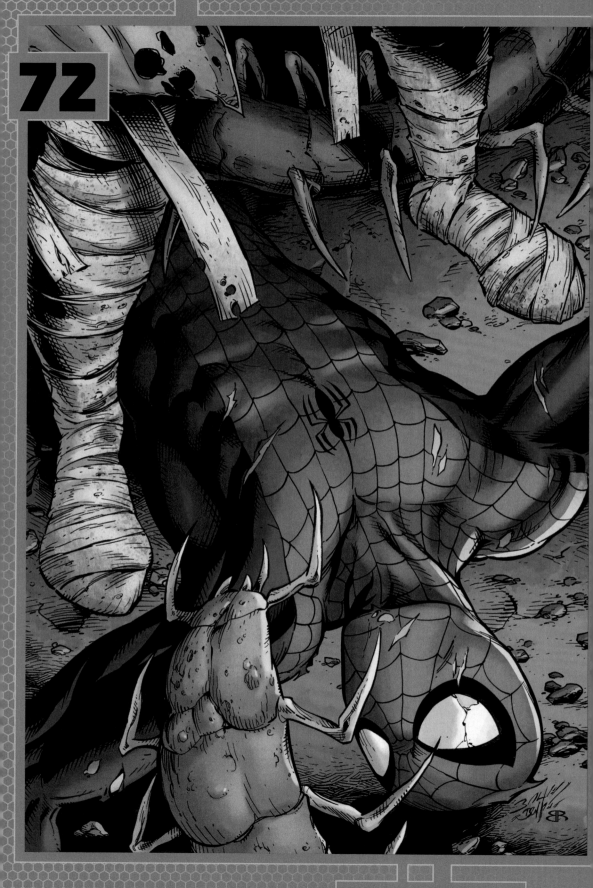

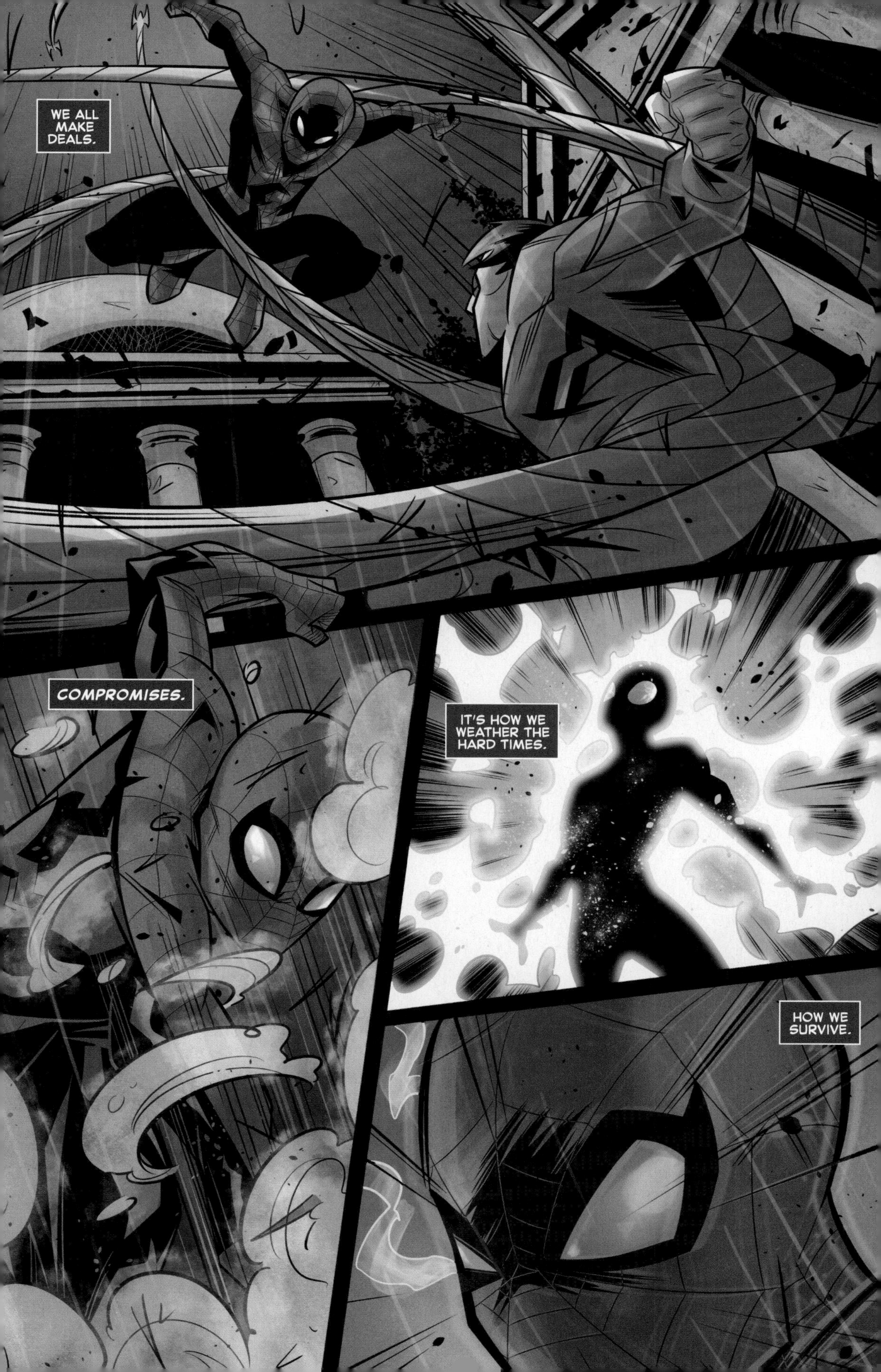
WE ALL MAKE DEALS.
COMPROMISES.
IT'S HOW WE WEATHER THE HARD TIMES.
HOW WE SURVIVE.

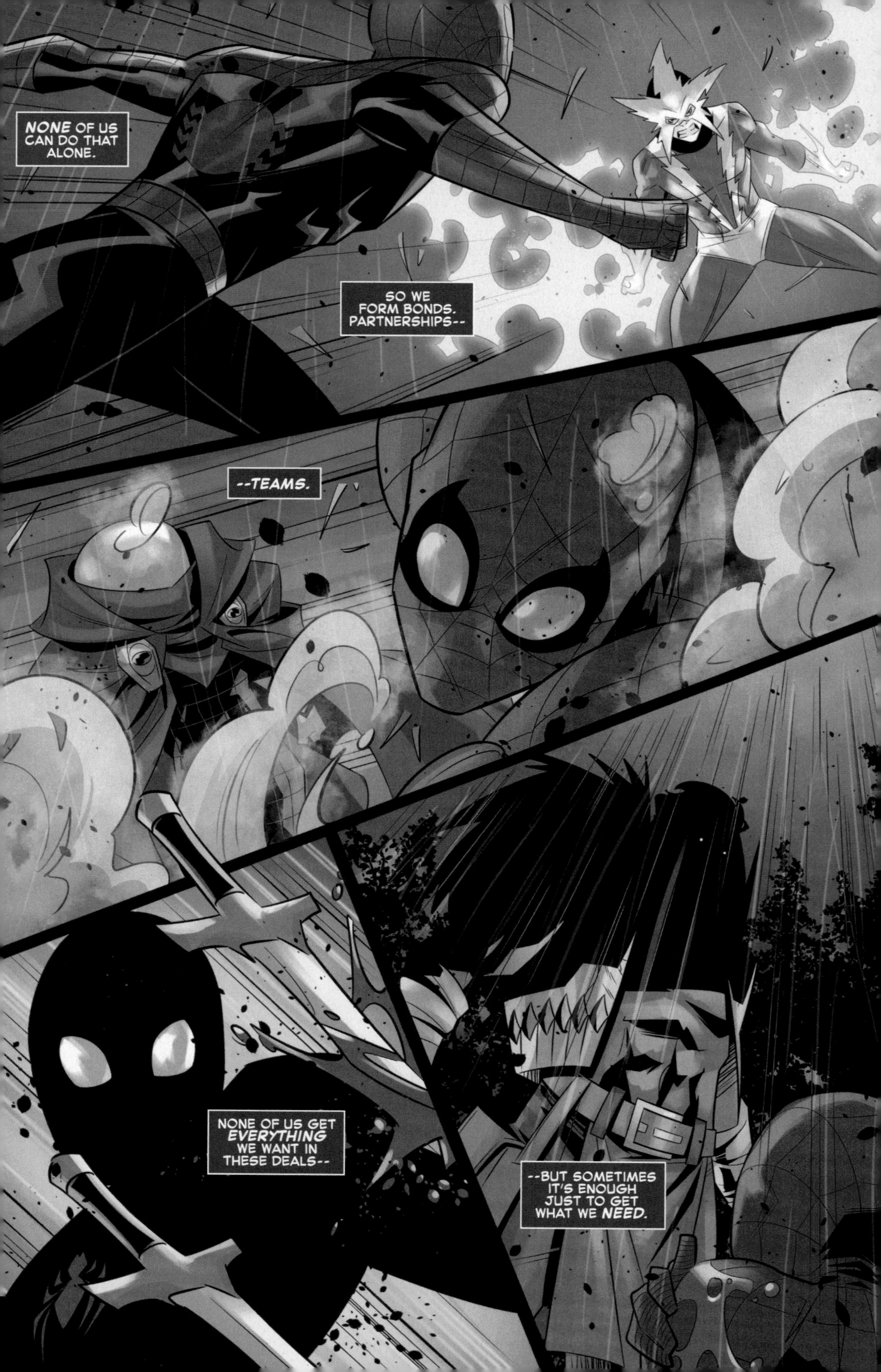
NONE OF US CAN DO THAT ALONE.
SO WE FORM BONDS. PARTNERSHIPS--
--TEAMS.
NONE OF US GET EVERYTHING WE WANT IN THESE DEALS--
--BUT SOMETIMES IT'S ENOUGH JUST TO GET WHAT WE NEED.

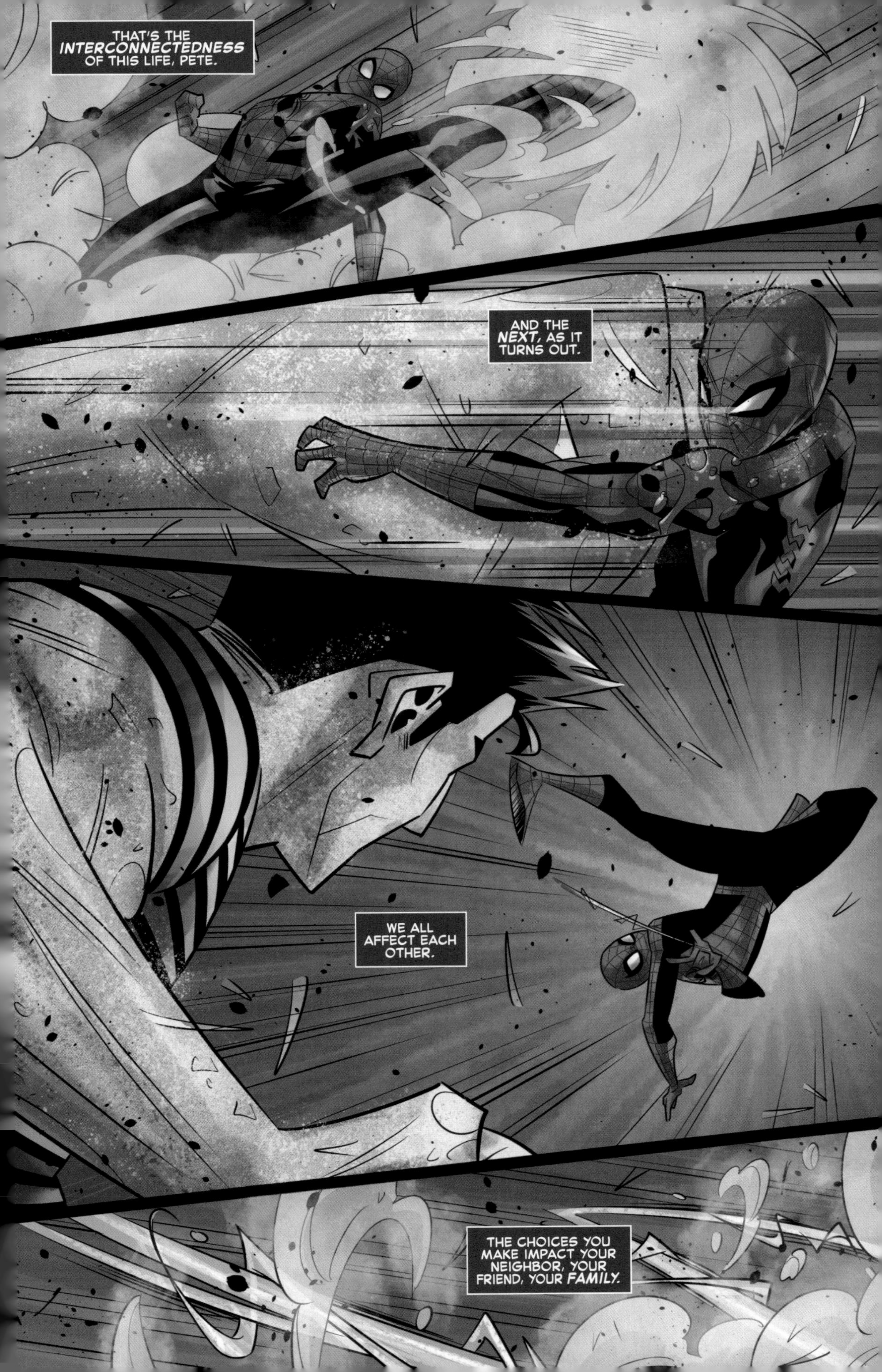
THAT'S THE INTERCONNECTEDNESS OF THIS LIFE, PETE.
AND THE NEXT, AS IT TURNS OUT.
WE ALL AFFECT EACH OTHER.
THE CHOICES YOU MAKE IMPACT YOUR NEIGHBOR, YOUR FRIEND, YOUR FAMILY.

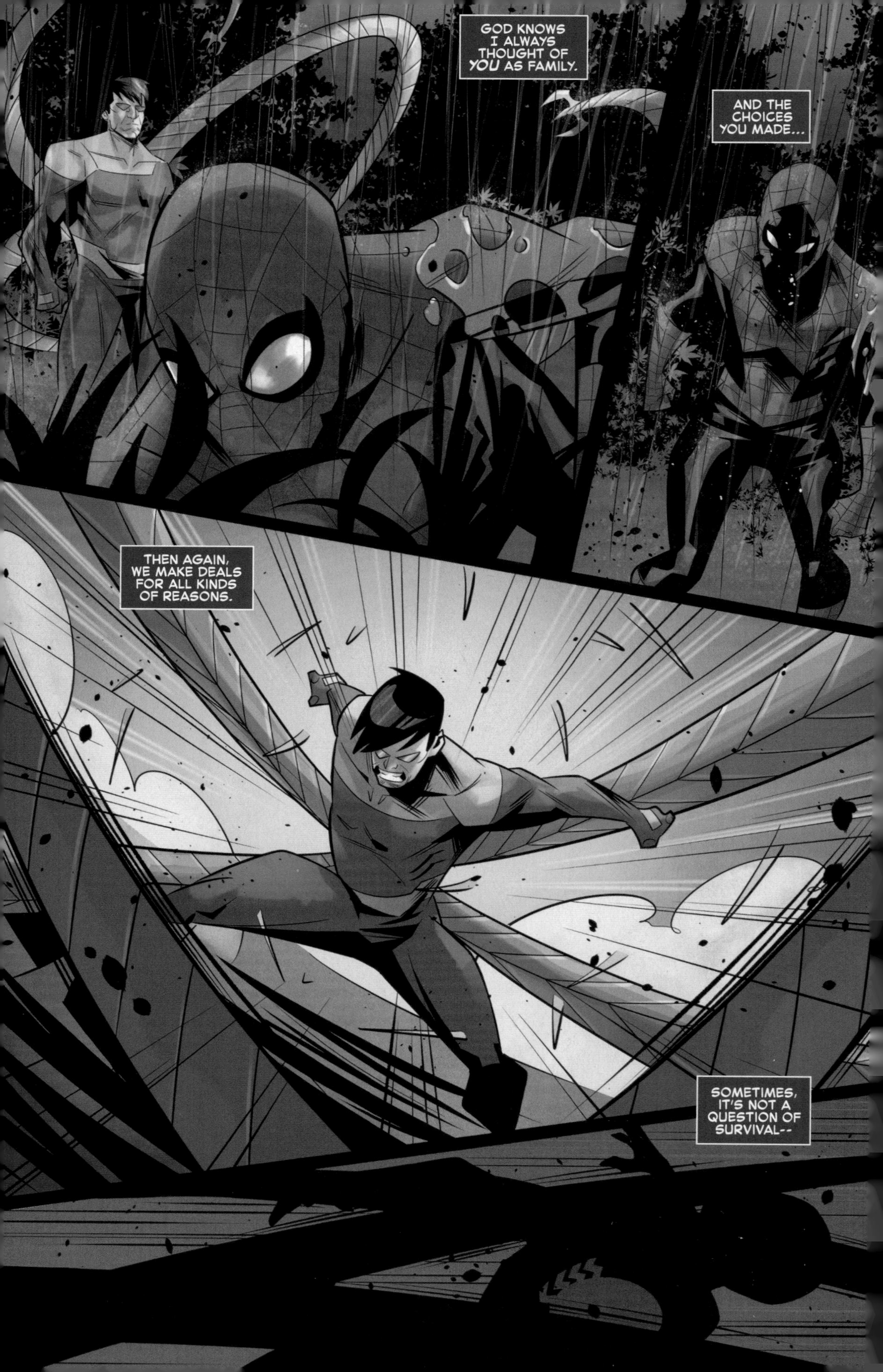
GOD KNOWS I ALWAYS THOUGHT OF YOU AS FAMILY.
AND THE CHOICES YOU MADE...
THEN AGAIN, WE MAKE DEALS FOR ALL KINDS OF REASONS.
SOMETIMES, IT'S NOT A QUESTION OF SURVIVAL--

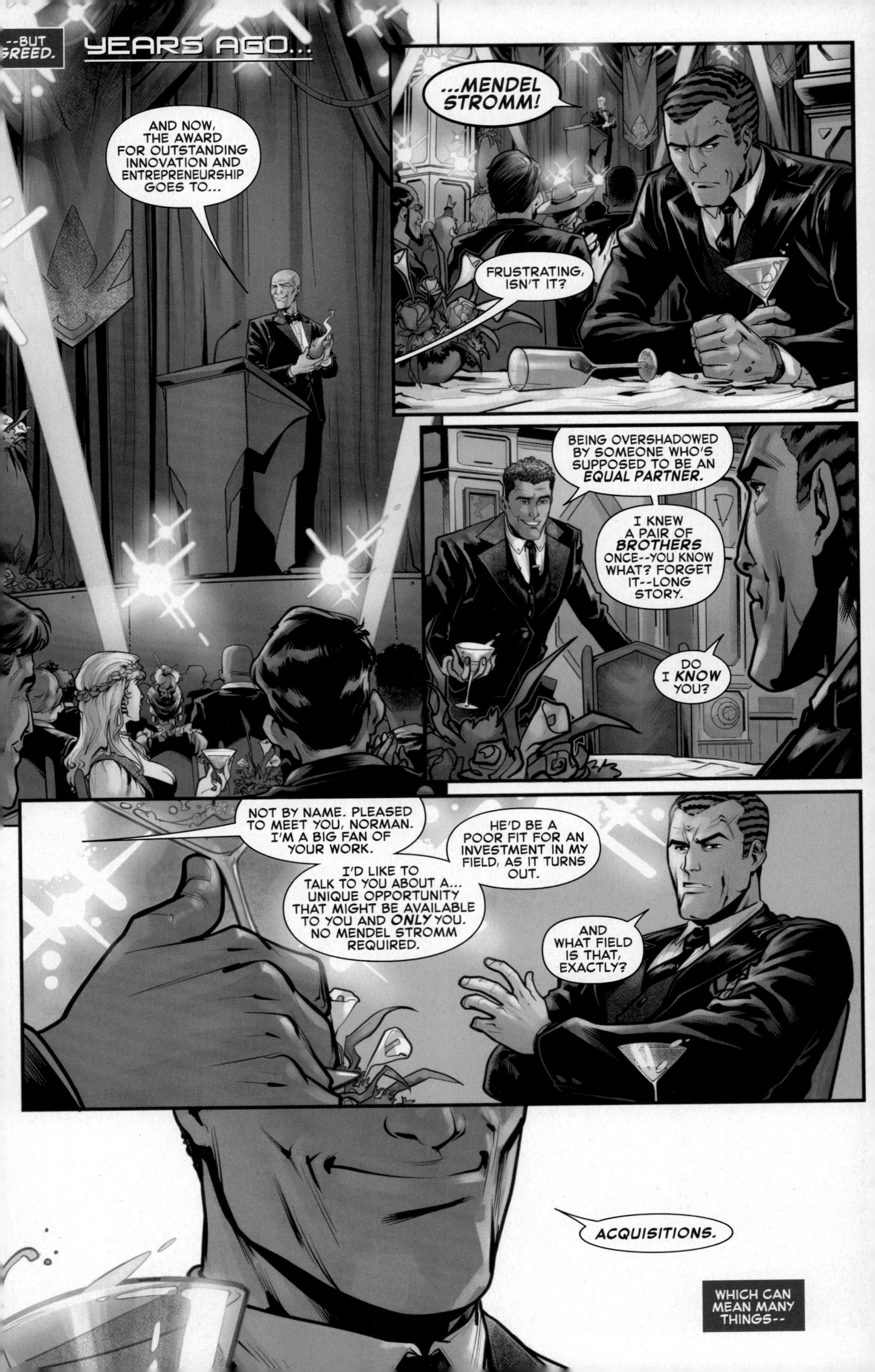
--BUT
GREED.
YEARS AGO...
AND NOW, THE AWARD FOR OUTSTANDING INNOVATION AND ENTREPRENEURSHIP GOES TO...
...MENDEL STROMM!
FRUSTRATING, ISN'T IT?
BEING OVERSHADOWED BY SOMEONE WHO'S SUPPOSED TO BE AN EQUAL PARTNER.
I KNEW A PAIR OF BROTHERS ONCE--YOU KNOW WHAT? FORGET IT--LONG STORY.
DO I KNOW YOU?
NOT BY NAME. PLEASED TO MEET YOU, NORMAN. I'M A BIG FAN OF YOUR WORK.
I'D LIKE TO TALK TO YOU ABOUT A... UNIQUE OPPORTUNITY THAT MIGHT BE AVAILABLE TO YOU AND ONLY YOU. NO MENDEL STROMM REQUIRED.
HE'D BE A POOR FIT FOR AN INVESTMENT IN MY FIELD, AS IT TURNS OUT.
AND WHAT FIELD IS THAT, EXACTLY?
ACQUISITIONS.
WHICH CAN MEAN MANY THINGS--

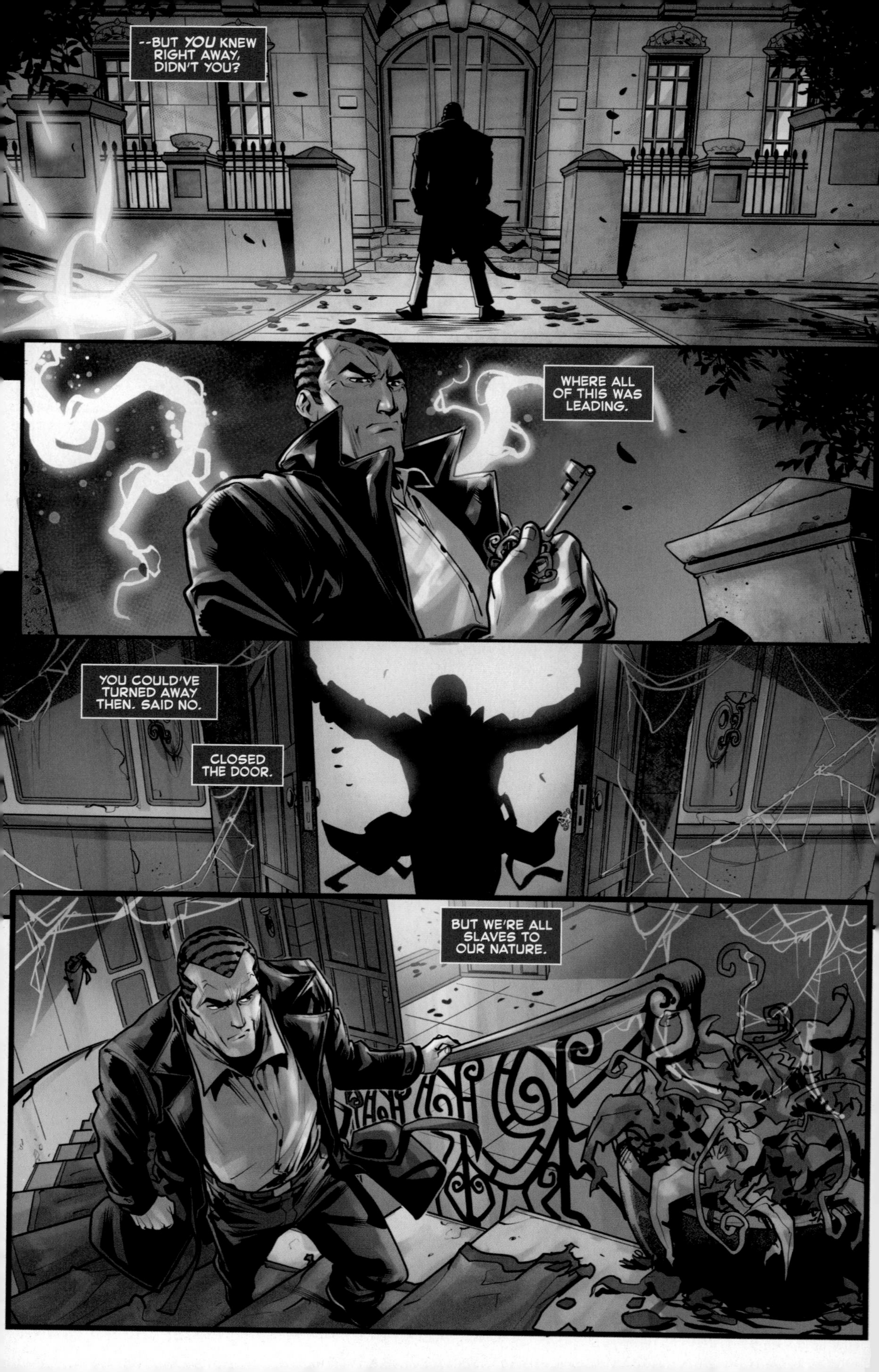
--BUT YOU KNEW RIGHT AWAY, DIDN'T YOU?
WHERE ALL OF THIS WAS LEADING.
YOU COULD'VE TURNED AWAY THEN. SAID NO.
CLOSED THE DOOR.
BUT WE'RE ALL SLAVES TO OUR NATURE.

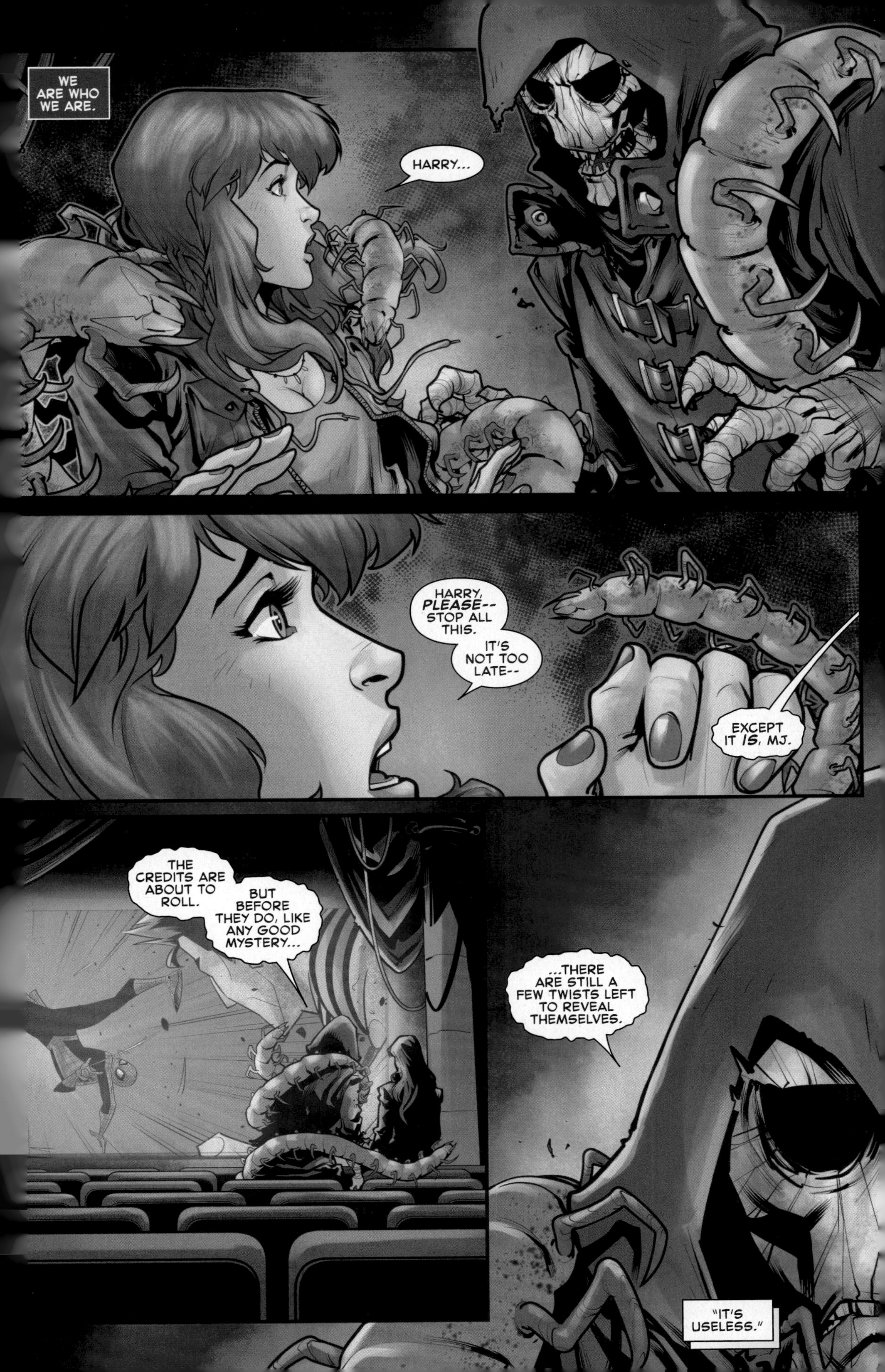
WE ARE WHO WE ARE.
HARRY...
HARRY, *PLEASE*-- STOP ALL THIS.
IT'S NOT TOO LATE--
EXCEPT IT *IS*, MJ.
THE CREDITS ARE ABOUT TO ROLL.
BUT BEFORE THEY DO, LIKE ANY GOOD MYSTERY...
...THERE ARE STILL A FEW TWISTS LEFT TO REVEAL THEMSELVES.
"IT'S USELESS."

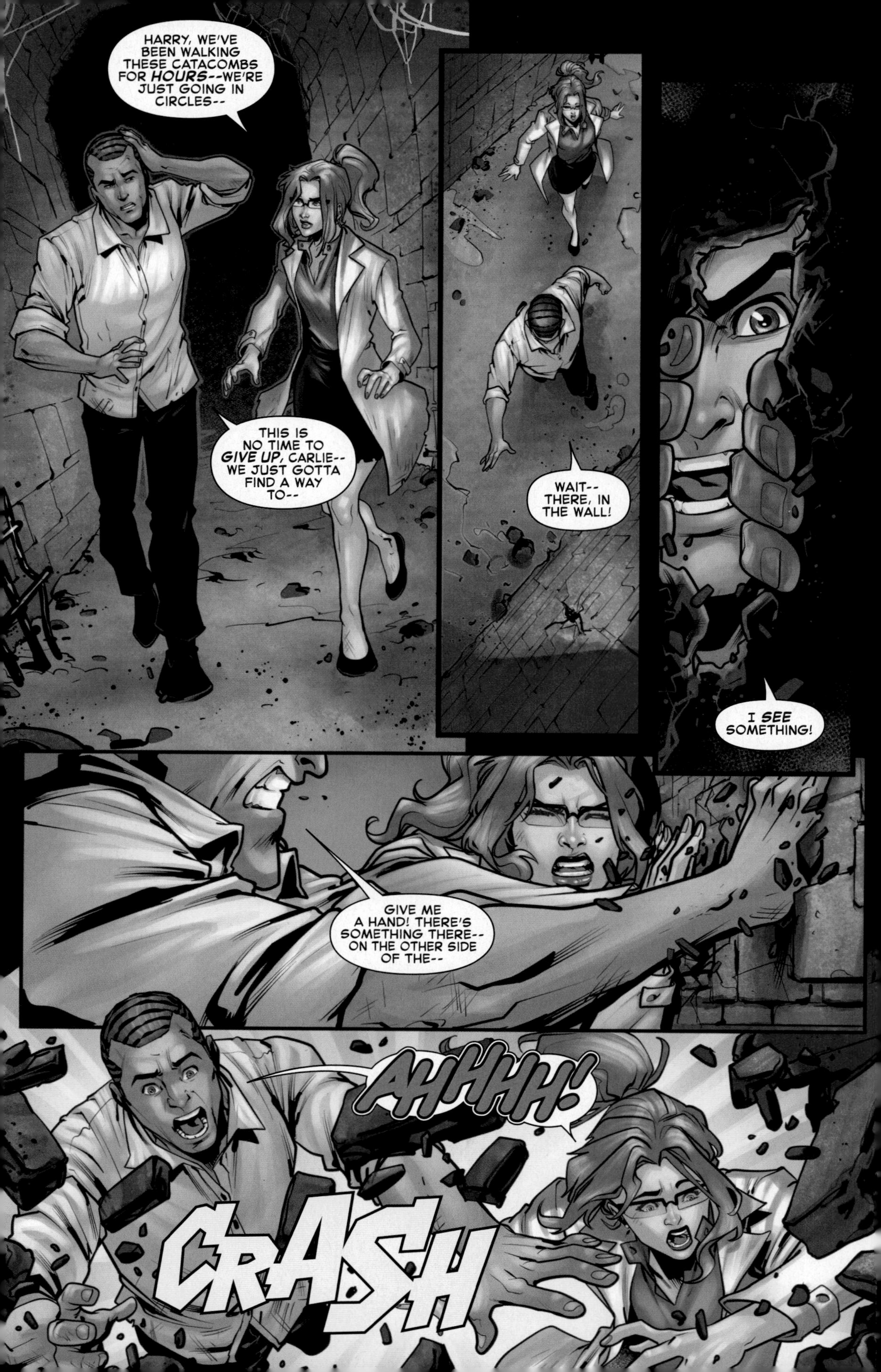
HARRY, WE'VE BEEN WALKING THESE CATACOMBS FOR HOURS--WE'RE JUST GOING IN CIRCLES--
THIS IS NO TIME TO GIVE UP, CARLIE--WE JUST GOTTA FIND A WAY TO--
WAIT--THERE, IN THE WALL!
I SEE SOMETHING!
GIVE ME A HAND! THERE'S SOMETHING THERE--ON THE OTHER SIDE OF THE--
AHHHH!
CRASH

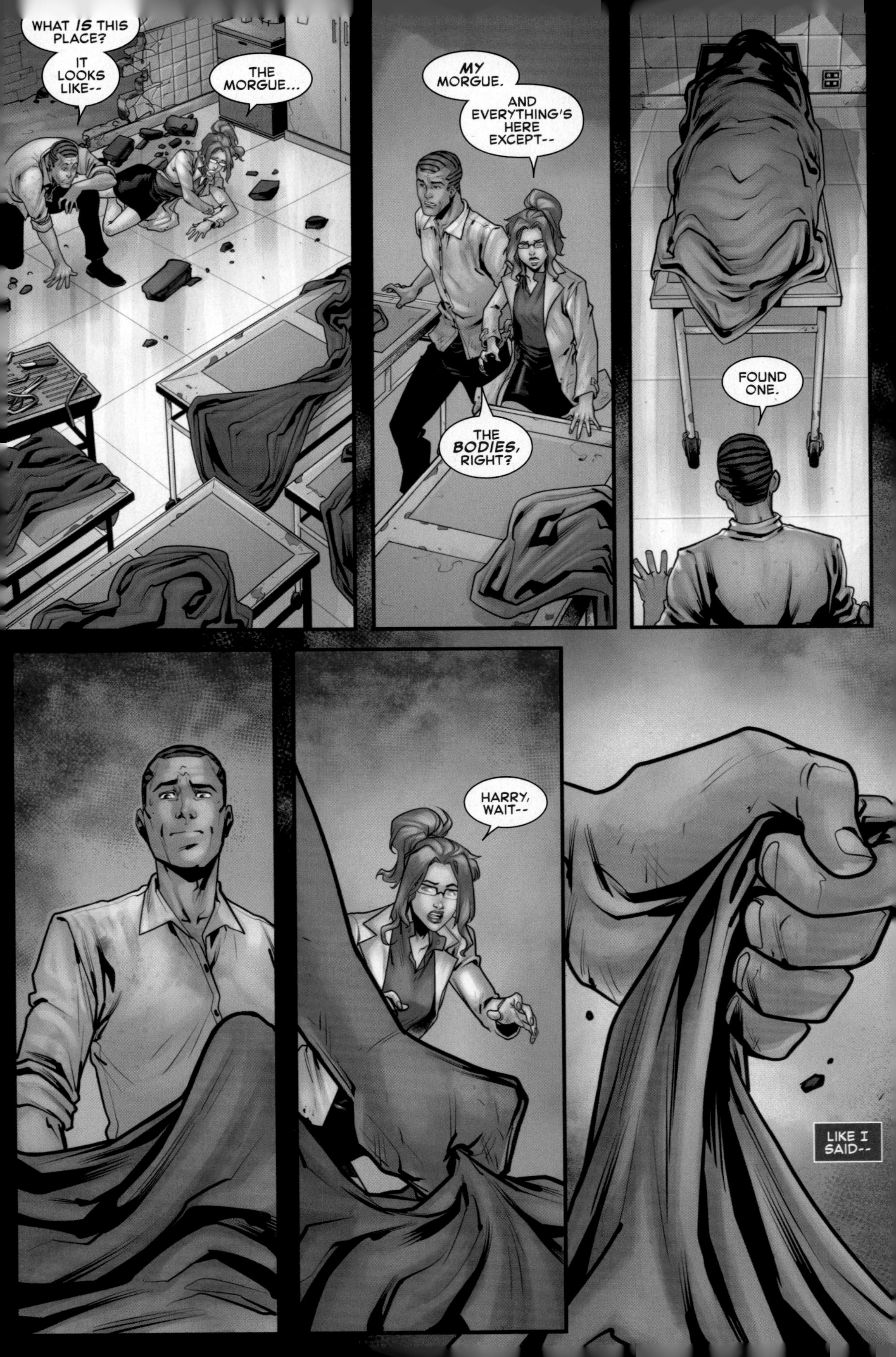
WHAT IS THIS PLACE?
IT LOOKS LIKE--
THE MORGUE...
MY MORGUE.
AND EVERYTHING'S HERE EXCEPT--
THE BODIES, RIGHT?
FOUND ONE.
HARRY, WAIT--
LIKE I SAID--

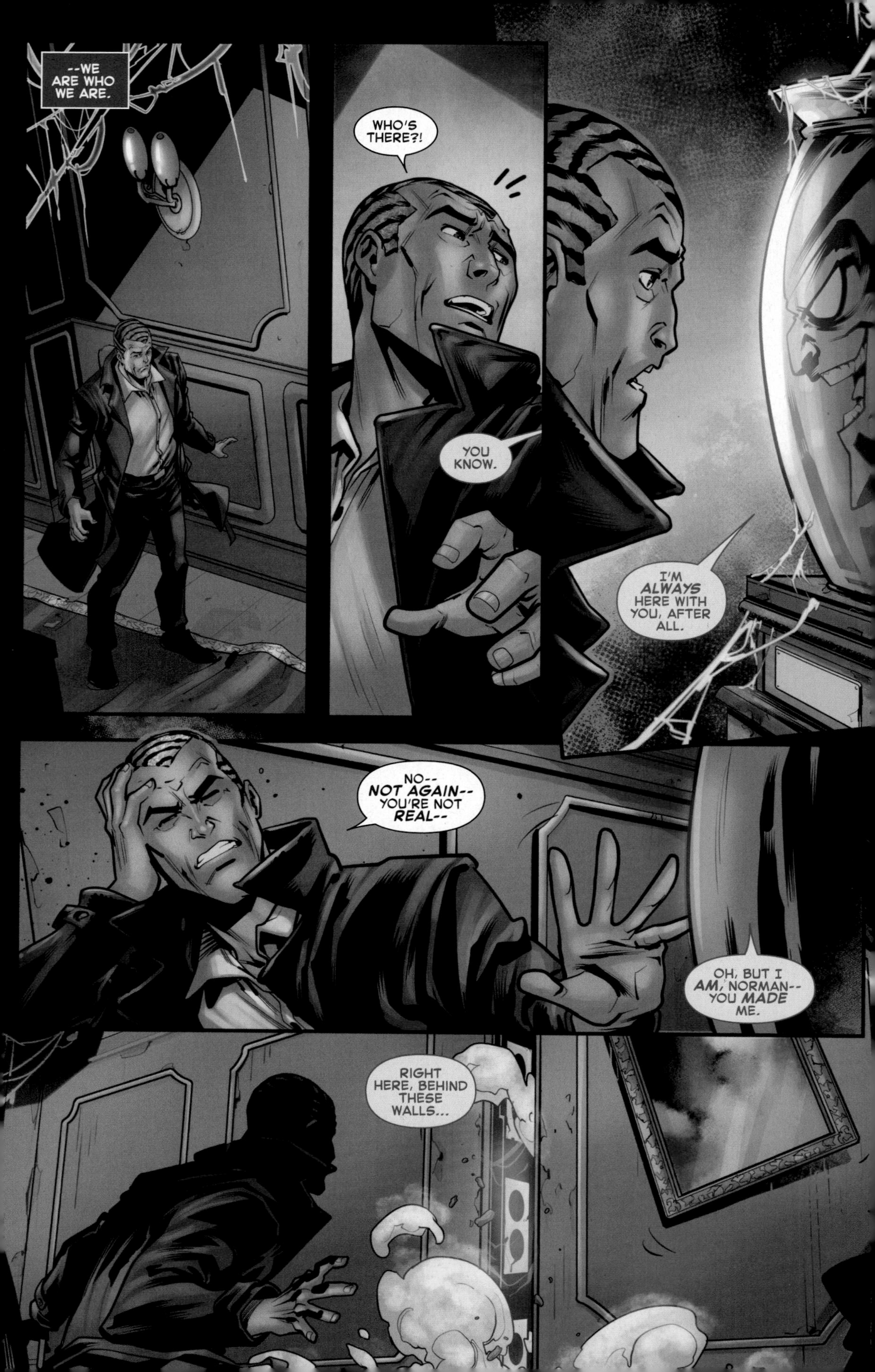
--WE ARE WHO WE ARE.
WHO'S THERE?!
YOU KNOW.
I'M ALWAYS HERE WITH YOU, AFTER ALL.
NO-- NOT AGAIN-- YOU'RE NOT REAL--
OH, BUT I AM, NORMAN-- YOU MADE ME.
RIGHT HERE, BEHIND THESE WALLS...

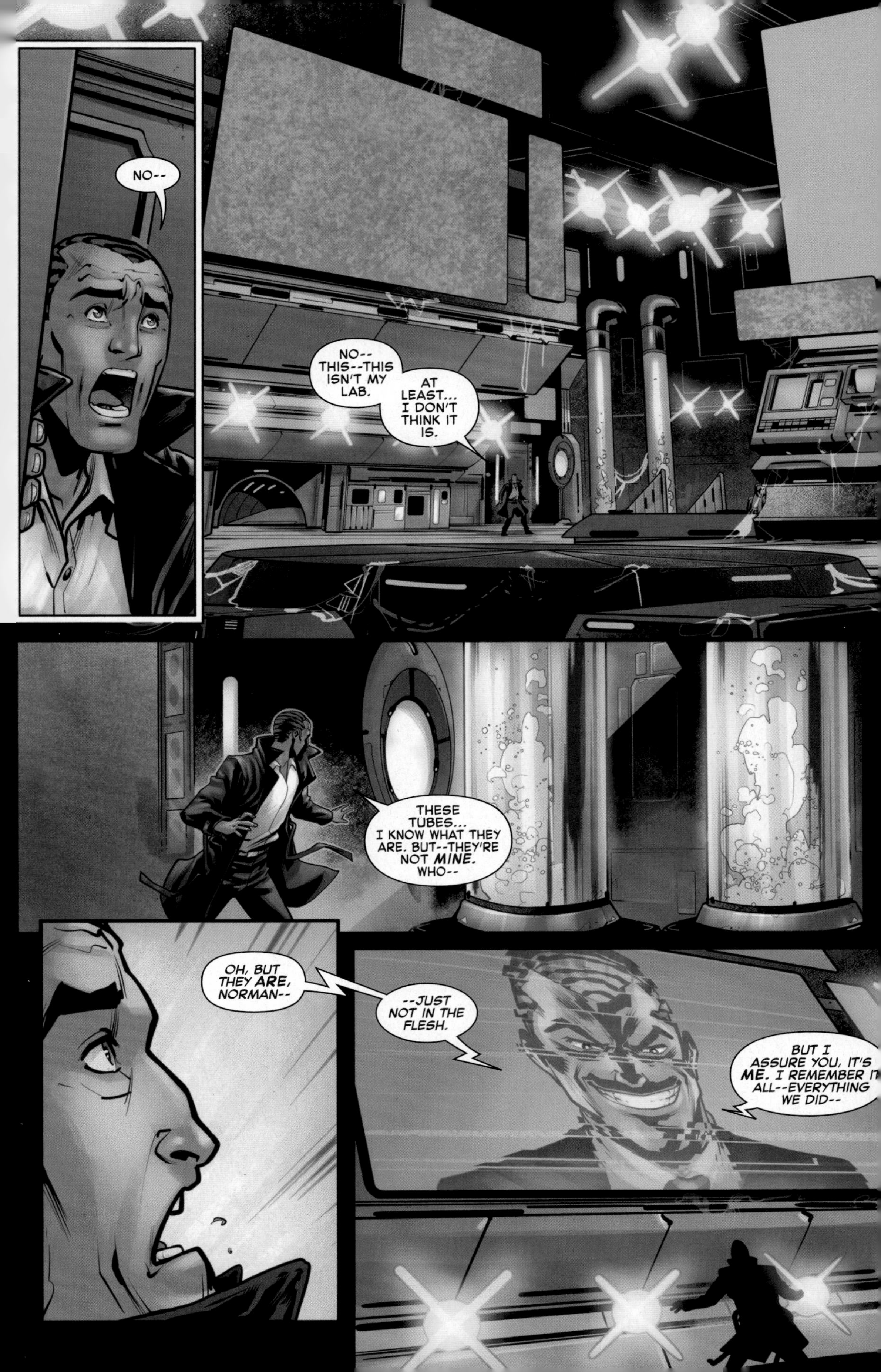
NO--
NO-- THIS--THIS ISN'T MY LAB.
AT LEAST... I DON'T THINK IT IS.
THESE TUBES... I KNOW WHAT THEY ARE. BUT--THEY'RE NOT MINE. WHO--
OH, BUT THEY ARE, NORMAN--
--JUST NOT IN THE FLESH.
BUT I ASSURE YOU, IT'S ME. I REMEMBER IT ALL--EVERYTHING WE DID--

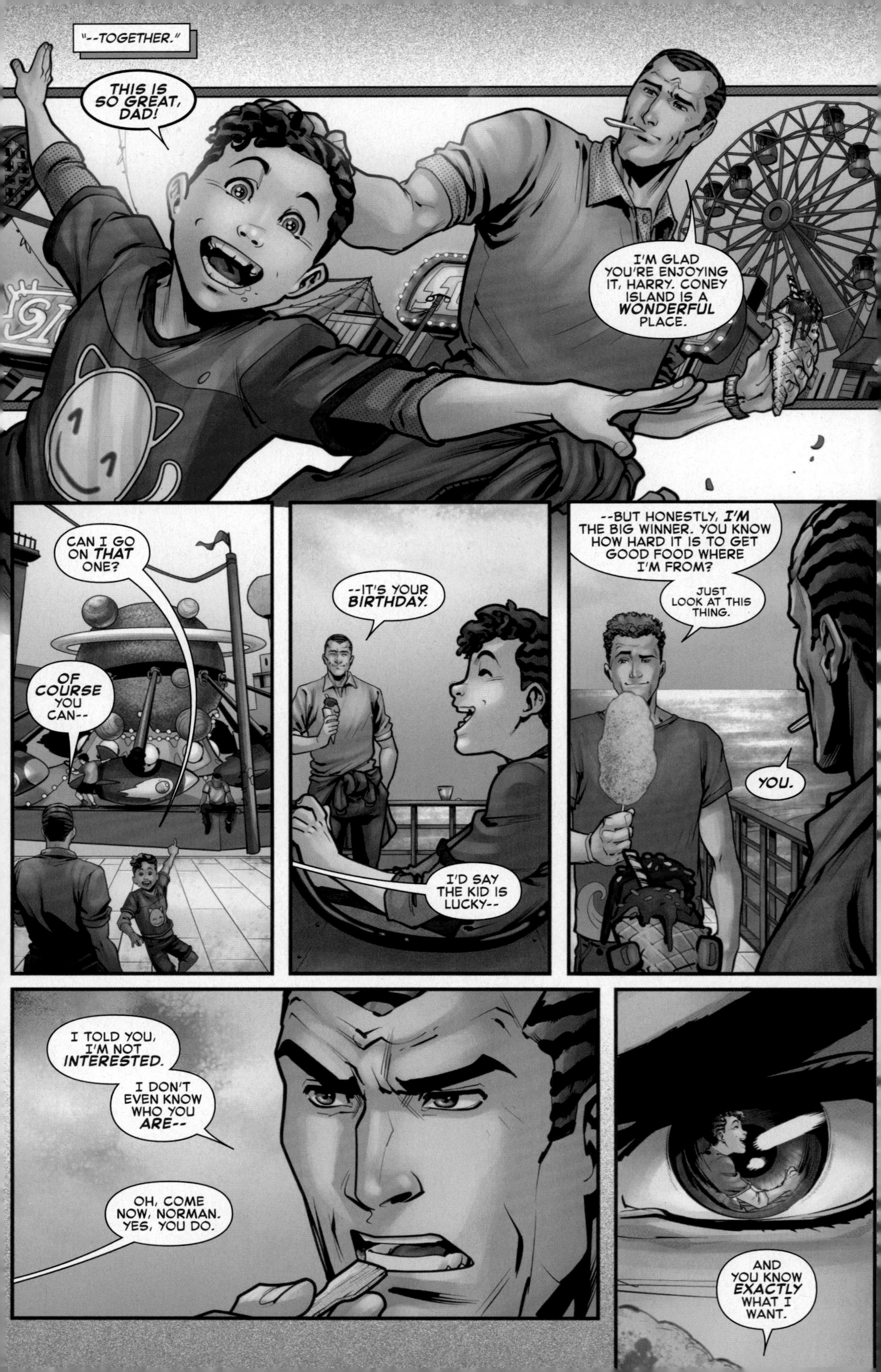
"--TOGETHER."
THIS IS SO GREAT, DAD!
I'M GLAD YOU'RE ENJOYING IT, HARRY. CONEY ISLAND IS A WONDERFUL PLACE.
CAN I GO ON THAT ONE?
OF COURSE YOU CAN--
--IT'S YOUR BIRTHDAY.
I'D SAY THE KID IS LUCKY--
--BUT HONESTLY, I'M THE BIG WINNER. YOU KNOW HOW HARD IT IS TO GET GOOD FOOD WHERE I'M FROM?
JUST LOOK AT THIS THING.
YOU.
I TOLD YOU, I'M NOT INTERESTED.
I DON'T EVEN KNOW WHO YOU ARE--
OH, COME NOW, NORMAN. YES, YOU DO.
AND YOU KNOW EXACTLY WHAT I WANT.

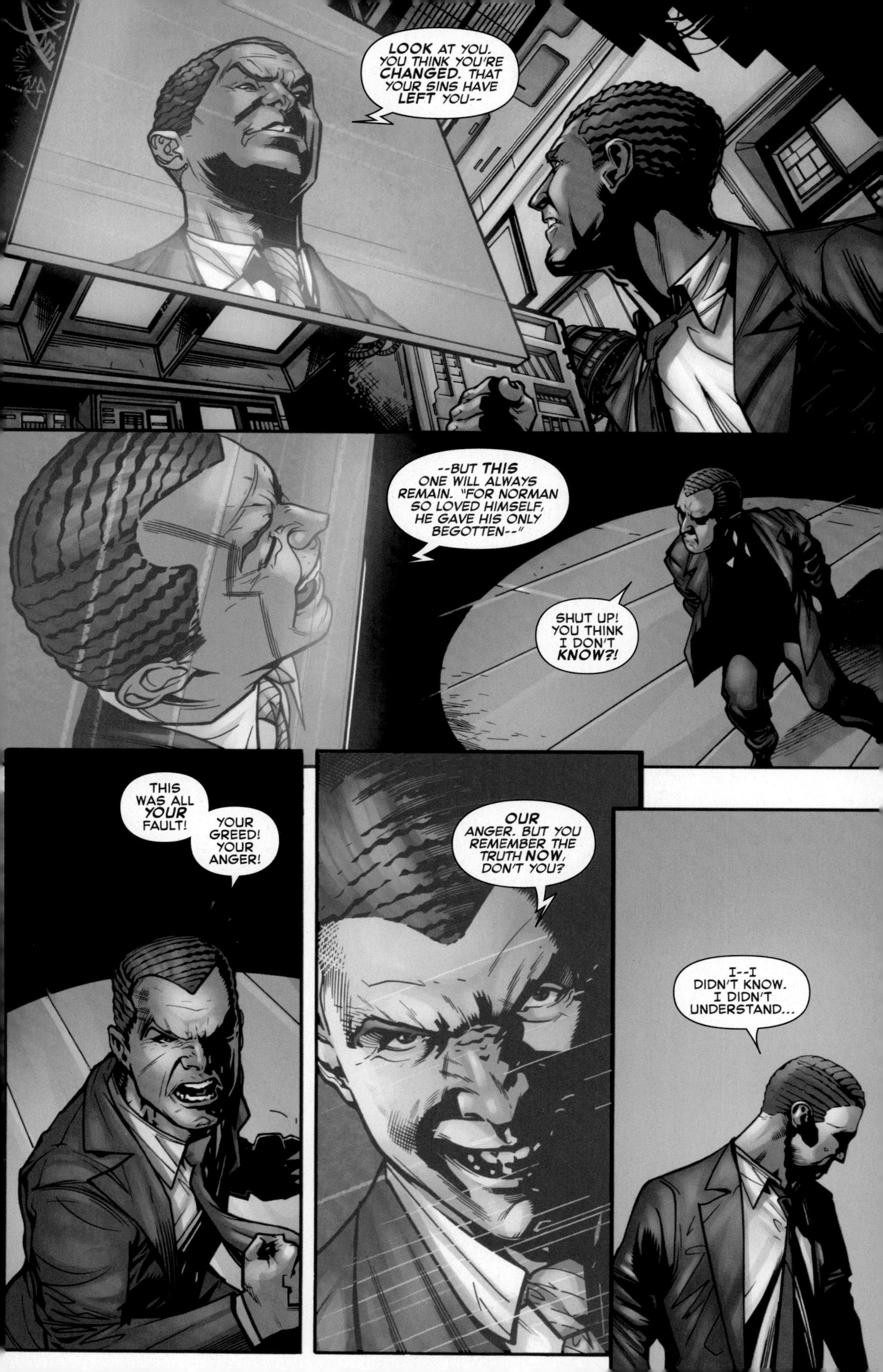
LOOK AT YOU. YOU THINK YOU'RE CHANGED. THAT YOUR SINS HAVE LEFT YOU--
--BUT THIS ONE WILL ALWAYS REMAIN. "FOR NORMAN SO LOVED HIMSELF, HE GAVE HIS ONLY BEGOTTEN--"
SHUT UP! YOU THINK I DON'T KNOW?!
THIS WAS ALL YOUR FAULT!
YOUR GREED! YOUR ANGER!
OUR ANGER. BUT YOU REMEMBER THE TRUTH NOW, DON'T YOU?
I--I DIDN'T KNOW. I DIDN'T UNDERSTAND...

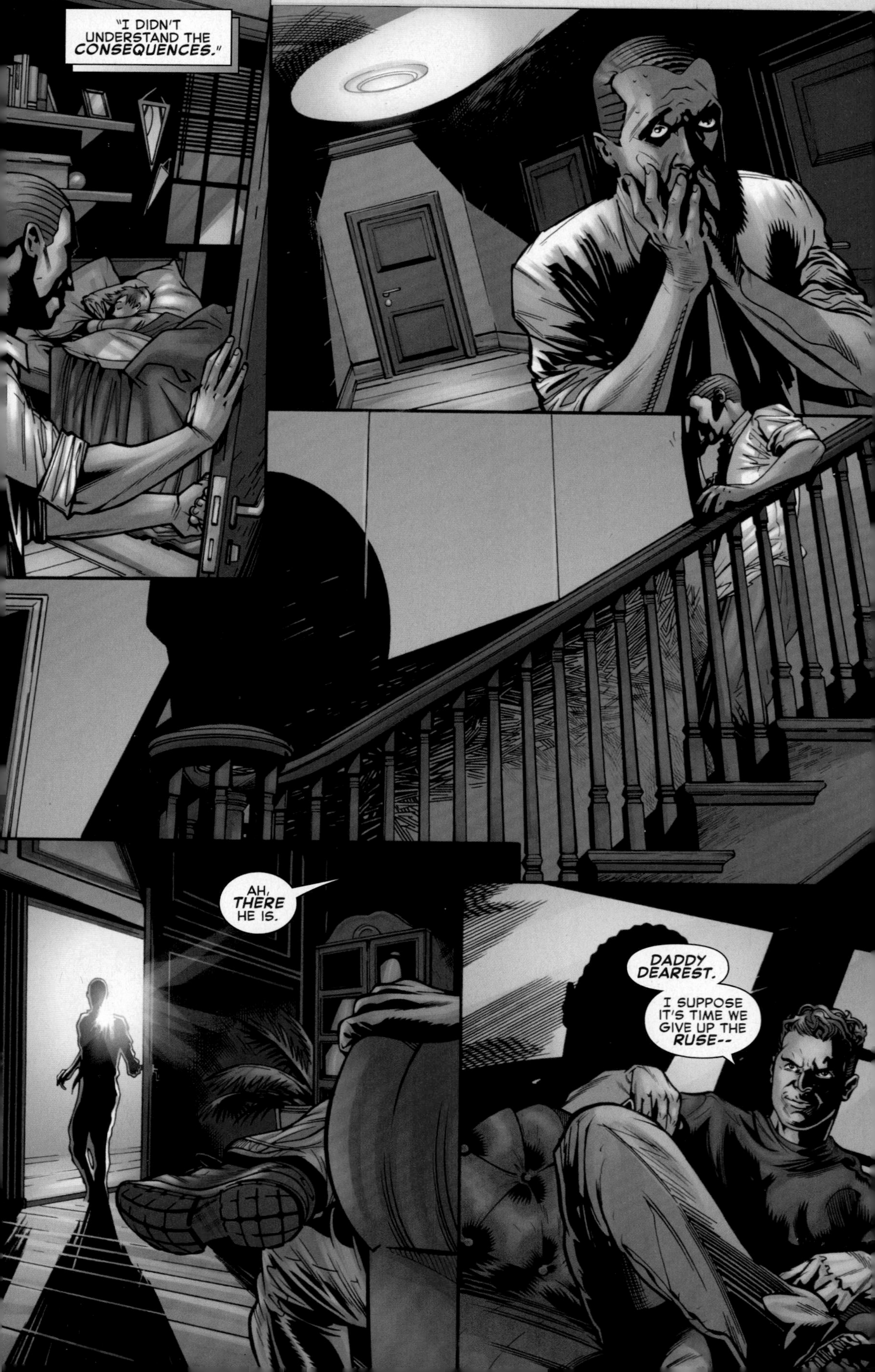
"I DIDN'T UNDERSTAND THE CONSEQUENCES."
AH, THERE HE IS.
DADDY DEAREST.
I SUPPOSE IT'S TIME WE GIVE UP THE RUSE--

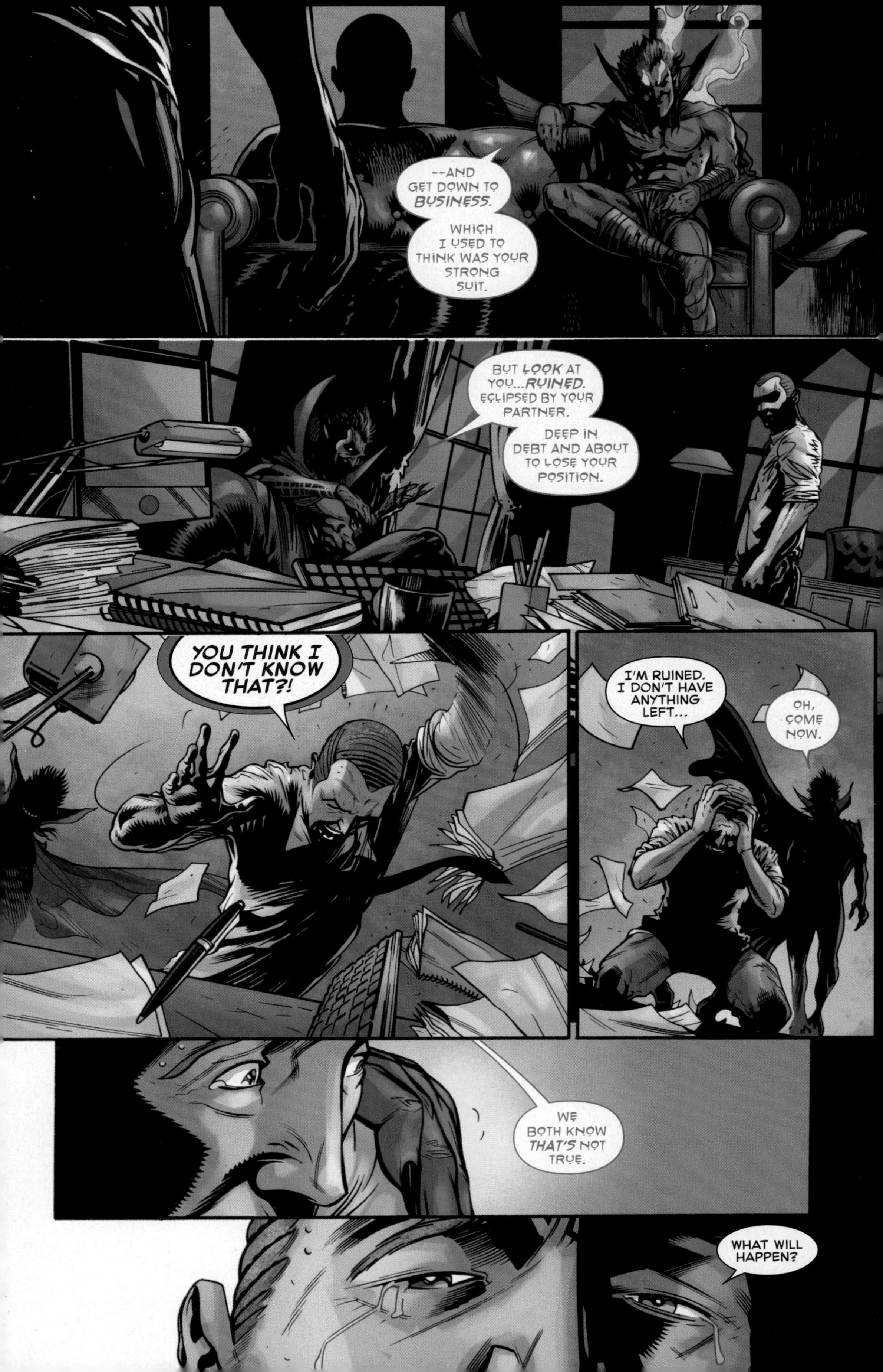
--AND GET DOWN TO BUSINESS.
WHICH I USED TO THINK WAS YOUR STRONG SUIT.
BUT LOOK AT YOU...RUINED. ECLIPSED BY YOUR PARTNER.
DEEP IN DEBT AND ABOUT TO LOSE YOUR POSITION.
YOU THINK I DON'T KNOW THAT?!
I'M RUINED. I DON'T HAVE ANYTHING LEFT...
OH, COME NOW.
WE BOTH KNOW THAT'S NOT TRUE.
WHAT WILL HAPPEN?

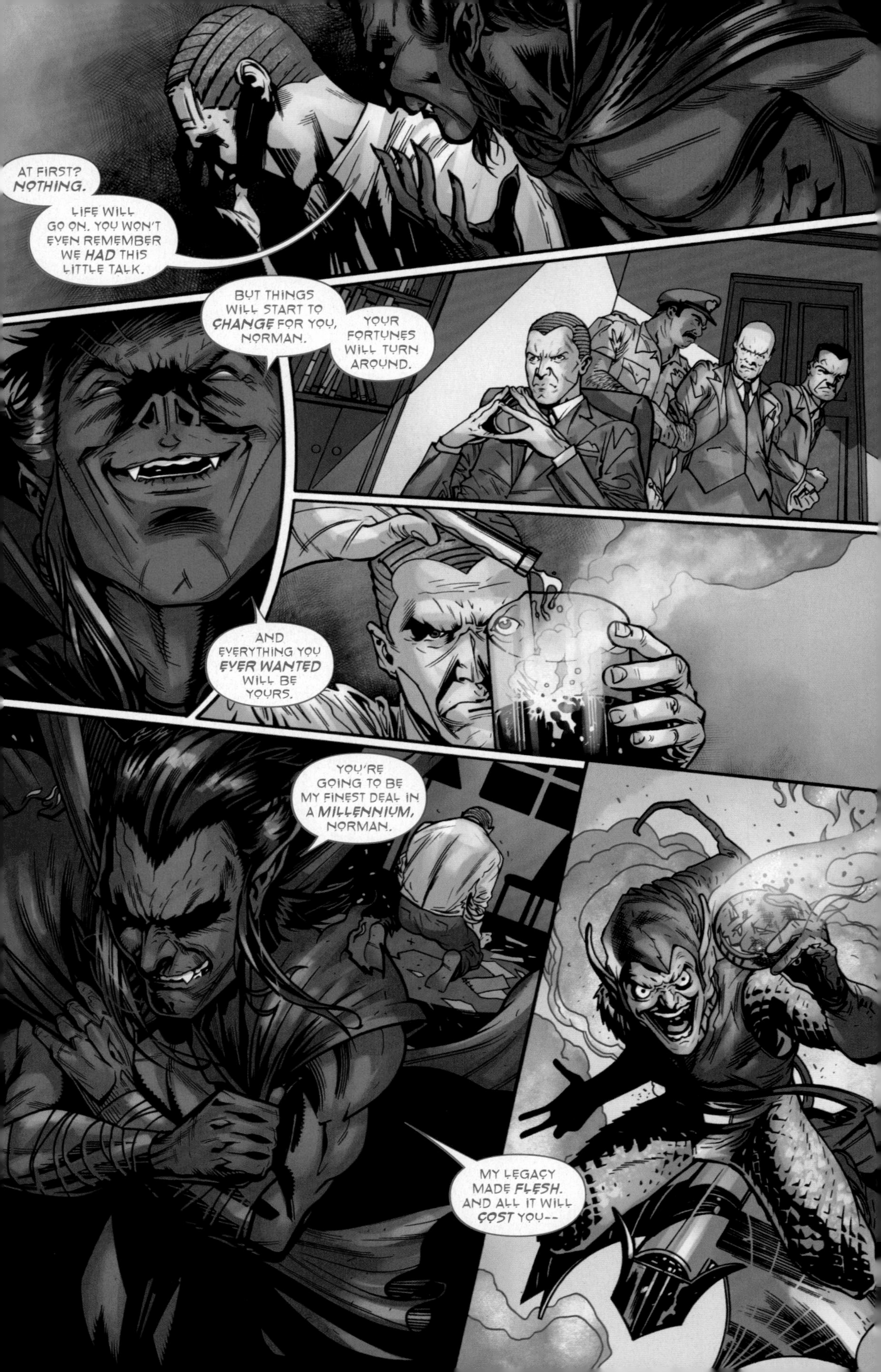
AT FIRST? NOTHING.
LIFE WILL GO ON. YOU WON'T EVEN REMEMBER WE HAD THIS LITTLE TALK.
BUT THINGS WILL START TO CHANGE FOR YOU, NORMAN.
YOUR FORTUNES WILL TURN AROUND.
AND EVERYTHING YOU EVER WANTED WILL BE YOURS.
YOU'RE GOING TO BE MY FINEST DEAL IN A MILLENNIUM, NORMAN.
MY LEGACY MADE FLESH. AND ALL IT WILL COST YOU--

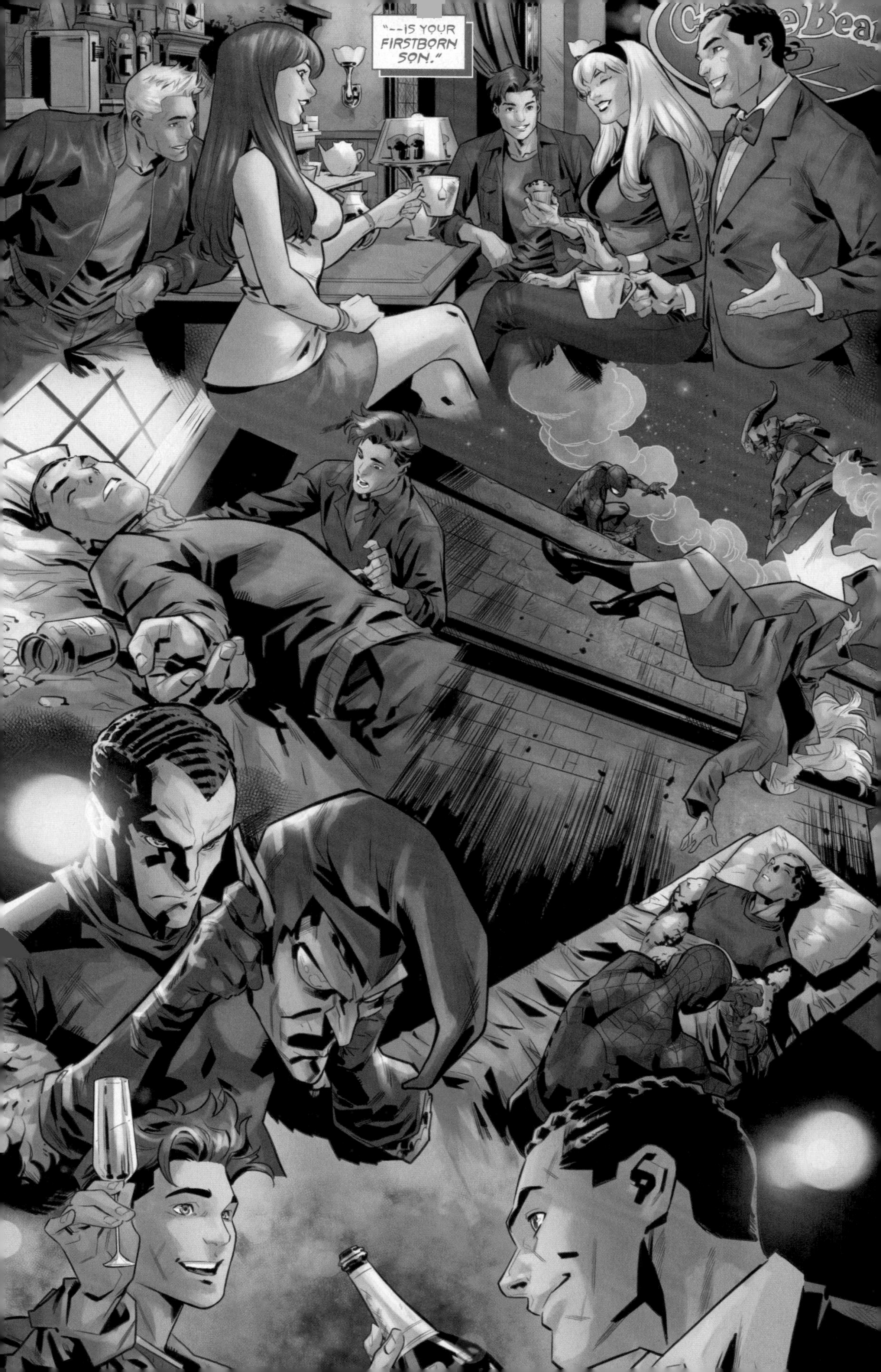
"--IS YOUR FIRSTBORN SON."

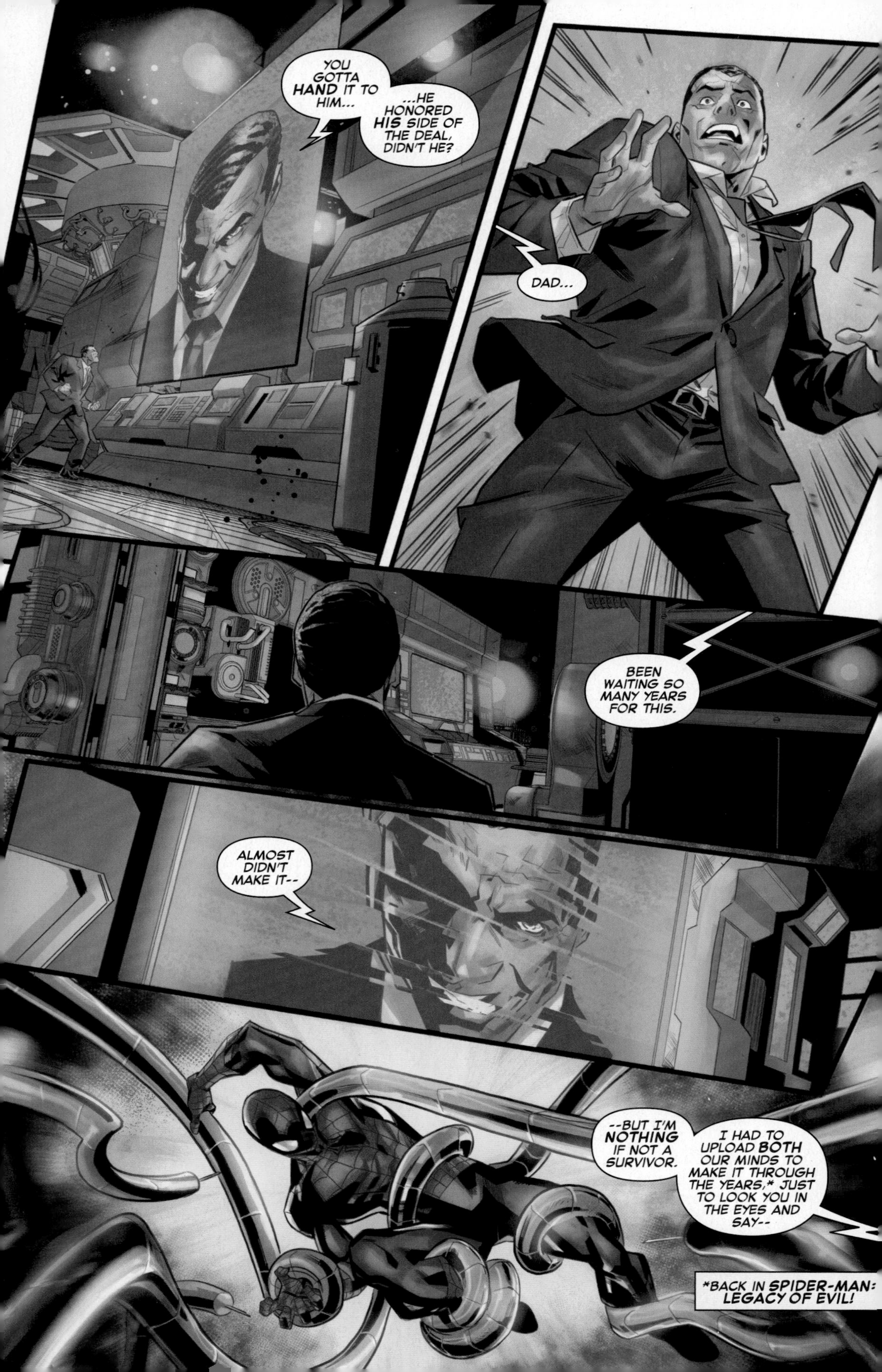
YOU GOTTA HAND IT TO HIM...
...HE HONORED HIS SIDE OF THE DEAL, DIDN'T HE?
DAD...
BEEN WAITING SO MANY YEARS FOR THIS.
ALMOST DIDN'T MAKE IT--
--BUT I'M NOTHING IF NOT A SURVIVOR.
I HAD TO UPLOAD BOTH OUR MINDS TO MAKE IT THROUGH THE YEARS,* JUST TO LOOK YOU IN THE EYES AND SAY--
*BACK IN SPIDER-MAN: LEGACY OF EVIL!

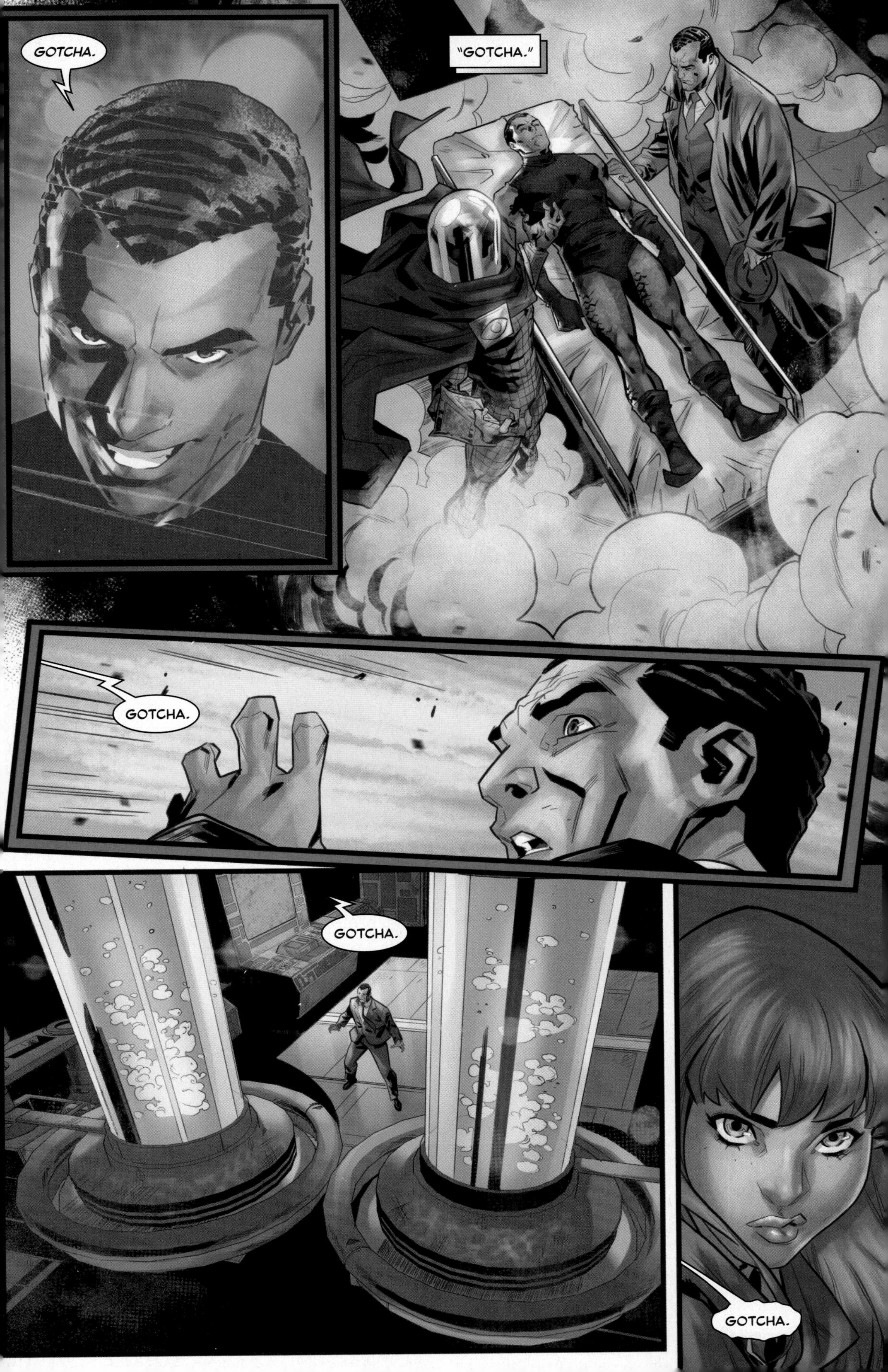
GOTCHA.
"GOTCHA."
GOTCHA.
GOTCHA.
GOTCHA.

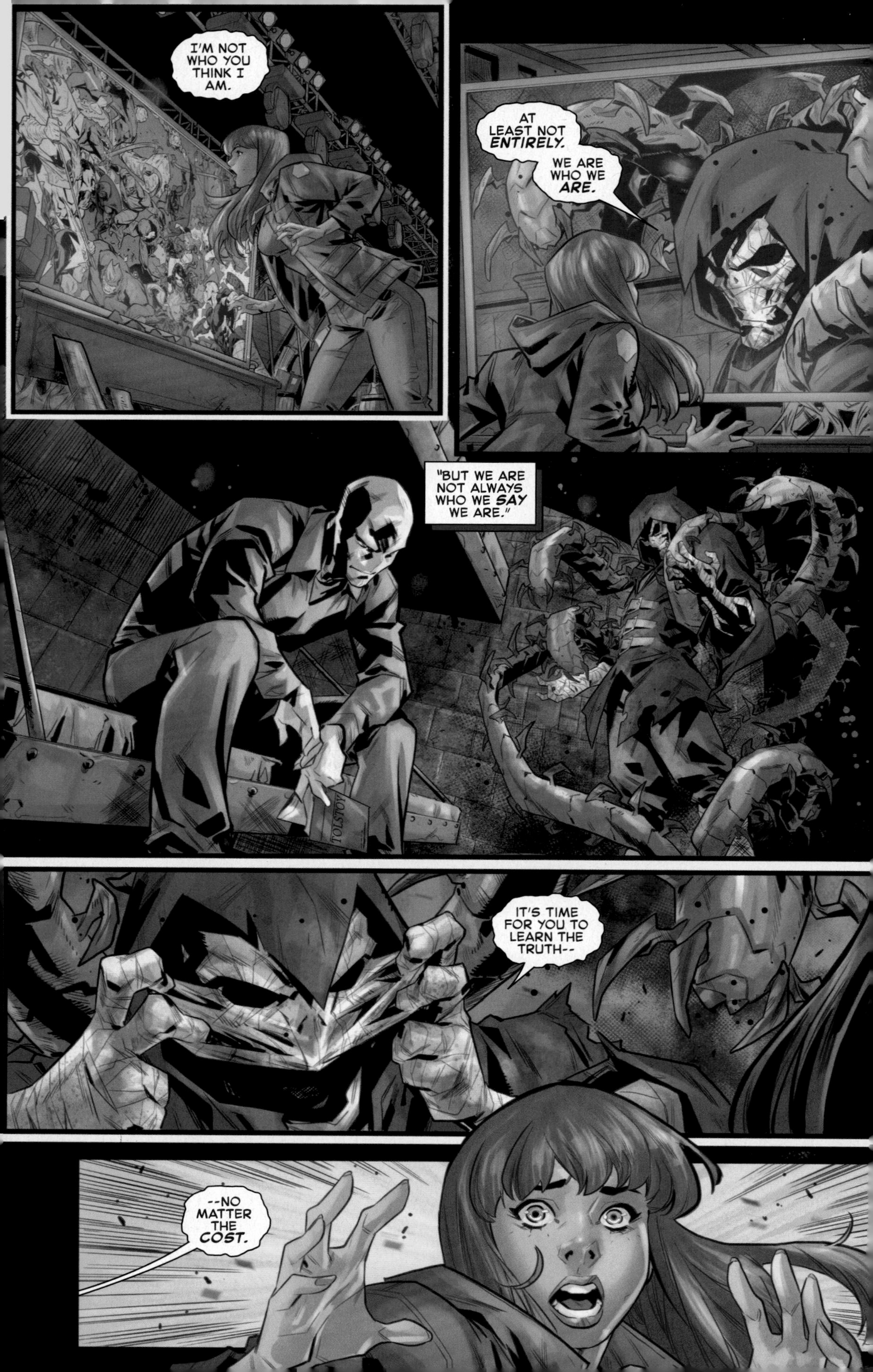

I'M NOT WHO YOU THINK I AM.
AT LEAST NOT ENTIRELY.
WE ARE WHO WE ARE.
"BUT WE ARE NOT ALWAYS WHO WE SAY WE ARE."
TOLSTOY
IT'S TIME FOR YOU TO LEARN THE TRUTH--
--NO MATTER THE COST.

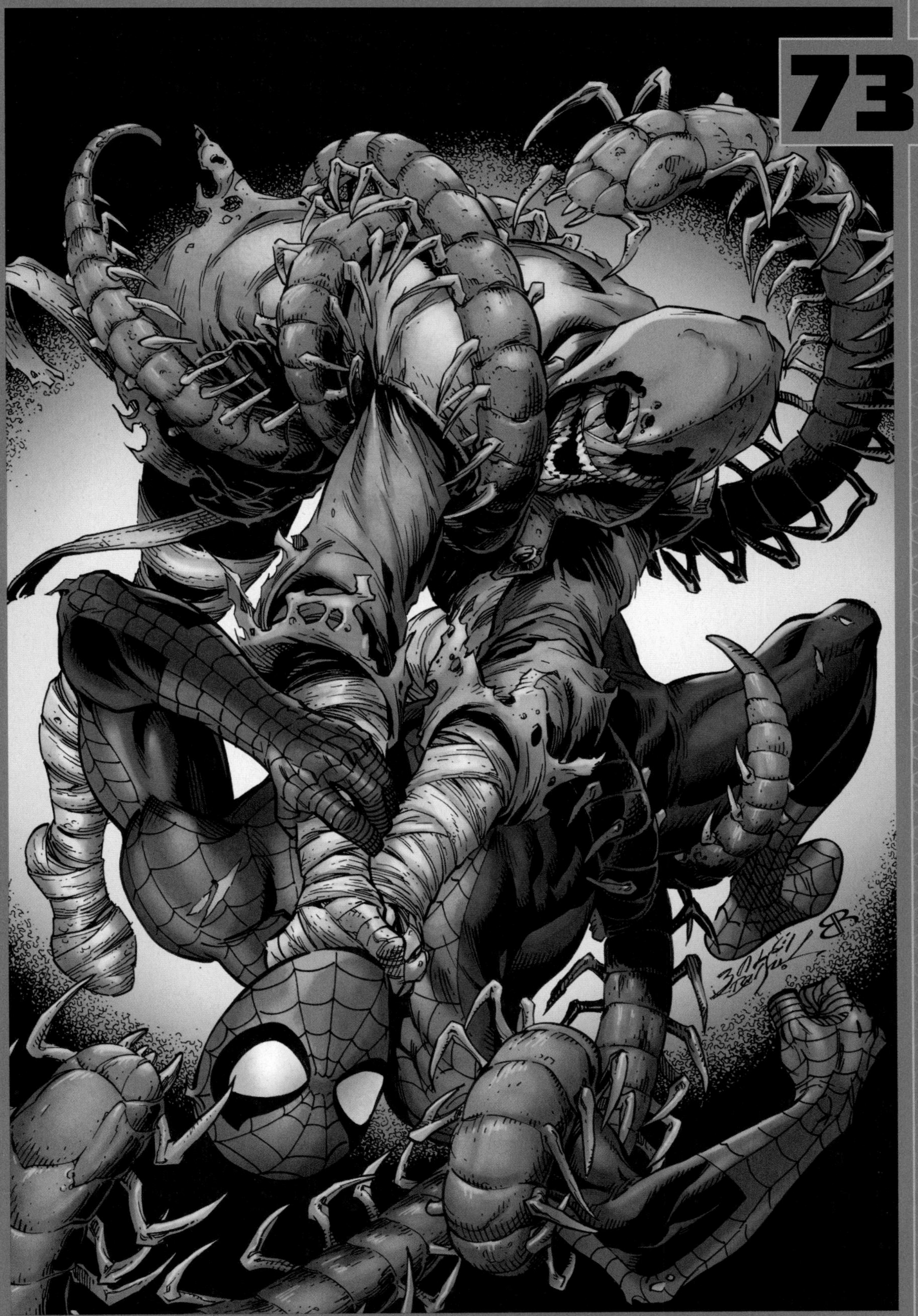

SINS OF OUR FATHERS

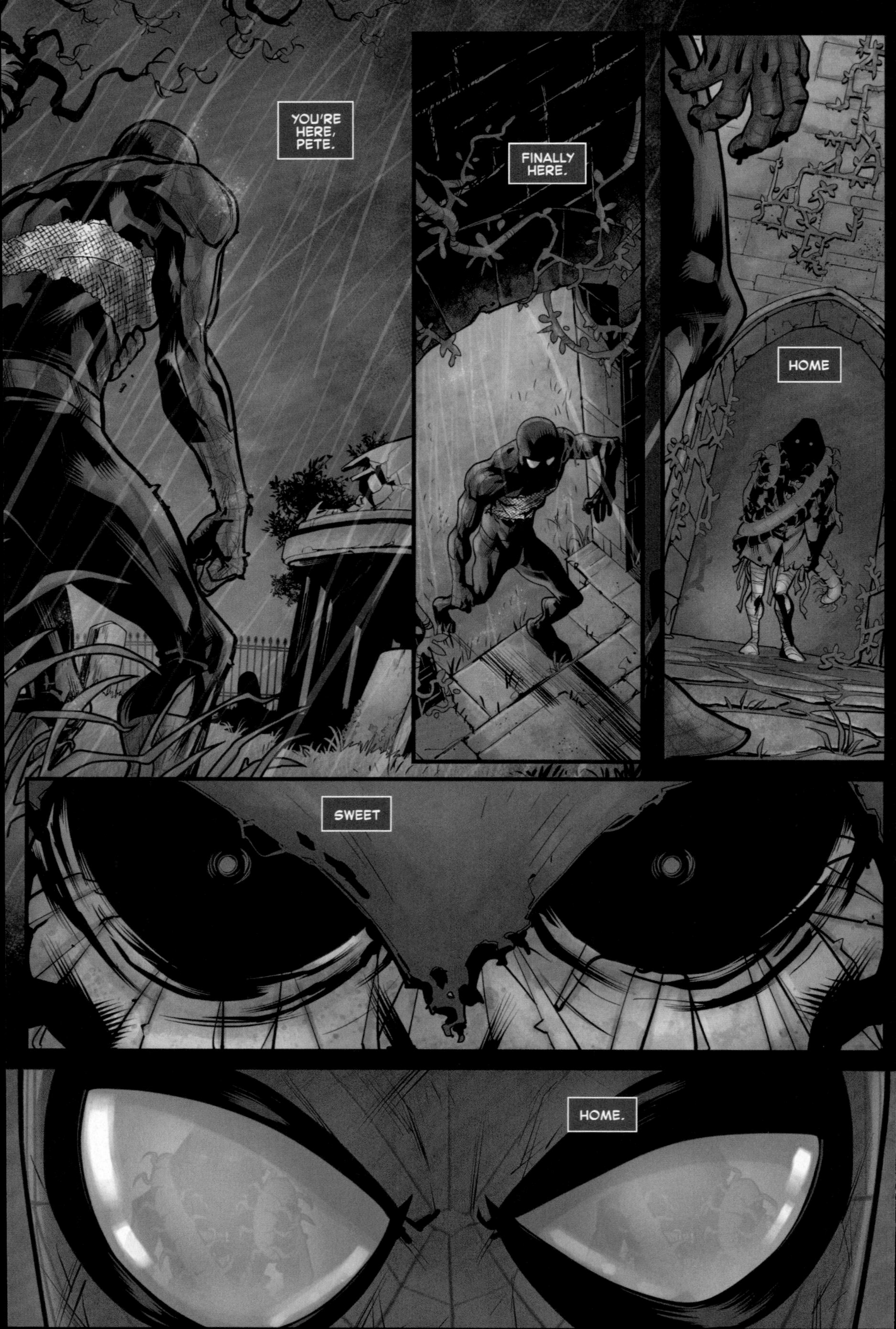
YOU'RE HERE, PETE.
FINALLY HERE.
HOME
SWEET
HOME.

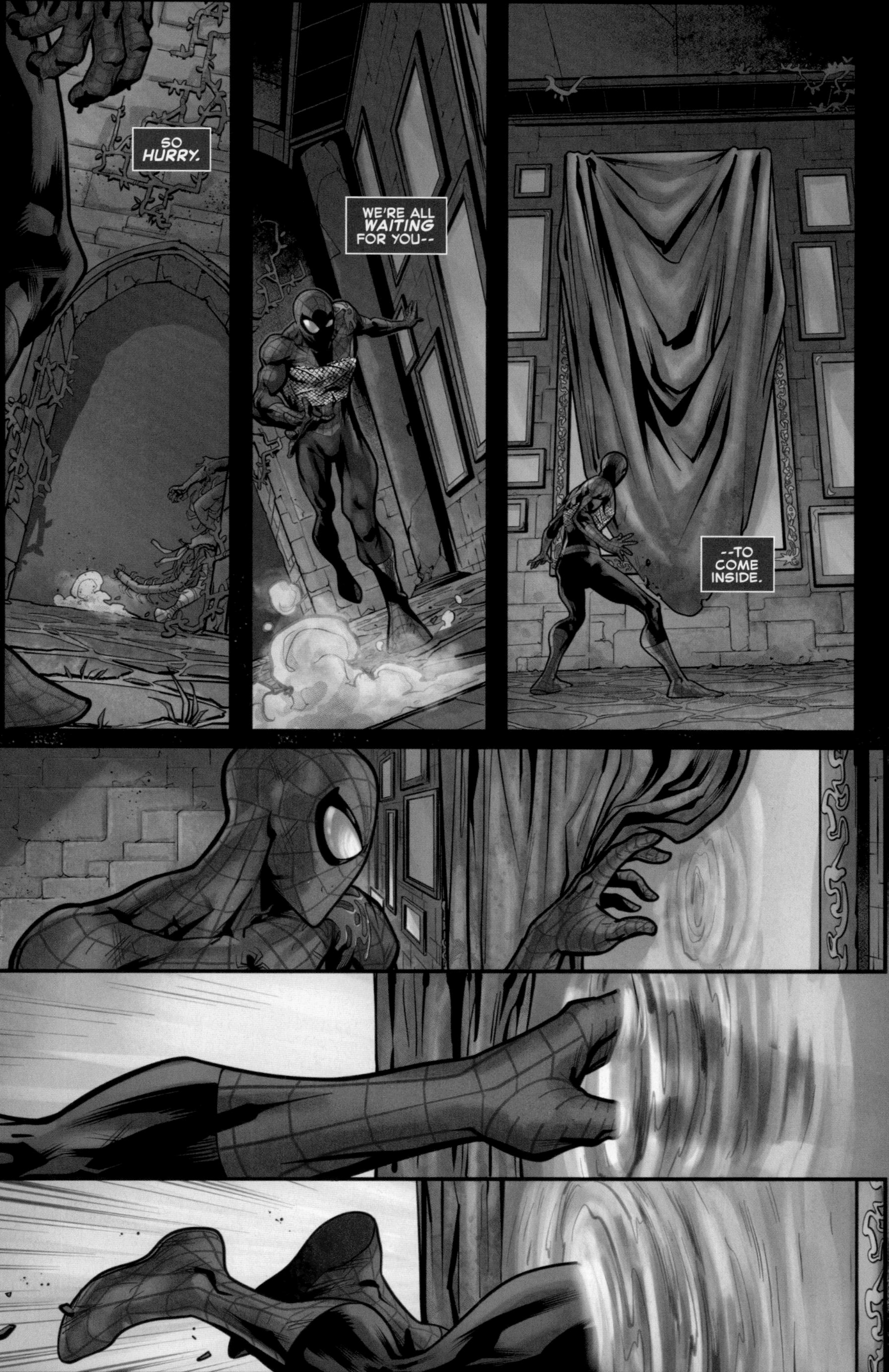
SO HURRY.
WE'RE ALL WAITING FOR YOU--
--TO COME INSIDE.

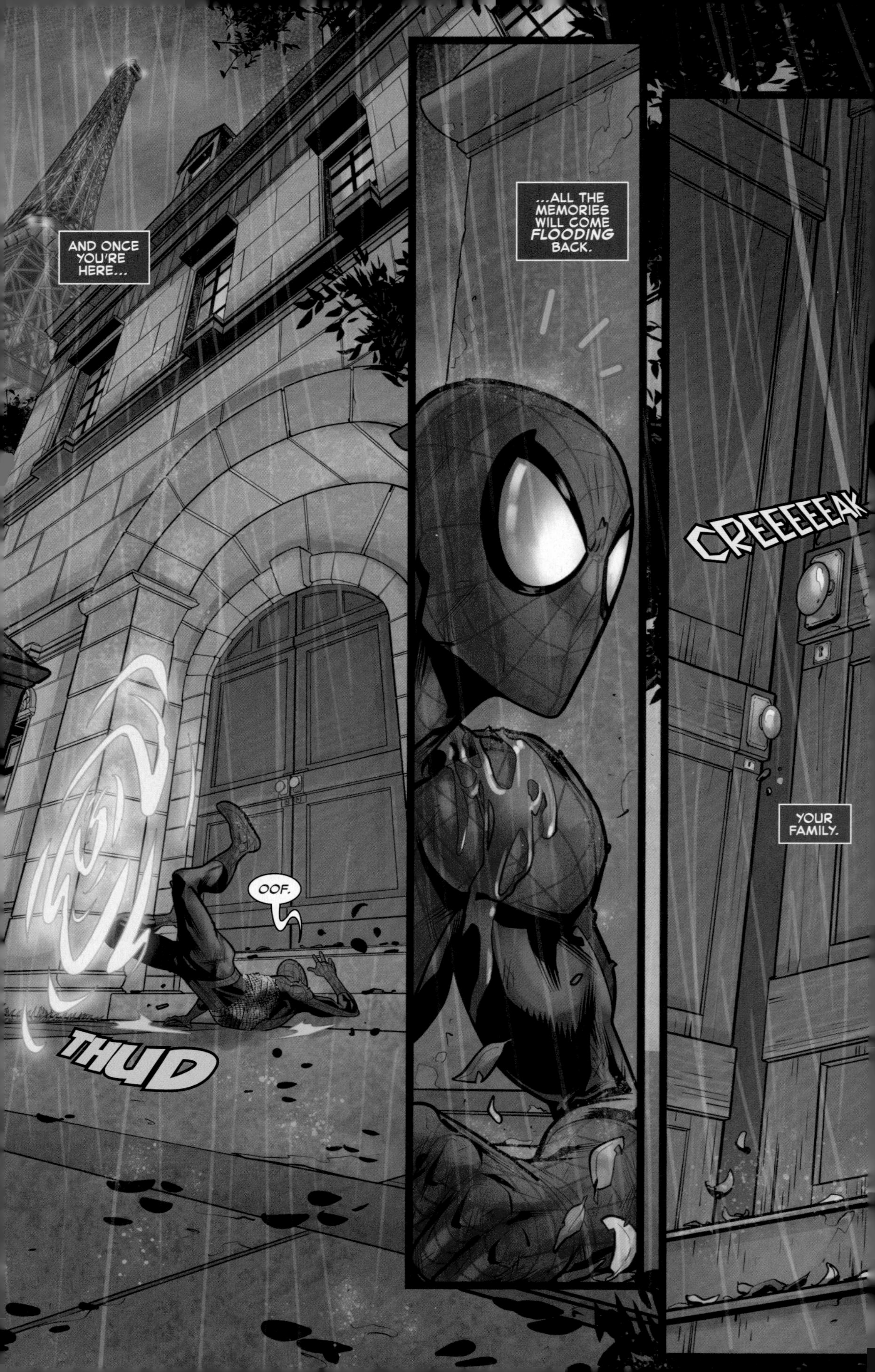
AND ONCE YOU'RE HERE...
OOF.
THUD
...ALL THE MEMORIES WILL COME FLOODING BACK.
CREEEEEAK
YOUR FAMILY.

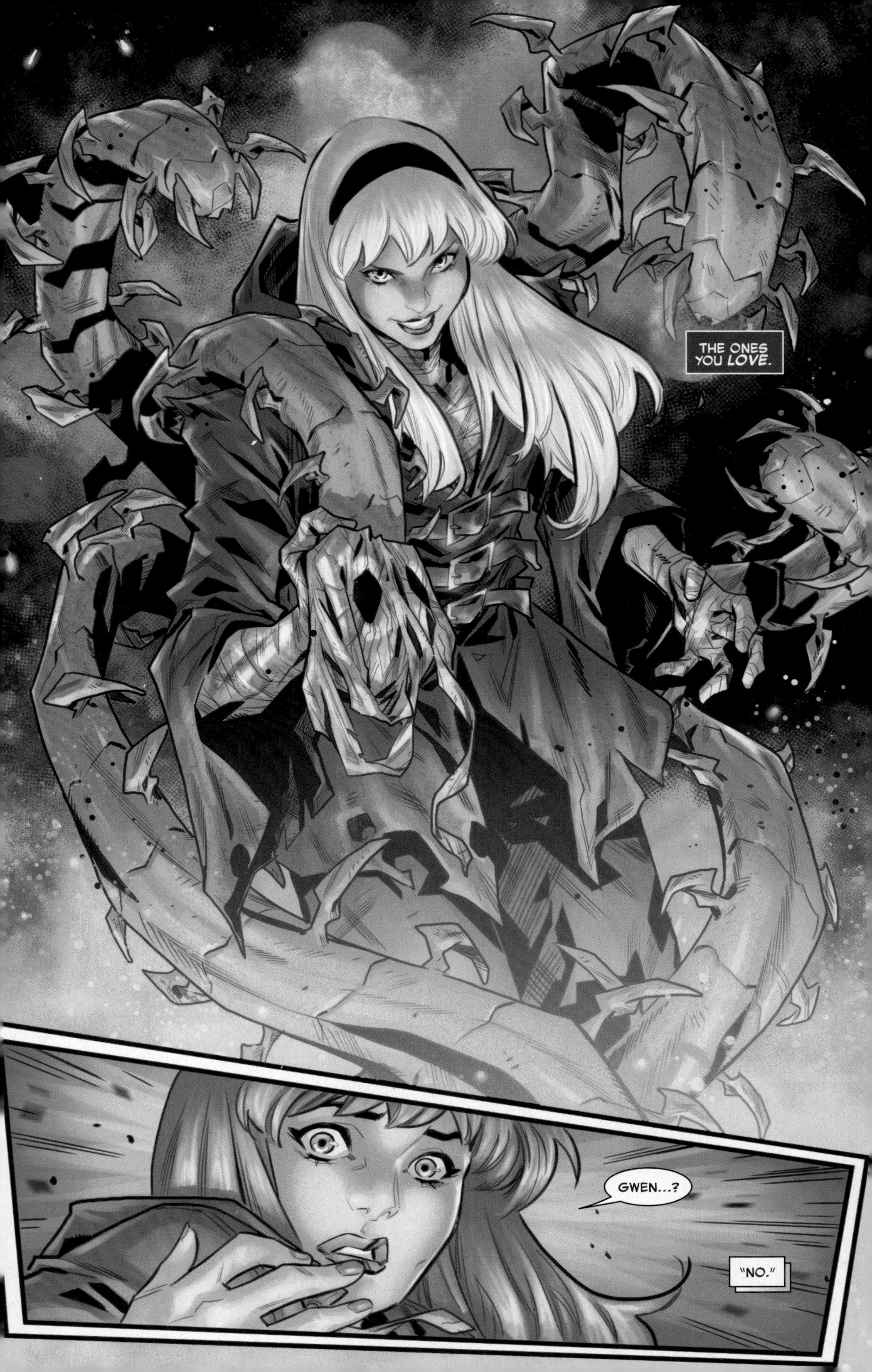
THE ONES YOU *LOVE*.
GWEN...?
"NO."

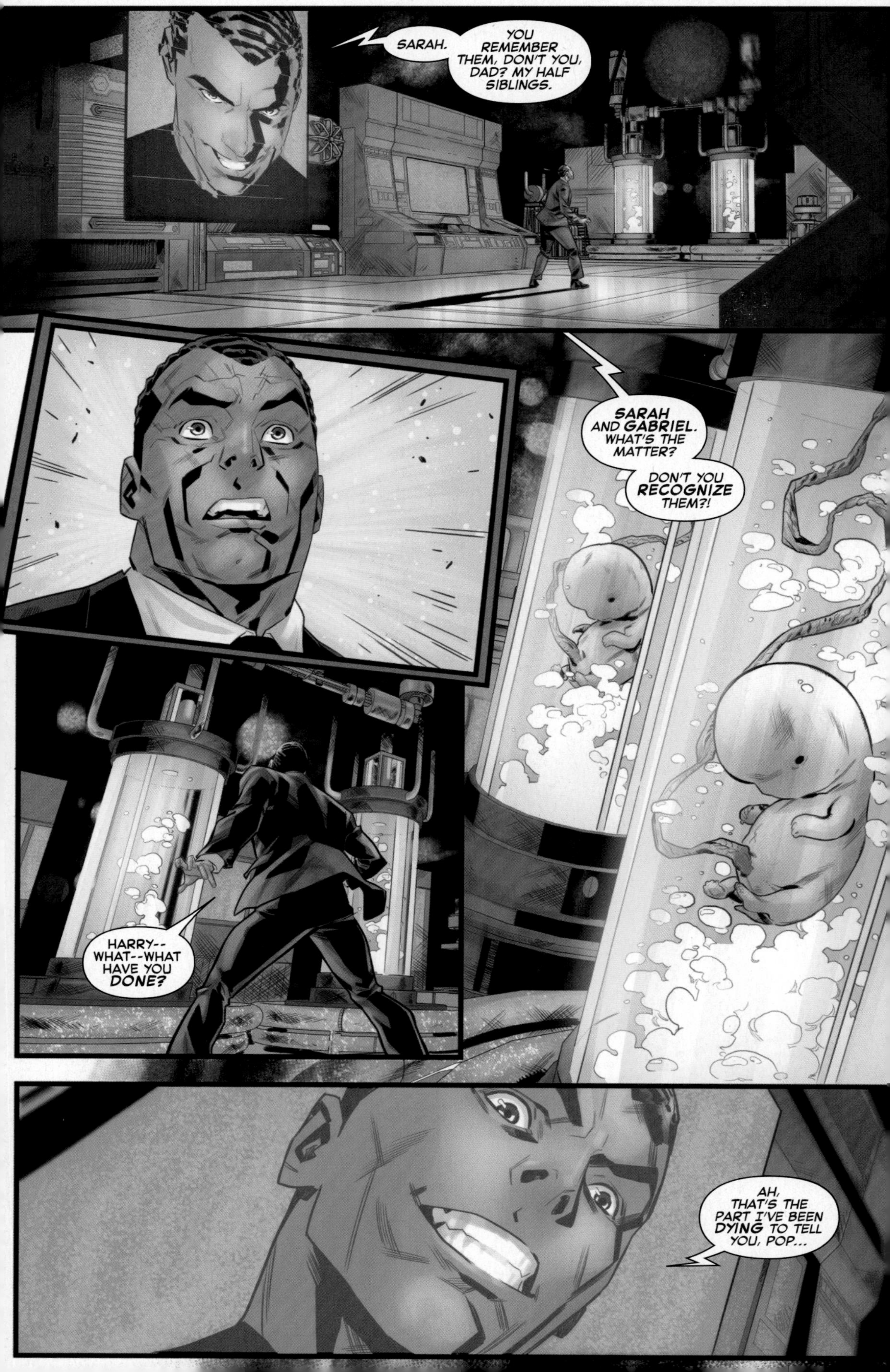
SARAH.
YOU REMEMBER THEM, DON'T YOU, DAD? MY HALF SIBLINGS.
SARAH AND GABRIEL. WHAT'S THE MATTER?
DON'T YOU RECOGNIZE THEM?!
HARRY-- WHAT--WHAT HAVE YOU DONE?
AH, THAT'S THE PART I'VE BEEN DYING TO TELL YOU, POP...

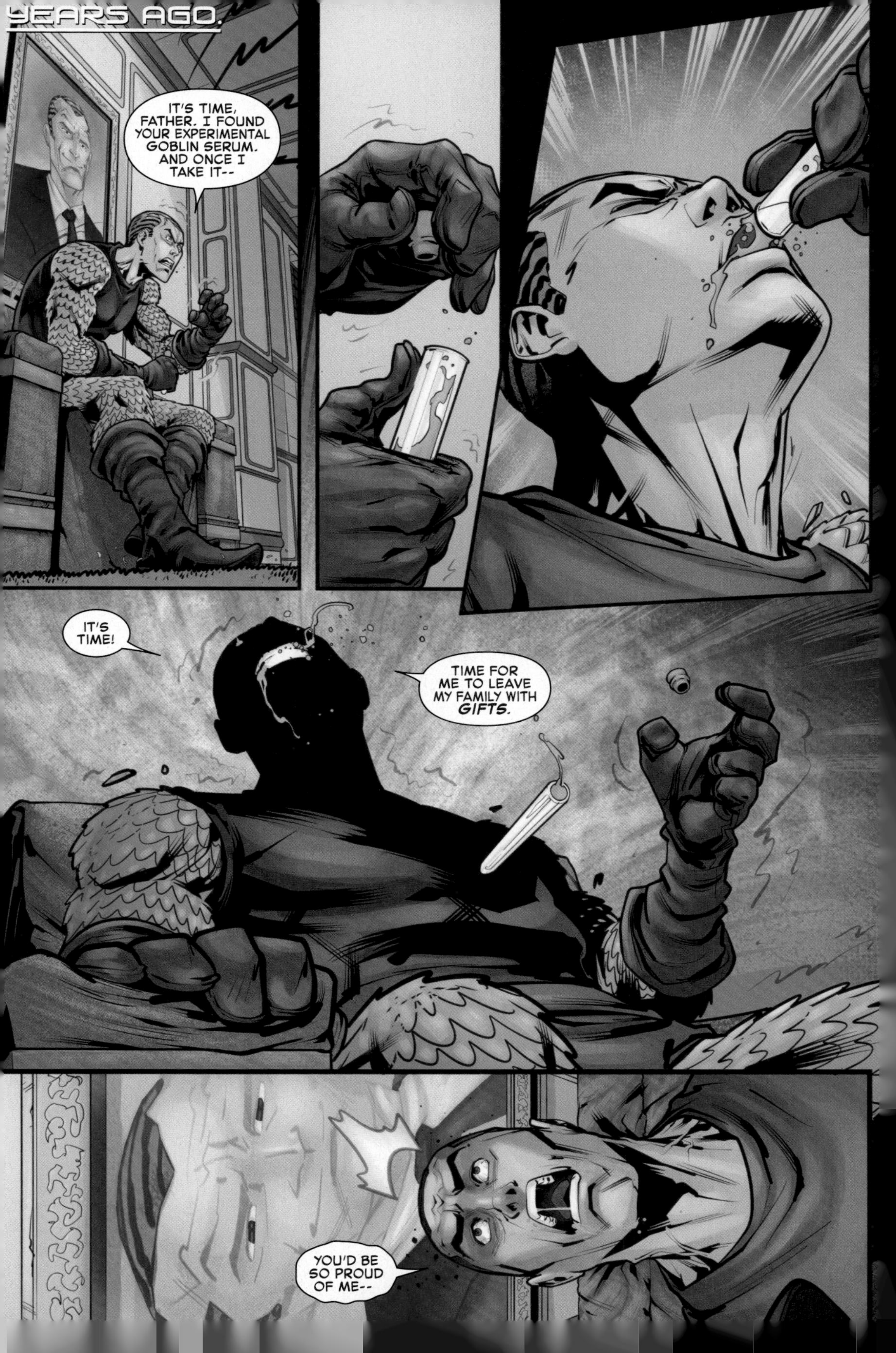
YEARS AGO.
IT'S TIME, FATHER. I FOUND YOUR EXPERIMENTAL GOBLIN SERUM. AND ONCE I TAKE IT--
IT'S TIME!
TIME FOR ME TO LEAVE MY FAMILY WITH GIFTS.
YOU'D BE SO PROUD OF ME--

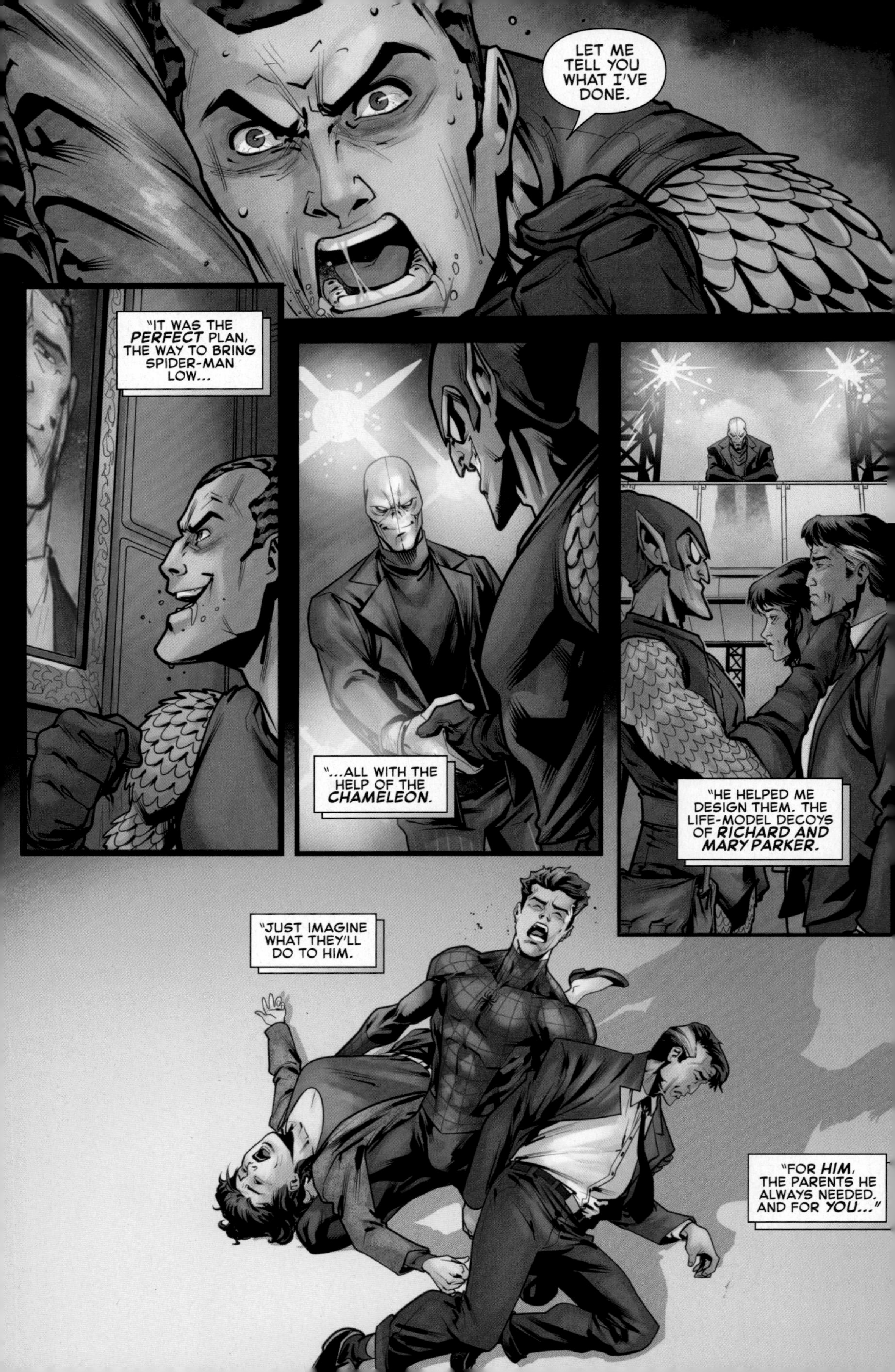
LET ME TELL YOU WHAT I'VE DONE.
"IT WAS THE PERFECT PLAN, THE WAY TO BRING SPIDER-MAN LOW...
"...ALL WITH THE HELP OF THE CHAMELEON.
"HE HELPED ME DESIGN THEM. THE LIFE-MODEL DECOYS OF RICHARD AND MARY PARKER.
"JUST IMAGINE WHAT THEY'LL DO TO HIM.
"FOR HIM, THE PARENTS HE ALWAYS NEEDED. AND FOR YOU..."

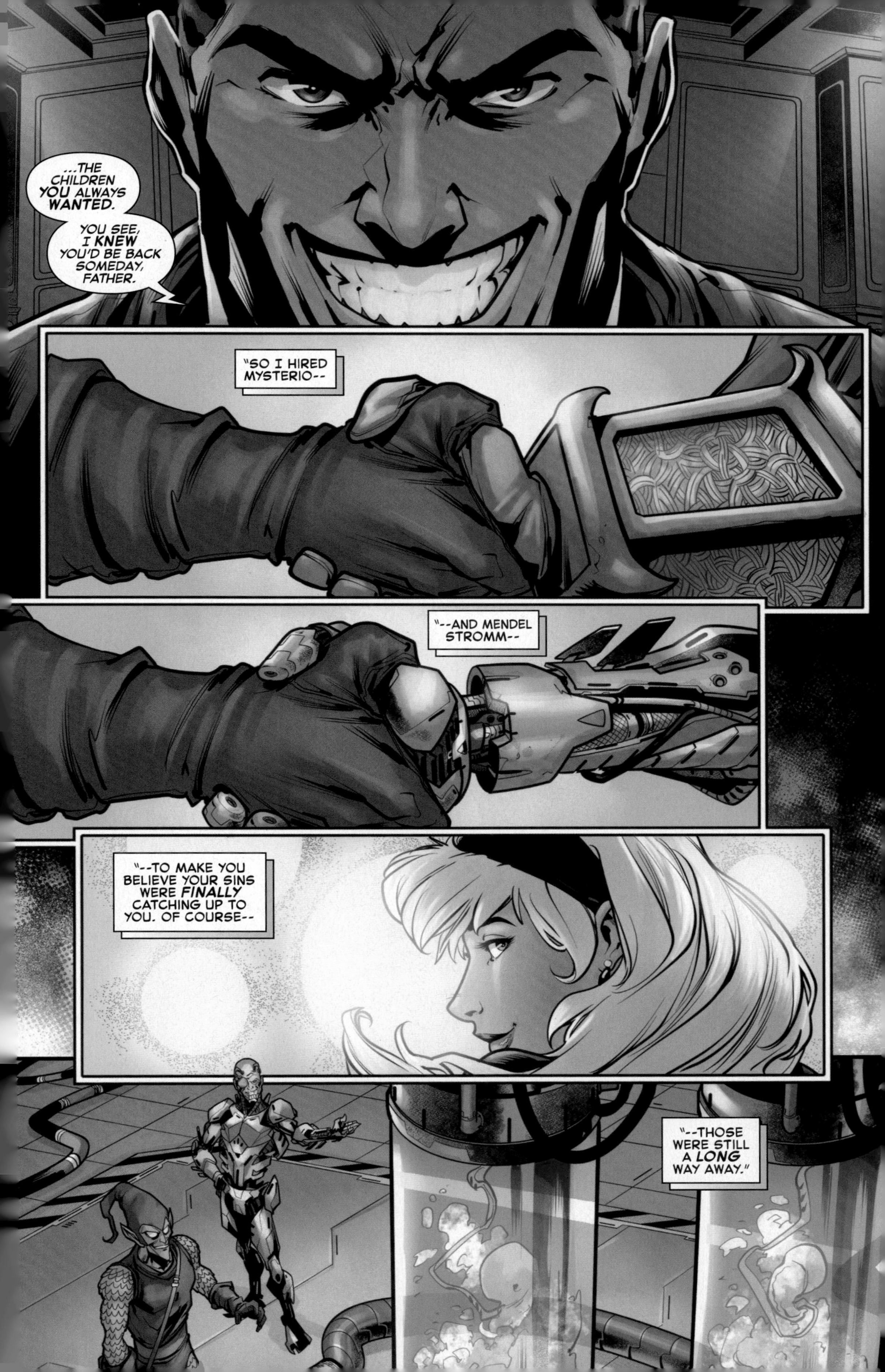
...THE CHILDREN YOU ALWAYS WANTED.
YOU SEE, I KNEW YOU'D BE BACK SOMEDAY, FATHER.
"SO I HIRED MYSTERIO--
"--AND MENDEL STROMM--
"--TO MAKE YOU BELIEVE YOUR SINS WERE FINALLY CATCHING UP TO YOU. OF COURSE--
"--THOSE WERE STILL A LONG WAY AWAY."

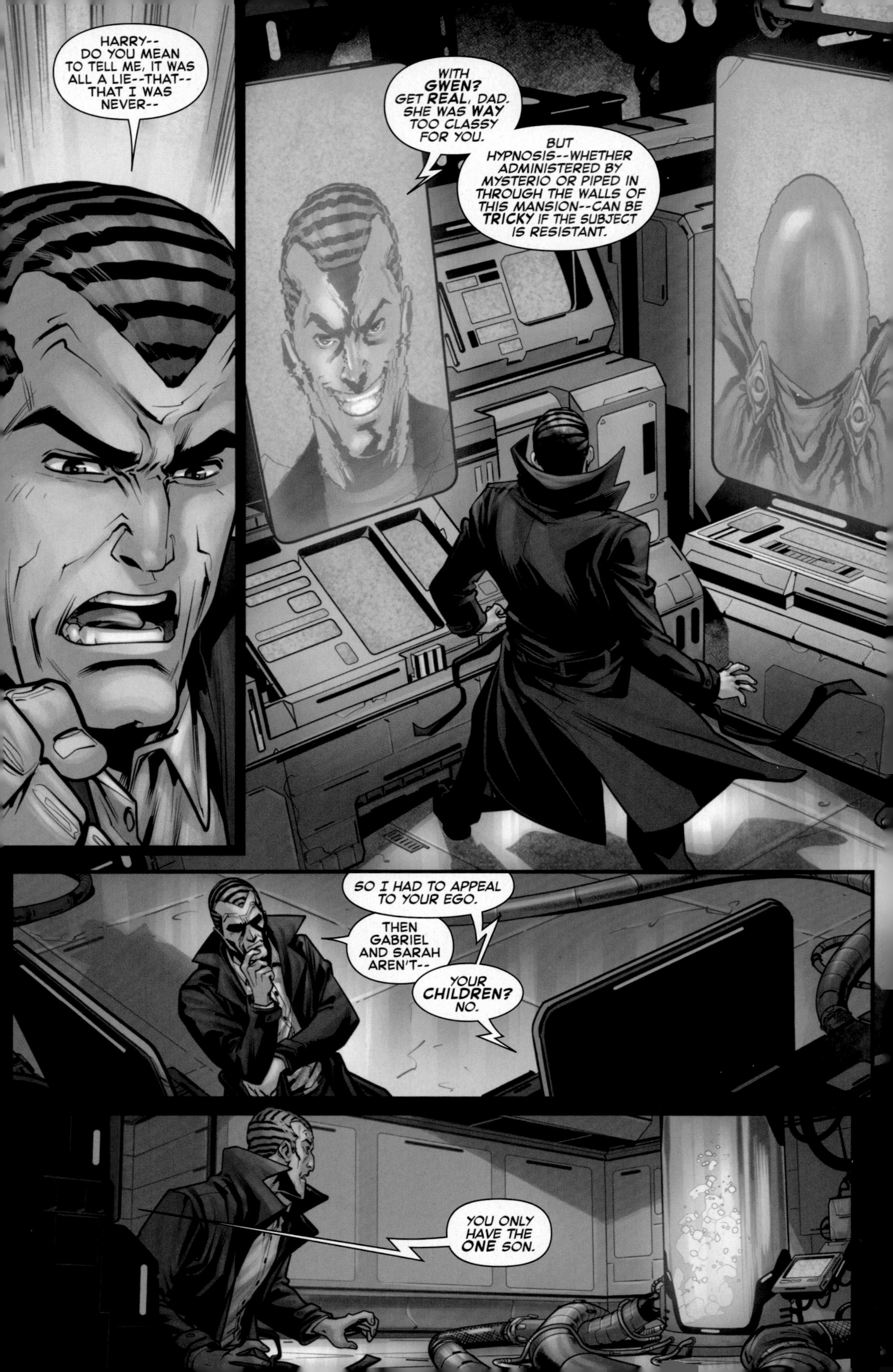
HARRY-- DO YOU MEAN TO TELL ME, IT WAS ALL A LIE--THAT-- THAT I WAS NEVER--
WITH GWEN? GET REAL, DAD. SHE WAS WAY TOO CLASSY FOR YOU.
BUT HYPNOSIS--WHETHER ADMINISTERED BY MYSTERIO OR PIPED IN THROUGH THE WALLS OF THIS MANSION--CAN BE TRICKY IF THE SUBJECT IS RESISTANT.
SO I HAD TO APPEAL TO YOUR EGO.
THEN GABRIEL AND SARAH AREN'T--
YOUR CHILDREN? NO.
YOU ONLY HAVE THE ONE SON.

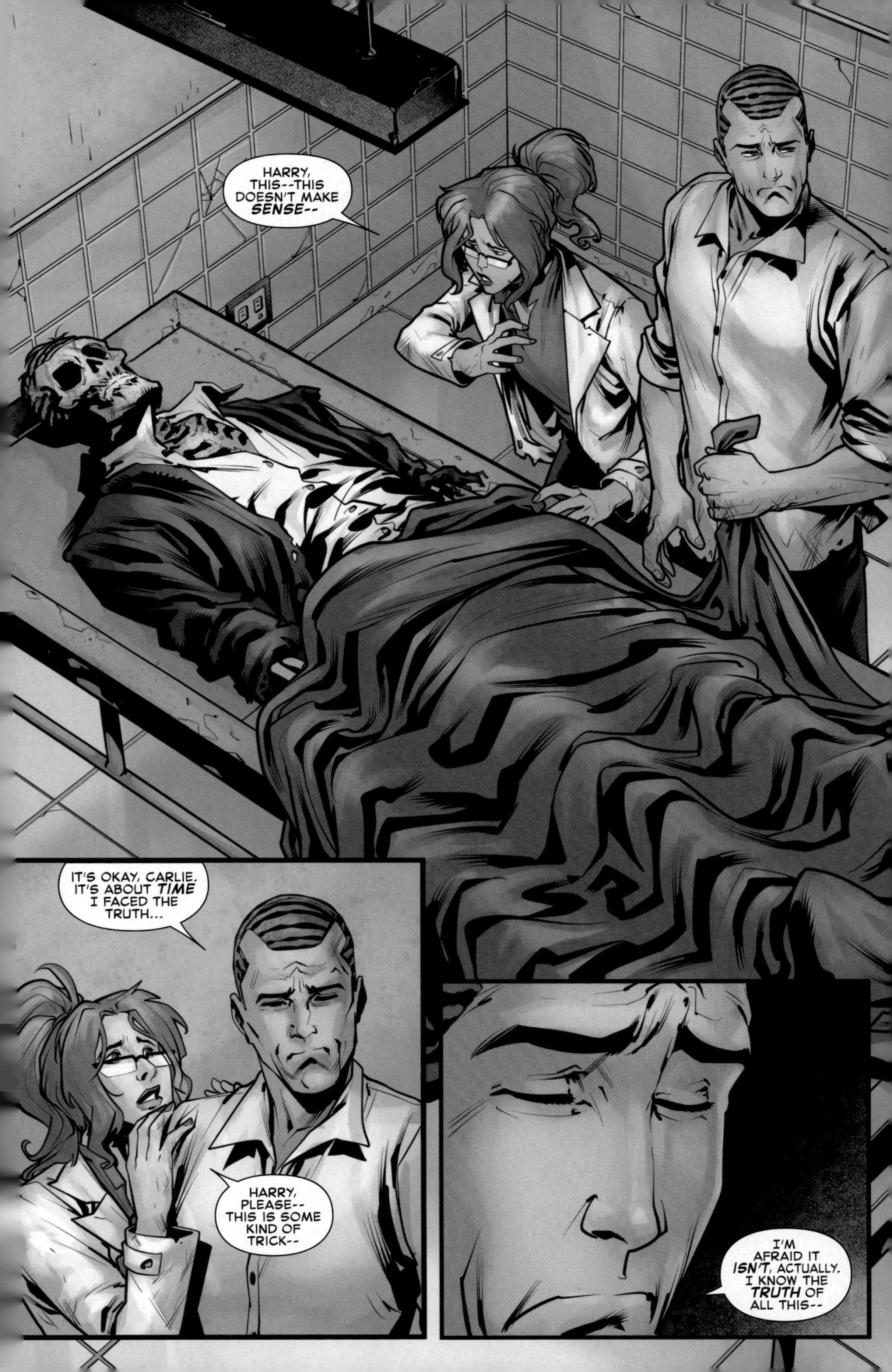
HARRY, THIS--THIS DOESN'T MAKE *SENSE*--
IT'S OKAY, CARLIE. IT'S ABOUT *TIME* I FACED THE TRUTH...
HARRY, PLEASE-- THIS IS SOME KIND OF TRICK--
I'M AFRAID IT *ISN'T*, ACTUALLY. I KNOW THE *TRUTH* OF ALL THIS--

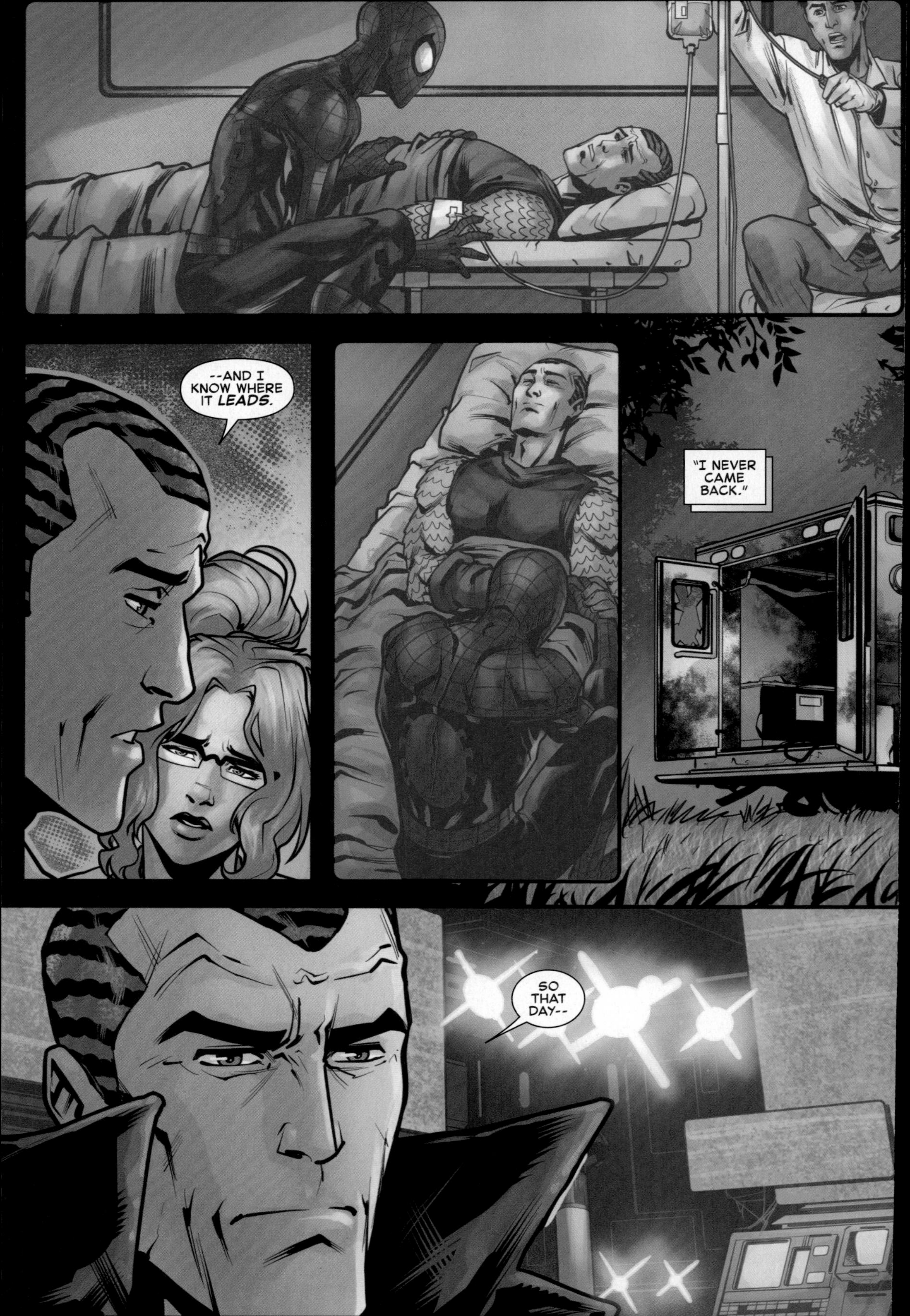
--AND I KNOW WHERE IT *LEADS*.
"I NEVER CAME BACK."
SO THAT DAY--

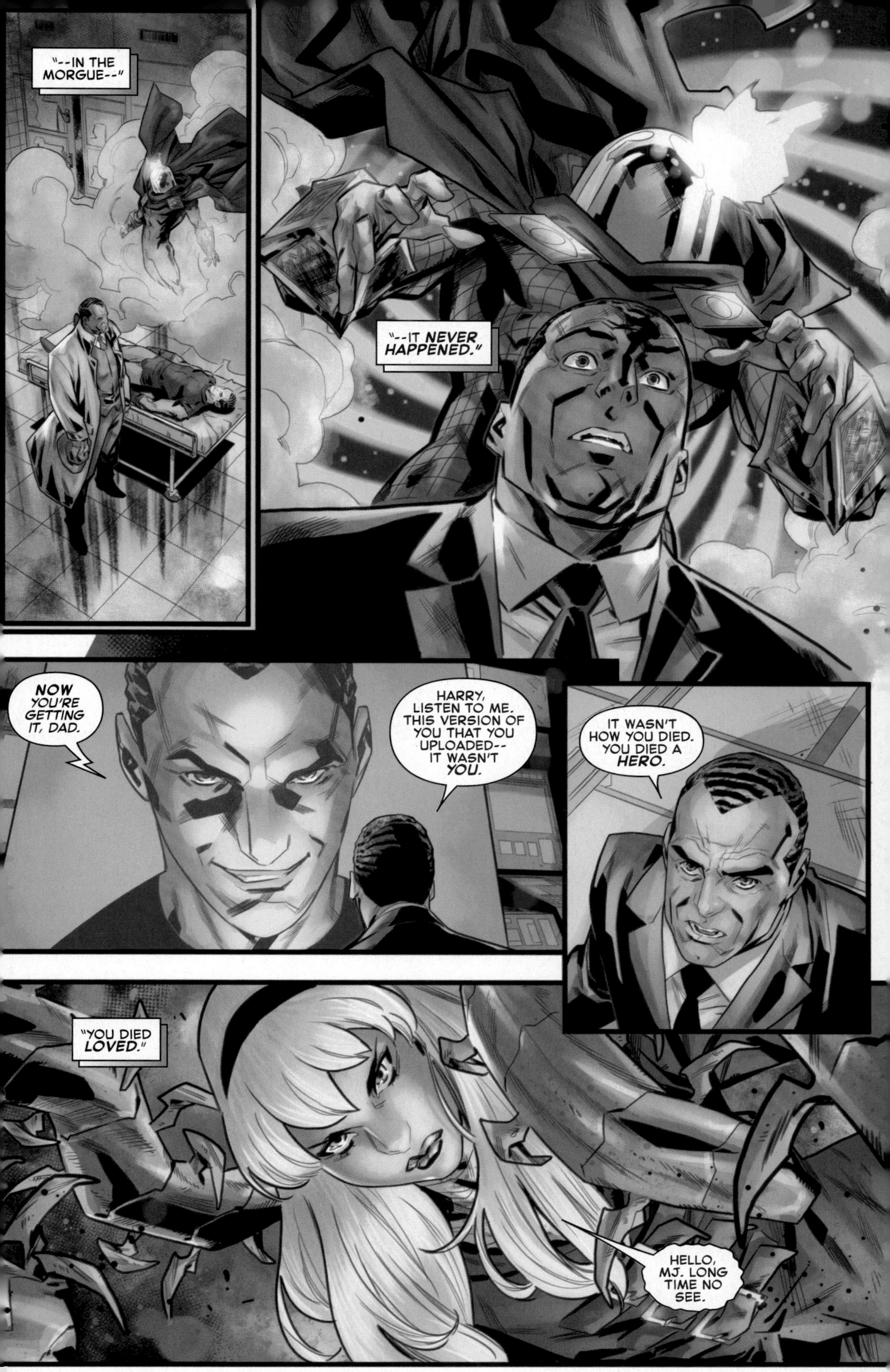
"--IN THE MORGUE--"
"--IT NEVER HAPPENED."
NOW YOU'RE GETTING IT, DAD.
HARRY, LISTEN TO ME. THIS VERSION OF YOU THAT YOU UPLOADED-- IT WASN'T YOU.
IT WASN'T HOW YOU DIED. YOU DIED A HERO.
"YOU DIED LOVED."
HELLO, MJ. LONG TIME NO SEE.

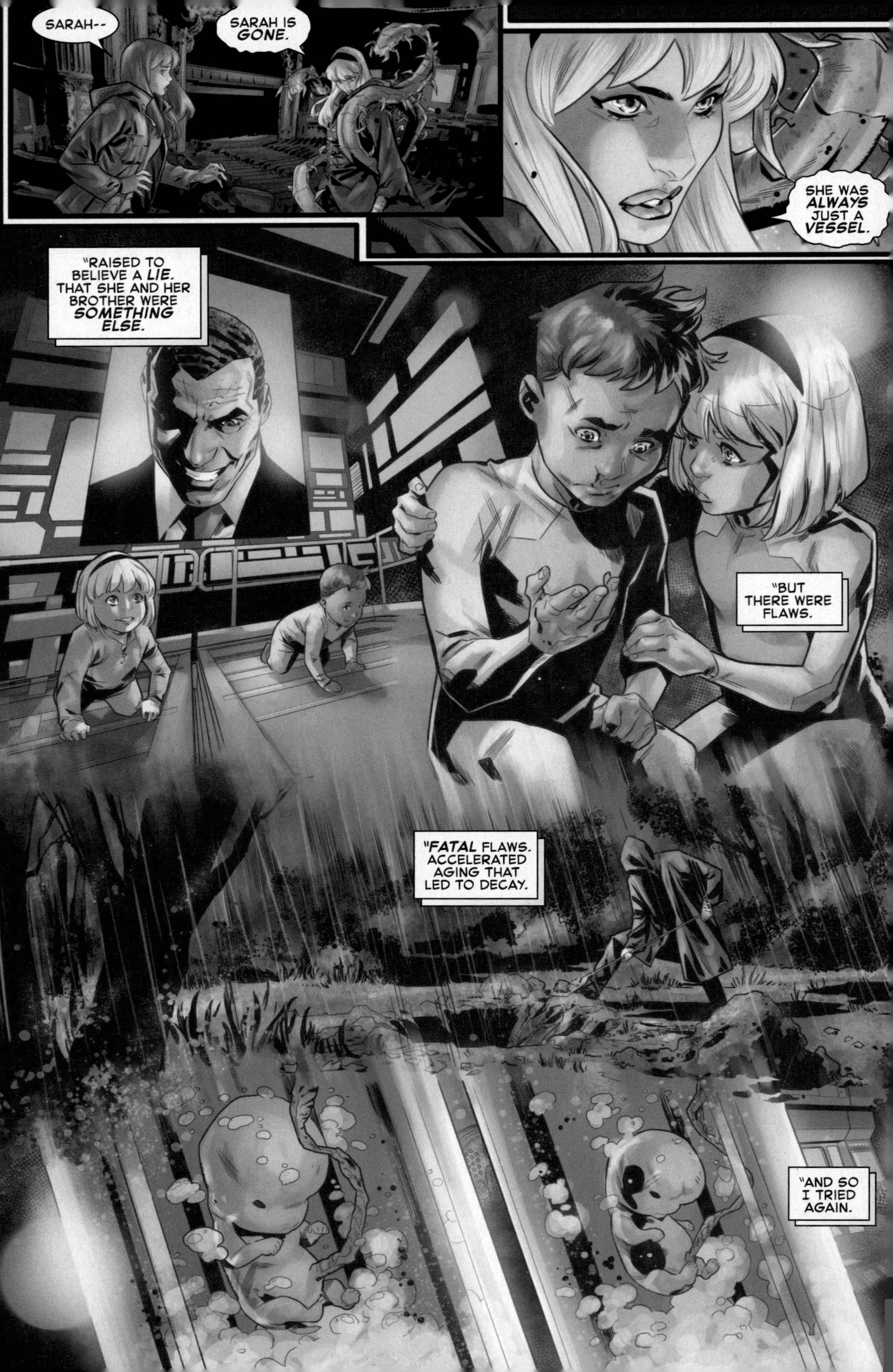
SARAH--
SARAH IS GONE.
SHE WAS ALWAYS JUST A VESSEL.
"RAISED TO BELIEVE A LIE. THAT SHE AND HER BROTHER WERE SOMETHING ELSE.
"BUT THERE WERE FLAWS.
"FATAL FLAWS. ACCELERATED AGING THAT LED TO DECAY.
"AND SO I TRIED AGAIN.

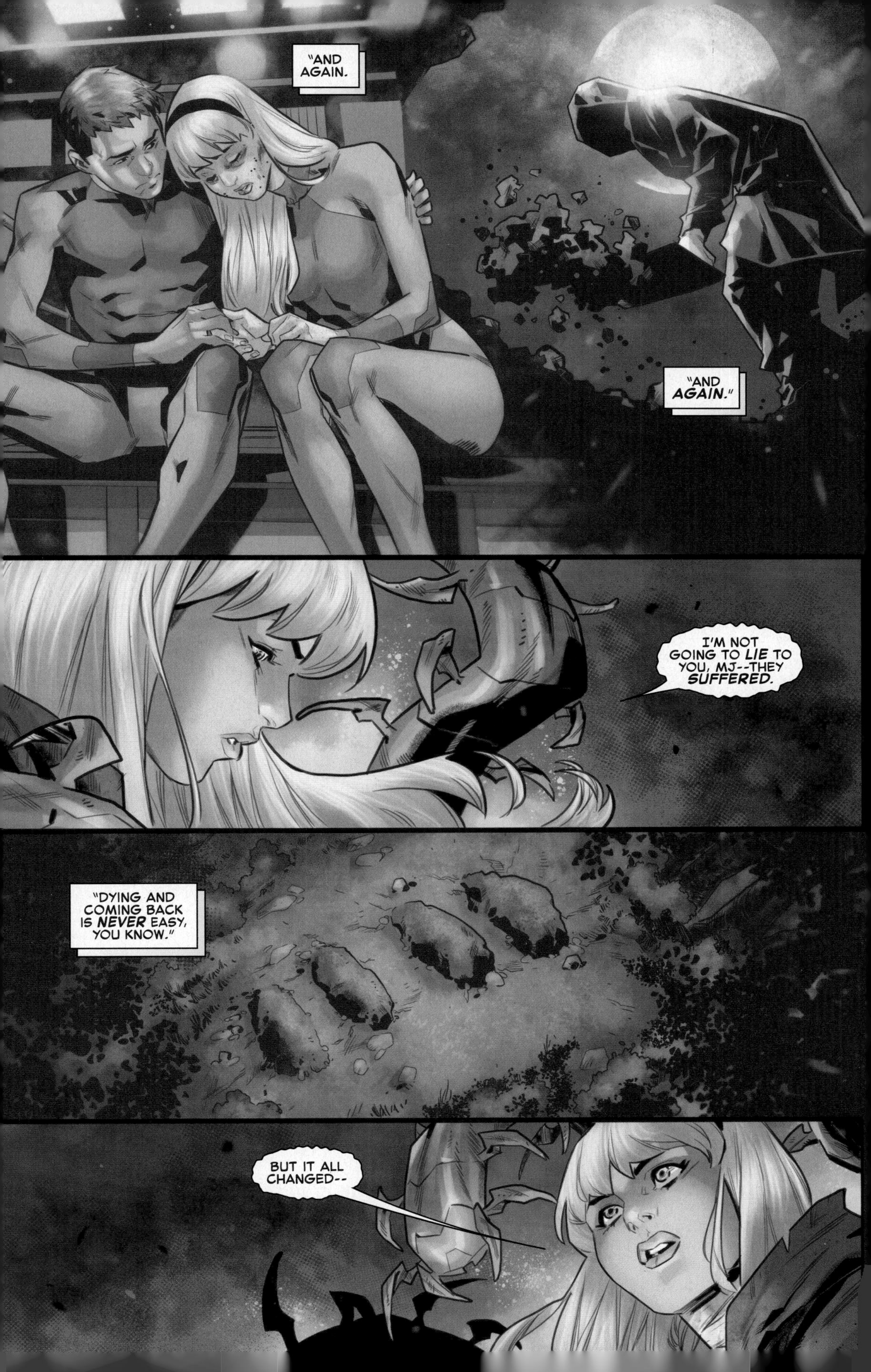
"AND AGAIN.
"AND AGAIN."
I'M NOT GOING TO LIE TO YOU, MJ--THEY SUFFERED.
"DYING AND COMING BACK IS NEVER EASY, YOU KNOW."
BUT IT ALL CHANGED--

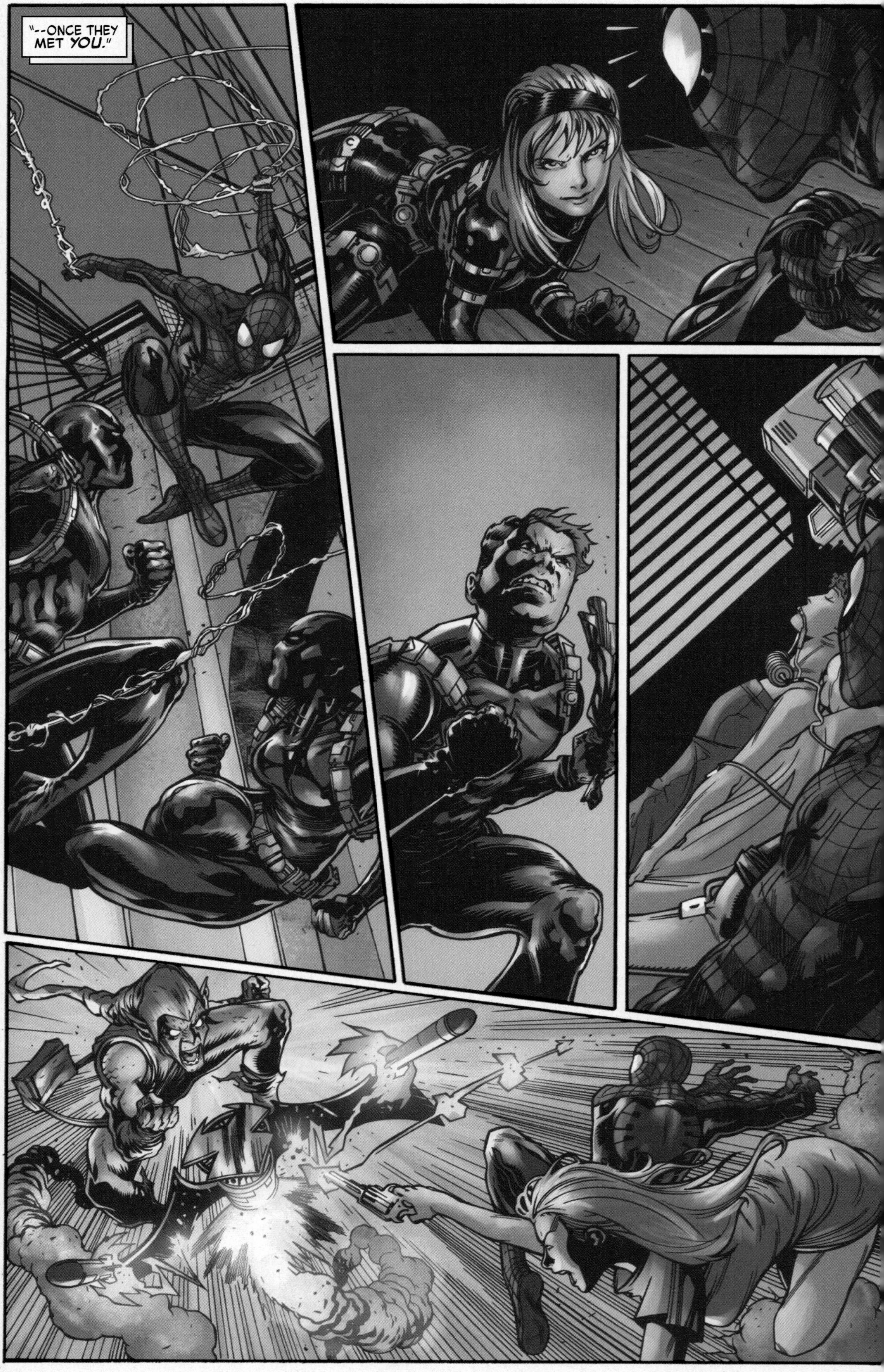
"--ONCE THEY MET YOU."

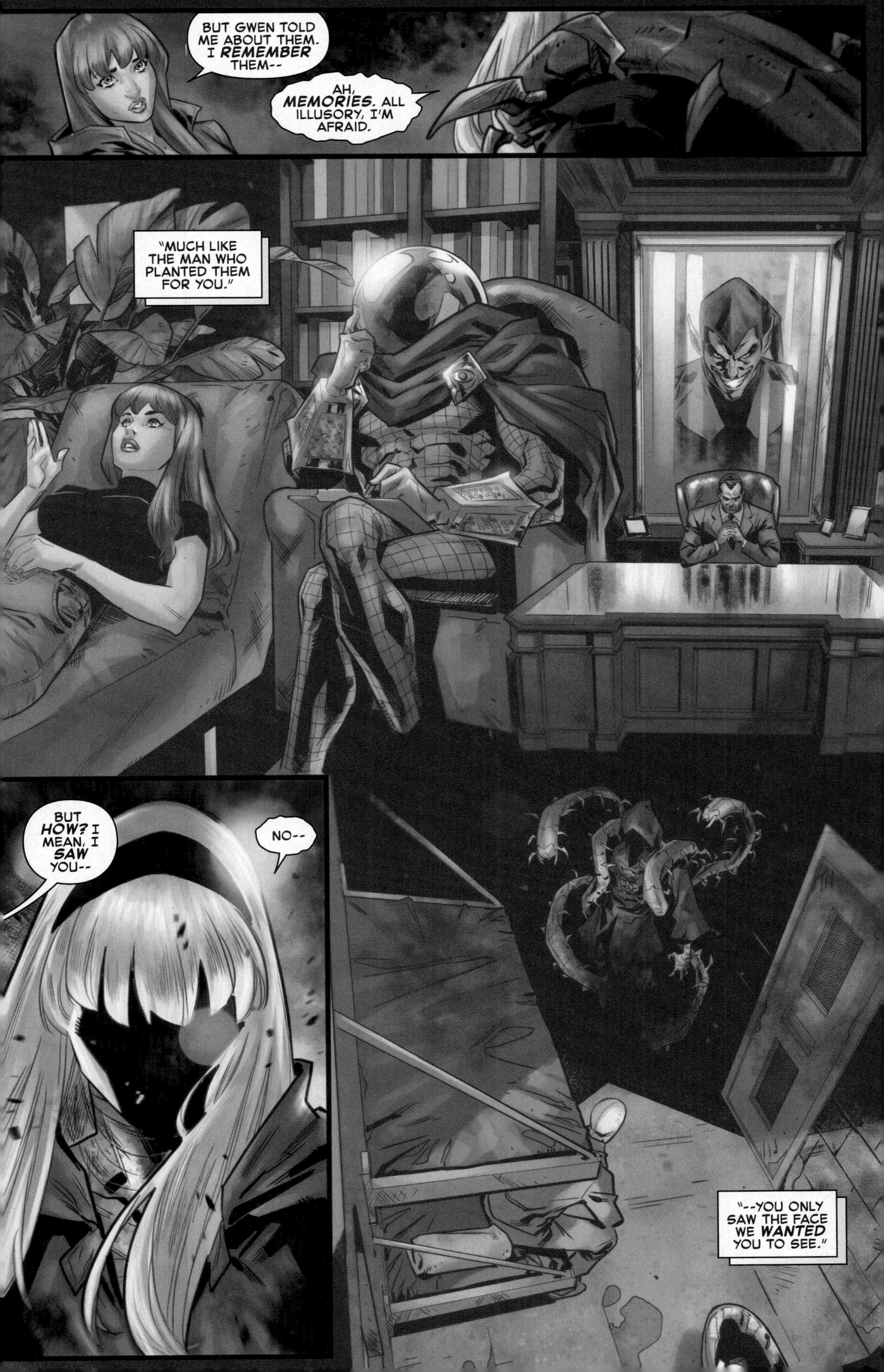
BUT GWEN TOLD ME ABOUT THEM. I REMEMBER THEM--
AH, MEMORIES. ALL ILLUSORY, I'M AFRAID.
"MUCH LIKE THE MAN WHO PLANTED THEM FOR YOU."
BUT HOW? I MEAN, I SAW YOU--
NO--
"--YOU ONLY SAW THE FACE WE WANTED YOU TO SEE."

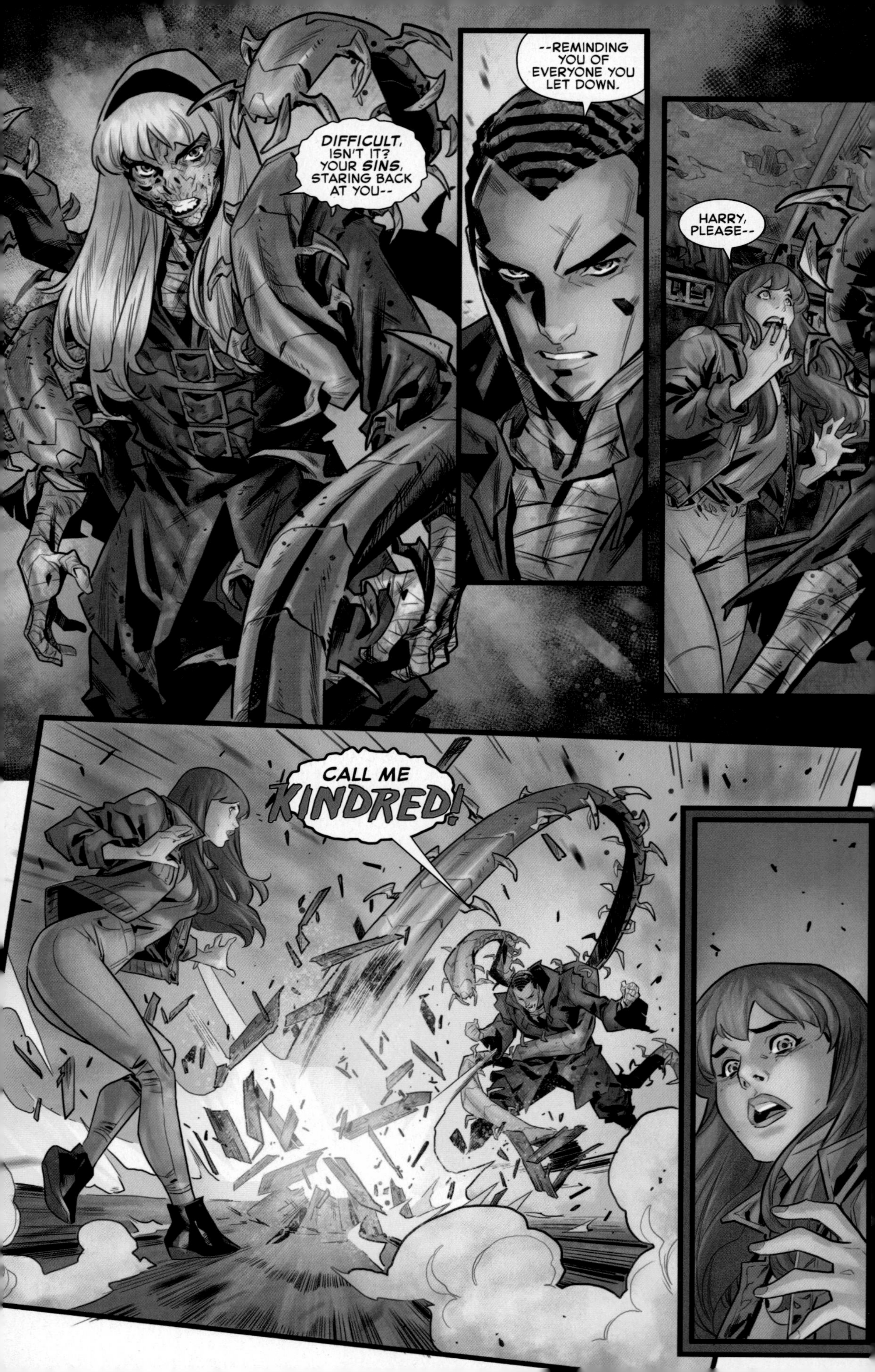
DIFFICULT, ISN'T IT? YOUR SINS, STARING BACK AT YOU--
--REMINDING YOU OF EVERYONE YOU LET DOWN.
HARRY, PLEASE--
CALL ME KINDRED!

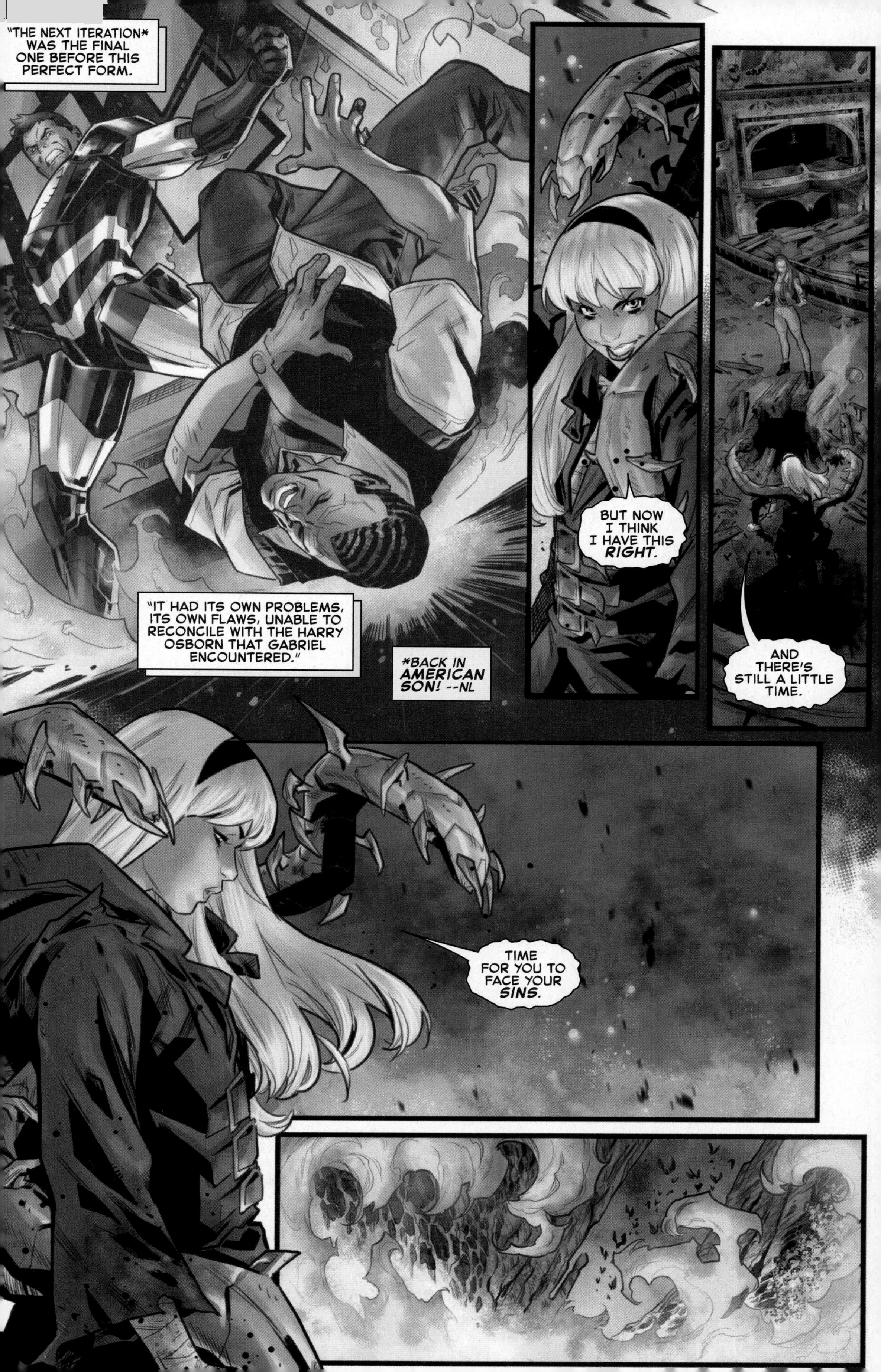

"THE NEXT ITERATION* WAS THE FINAL ONE BEFORE THIS PERFECT FORM.
"IT HAD ITS OWN PROBLEMS, ITS OWN FLAWS, UNABLE TO RECONCILE WITH THE HARRY OSBORN THAT GABRIEL ENCOUNTERED."
*BACK IN AMERICAN SON! --NL
BUT NOW I THINK I HAVE THIS RIGHT.
AND THERE'S STILL A LITTLE TIME.
TIME FOR YOU TO FACE YOUR SINS.

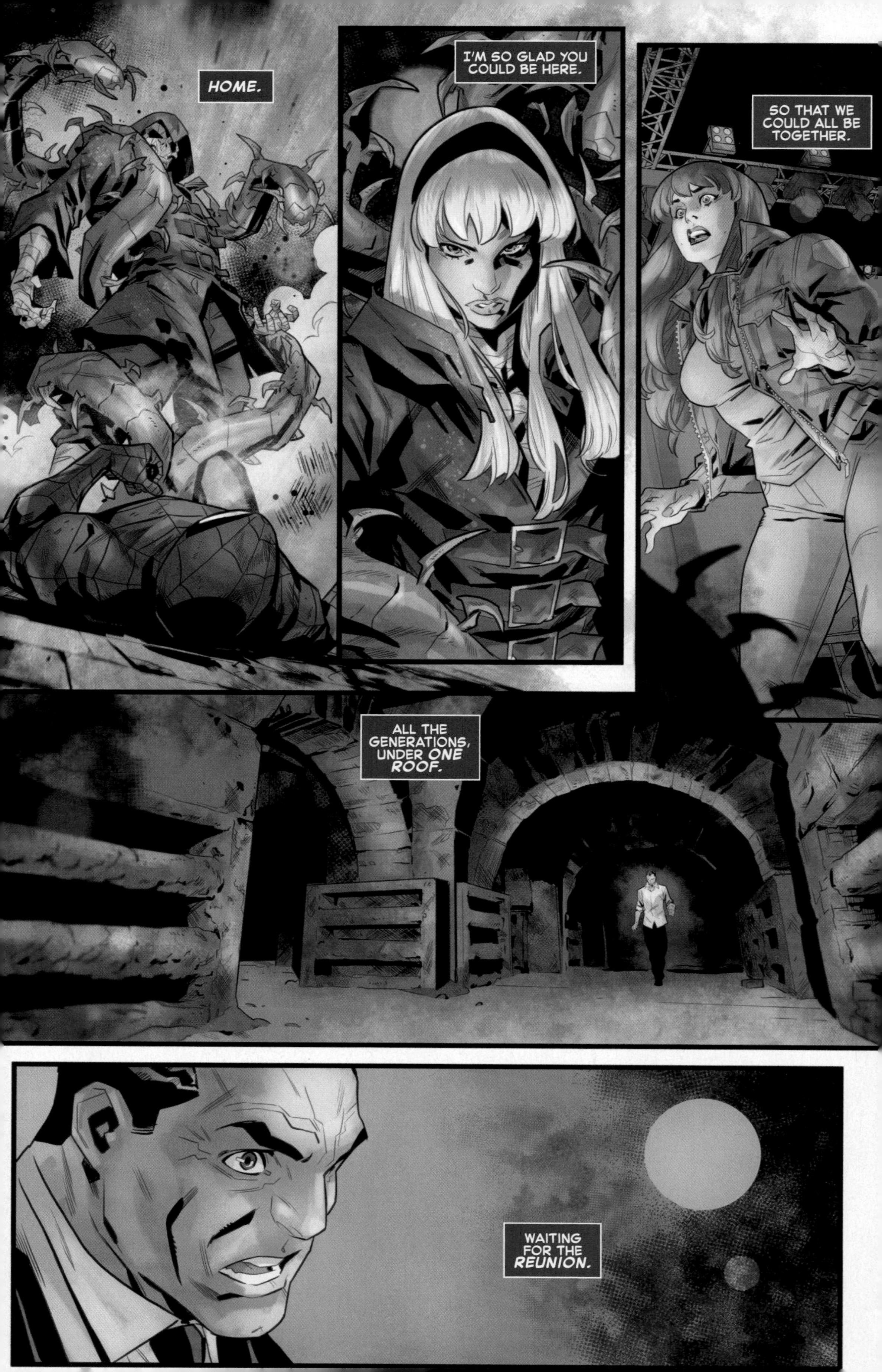
HOME.
I'M SO GLAD YOU COULD BE HERE.
SO THAT WE COULD ALL BE TOGETHER.
ALL THE GENERATIONS, UNDER ONE ROOF.
WAITING FOR THE REUNION.

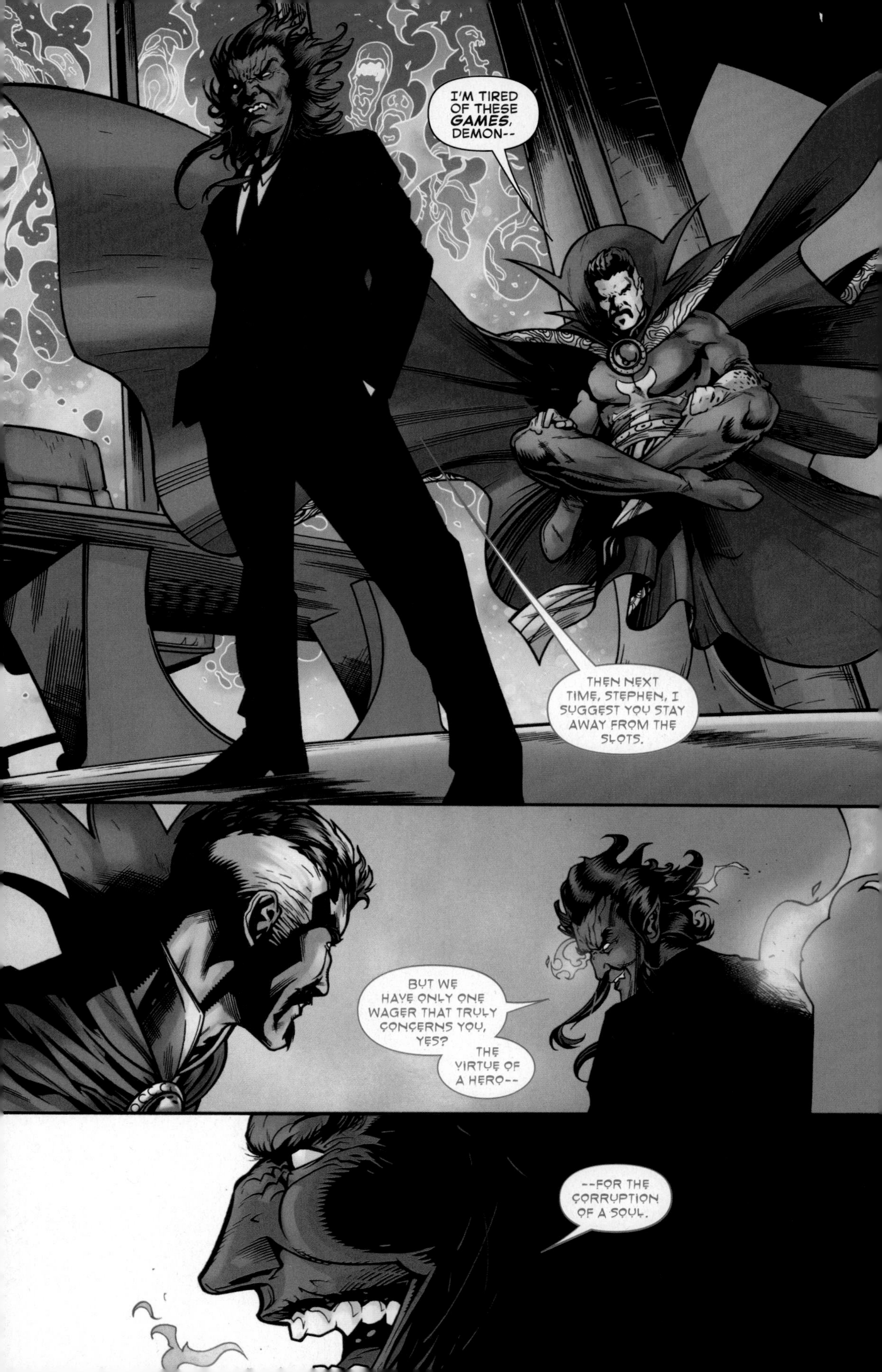
I'M TIRED OF THESE GAMES, DEMON--
THEN NEXT TIME, STEPHEN, I SUGGEST YOU STAY AWAY FROM THE SLOTS.
BUT WE HAVE ONLY ONE WAGER THAT TRULY CONCERNS YOU, YES?
THE VIRTUE OF A HERO--
--FOR THE CORRUPTION OF A SOUL.

74

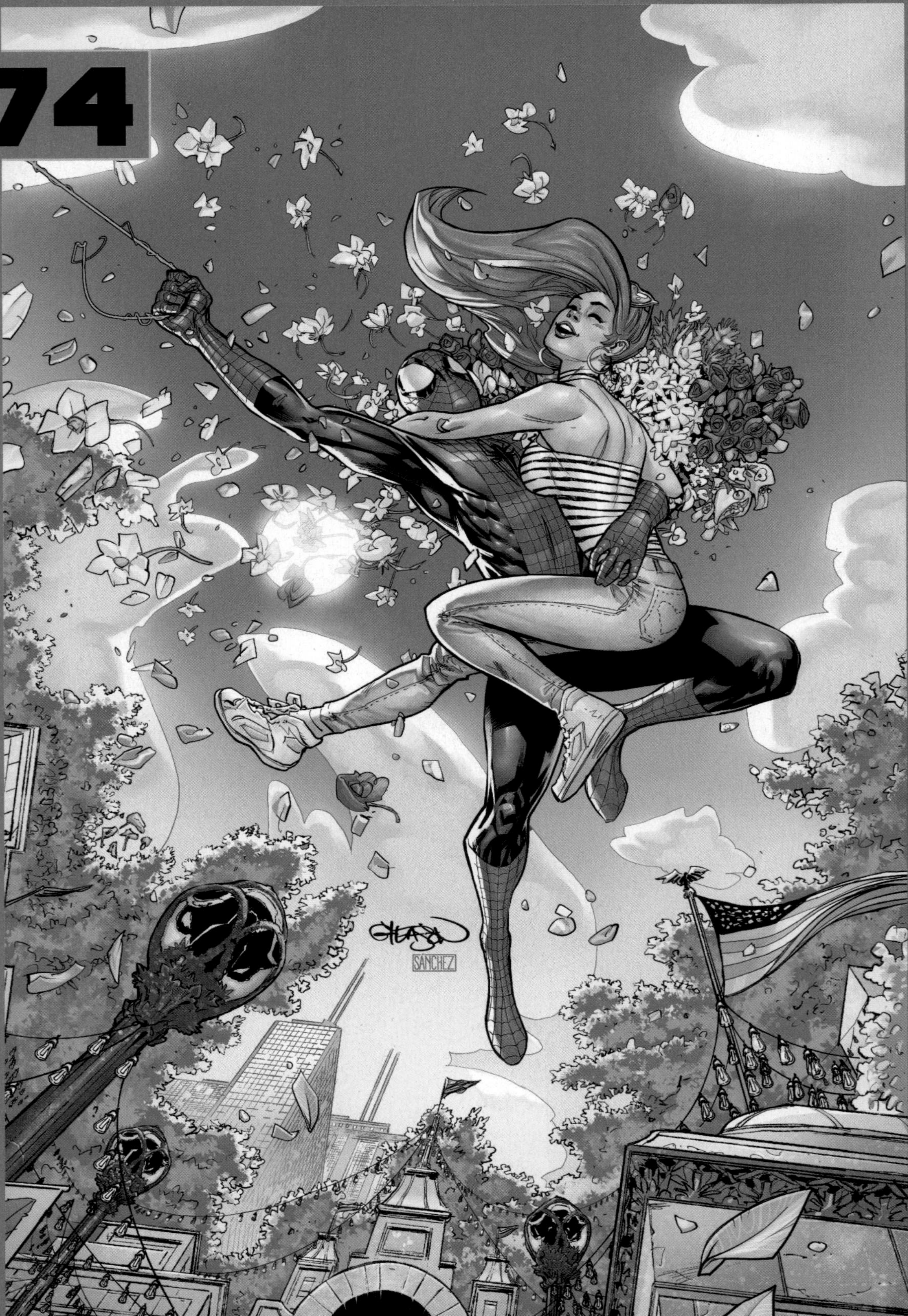
SÁNCHEZ

WHAT COST VICTORY?

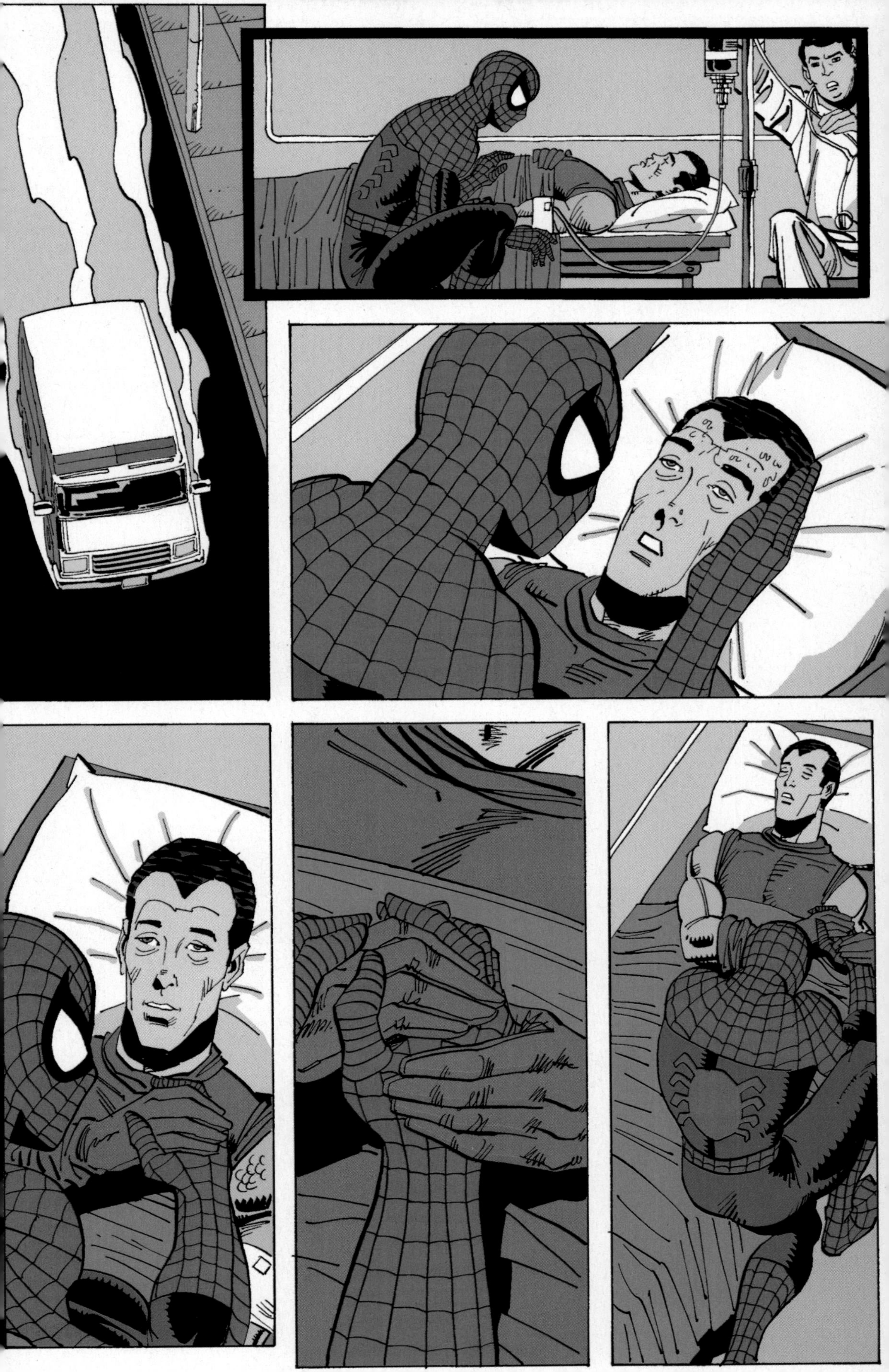

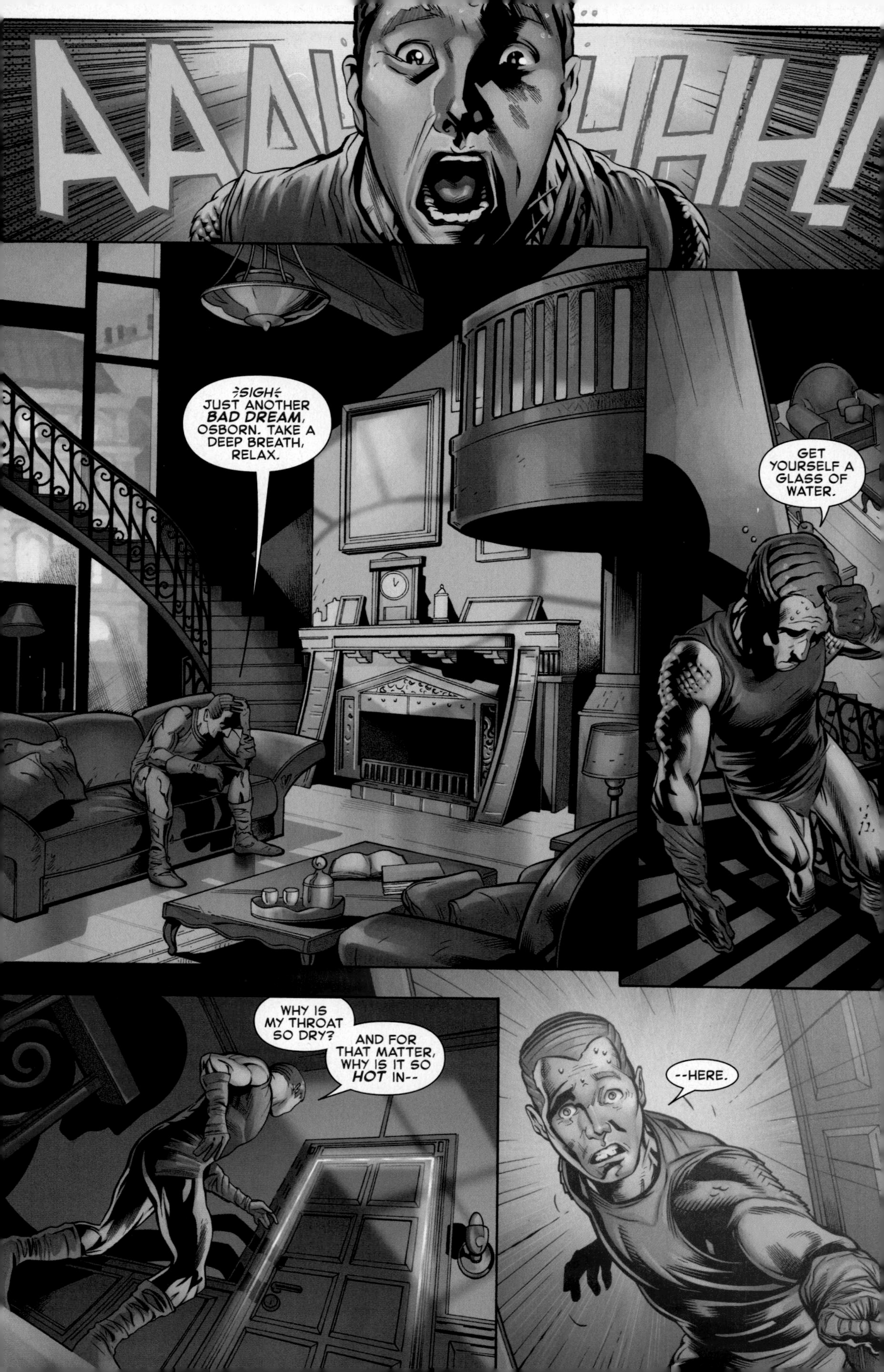
AAAUUHHH!
≶SIGH≶ JUST ANOTHER BAD DREAM, OSBORN. TAKE A DEEP BREATH, RELAX.
GET YOURSELF A GLASS OF WATER.
WHY IS MY THROAT SO DRY?
AND FOR THAT MATTER, WHY IS IT SO HOT IN--
--HERE.

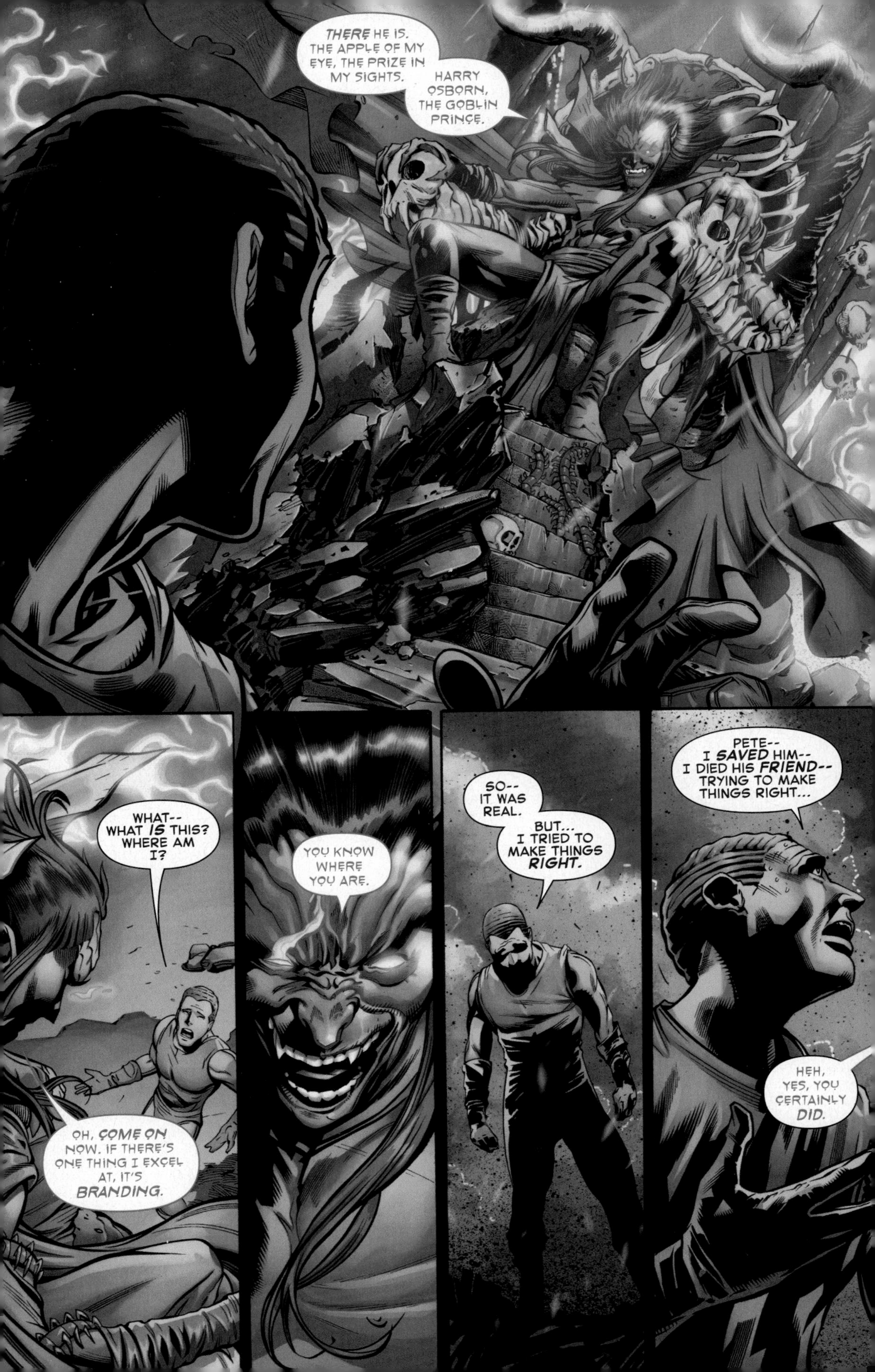
THERE HE IS. THE APPLE OF MY EYE, THE PRIZE IN MY SIGHTS.
HARRY OSBORN, THE GOBLIN PRINCE.
WHAT-- WHAT IS THIS? WHERE AM I?
OH, COME ON NOW. IF THERE'S ONE THING I EXCEL AT, IT'S BRANDING.
YOU KNOW WHERE YOU ARE.
SO-- IT WAS REAL.
BUT... I TRIED TO MAKE THINGS RIGHT.
PETE-- I SAVED HIM-- I DIED HIS FRIEND-- TRYING TO MAKE THINGS RIGHT...
HEH, YES, YOU CERTAINLY DID.

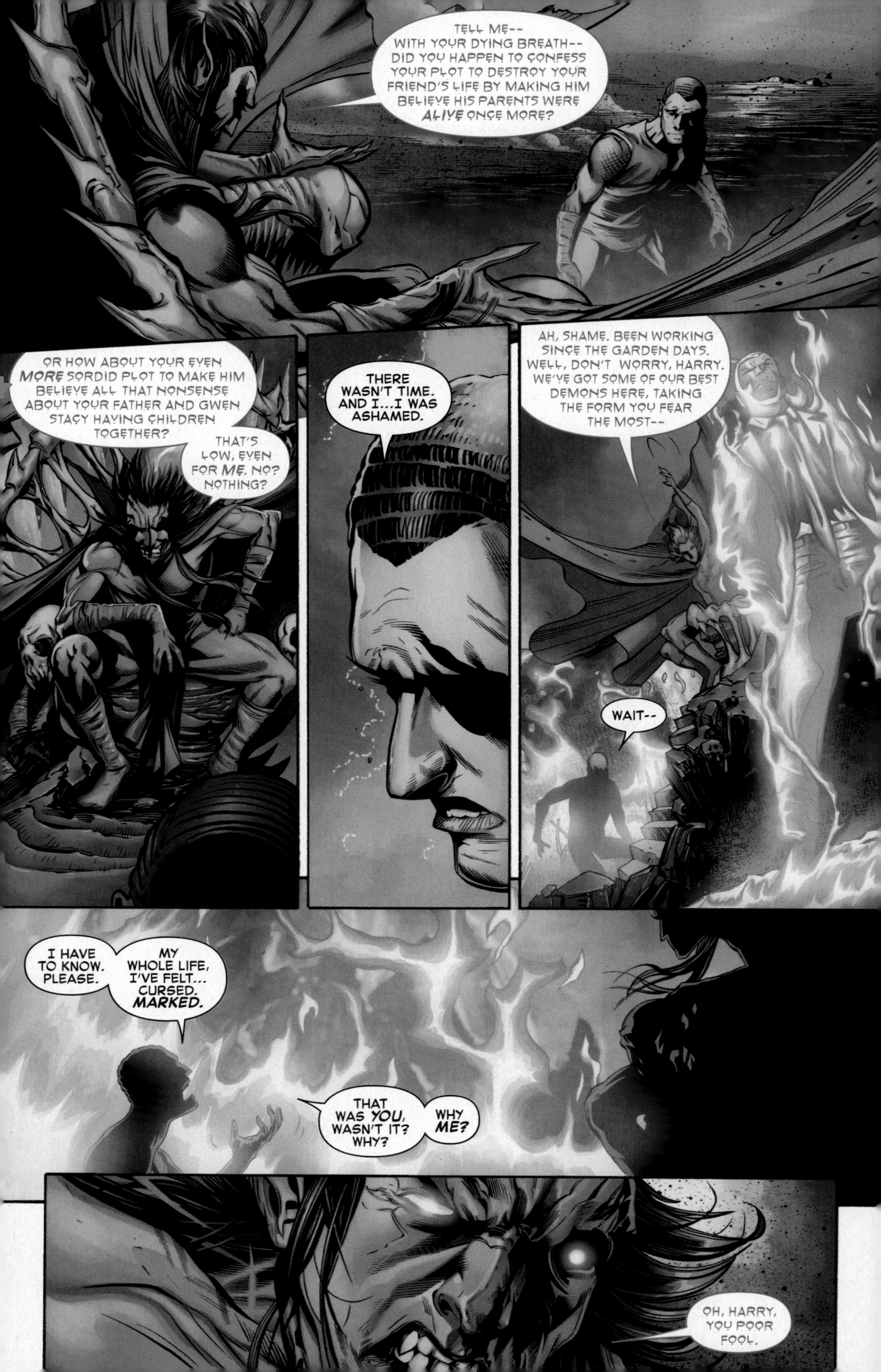
TELL ME-- WITH YOUR DYING BREATH-- DID YOU HAPPEN TO CONFESS YOUR PLOT TO DESTROY YOUR FRIEND'S LIFE BY MAKING HIM BELIEVE HIS PARENTS WERE ALIVE ONCE MORE?
OR HOW ABOUT YOUR EVEN MORE SORDID PLOT TO MAKE HIM BELIEVE ALL THAT NONSENSE ABOUT YOUR FATHER AND GWEN STACY HAVING CHILDREN TOGETHER?
THAT'S LOW, EVEN FOR ME. NO? NOTHING?
THERE WASN'T TIME. AND I...I WAS ASHAMED.
AH, SHAME. BEEN WORKING SINCE THE GARDEN DAYS. WELL, DON'T WORRY, HARRY. WE'VE GOT SOME OF OUR BEST DEMONS HERE, TAKING THE FORM YOU FEAR THE MOST--
WAIT--
I HAVE TO KNOW. PLEASE.
MY WHOLE LIFE, I'VE FELT... CURSED. MARKED.
THAT WAS YOU, WASN'T IT? WHY?
WHY ME?
OH, HARRY, YOU POOR FOOL.

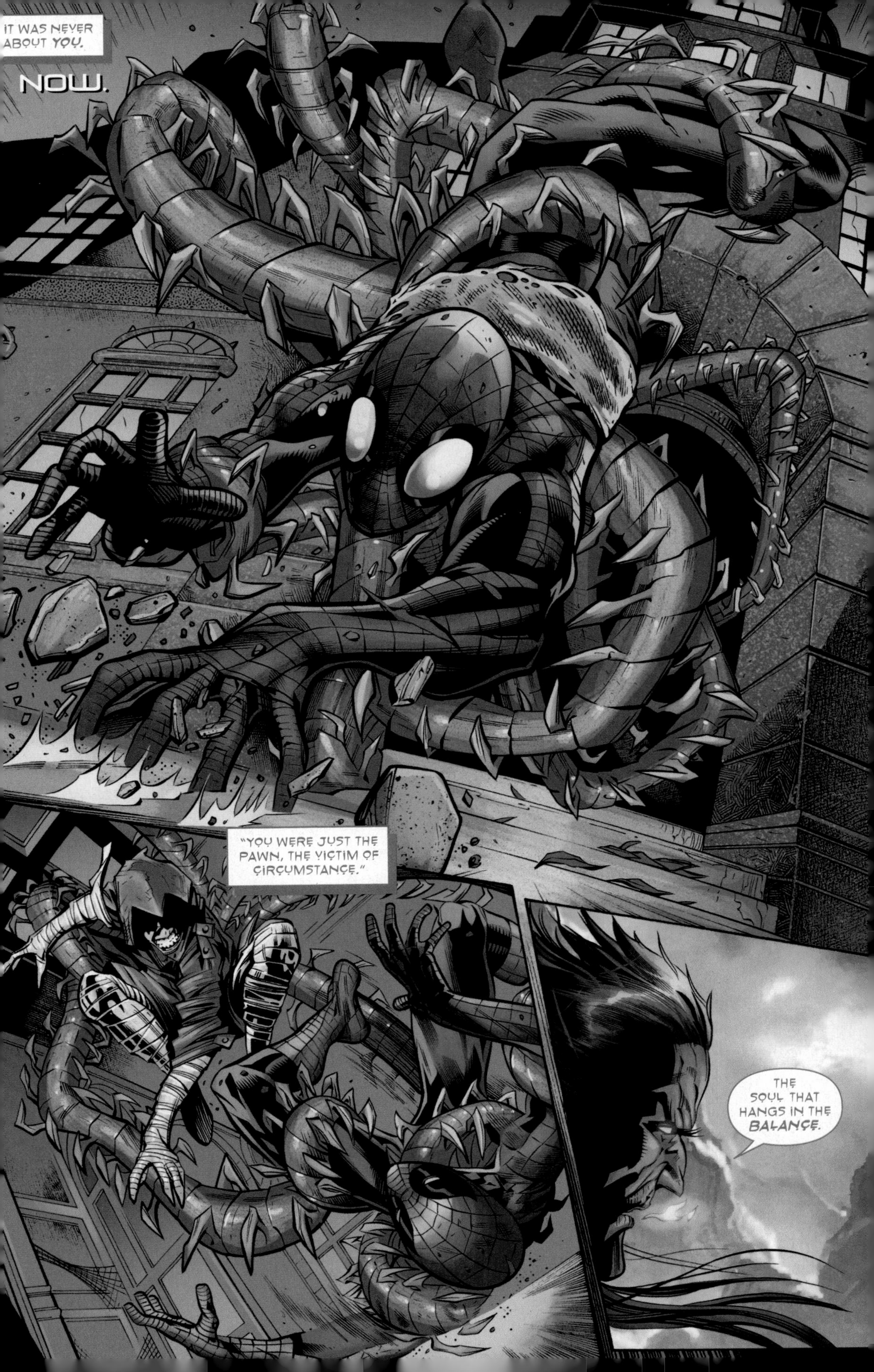
IT WAS NEVER ABOUT YOU.
NOW.
"YOU WERE JUST THE PAWN, THE VICTIM OF CIRCUMSTANCE."
THE SOUL THAT HANGS IN THE BALANCE.

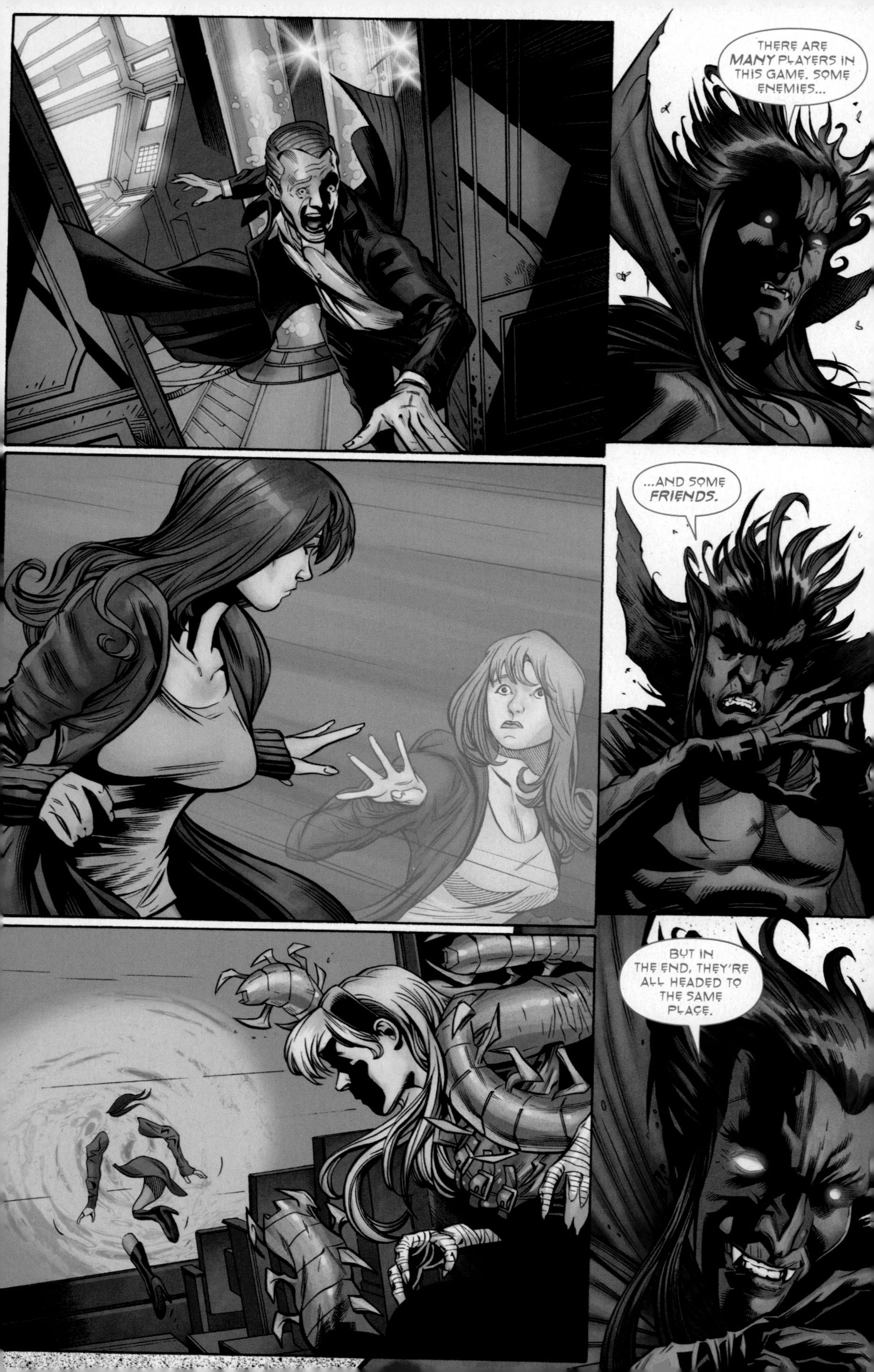
THERE ARE MANY PLAYERS IN THIS GAME. SOME ENEMIES...
...AND SOME FRIENDS.
BUT IN THE END, THEY'RE ALL HEADED TO THE SAME PLACE.

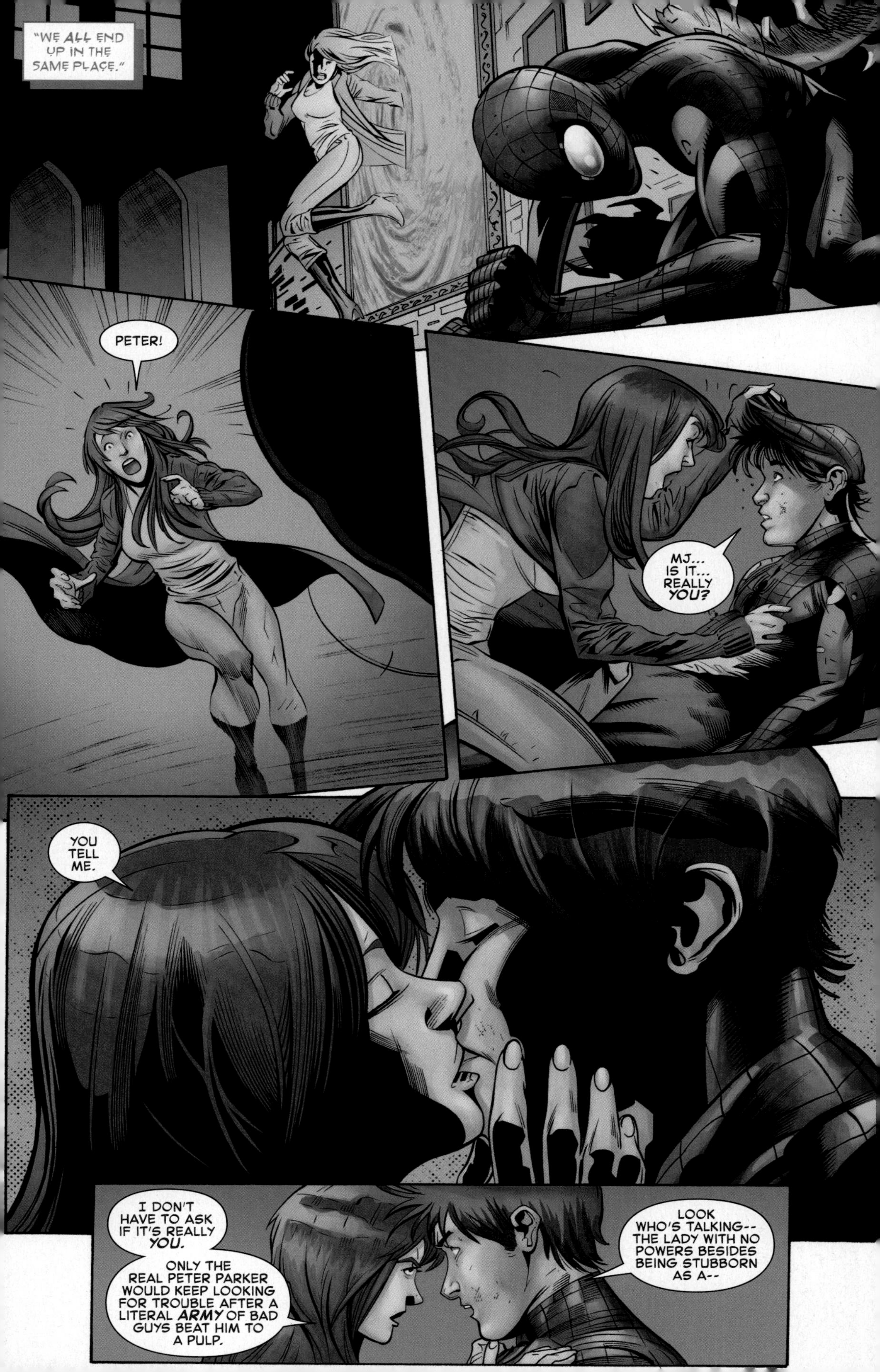
"WE ALL END UP IN THE SAME PLACE."
PETER!
MJ... IS IT... REALLY YOU?
YOU TELL ME.
I DON'T HAVE TO ASK IF IT'S REALLY YOU.
ONLY THE REAL PETER PARKER WOULD KEEP LOOKING FOR TROUBLE AFTER A LITERAL ARMY OF BAD GUYS BEAT HIM TO A PULP.
LOOK WHO'S TALKING-- THE LADY WITH NO POWERS BESIDES BEING STUBBORN AS A--

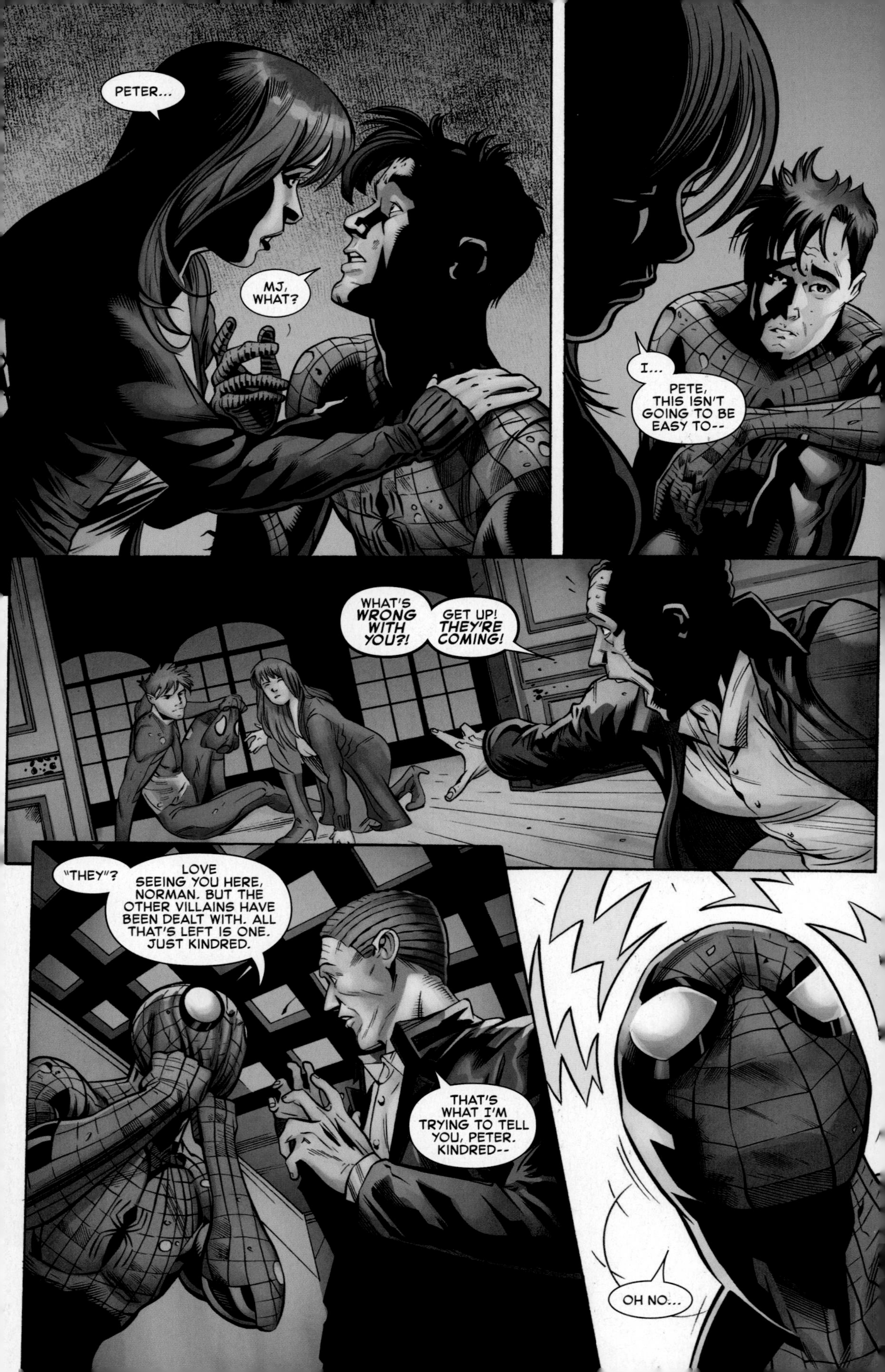
PETER...
MJ, WHAT?
I...
PETE, THIS ISN'T GOING TO BE EASY TO--
WHAT'S WRONG WITH YOU?!
GET UP! THEY'RE COMING!
"THEY"?
LOVE SEEING YOU HERE, NORMAN. BUT THE OTHER VILLAINS HAVE BEEN DEALT WITH. ALL THAT'S LEFT IS ONE. JUST KINDRED.
THAT'S WHAT I'M TRYING TO TELL YOU, PETER. KINDRED--
OH NO...

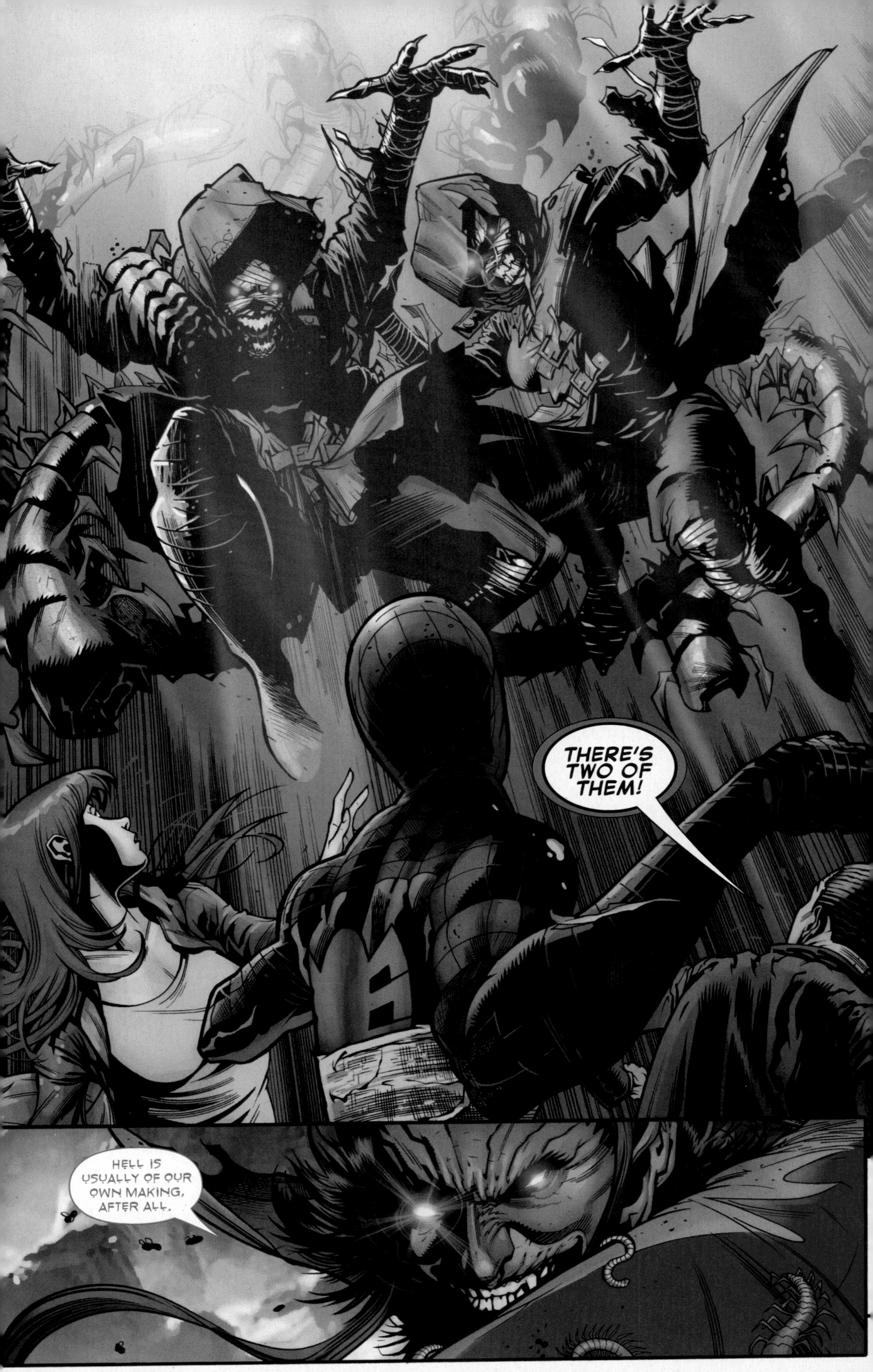
THERE'S TWO OF THEM!
HELL IS USUALLY OF OUR OWN MAKING, AFTER ALL.

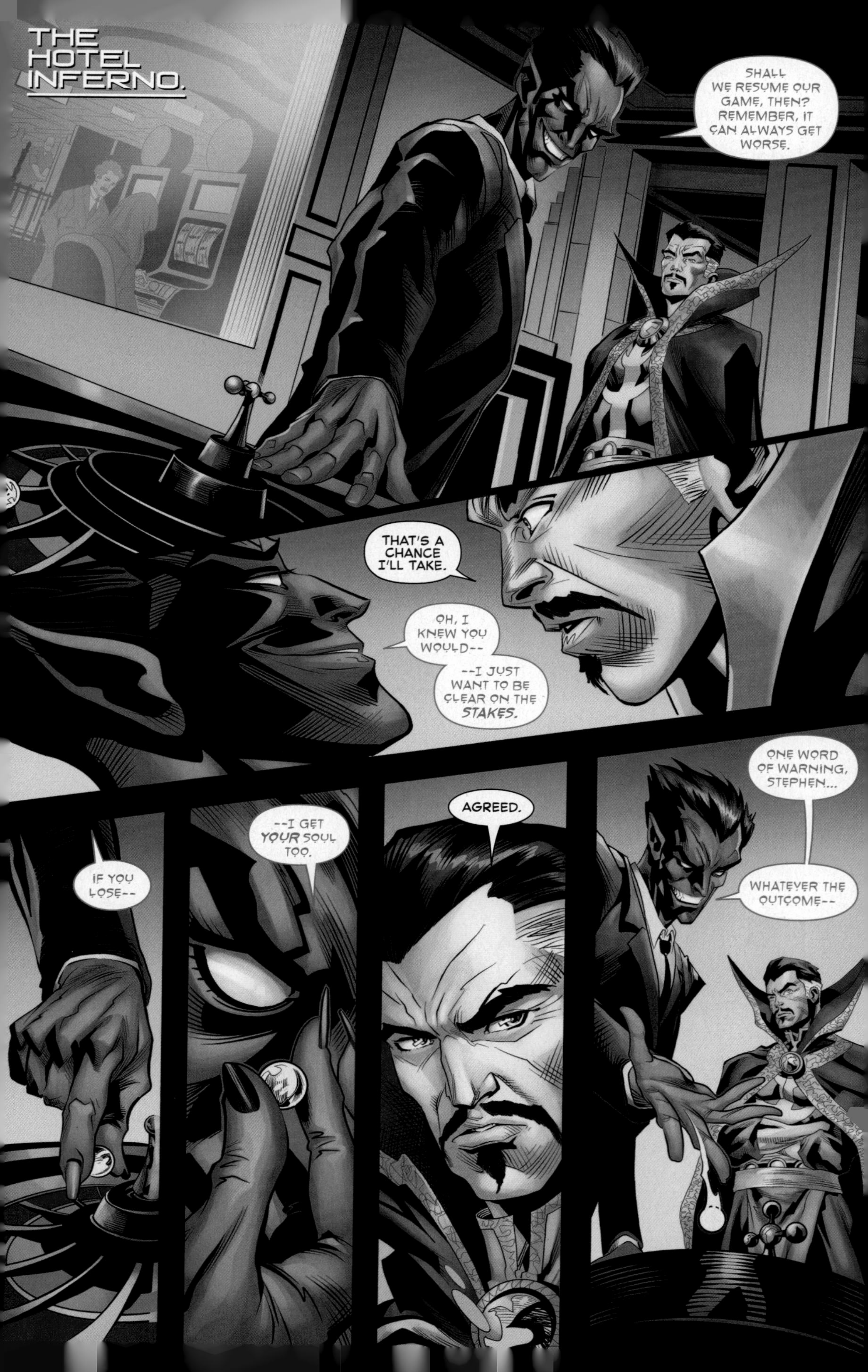
THE HOTEL INFERNO.
SHALL WE RESUME OUR GAME, THEN? REMEMBER, IT CAN ALWAYS GET WORSE.
THAT'S A CHANCE I'LL TAKE.
OH, I KNEW YOU WOULD--
--I JUST WANT TO BE CLEAR ON THE STAKES.
IF YOU LOSE--
--I GET YOUR SOUL TOO.
AGREED.
ONE WORD OF WARNING, STEPHEN...
WHATEVER THE OUTCOME--

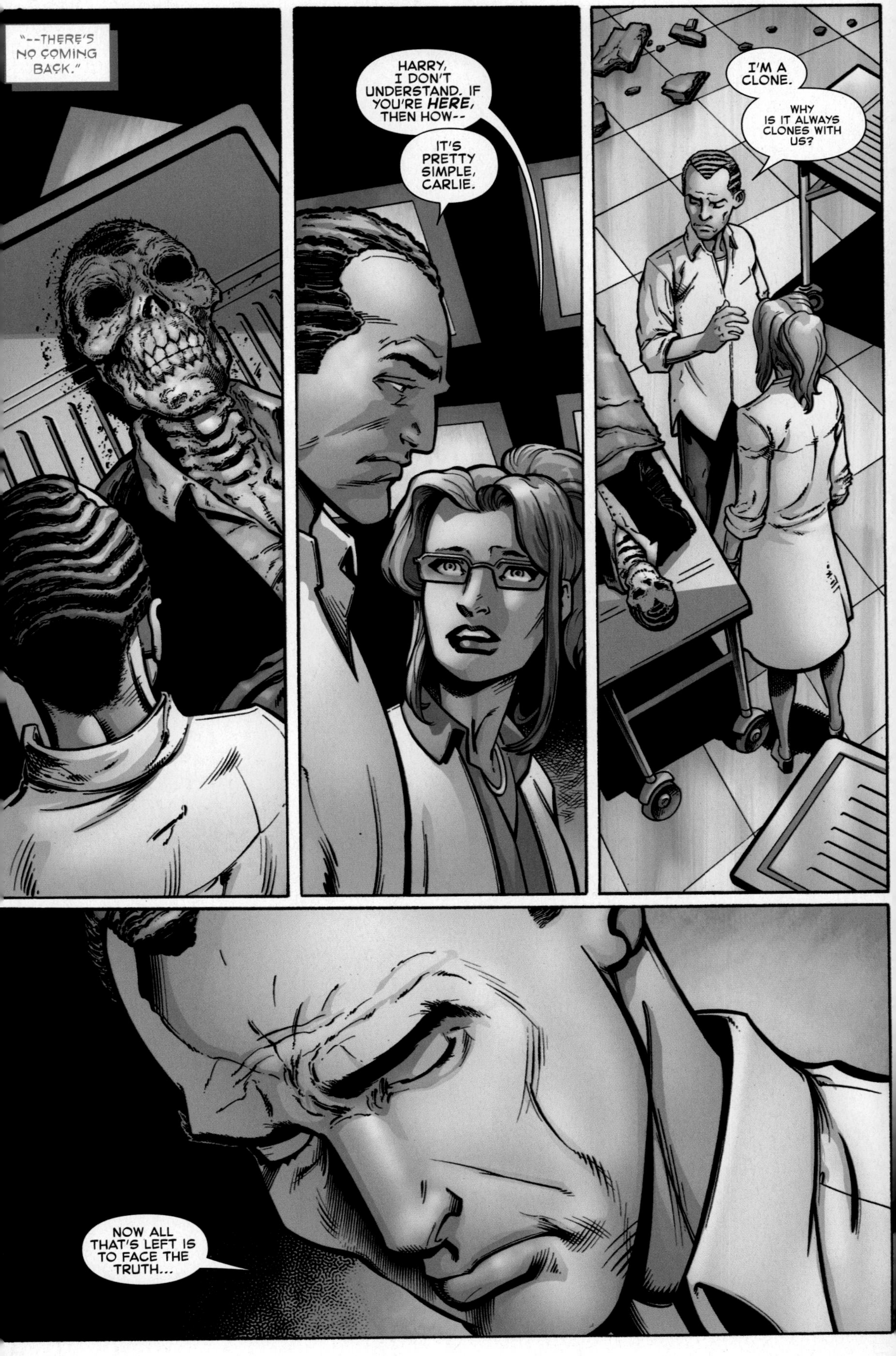
"--THERE'S NO COMING BACK."
HARRY, I DON'T UNDERSTAND. IF YOU'RE HERE, THEN HOW--
IT'S PRETTY SIMPLE, CARLIE.
I'M A CLONE.
WHY IS IT ALWAYS CLONES WITH US?
NOW ALL THAT'S LEFT IS TO FACE THE TRUTH...

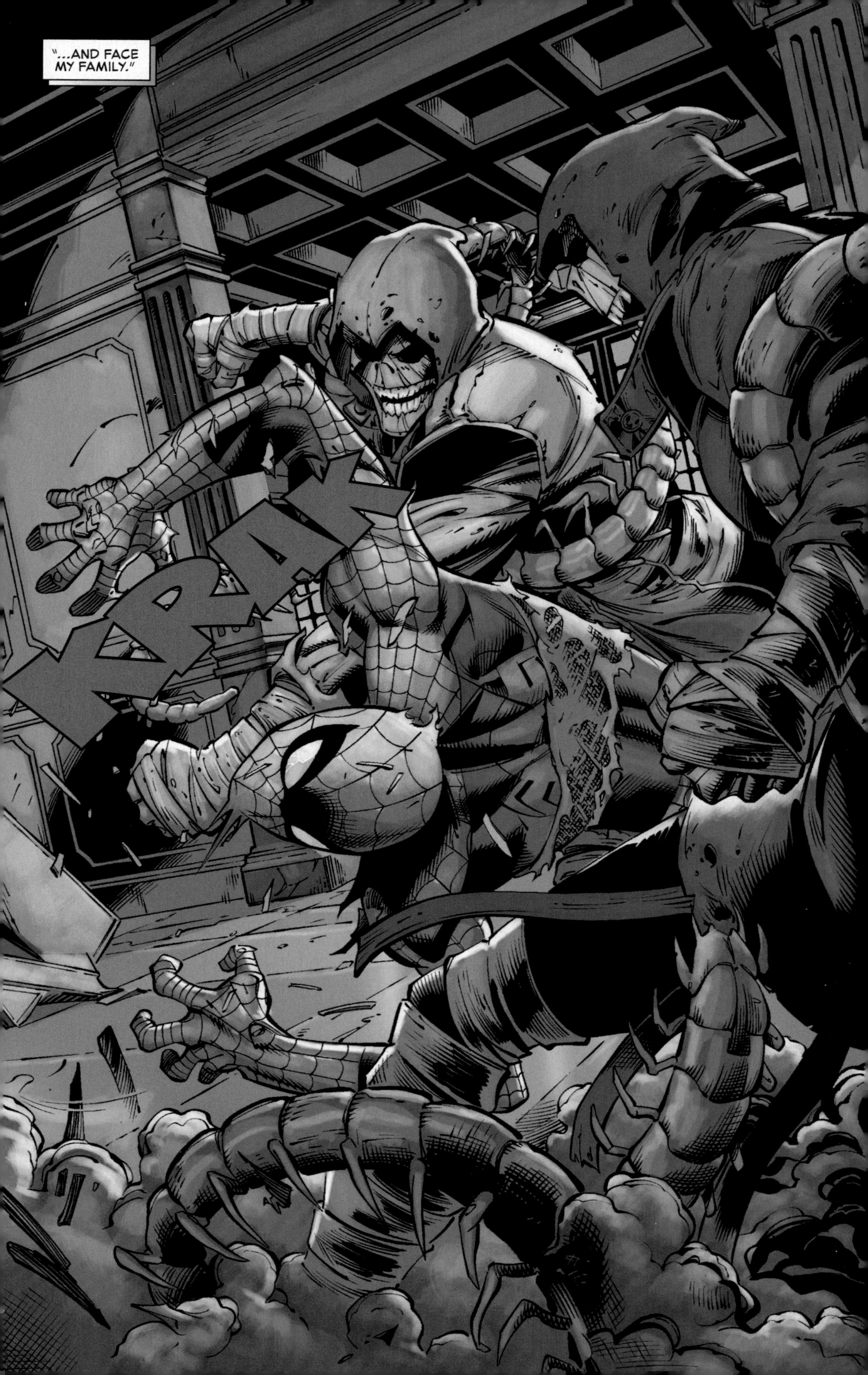
"...AND FACE MY FAMILY."
KRAK

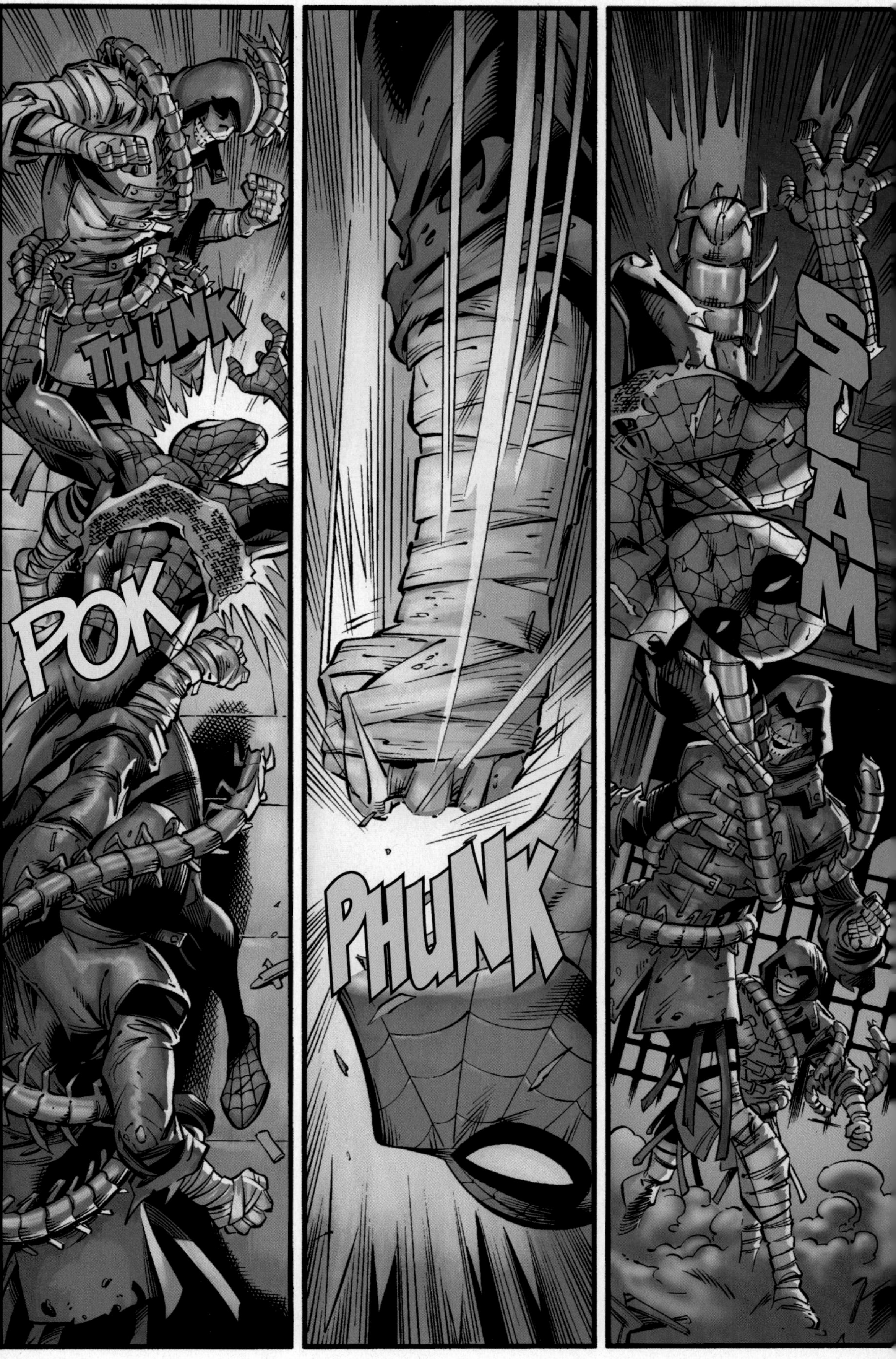
THUNK
POK
PHUNK
SLAM

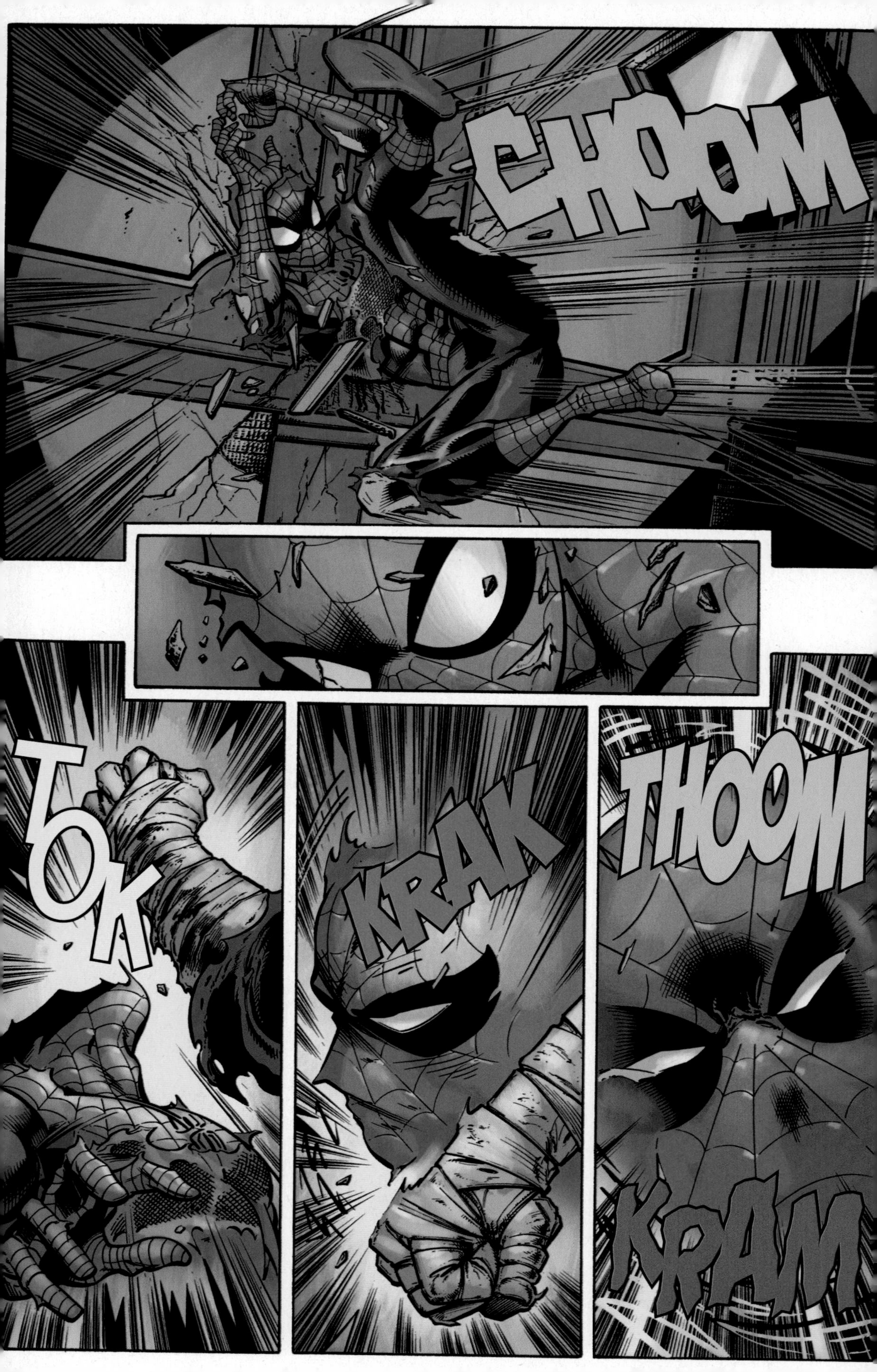
CHOOM
TOK
KRAK
THOOM
KRAM

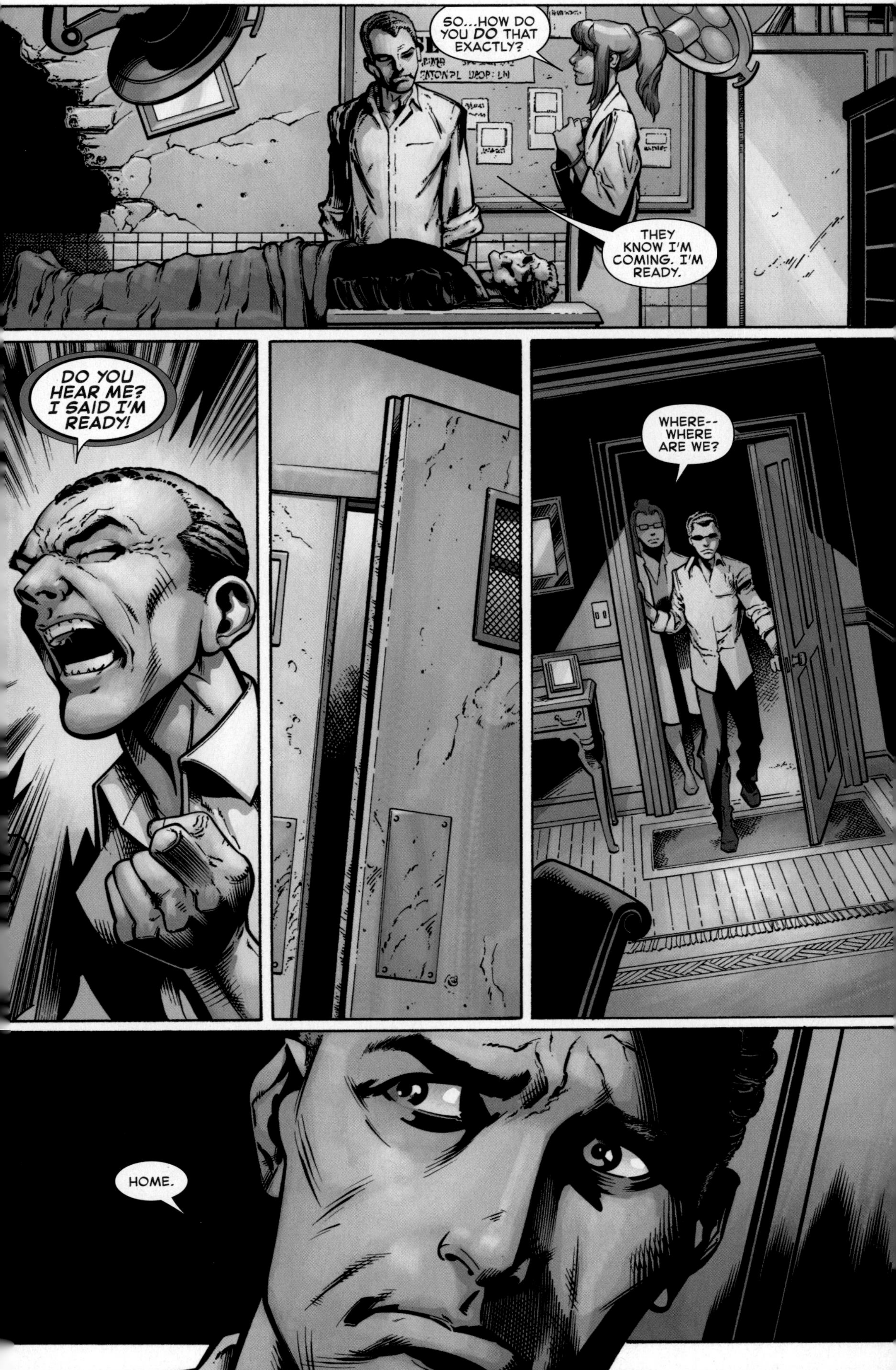
SO...HOW DO YOU DO THAT EXACTLY?
THEY KNOW I'M COMING. I'M READY.
DO YOU HEAR ME? I SAID I'M READY!
WHERE-- WHERE ARE WE?
HOME.

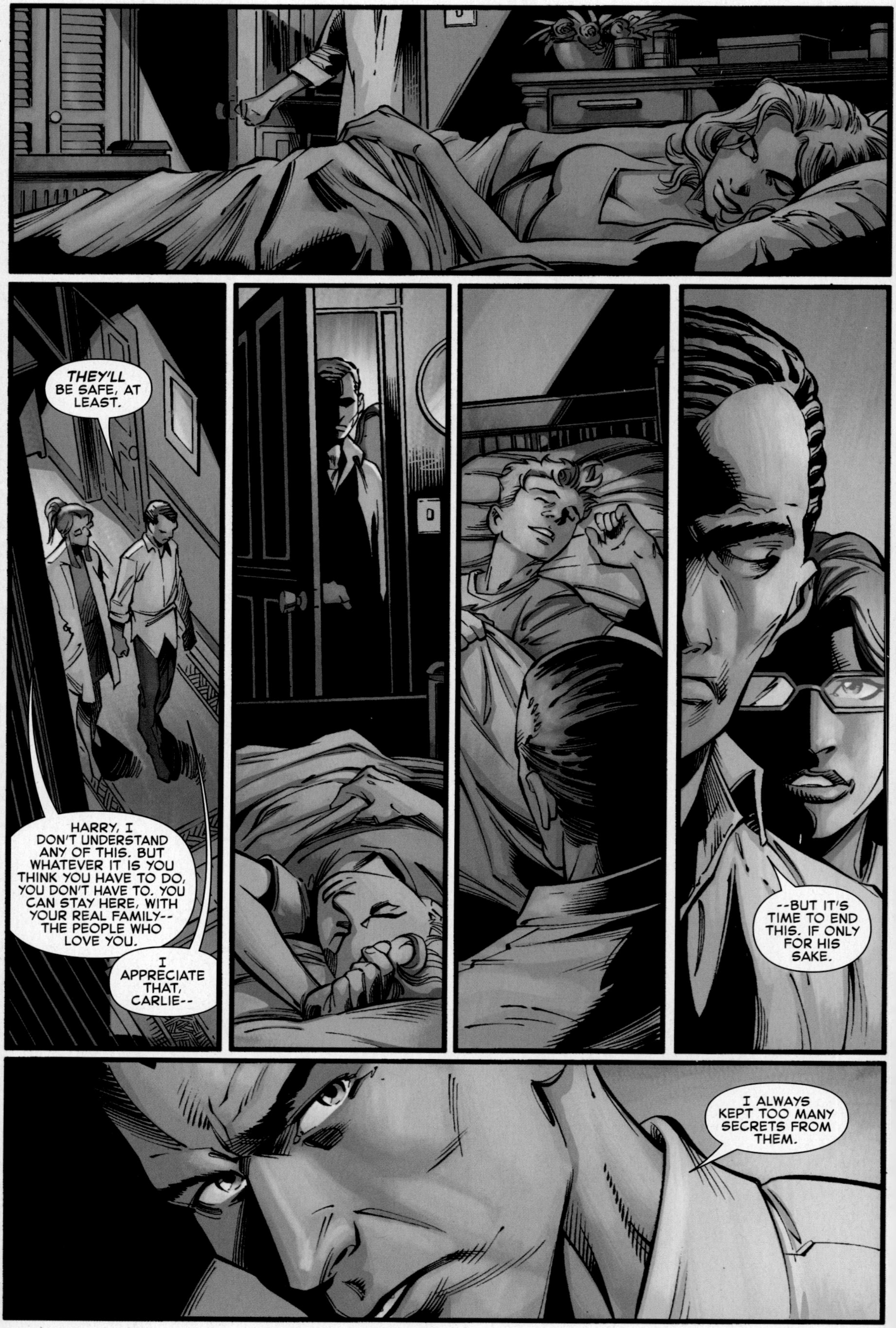
THEY'LL BE SAFE, AT LEAST.
HARRY, I DON'T UNDERSTAND ANY OF THIS. BUT WHATEVER IT IS YOU THINK YOU HAVE TO DO, YOU DON'T HAVE TO. YOU CAN STAY HERE, WITH YOUR REAL FAMILY-- THE PEOPLE WHO LOVE YOU.
I APPRECIATE THAT, CARLIE--
--BUT IT'S TIME TO END THIS. IF ONLY FOR HIS SAKE.
I ALWAYS KEPT TOO MANY SECRETS FROM THEM.

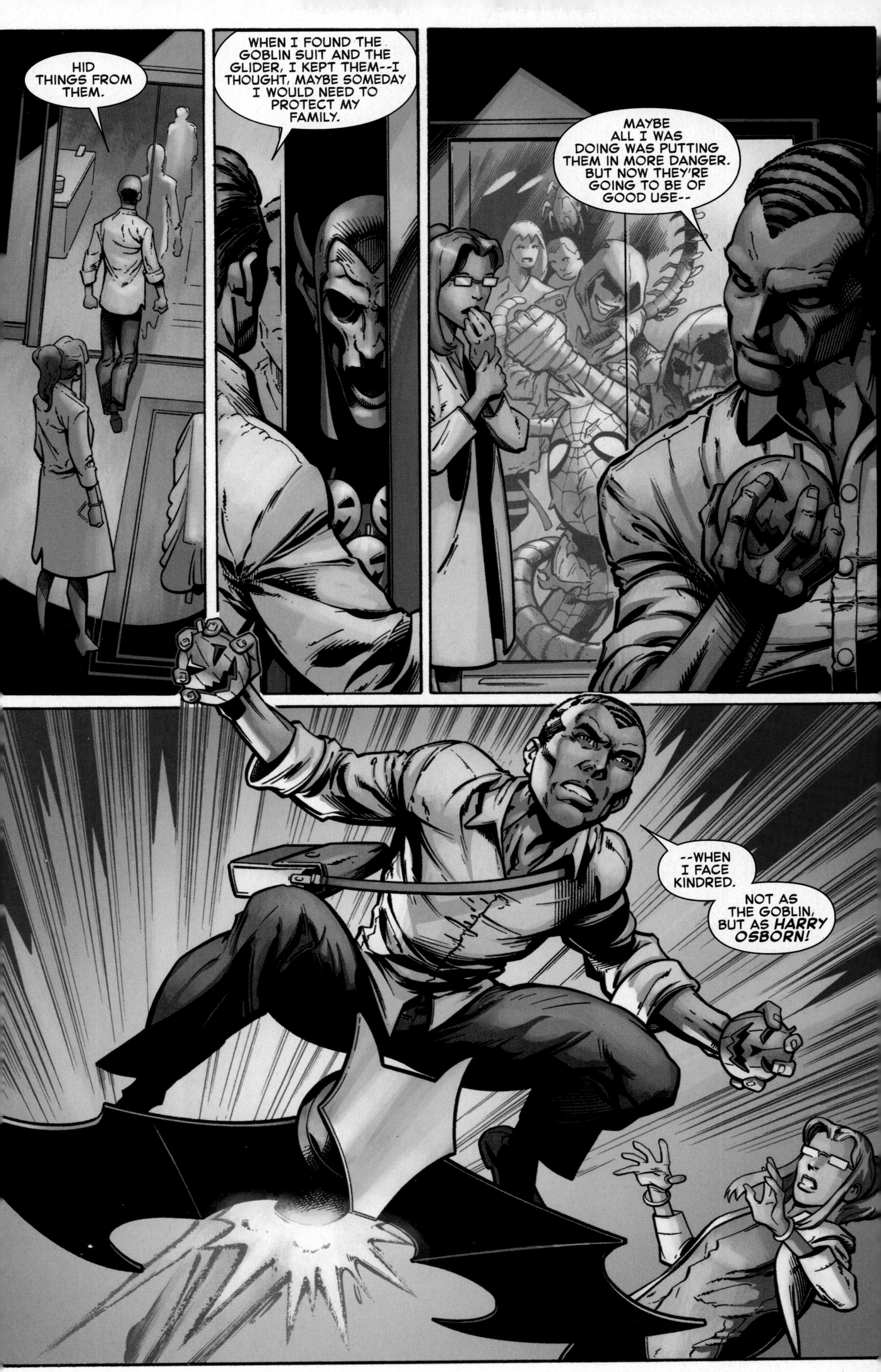
HID THINGS FROM THEM.
WHEN I FOUND THE GOBLIN SUIT AND THE GLIDER, I KEPT THEM--I THOUGHT, MAYBE SOMEDAY I WOULD NEED TO PROTECT MY FAMILY.
MAYBE ALL I WAS DOING WAS PUTTING THEM IN MORE DANGER. BUT NOW THEY'RE GOING TO BE OF GOOD USE--
--WHEN I FACE KINDRED.
NOT AS THE GOBLIN, BUT AS *HARRY OSBORN!*

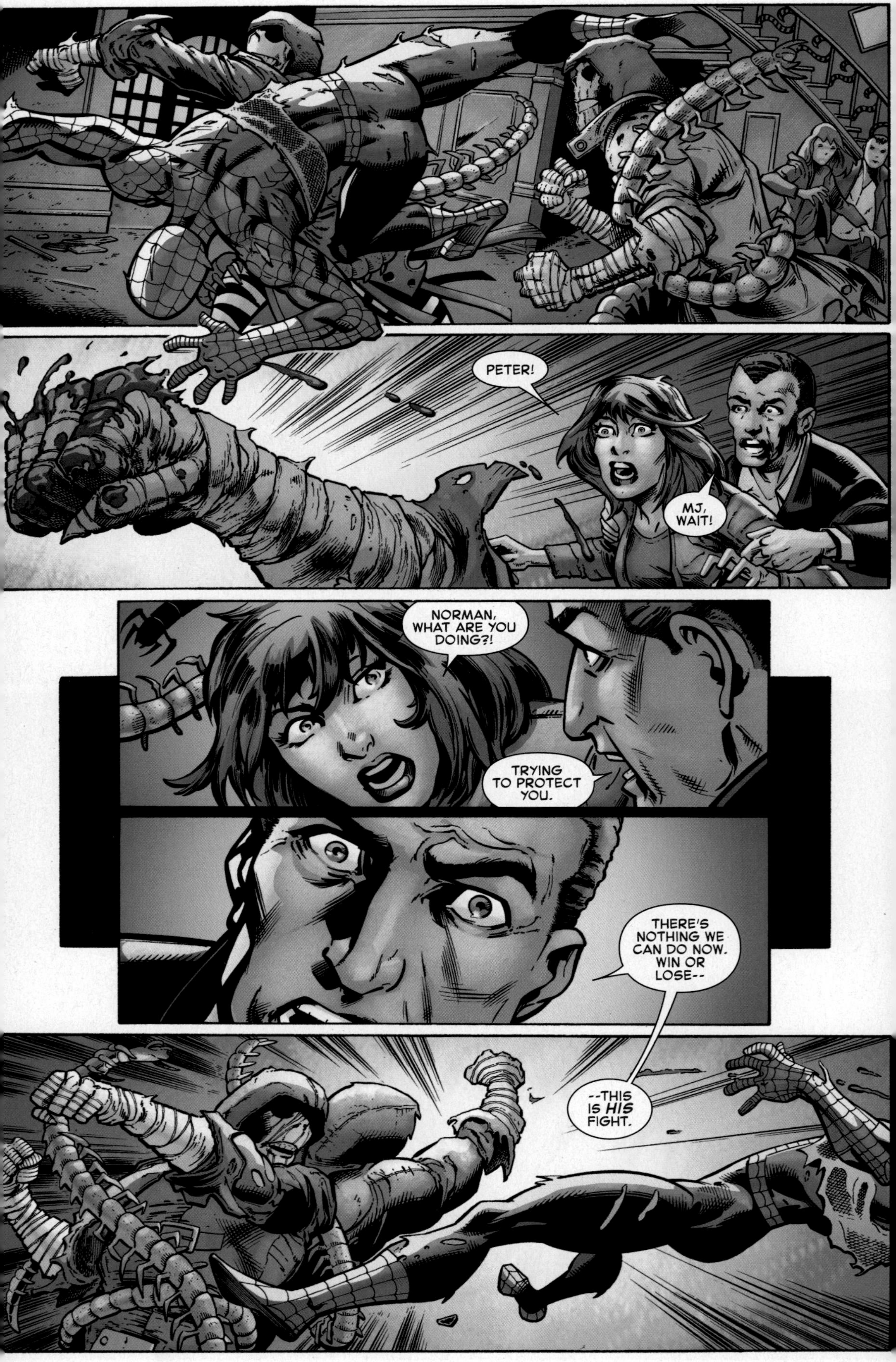
PETER!
MJ, WAIT!
NORMAN, WHAT ARE YOU DOING?!
TRYING TO PROTECT YOU.
THERE'S NOTHING WE CAN DO NOW. WIN OR LOSE--
--THIS IS *HIS* FIGHT.

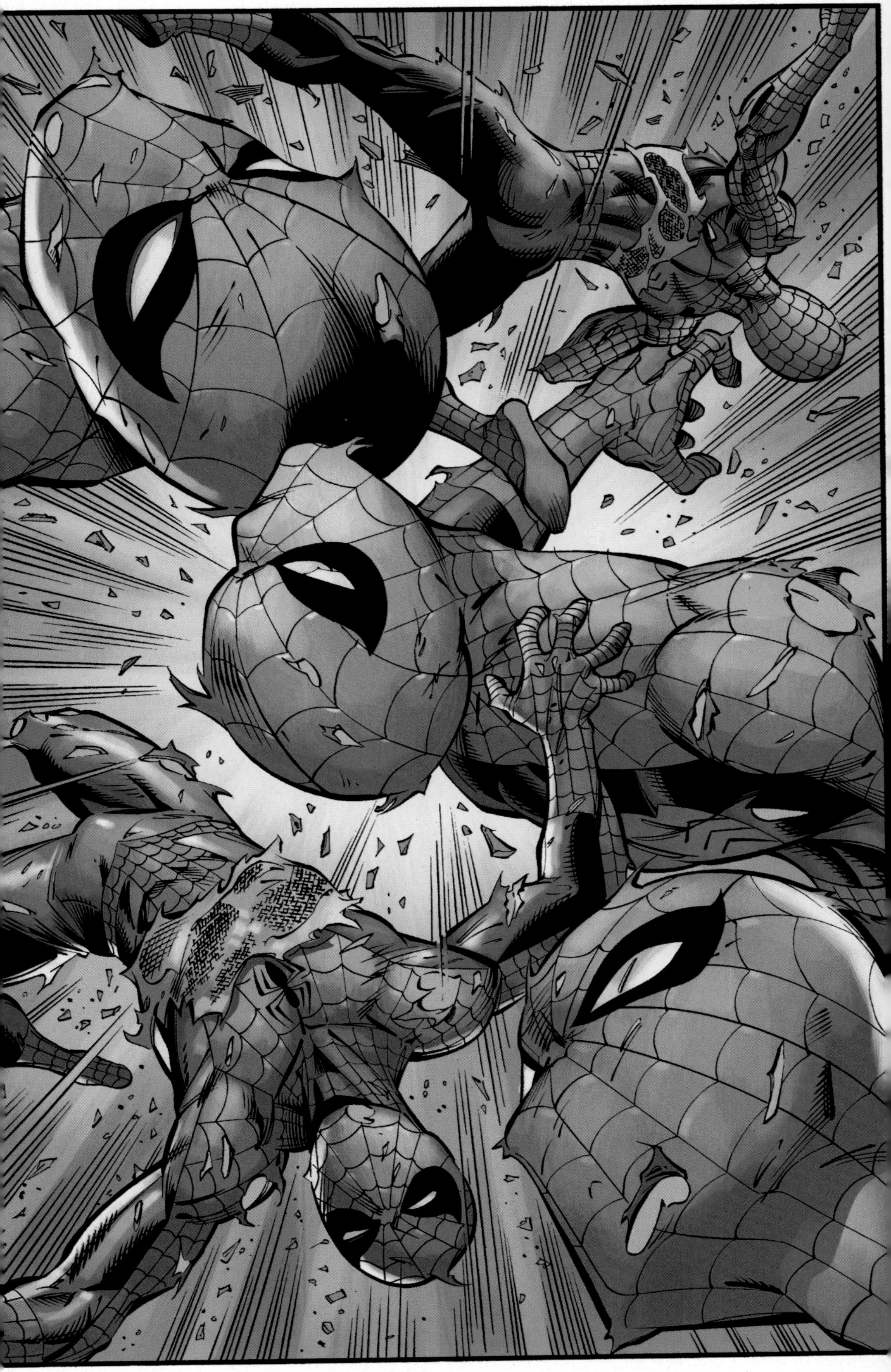

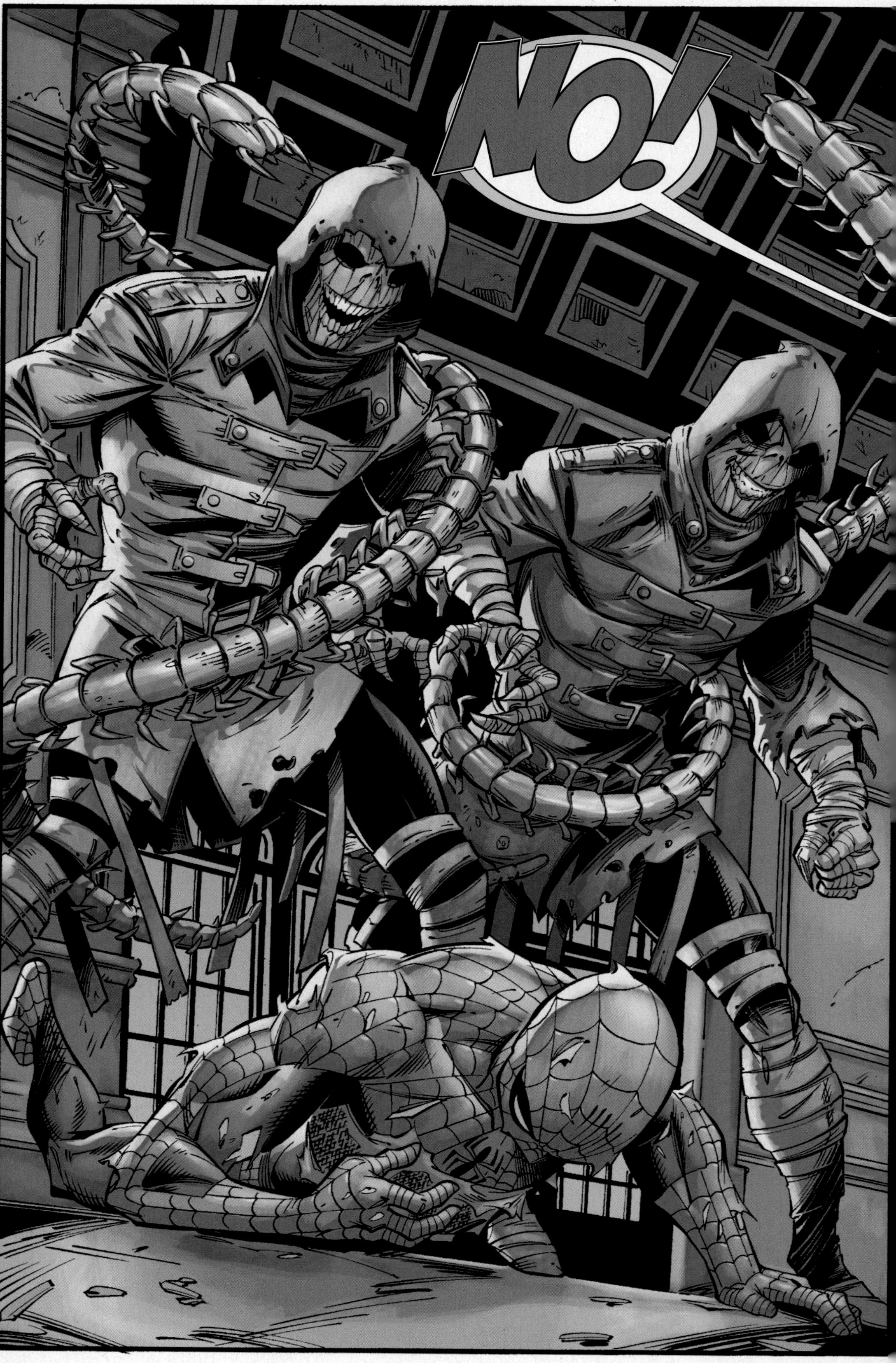
NO!

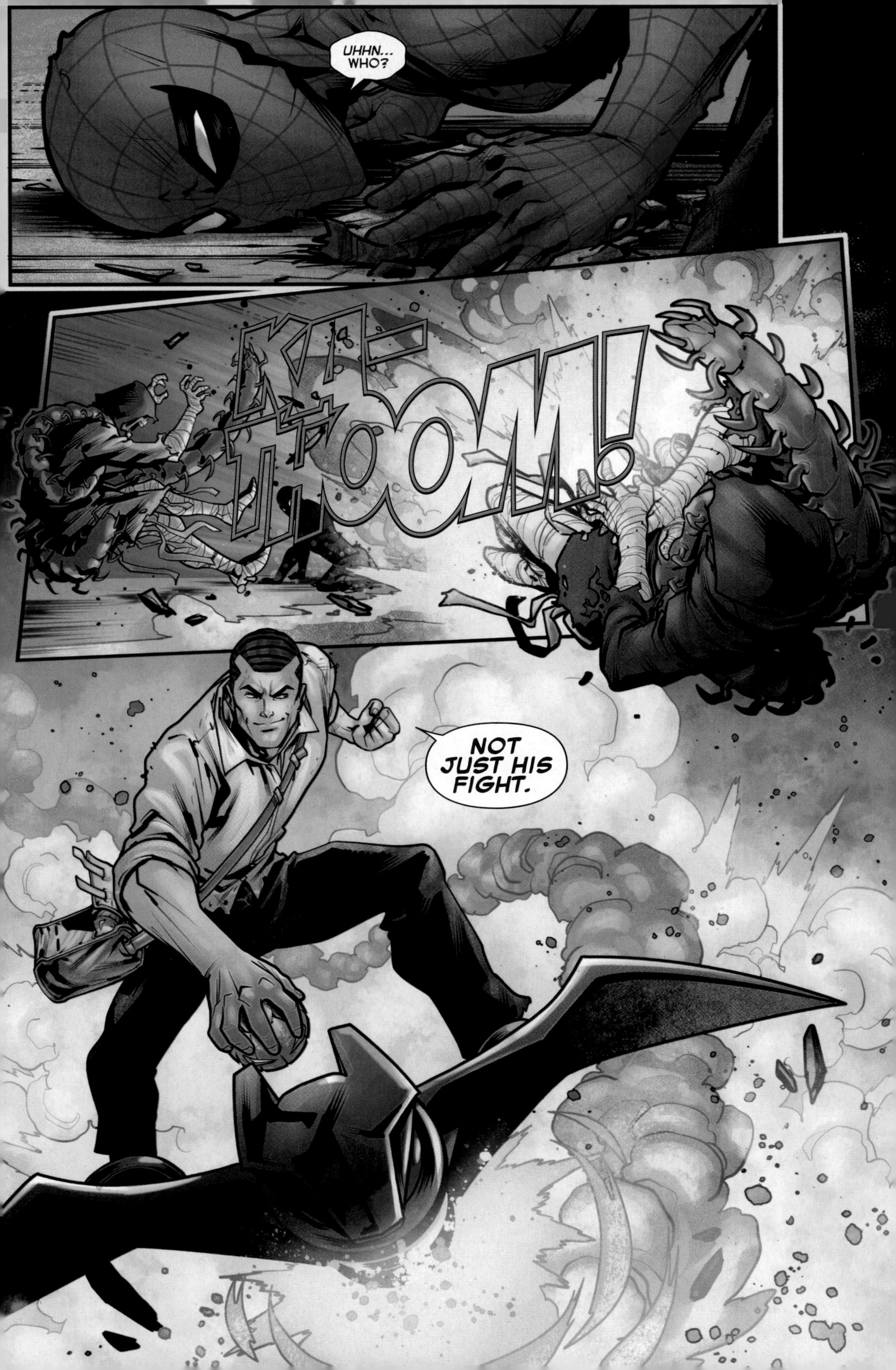
UHHN... WHO?
KA-THOOM!
NOT JUST HIS FIGHT.

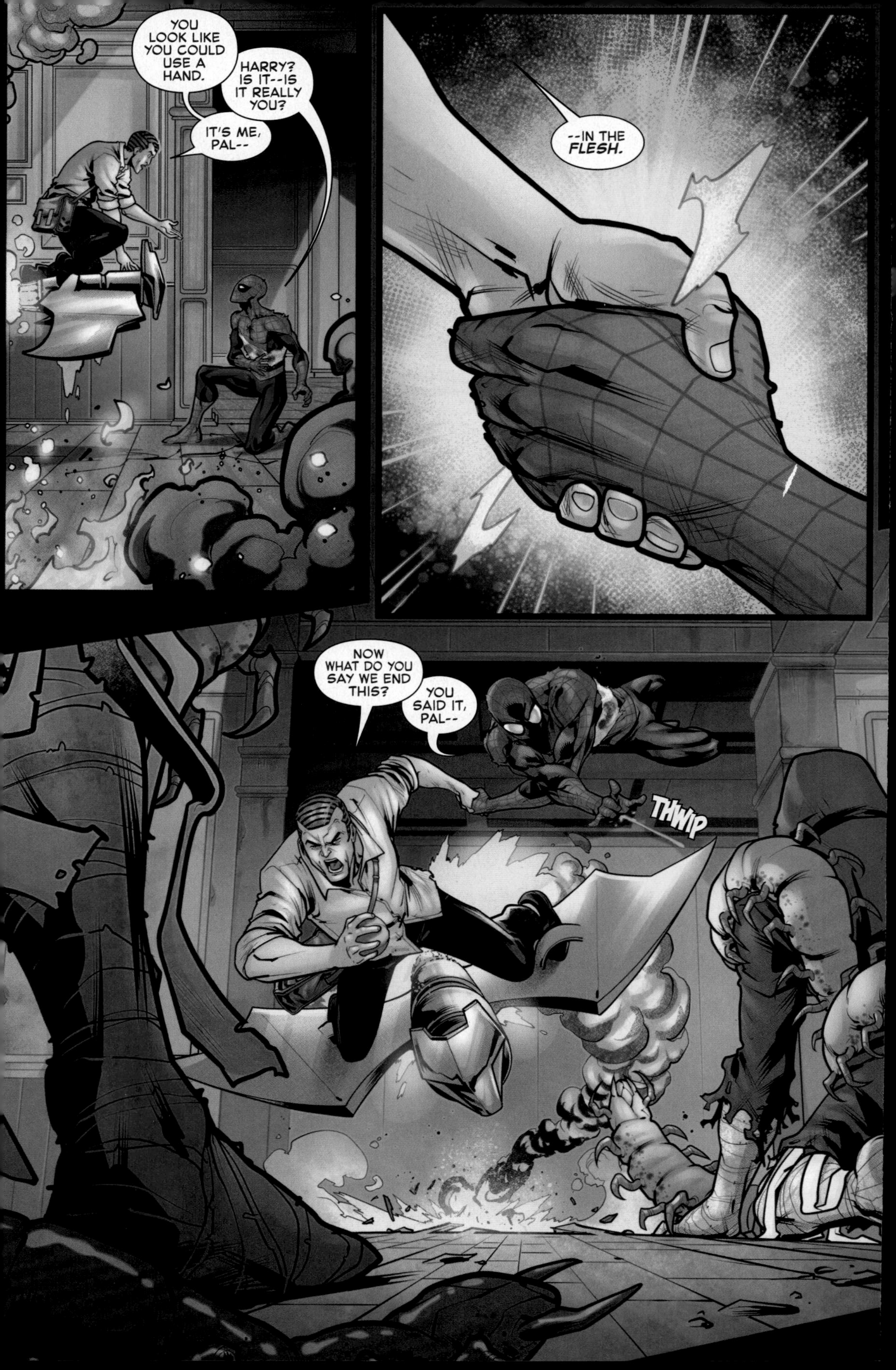
YOU LOOK LIKE YOU COULD USE A HAND.
HARRY? IS IT--IS IT REALLY YOU?
IT'S ME, PAL--
--IN THE FLESH.
NOW WHAT DO YOU SAY WE END THIS?
YOU SAID IT, PAL--
THWIP

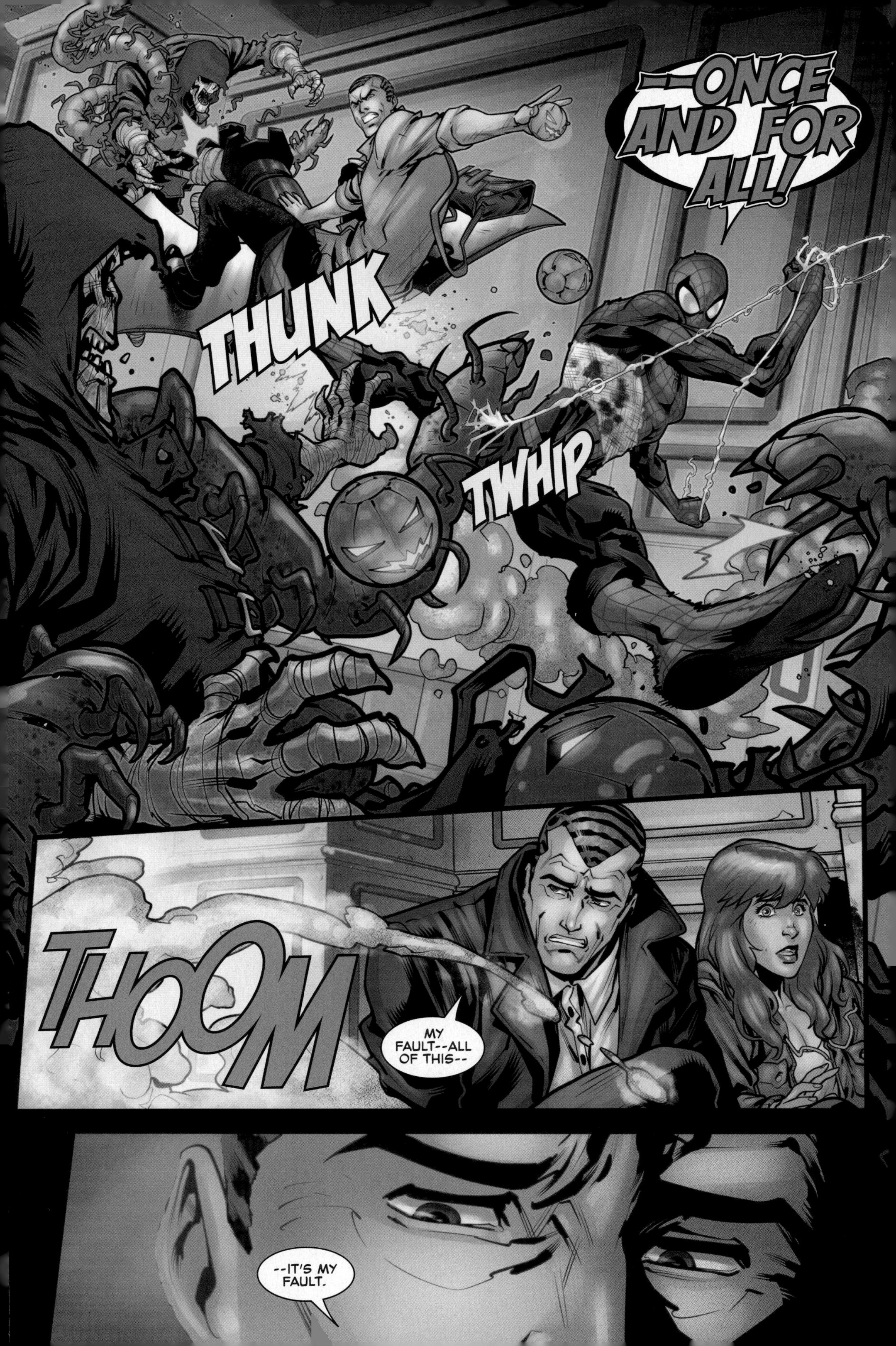
--ONCE AND FOR ALL!
THUNK
TWHIP
THOOM
MY FAULT--ALL OF THIS--
--IT'S MY FAULT.

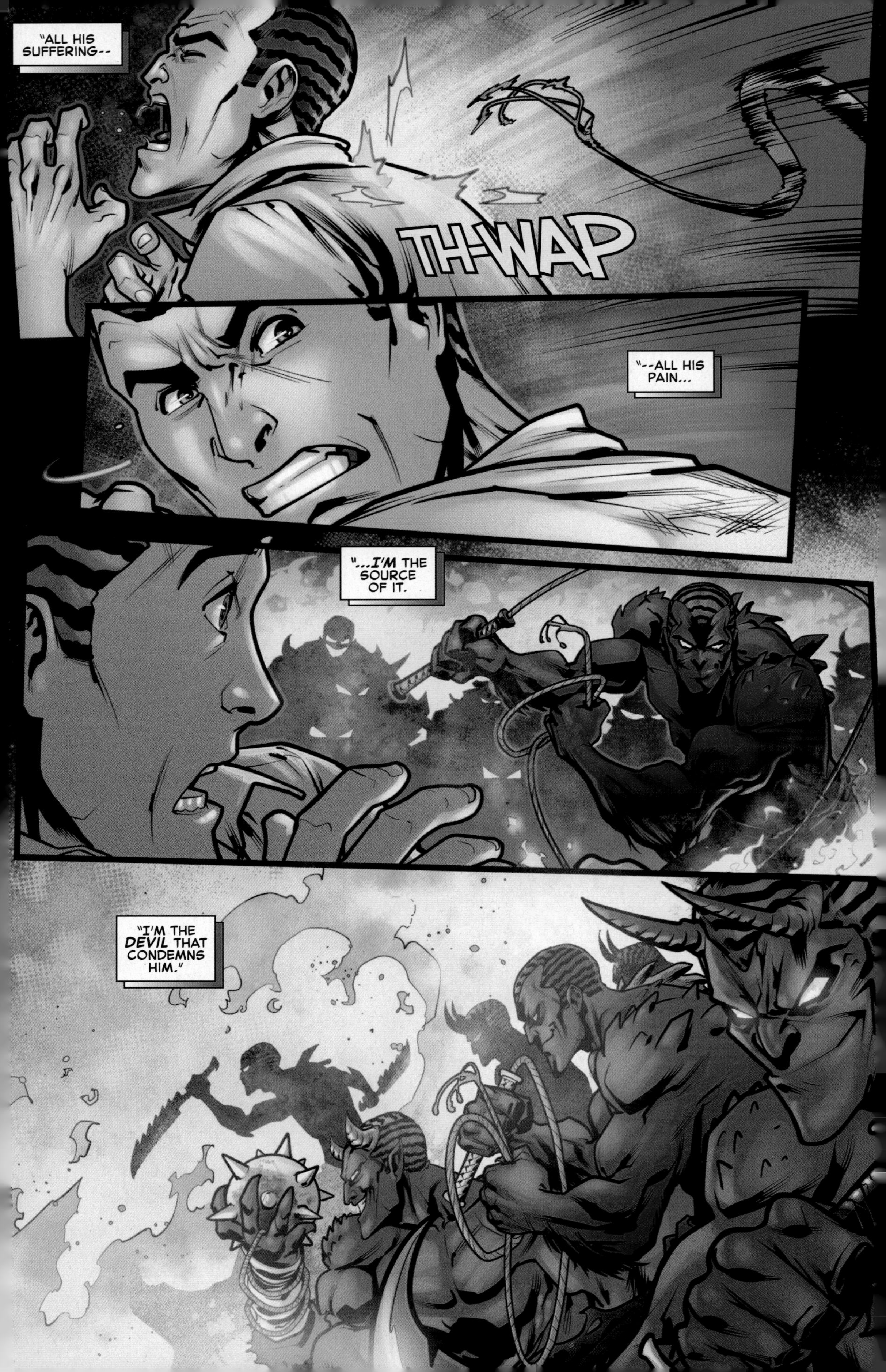
"ALL HIS SUFFERING--
TH-WAP
"--ALL HIS PAIN...
"...*I'M* THE SOURCE OF IT.
"I'M THE *DEVIL* THAT CONDEMNS HIM."

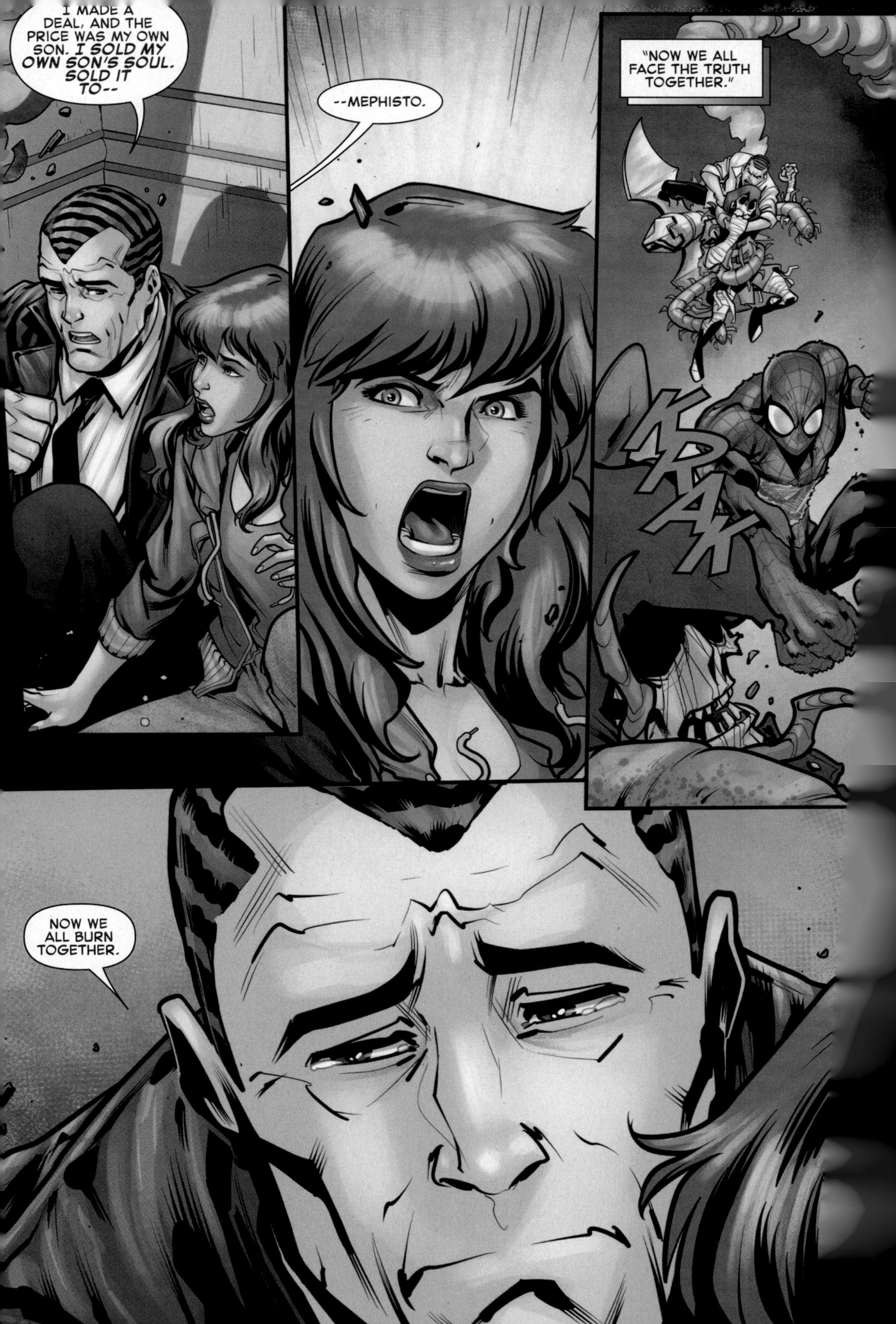
I MADE A DEAL, AND THE PRICE WAS MY OWN SON. I SOLD MY OWN SON'S SOUL. SOLD IT TO--
--MEPHISTO.
"NOW WE ALL FACE THE TRUTH TOGETHER."
KRAK
NOW WE ALL BURN TOGETHER.

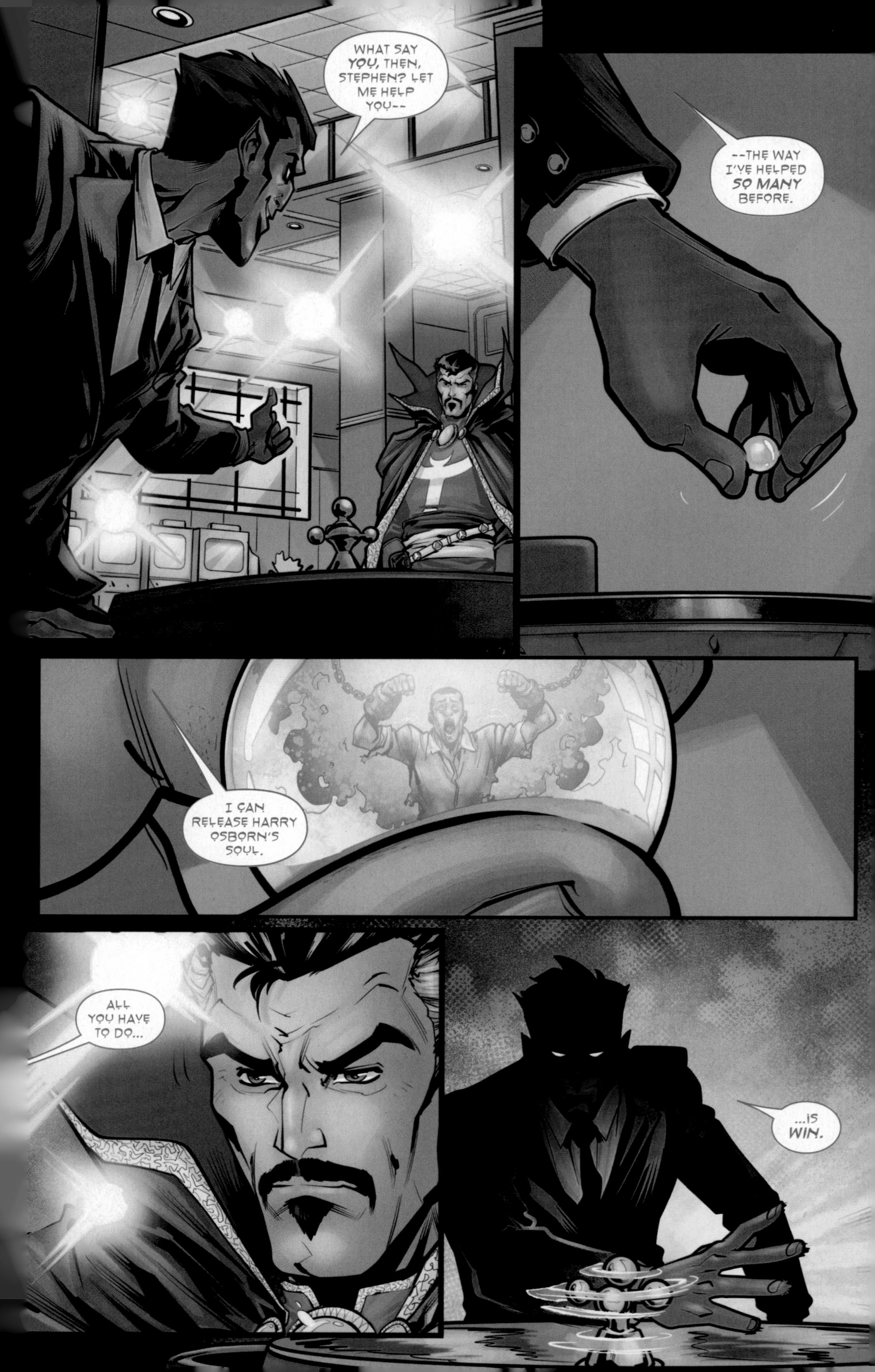
WHAT SAY YOU, THEN, STEPHEN? LET ME HELP YOU--
--THE WAY I'VE HELPED SO MANY BEFORE.
I CAN RELEASE HARRY OSBORN'S SOUL.
ALL YOU HAVE TO DO...
...IS WIN.

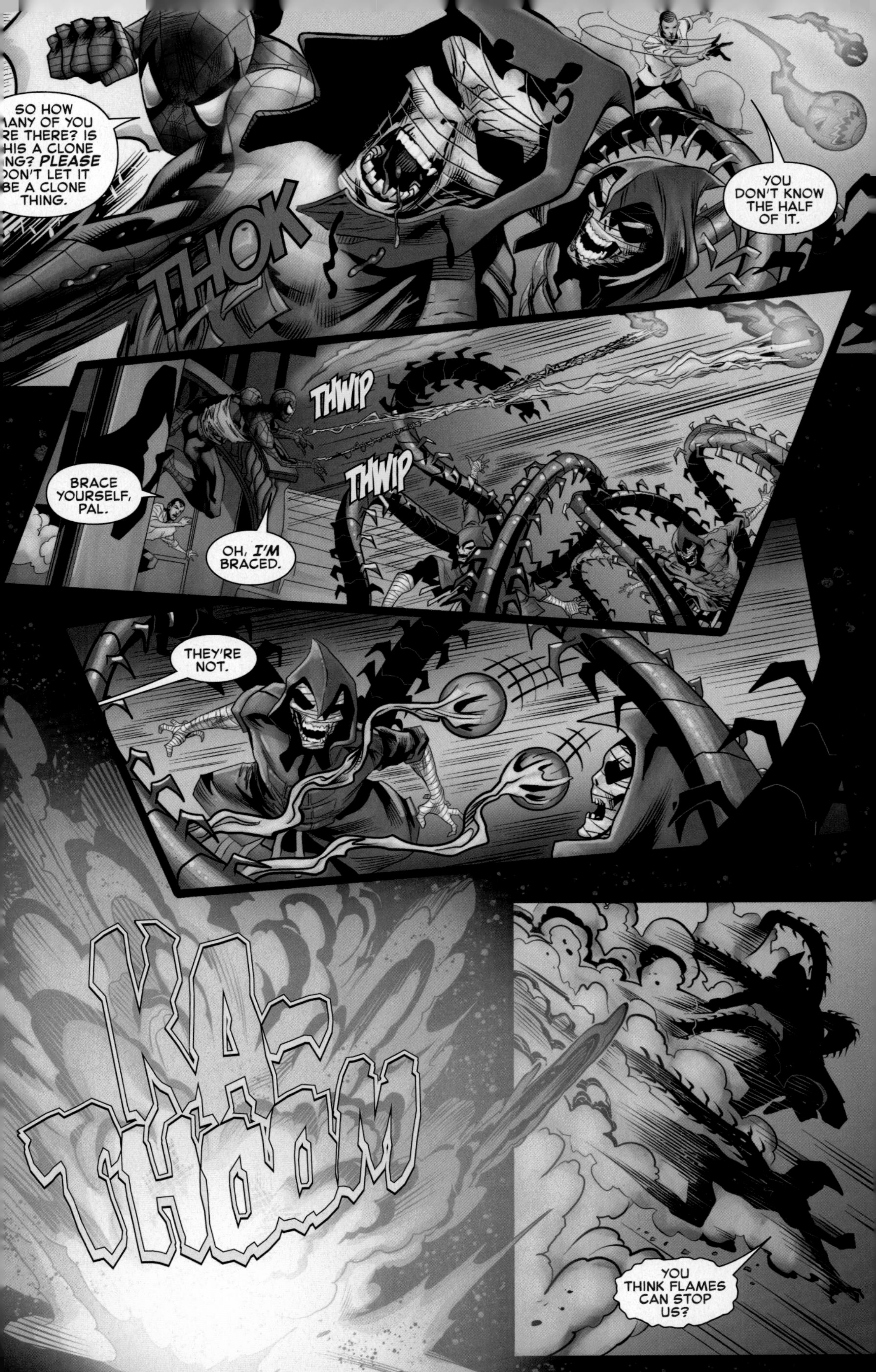
SO HOW ANY OF YOU RE THERE? IS HIS A CLONE NG? *PLEASE* ON'T LET IT BE A CLONE THING.
THOK
YOU DON'T KNOW THE HALF OF IT.
THWIP
THWIP
BRACE YOURSELF, PAL.
OH, *I'M* BRACED.
THEY'RE NOT.
KA-THOOM
YOU THINK FLAMES CAN STOP US?

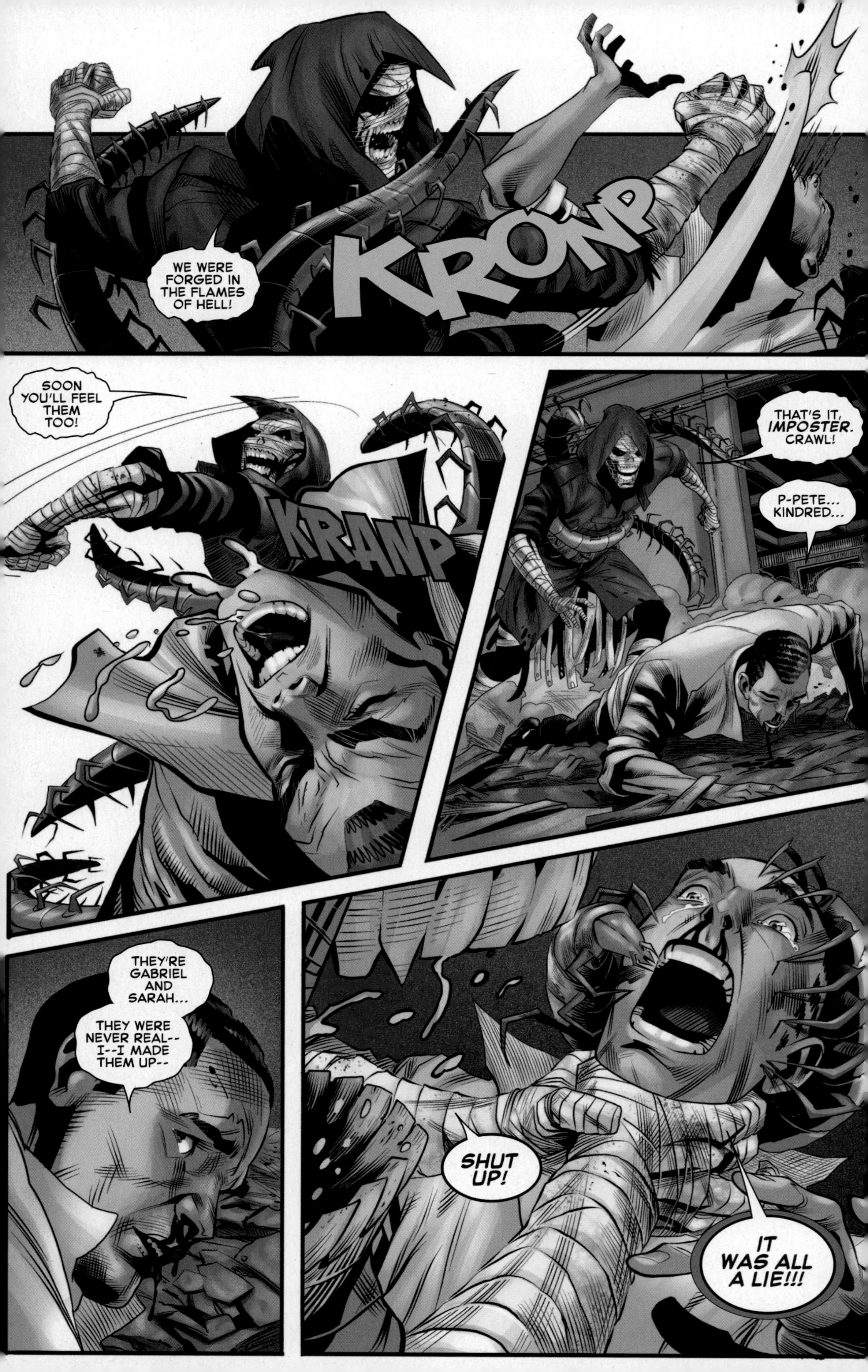

WE WERE FORGED IN THE FLAMES OF HELL!
KRONP
SOON YOU'LL FEEL THEM TOO!
KRANP
THAT'S IT, IMPOSTER. CRAWL!
P-PETE... KINDRED...
THEY'RE GABRIEL AND SARAH...
THEY WERE NEVER REAL-- I--I MADE THEM UP--
SHUT UP!
IT WAS ALL A LIE!!!

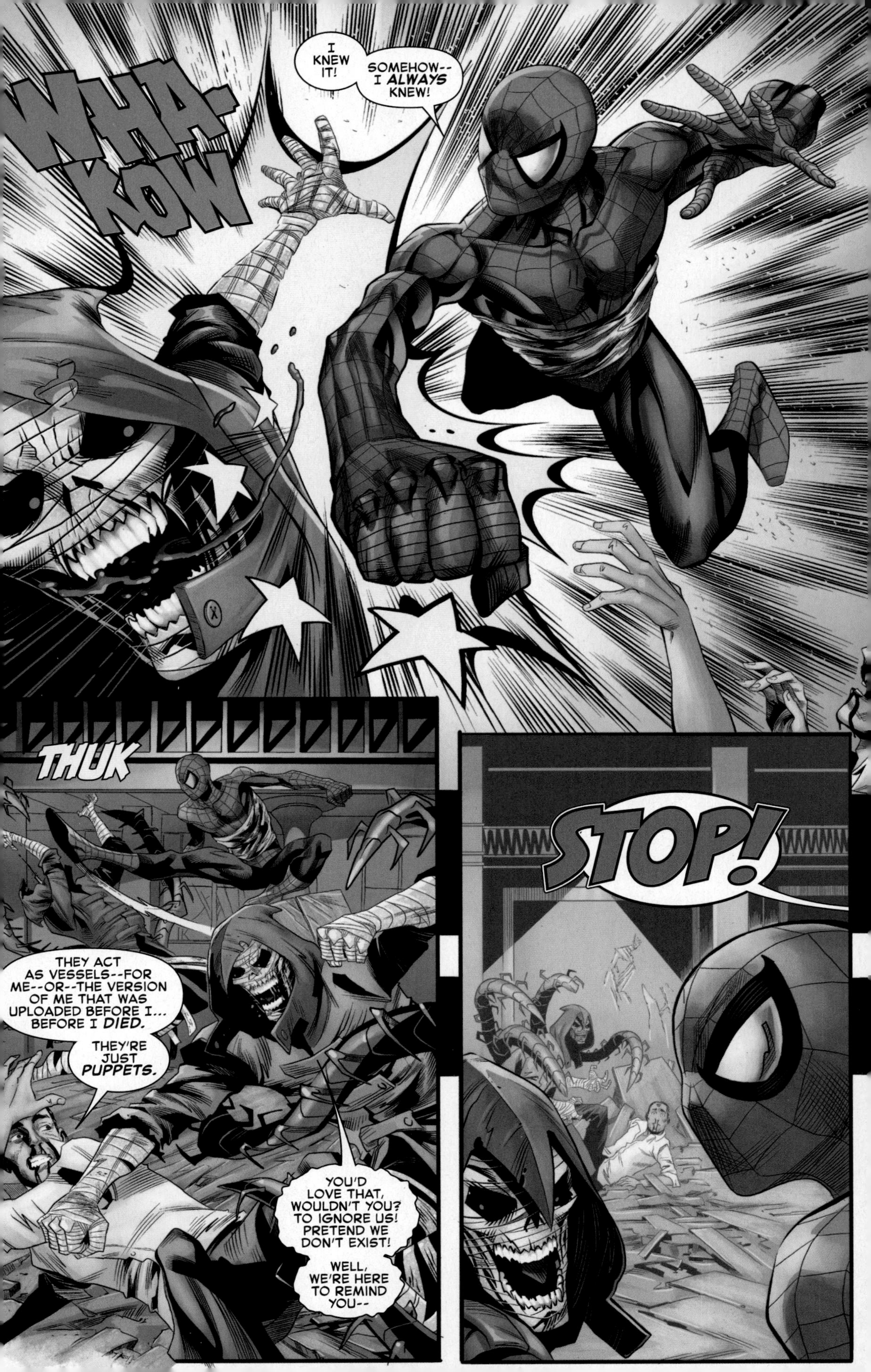
WHA-KOW
I KNEW IT!
SOMEHOW-- I ALWAYS KNEW!
THUK
THEY ACT AS VESSELS--FOR ME--OR--THE VERSION OF ME THAT WAS UPLOADED BEFORE I... BEFORE I DIED.
THEY'RE JUST PUPPETS.
YOU'D LOVE THAT, WOULDN'T YOU? TO IGNORE US! PRETEND WE DON'T EXIST!
WELL, WE'RE HERE TO REMIND YOU--
STOP!

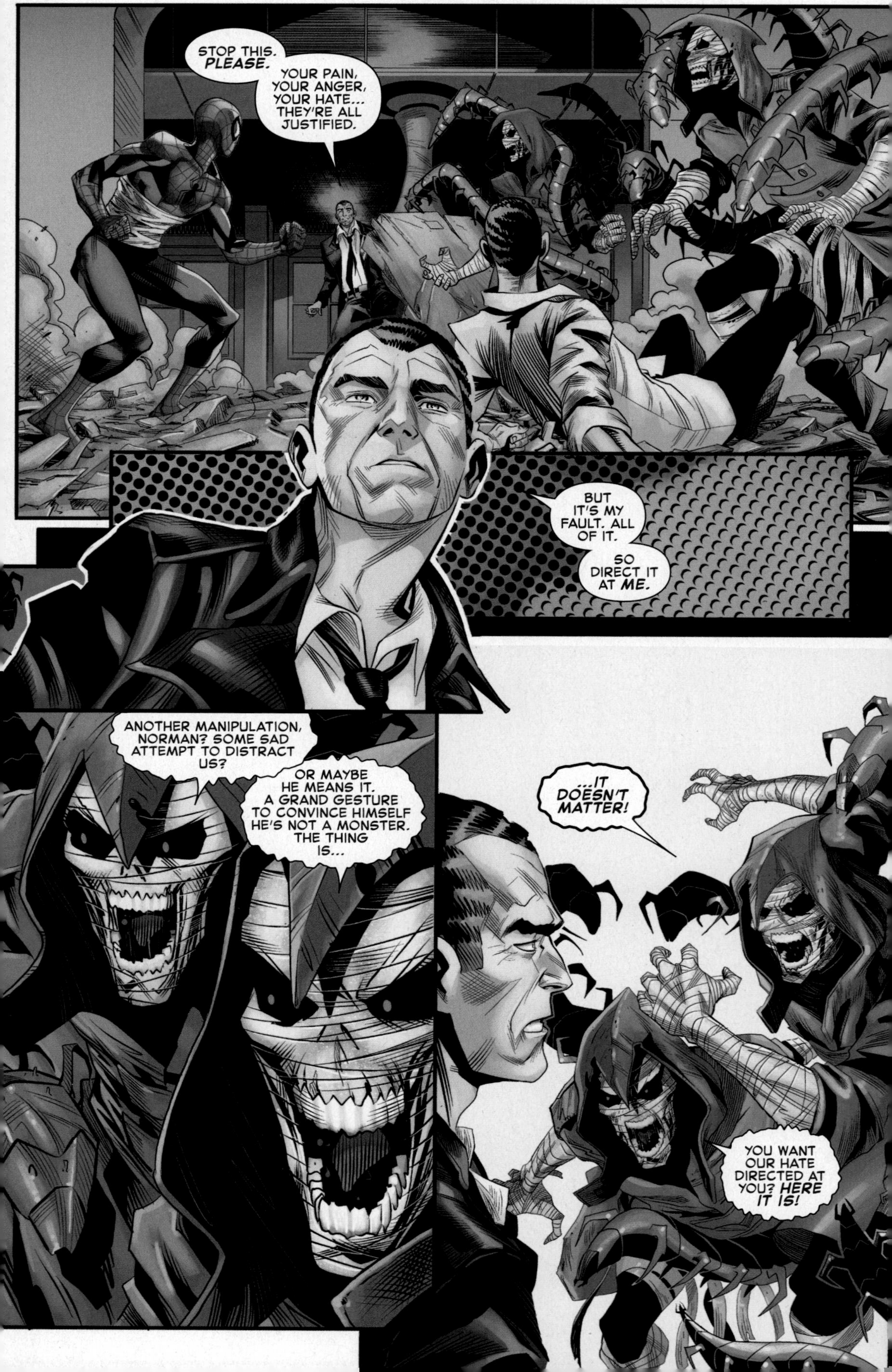
STOP THIS. PLEASE.
YOUR PAIN, YOUR ANGER, YOUR HATE... THEY'RE ALL JUSTIFIED.
BUT IT'S MY FAULT. ALL OF IT.
SO DIRECT IT AT ME.
ANOTHER MANIPULATION, NORMAN? SOME SAD ATTEMPT TO DISTRACT US?
OR MAYBE HE MEANS IT. A GRAND GESTURE TO CONVINCE HIMSELF HE'S NOT A MONSTER. THE THING IS...
...IT DOESN'T MATTER!
YOU WANT OUR HATE DIRECTED AT YOU? HERE IT IS!

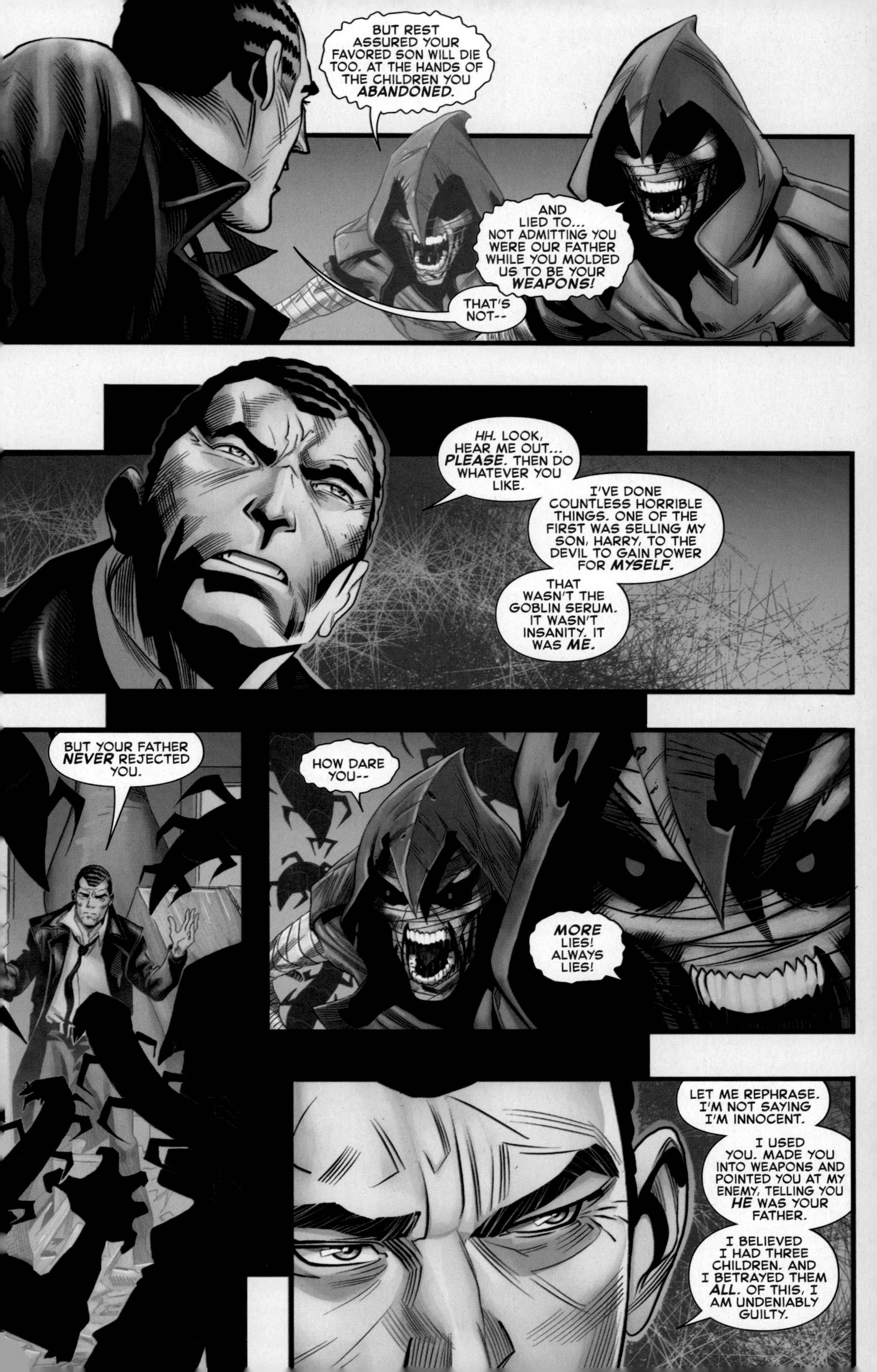

BUT REST ASSURED YOUR FAVORED SON WILL DIE TOO. AT THE HANDS OF THE CHILDREN YOU ABANDONED.
AND LIED TO... NOT ADMITTING YOU WERE OUR FATHER WHILE YOU MOLDED US TO BE YOUR WEAPONS!
THAT'S NOT--
HH. LOOK, HEAR ME OUT... PLEASE. THEN DO WHATEVER YOU LIKE.
I'VE DONE COUNTLESS HORRIBLE THINGS. ONE OF THE FIRST WAS SELLING MY SON, HARRY, TO THE DEVIL TO GAIN POWER FOR MYSELF.
THAT WASN'T THE GOBLIN SERUM. IT WASN'T INSANITY. IT WAS ME.
BUT YOUR FATHER NEVER REJECTED YOU.
HOW DARE YOU--
MORE LIES! ALWAYS LIES!
LET ME REPHRASE. I'M NOT SAYING I'M INNOCENT.
I USED YOU. MADE YOU INTO WEAPONS AND POINTED YOU AT MY ENEMY, TELLING YOU HE WAS YOUR FATHER.
I BELIEVED I HAD THREE CHILDREN. AND I BETRAYED THEM ALL. OF THIS, I AM UNDENIABLY GUILTY.

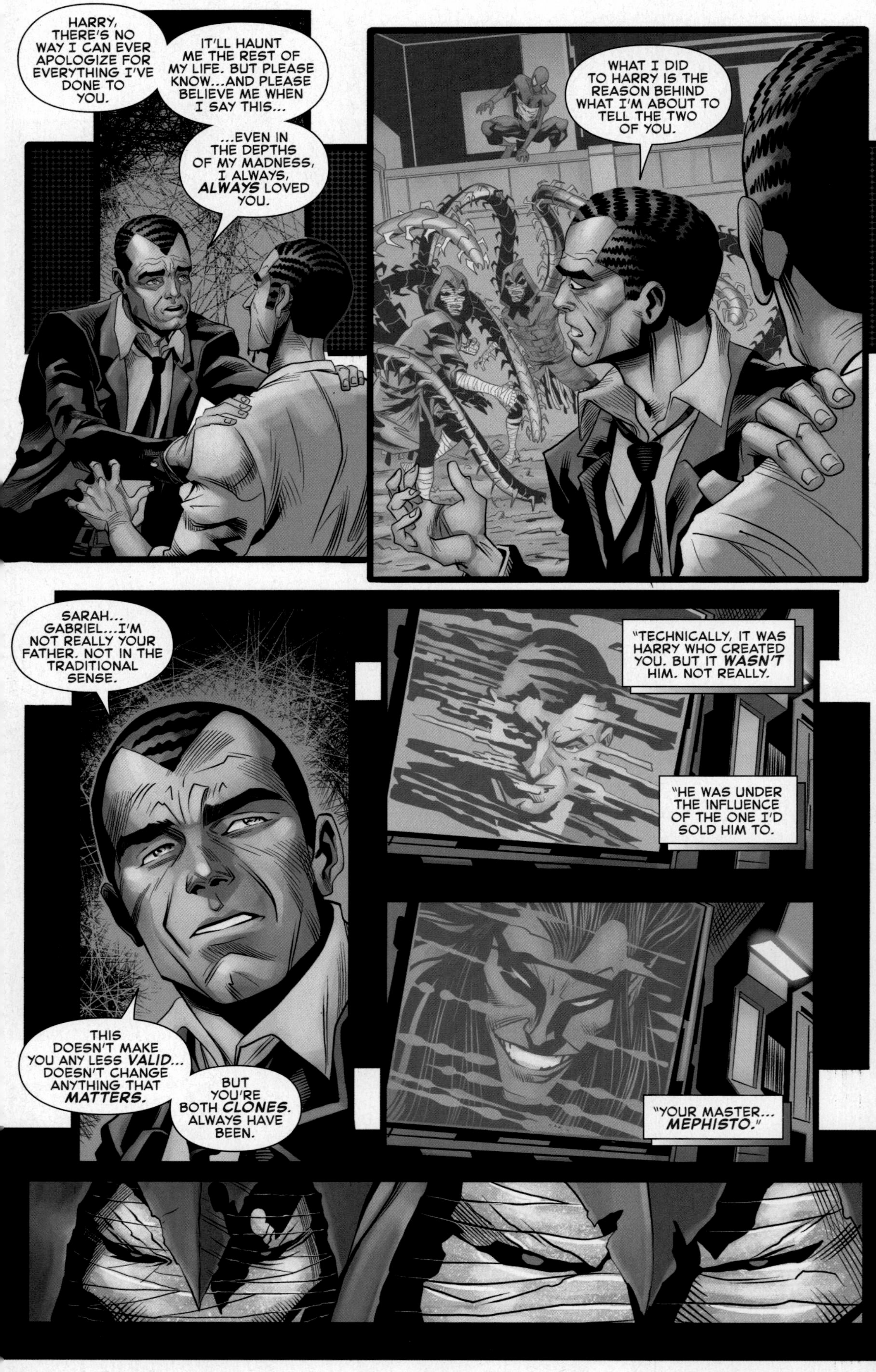
HARRY, THERE'S NO WAY I CAN EVER APOLOGIZE FOR EVERYTHING I'VE DONE TO YOU.
IT'LL HAUNT ME THE REST OF MY LIFE. BUT PLEASE KNOW...AND PLEASE BELIEVE ME WHEN I SAY THIS...
...EVEN IN THE DEPTHS OF MY MADNESS, I ALWAYS, ALWAYS LOVED YOU.
WHAT I DID TO HARRY IS THE REASON BEHIND WHAT I'M ABOUT TO TELL THE TWO OF YOU.
SARAH... GABRIEL...I'M NOT REALLY YOUR FATHER. NOT IN THE TRADITIONAL SENSE.
THIS DOESN'T MAKE YOU ANY LESS VALID... DOESN'T CHANGE ANYTHING THAT MATTERS.
BUT YOU'RE BOTH CLONES. ALWAYS HAVE BEEN.
"TECHNICALLY, IT WAS HARRY WHO CREATED YOU. BUT IT WASN'T HIM. NOT REALLY.
"HE WAS UNDER THE INFLUENCE OF THE ONE I'D SOLD HIM TO.
"YOUR MASTER... MEPHISTO."

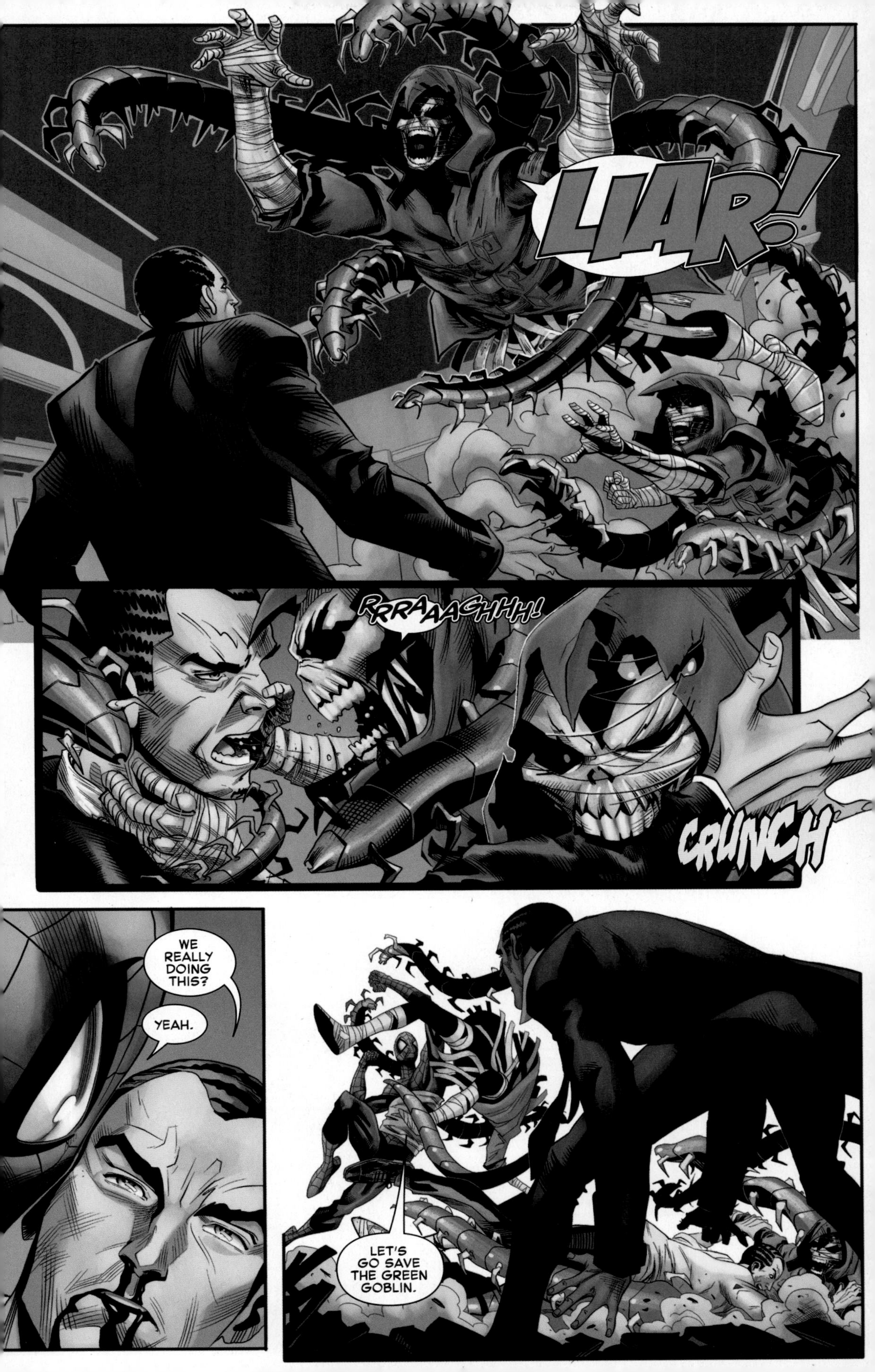
LIAR!
RRRAAAGHHH!
CRUNCH
WE REALLY DOING THIS?
YEAH.
LET'S GO SAVE THE GREEN GOBLIN.

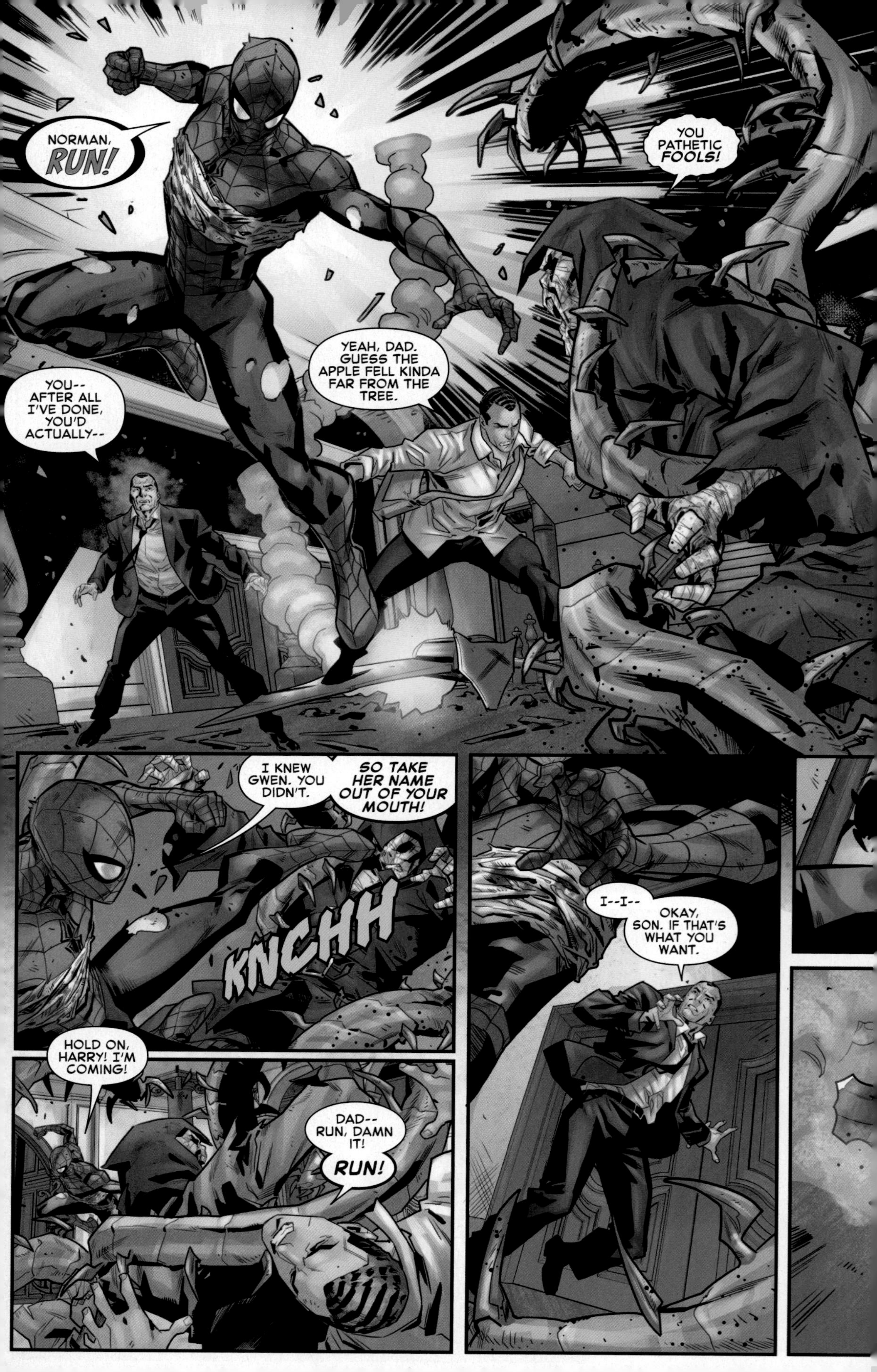
NORMAN, RUN!
YOU PATHETIC FOOLS!
YOU-- AFTER ALL I'VE DONE, YOU'D ACTUALLY--
YEAH, DAD. GUESS THE APPLE FELL KINDA FAR FROM THE TREE.
I KNEW GWEN. YOU DIDN'T.
SO TAKE HER NAME OUT OF YOUR MOUTH!
KNCHH
HOLD ON, HARRY! I'M COMING!
DAD-- RUN, DAMN IT!
RUN!
I--I--
OKAY, SON. IF THAT'S WHAT YOU WANT.

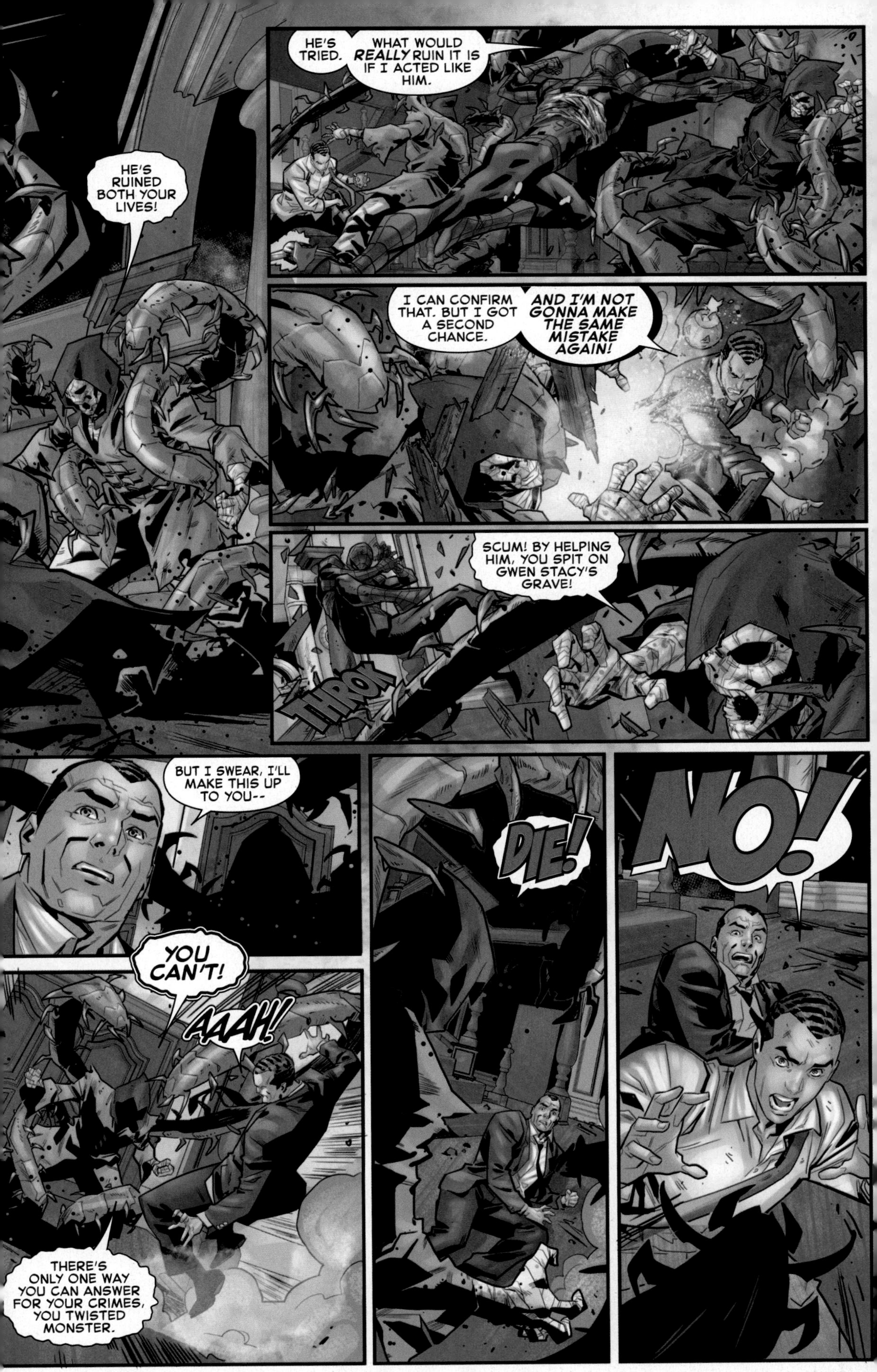
HE'S RUINED BOTH YOUR LIVES!
HE'S TRIED.
WHAT WOULD REALLY RUIN IT IS IF I ACTED LIKE HIM.
I CAN CONFIRM THAT. BUT I GOT A SECOND CHANCE.
AND I'M NOT GONNA MAKE THE SAME MISTAKE AGAIN!
SCUM! BY HELPING HIM, YOU SPIT ON GWEN STACY'S GRAVE!
THROK
BUT I SWEAR, I'LL MAKE THIS UP TO YOU--
YOU CAN'T!
AAAH!
THERE'S ONLY ONE WAY YOU CAN ANSWER FOR YOUR CRIMES, YOU TWISTED MONSTER.
DIE!
NO!

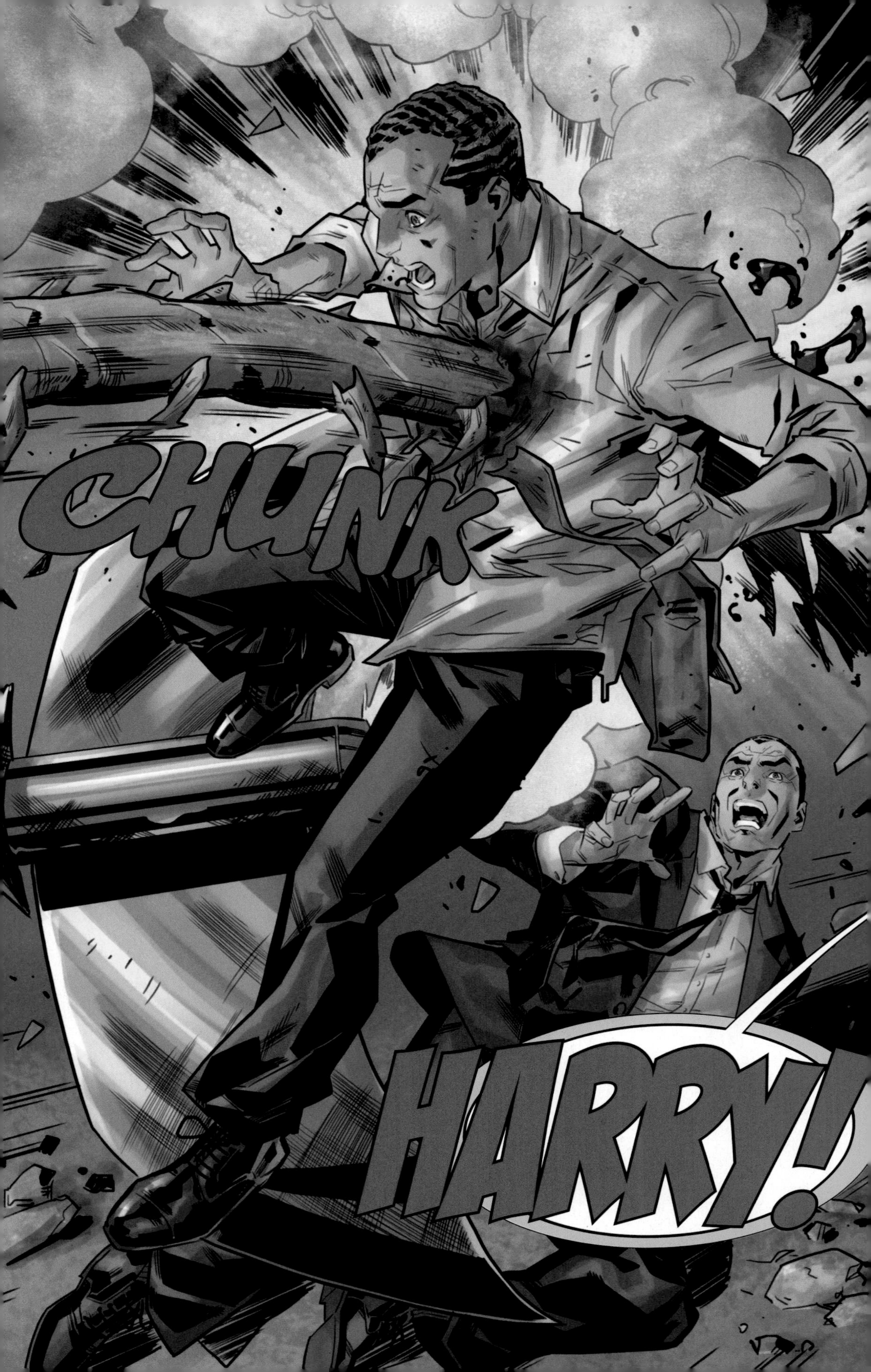
CHUNK
HARRY!

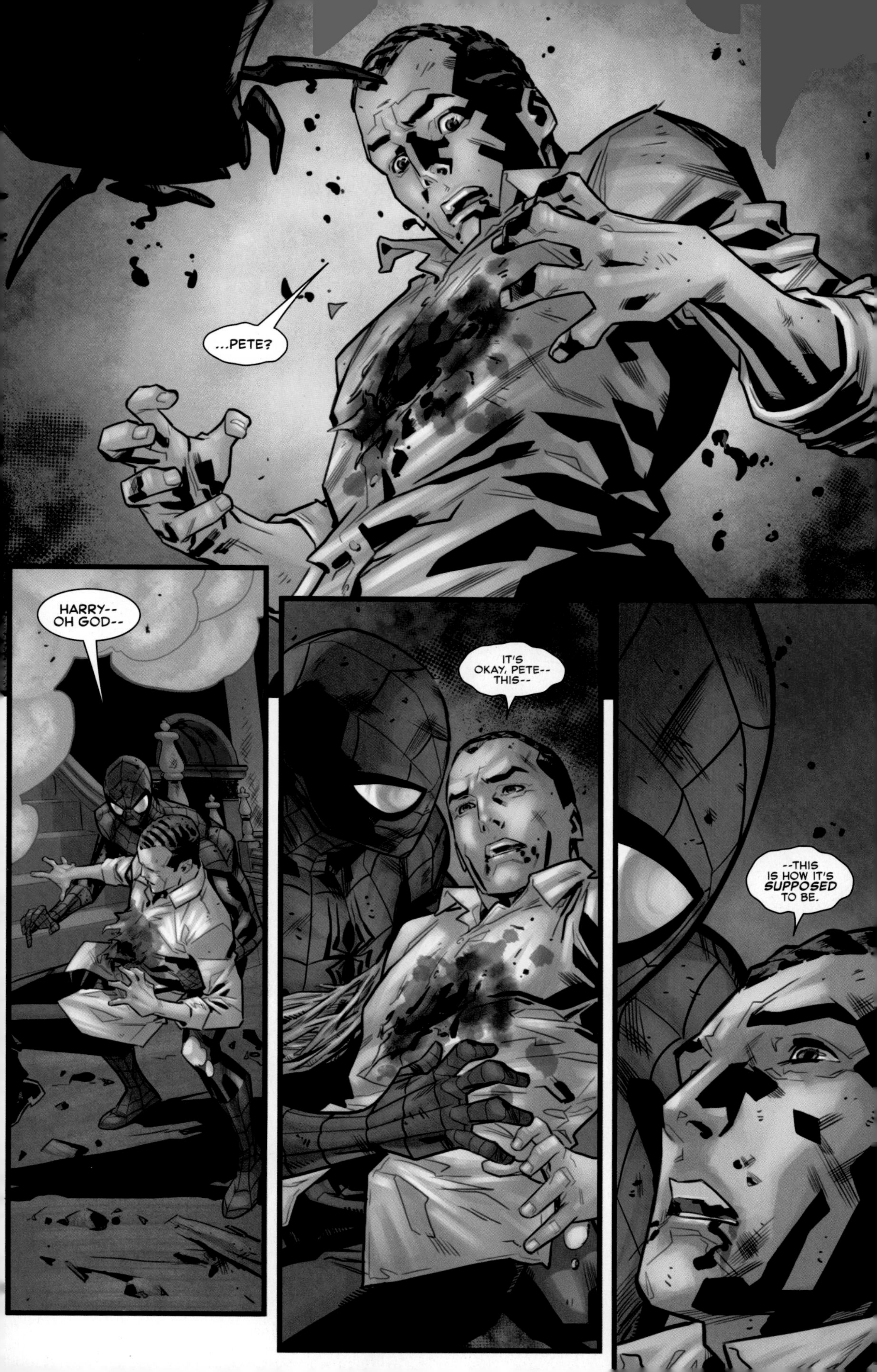
...PETE?
HARRY--
OH GOD--
IT'S
OKAY, PETE--
THIS--
--THIS
IS HOW IT'S
SUPPOSED
TO BE.

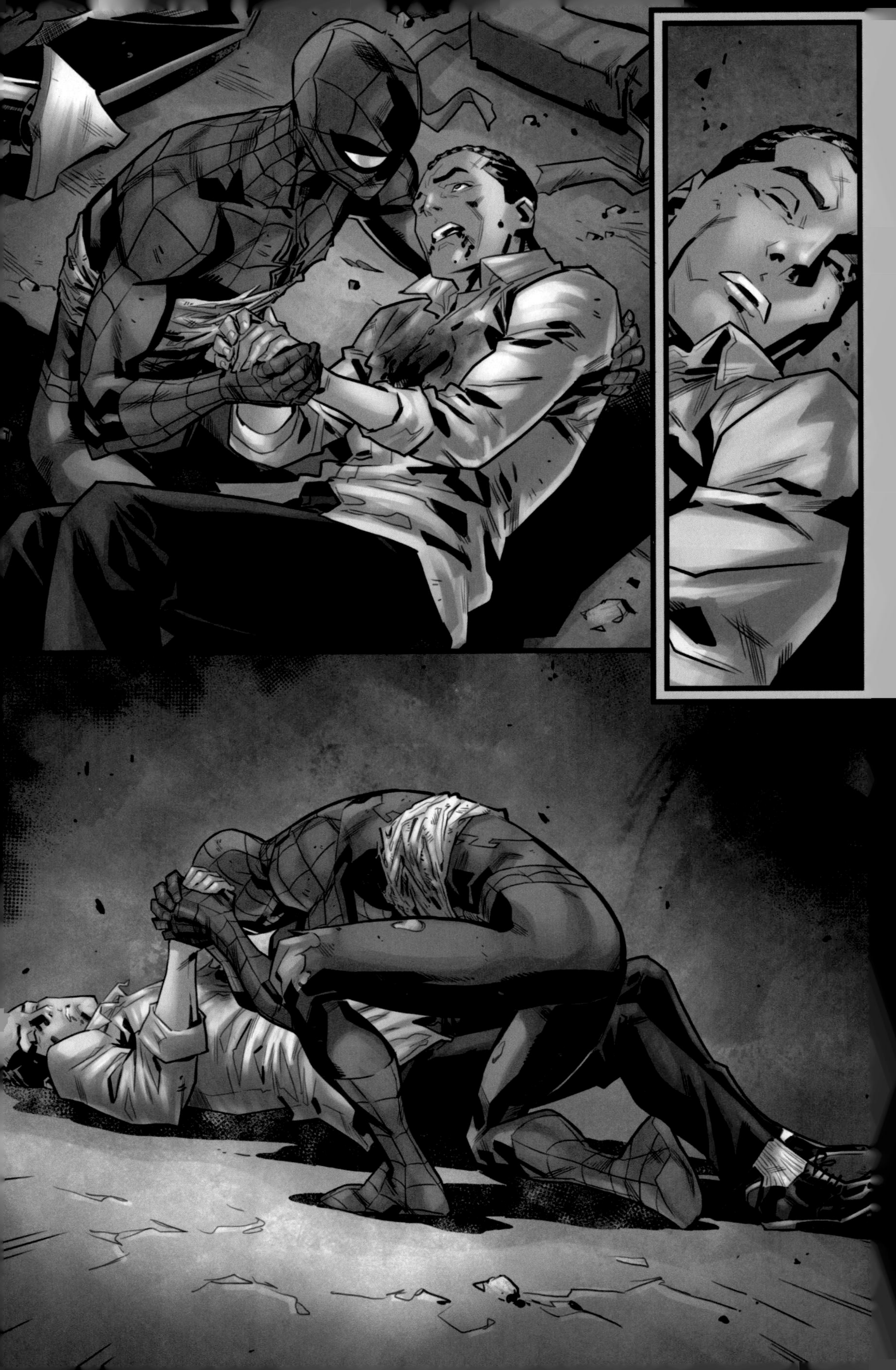

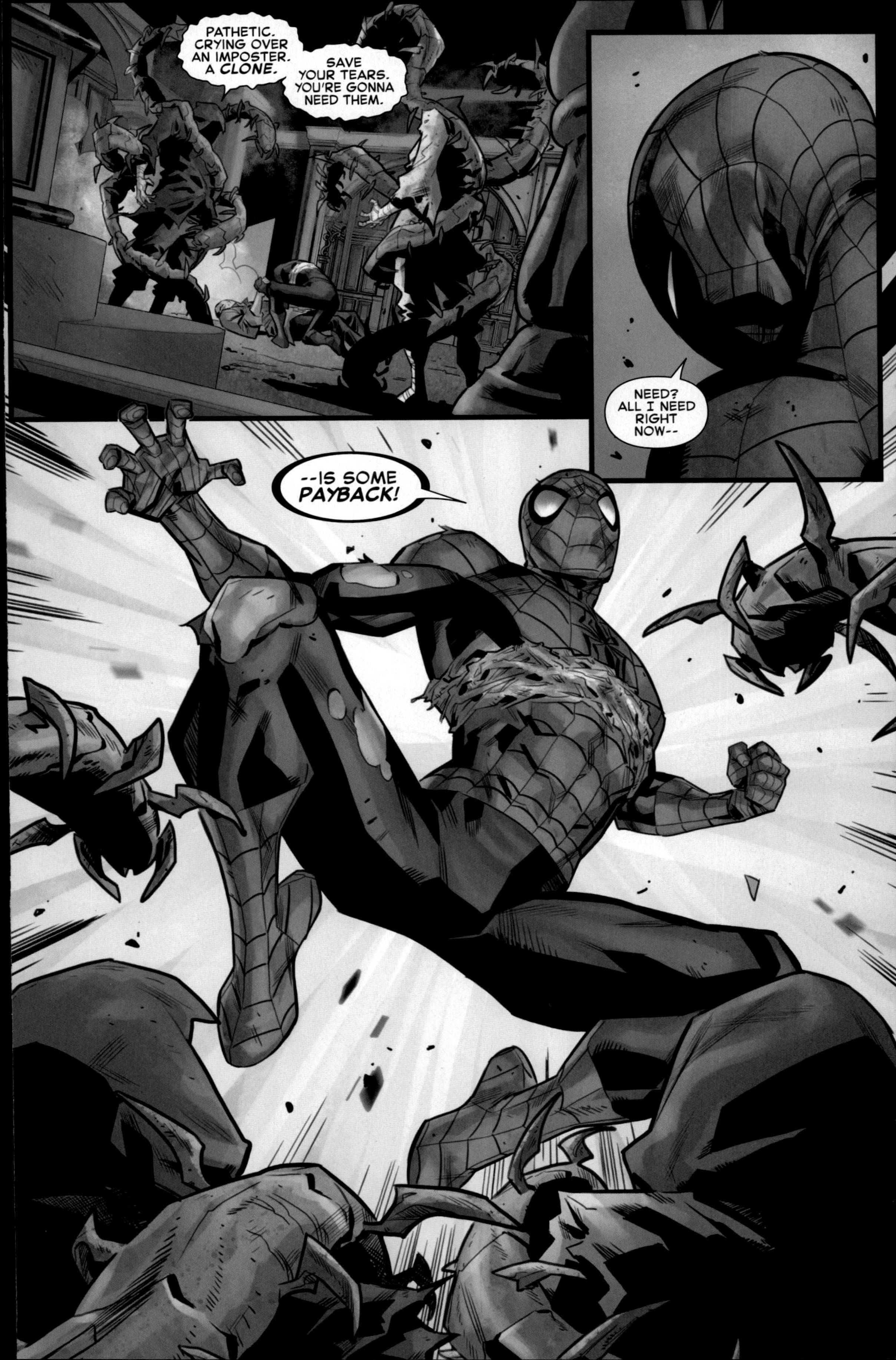
PATHETIC. CRYING OVER AN IMPOSTER. A CLONE.
SAVE YOUR TEARS. YOU'RE GONNA NEED THEM.
NEED? ALL I NEED RIGHT NOW--
--IS SOME PAYBACK!

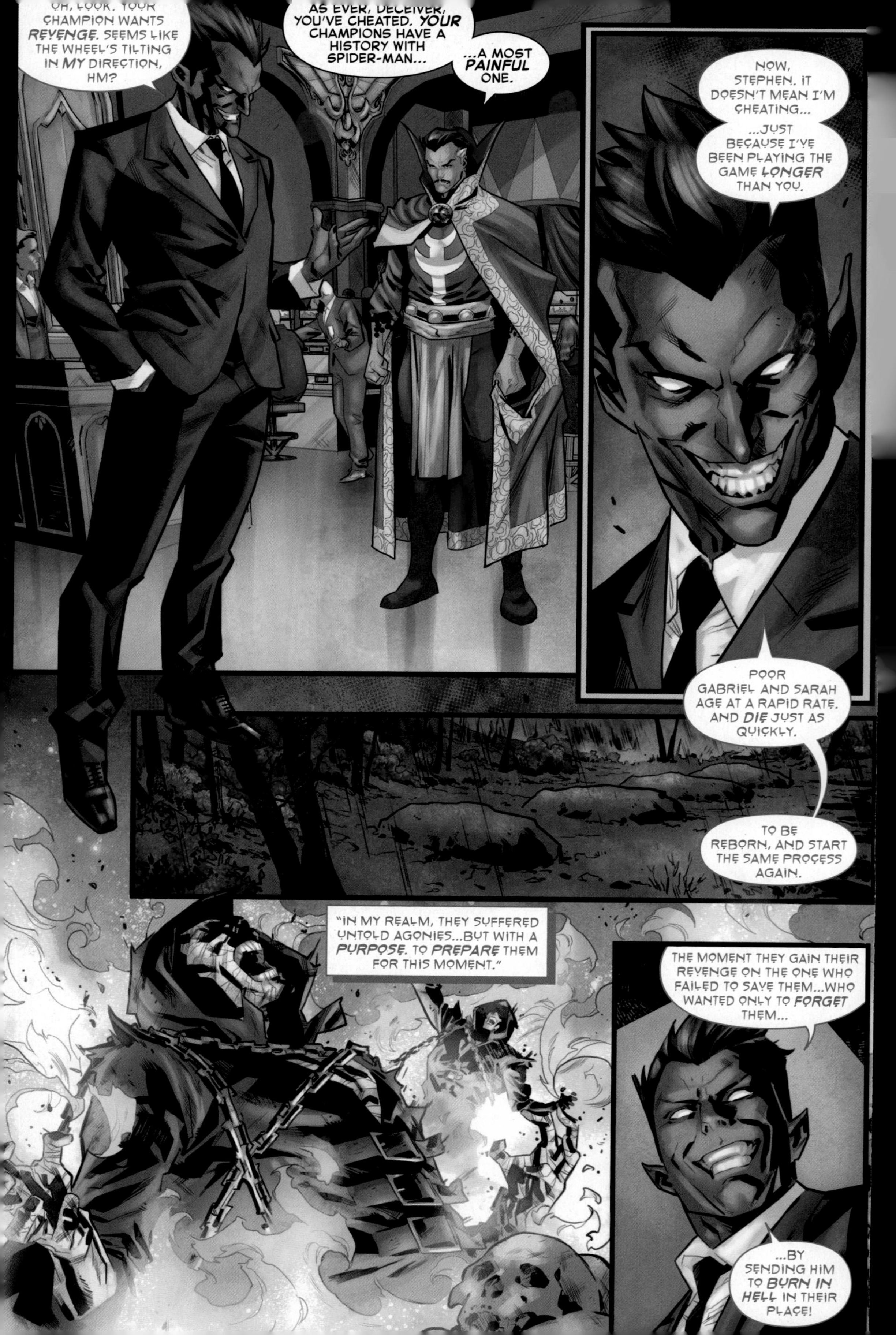
OH, LOOK. YOUR CHAMPION WANTS REVENGE. SEEMS LIKE THE WHEEL'S TILTING IN MY DIRECTION, HM?
AS EVER, DECEIVER, YOU'VE CHEATED. YOUR CHAMPIONS HAVE A HISTORY WITH SPIDER-MAN...
...A MOST PAINFUL ONE.
NOW, STEPHEN. IT DOESN'T MEAN I'M CHEATING...
...JUST BECAUSE I'VE BEEN PLAYING THE GAME LONGER THAN YOU.
POOR GABRIEL AND SARAH AGE AT A RAPID RATE. AND DIE JUST AS QUICKLY.
TO BE REBORN, AND START THE SAME PROCESS AGAIN.
"IN MY REALM, THEY SUFFERED UNTOLD AGONIES...BUT WITH A PURPOSE. TO PREPARE THEM FOR THIS MOMENT."
THE MOMENT THEY GAIN THEIR REVENGE ON THE ONE WHO FAILED TO SAVE THEM...WHO WANTED ONLY TO FORGET THEM...
...BY SENDING HIM TO BURN IN HELL IN THEIR PLACE!

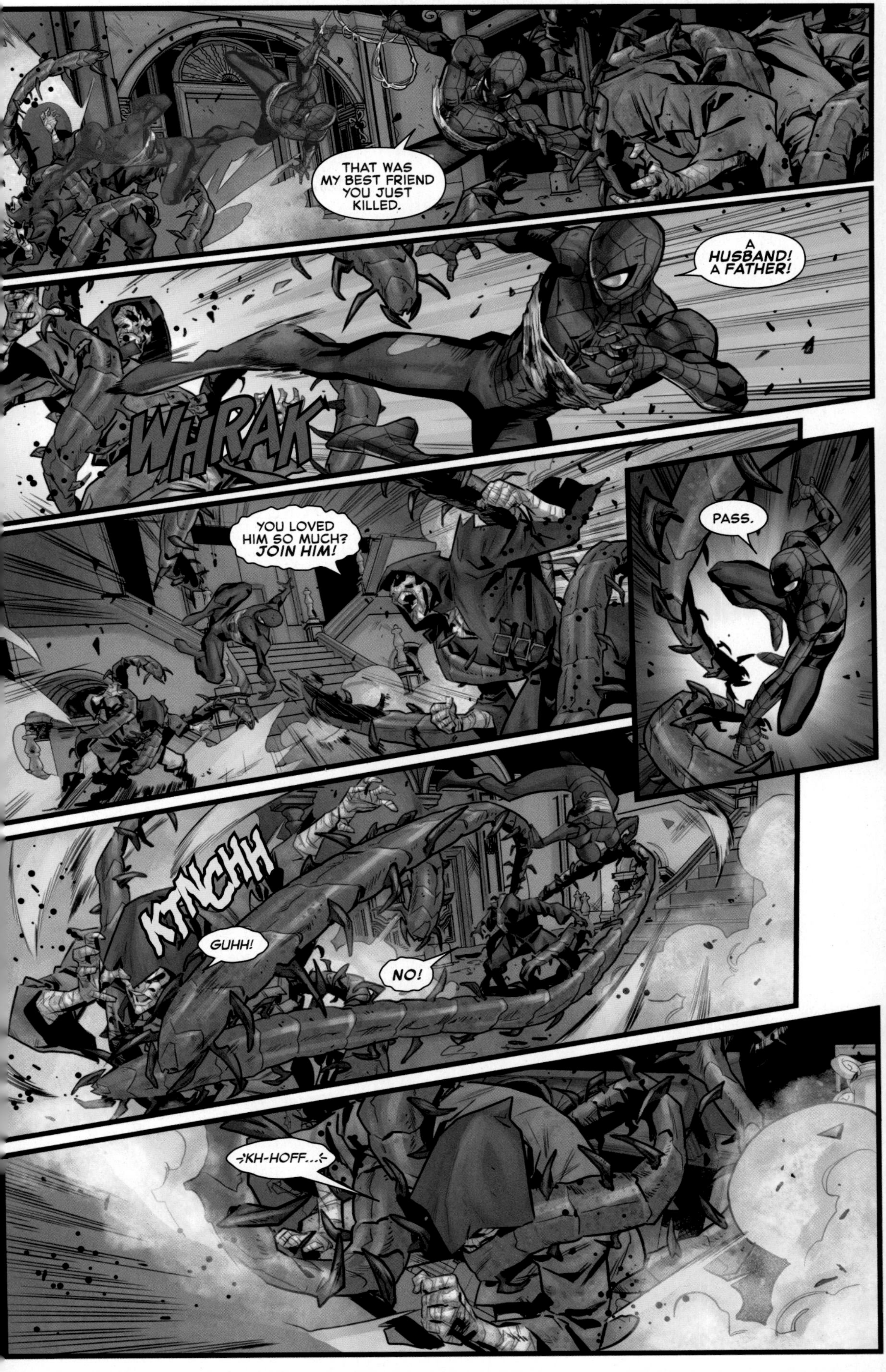
THAT WAS MY BEST FRIEND YOU JUST KILLED.
A HUSBAND! A FATHER!
WHRAK
YOU LOVED HIM SO MUCH? JOIN HIM!
PASS.
KTNCHH
GUHH!
NO!
KH-HOFF...

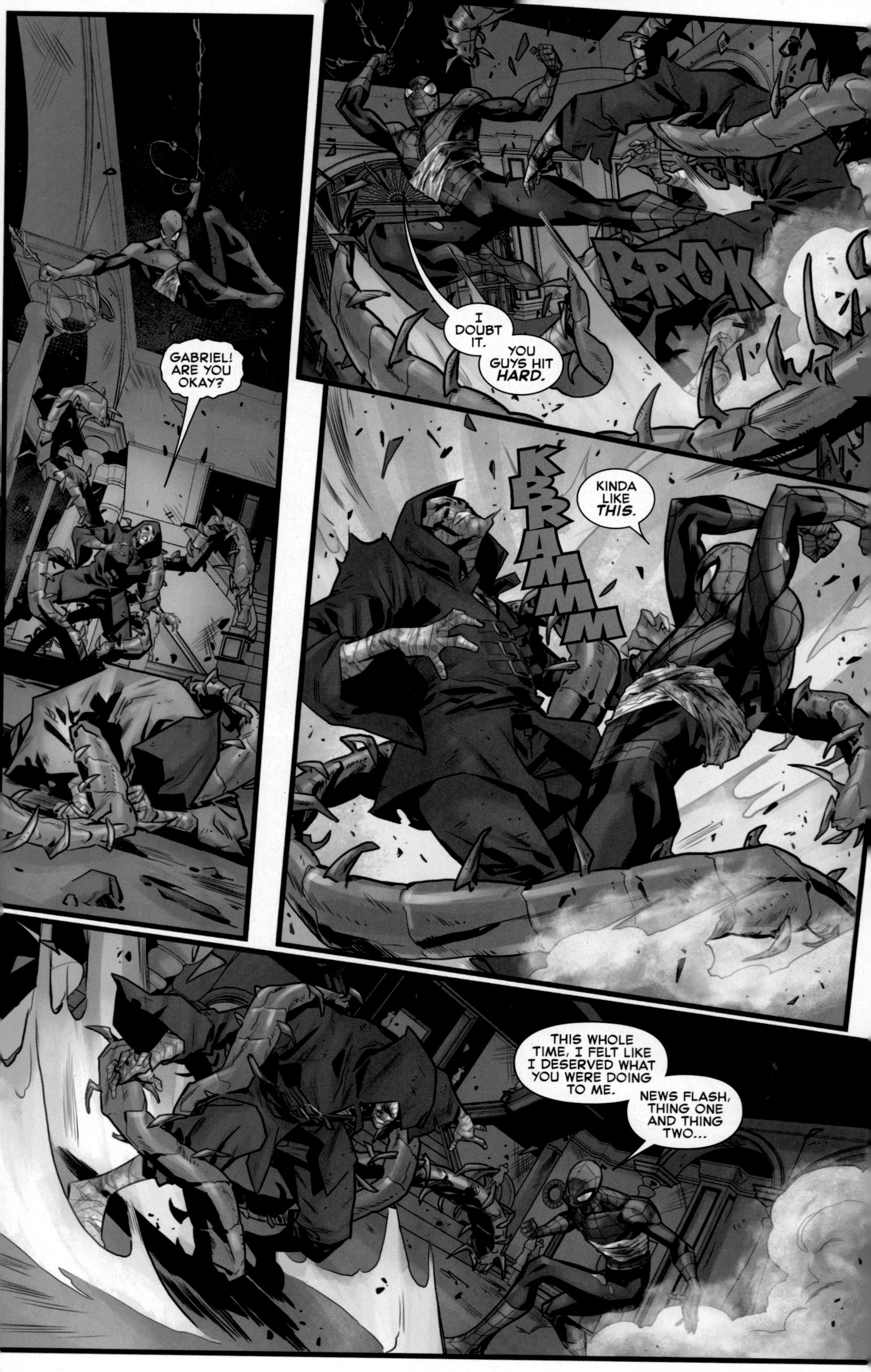
GABRIEL! ARE YOU OKAY?
I DOUBT IT.
YOU GUYS HIT HARD.
BROK
KBRAMMM
KINDA LIKE THIS.
THIS WHOLE TIME, I FELT LIKE I DESERVED WHAT YOU WERE DOING TO ME.
NEWS FLASH, THING ONE AND THING TWO...

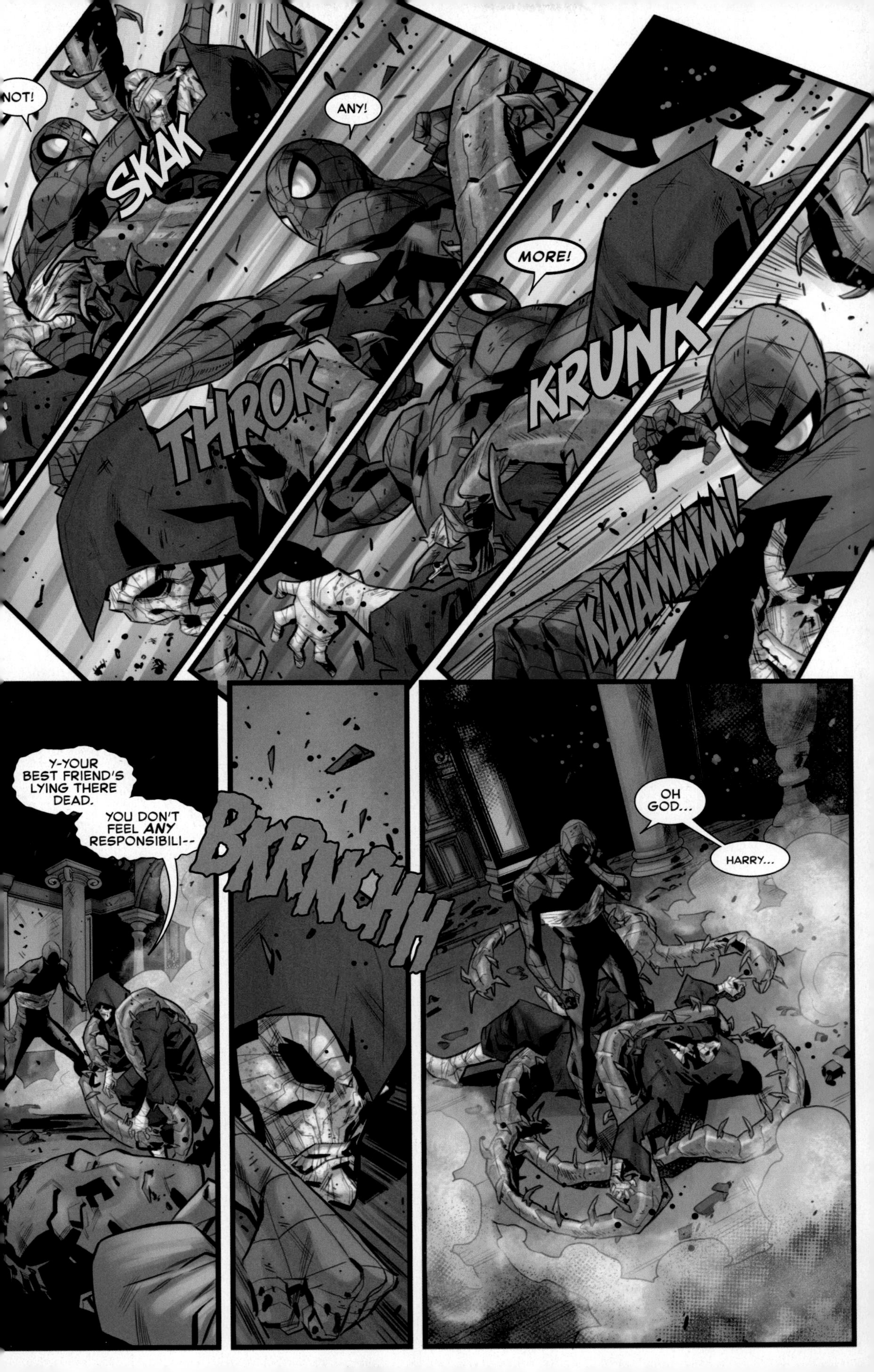
NOT!
SKAK
ANY!
THROK
MORE!
KRUNK
KATAMMM!
Y-YOUR BEST FRIEND'S LYING THERE DEAD.
YOU DON'T FEEL ANY RESPONSIBILI--
BKRNCHH
OH GOD...
HARRY...

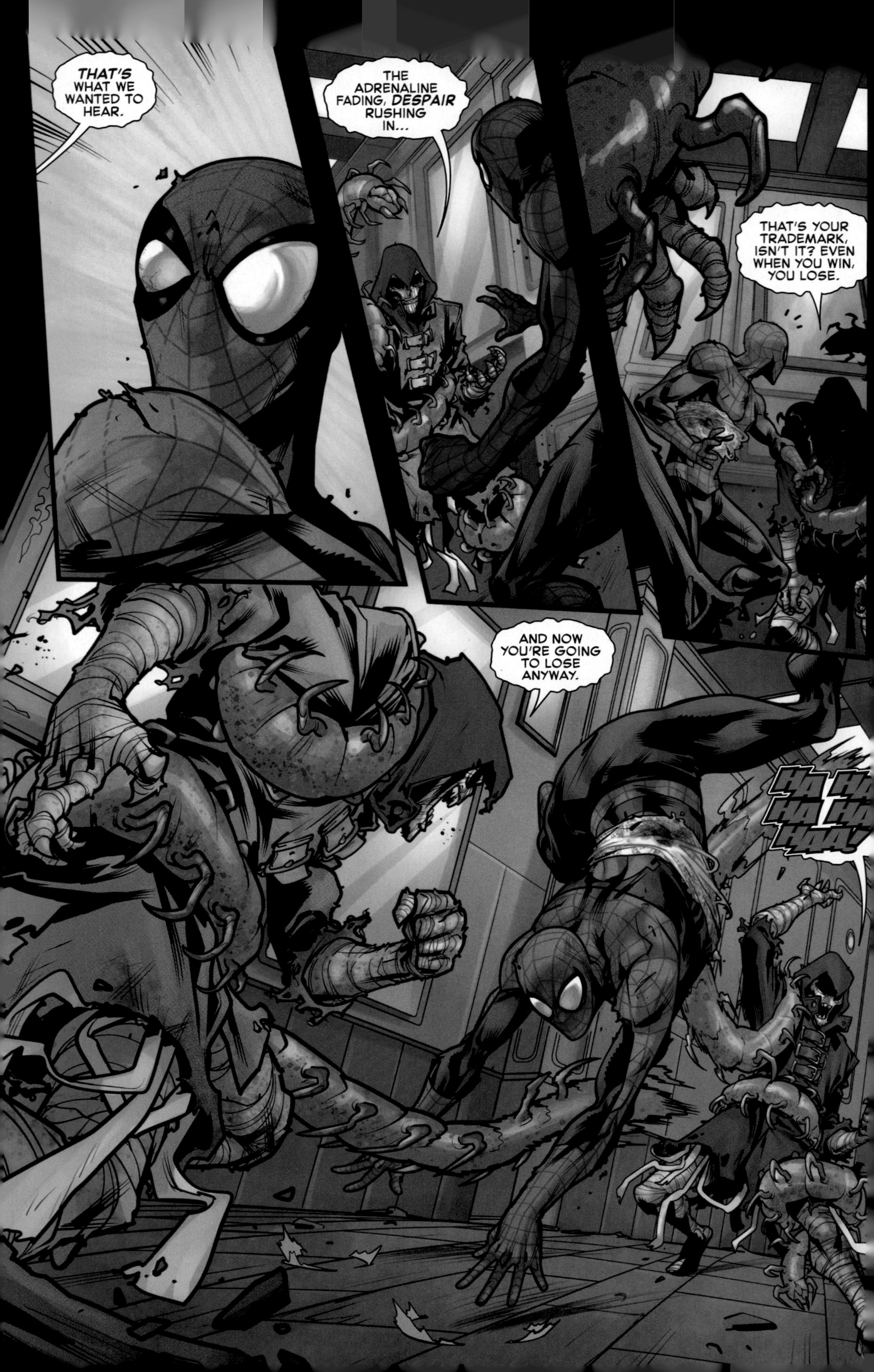

THAT'S WHAT WE WANTED TO HEAR.
THE ADRENALINE FADING, DESPAIR RUSHING IN...
THAT'S YOUR TRADEMARK, ISN'T IT? EVEN WHEN YOU WIN, YOU LOSE.
AND NOW YOU'RE GOING TO LOSE ANYWAY.
HA HA HA HA HAA!

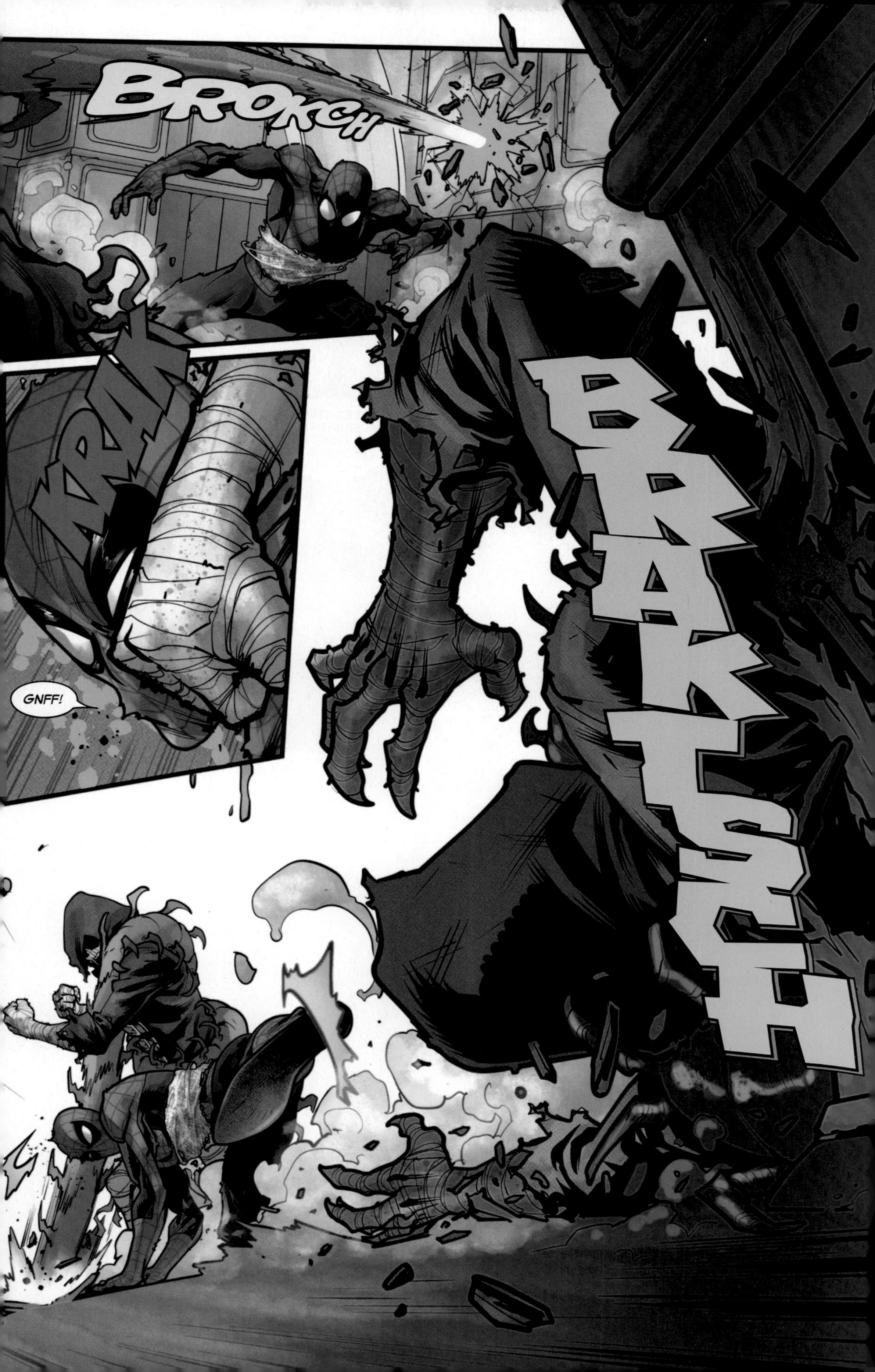
BROKCH
KRAK
GNFF!
BRAKSSH

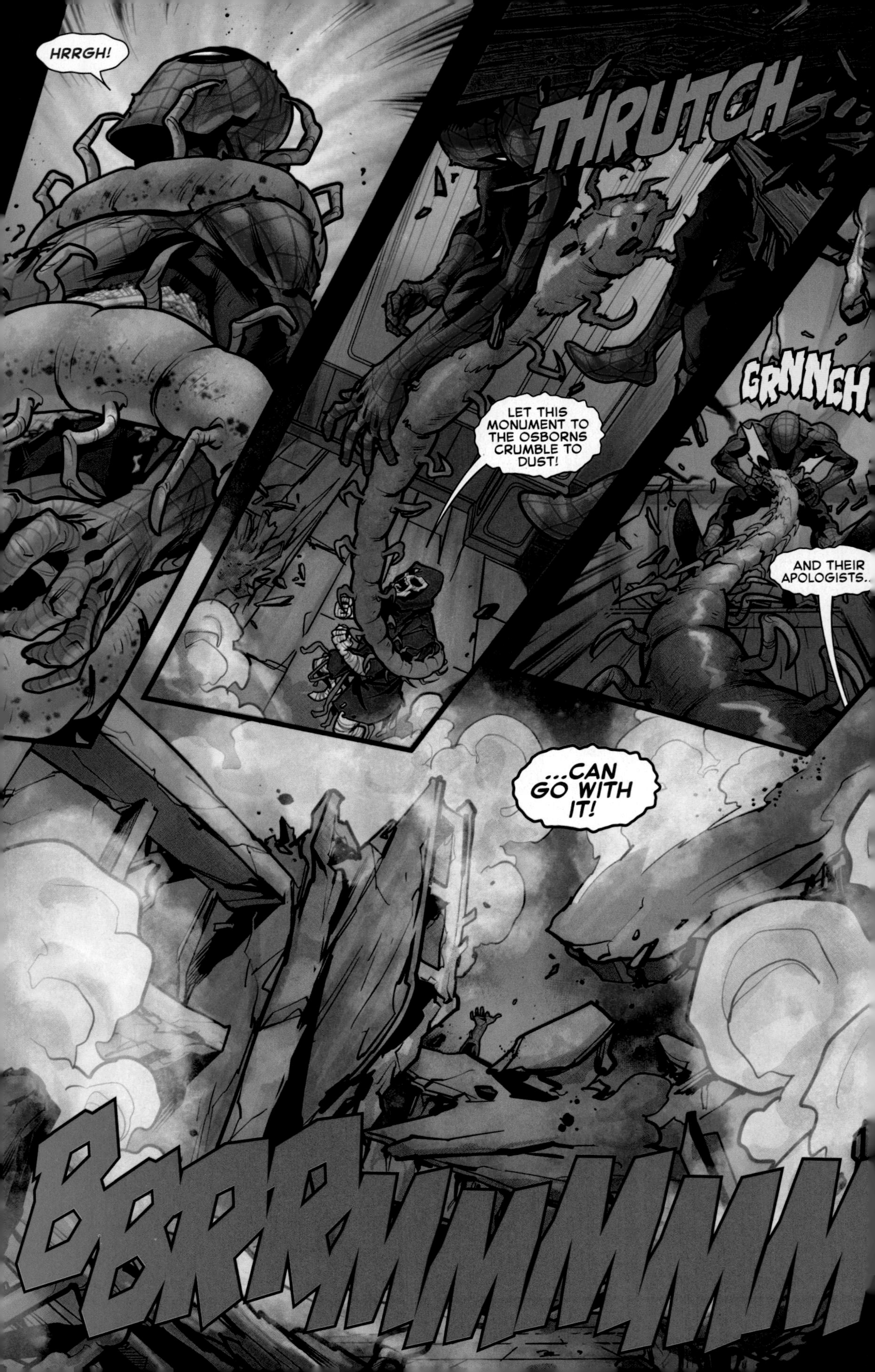
HRRGH!
THRUTCH
LET THIS MONUMENT TO THE OSBORNS CRUMBLE TO DUST!
GRNNCH
AND THEIR APOLOGISTS...
...CAN GO WITH IT!

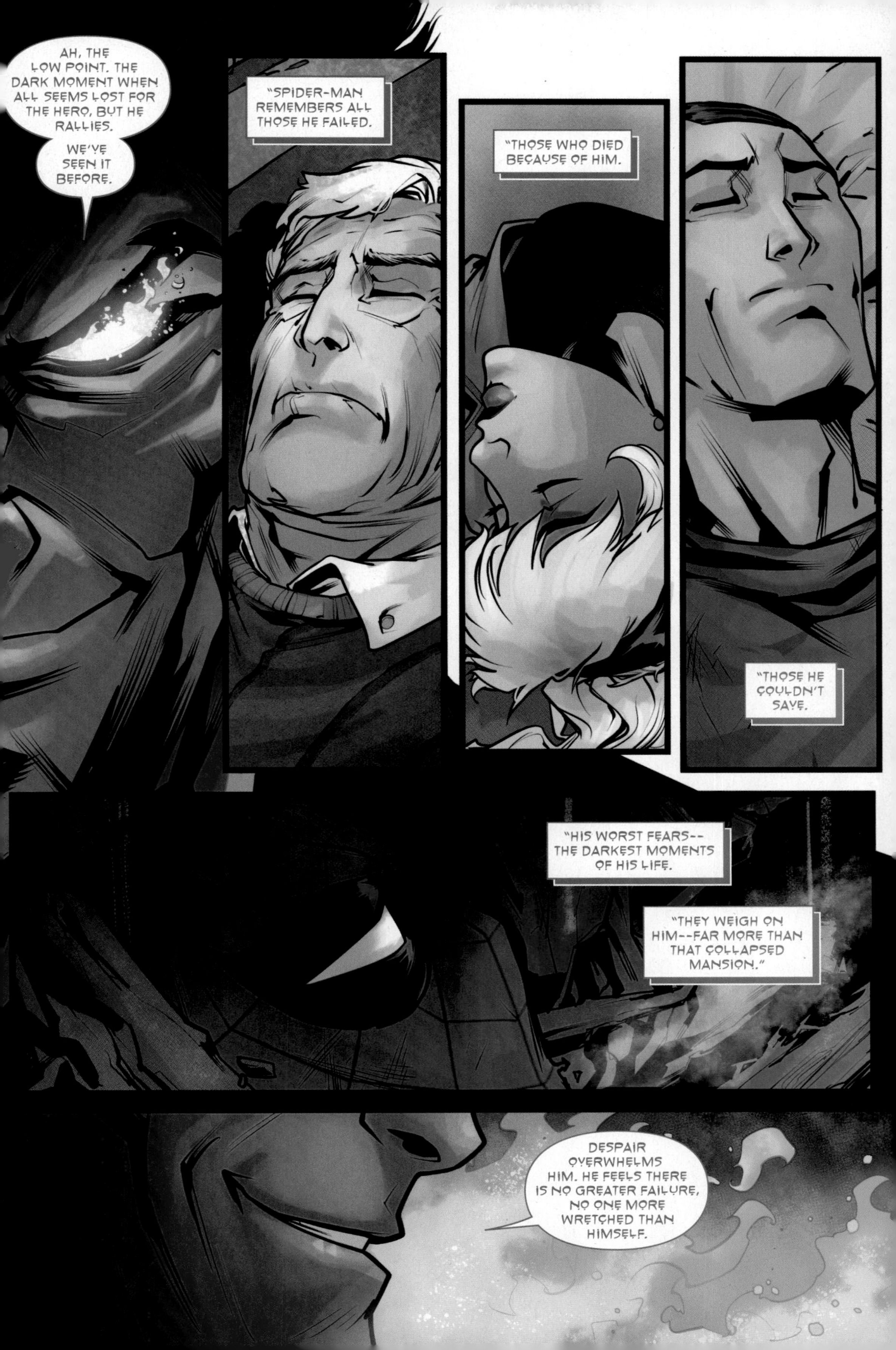
AH, THE LOW POINT. THE DARK MOMENT WHEN ALL SEEMS LOST FOR THE HERO, BUT HE RALLIES.
WE'VE SEEN IT BEFORE.
"SPIDER-MAN REMEMBERS ALL THOSE HE FAILED.
"THOSE WHO DIED BECAUSE OF HIM.
"THOSE HE COULDN'T SAVE.
"HIS WORST FEARS-- THE DARKEST MOMENTS OF HIS LIFE.
"THEY WEIGH ON HIM--FAR MORE THAN THAT COLLAPSED MANSION."
DESPAIR OVERWHELMS HIM. HE FEELS THERE IS NO GREATER FAILURE, NO ONE MORE WRETCHED THAN HIMSELF.

"BUT, LIKE EVERY TIME BEFORE--"

--THE HERO WILL RISE.

"REACH DEEP WITHIN HIMSELF--"

"--FIND UNTAPPED RESERVES--"

--OF COURAGE, STRENGTH, AND HOPE. AND HE WILL *LIFT THE IMPOSSIBLE WEIGHT...*

UNNHHH...

OH DEAR.

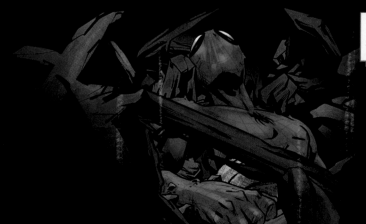

"IT SEEMS YOUR CHAMPION IS A BIT *SHORT* OF HOPE AT THE MOMENT, STEPHEN."

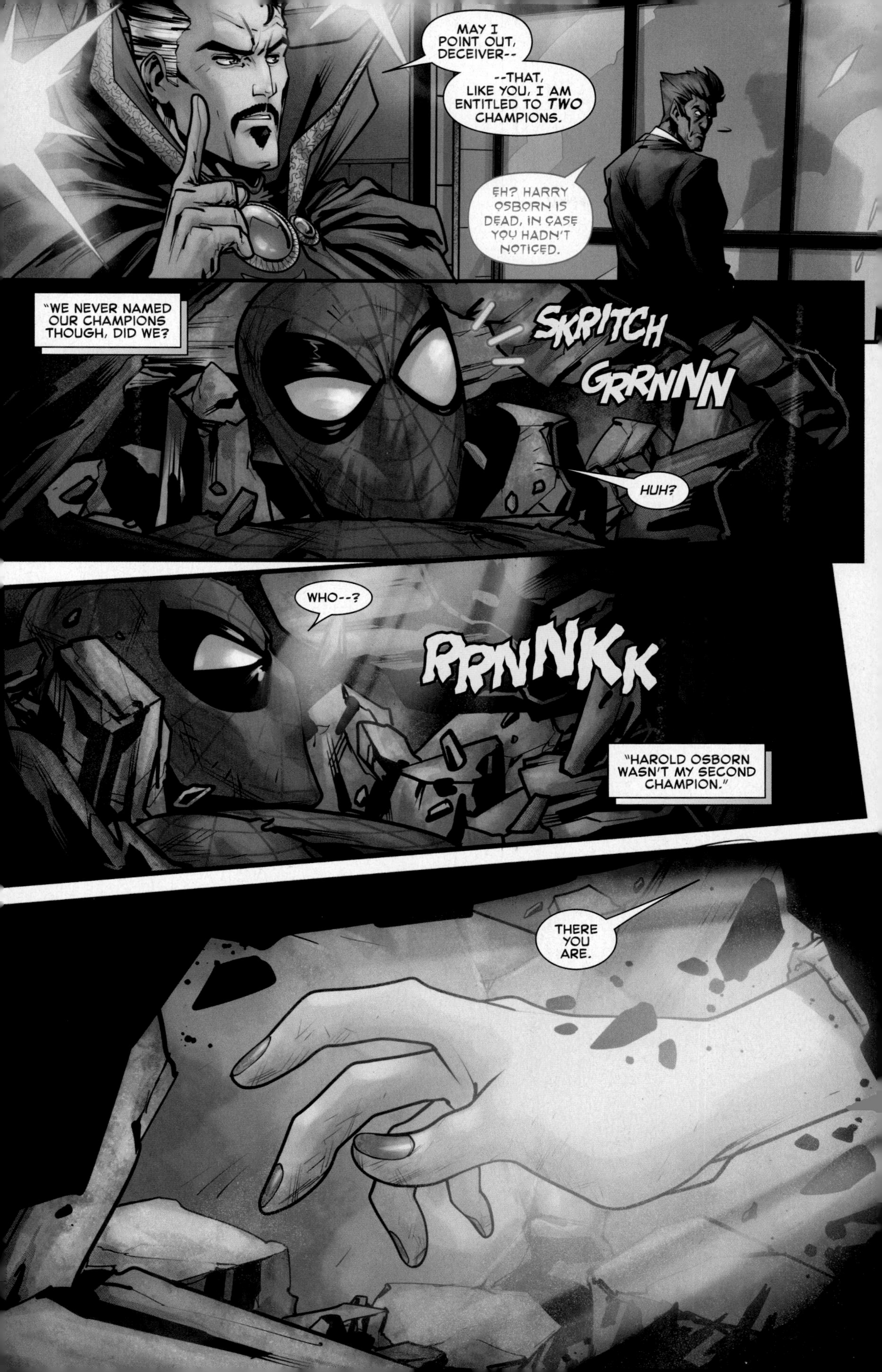
MAY I POINT OUT, DECEIVER--
--THAT, LIKE YOU, I AM ENTITLED TO TWO CHAMPIONS.
EH? HARRY OSBORN IS DEAD, IN CASE YOU HADN'T NOTICED.
"WE NEVER NAMED OUR CHAMPIONS THOUGH, DID WE?
SKRITCH
GRRNNN
HUH?
WHO--?
RRNNKK
"HAROLD OSBORN WASN'T MY SECOND CHAMPION."
THERE YOU ARE.

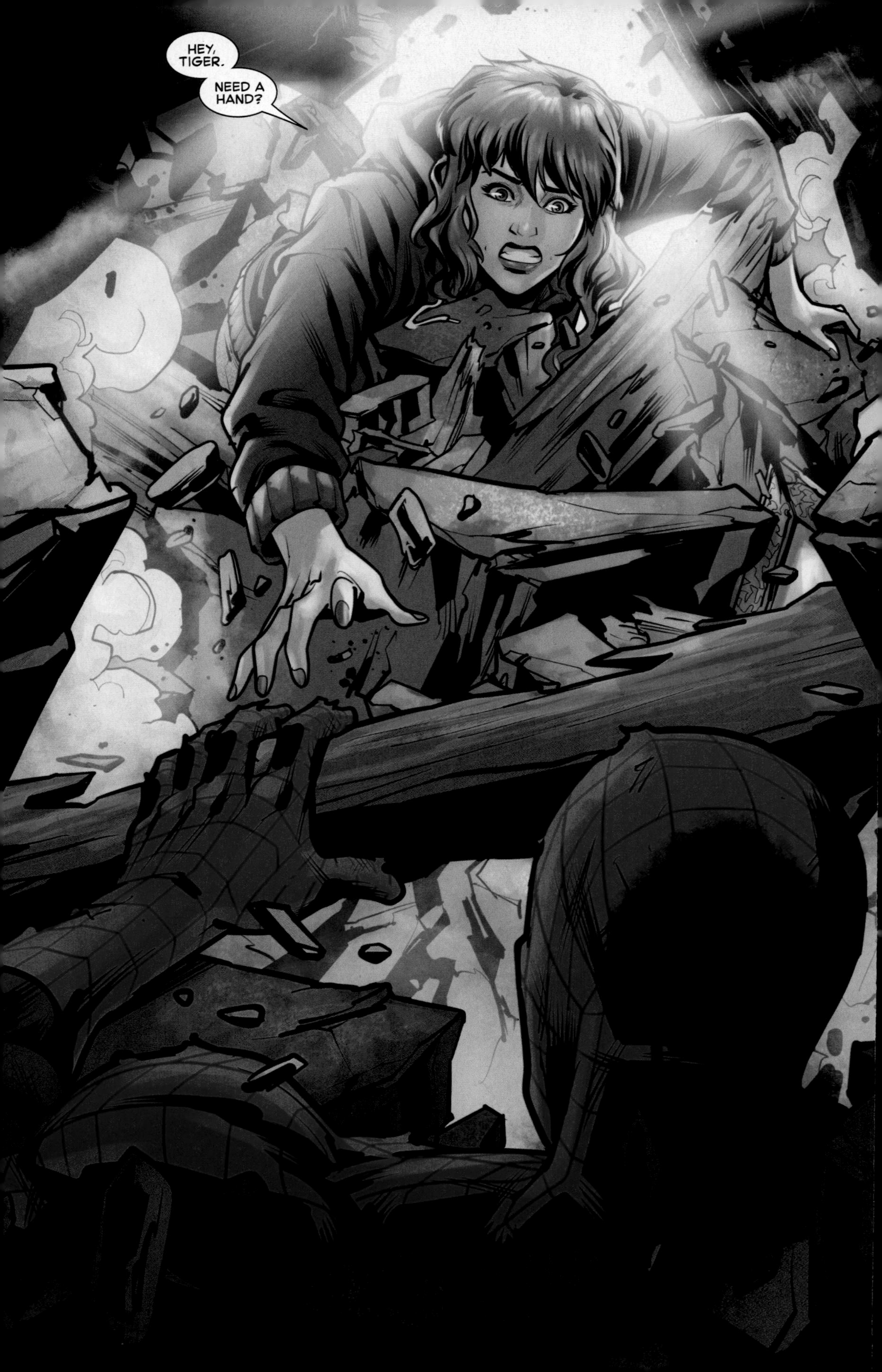
HEY, TIGER.
NEED A HAND?

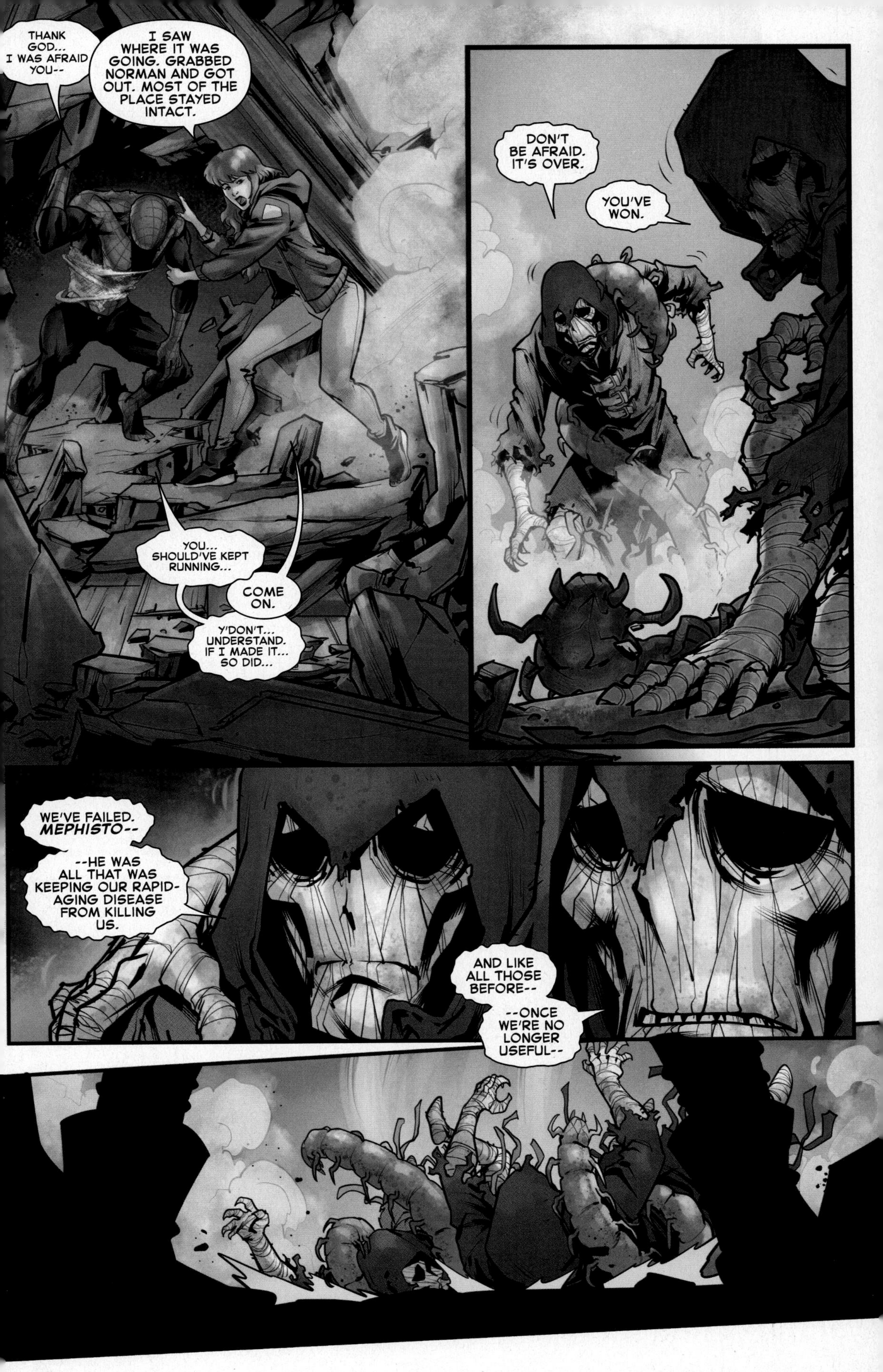

THANK GOD... I WAS AFRAID YOU--
I SAW WHERE IT WAS GOING. GRABBED NORMAN AND GOT OUT. MOST OF THE PLACE STAYED INTACT.
YOU... SHOULD'VE KEPT RUNNING...
COME ON.
Y'DON'T... UNDERSTAND. IF I MADE IT... SO DID...
DON'T BE AFRAID. IT'S OVER.
YOU'VE WON.
WE'VE FAILED. MEPHISTO--
--HE WAS ALL THAT WAS KEEPING OUR RAPID-AGING DISEASE FROM KILLING US.
AND LIKE ALL THOSE BEFORE--
--ONCE WE'RE NO LONGER USEFUL--

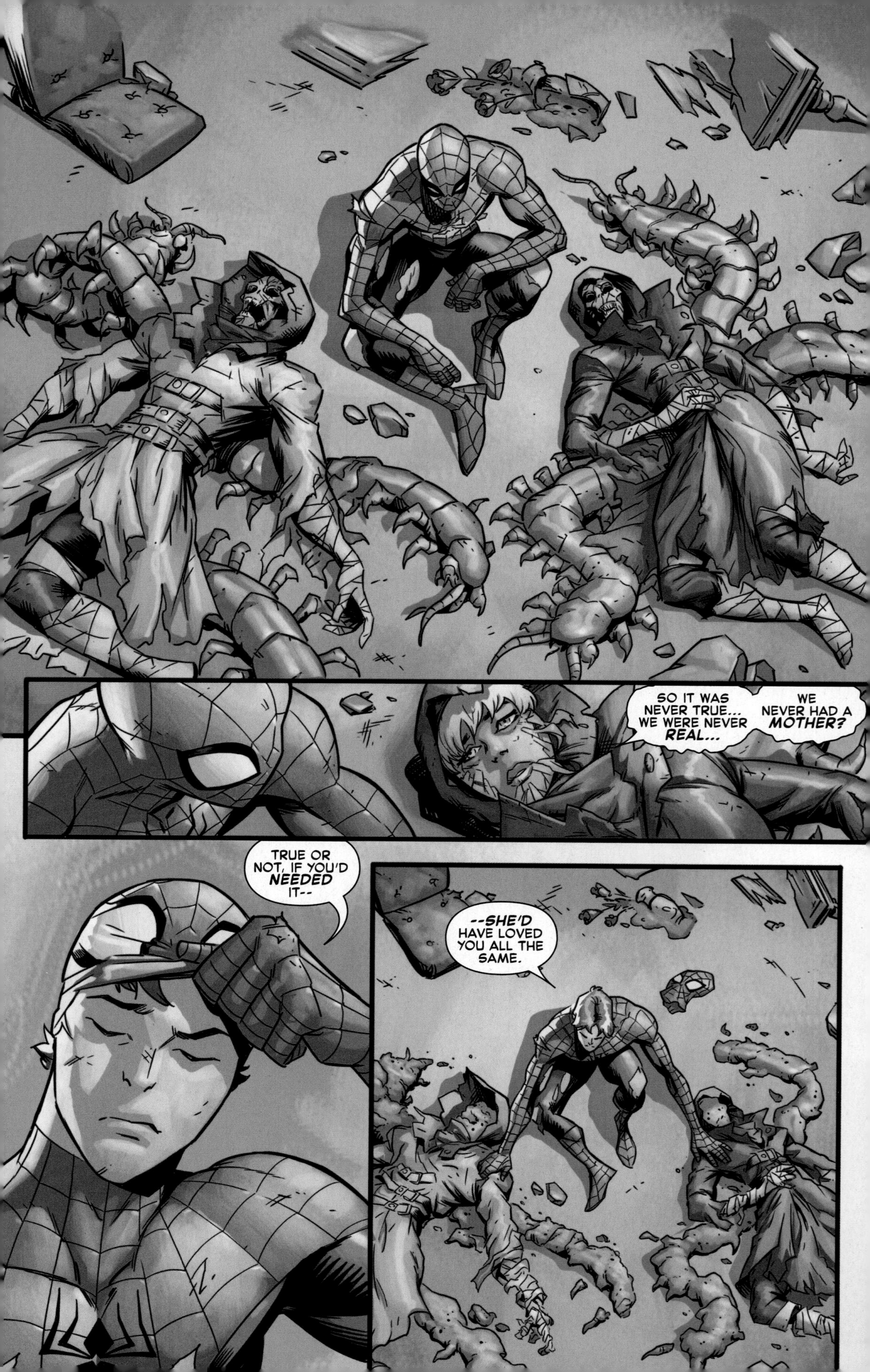
SO IT WAS NEVER TRUE... WE WERE NEVER REAL...
WE NEVER HAD A MOTHER?
TRUE OR NOT, IF YOU'D NEEDED IT--
--SHE'D HAVE LOVED YOU ALL THE SAME.

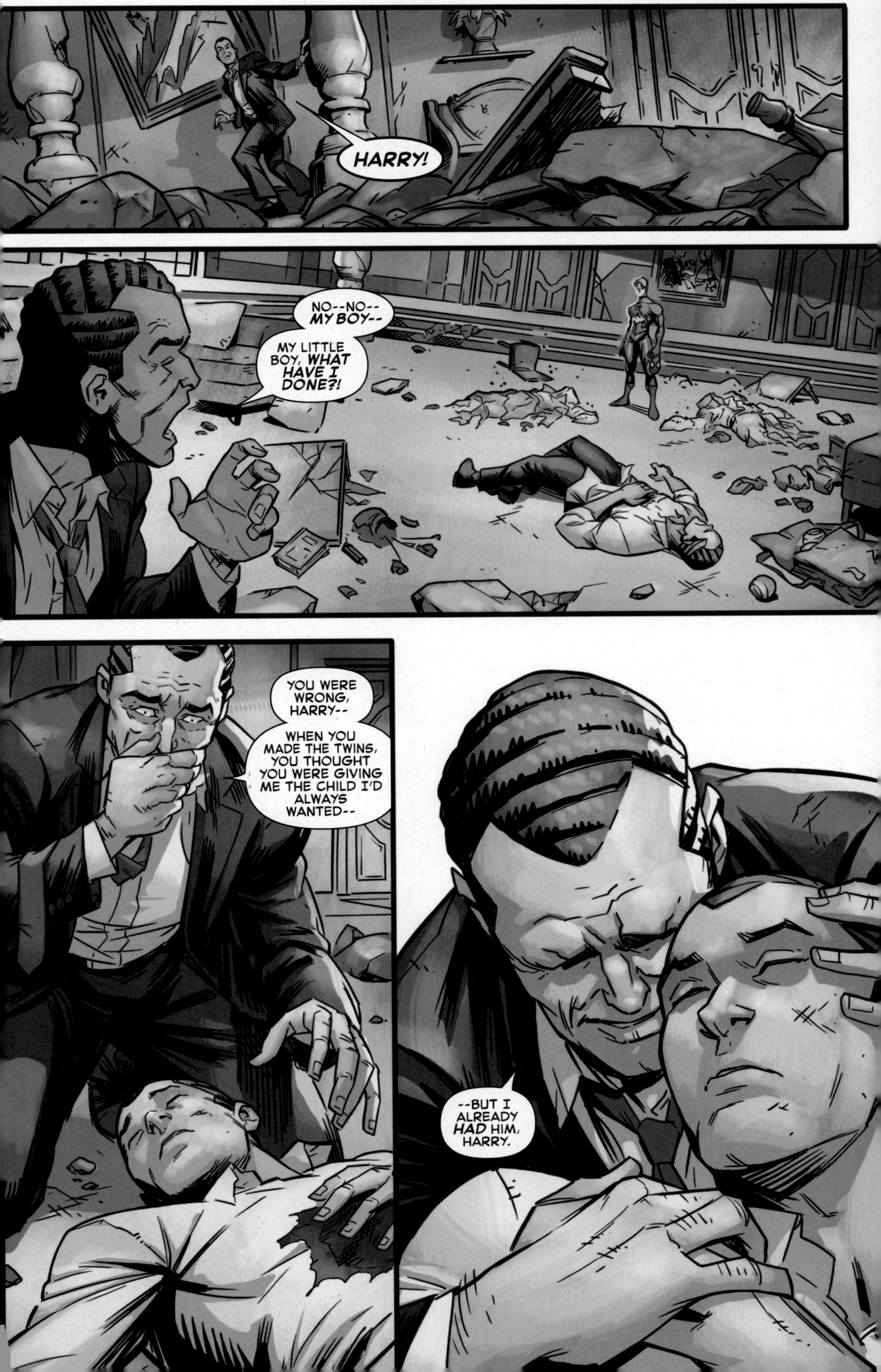
HARRY!
NO--NO--MY BOY--
MY LITTLE BOY, WHAT HAVE I DONE?!
YOU WERE WRONG, HARRY--
WHEN YOU MADE THE TWINS, YOU THOUGHT YOU WERE GIVING ME THE CHILD I'D ALWAYS WANTED--
--BUT I ALREADY HAD HIM, HARRY.

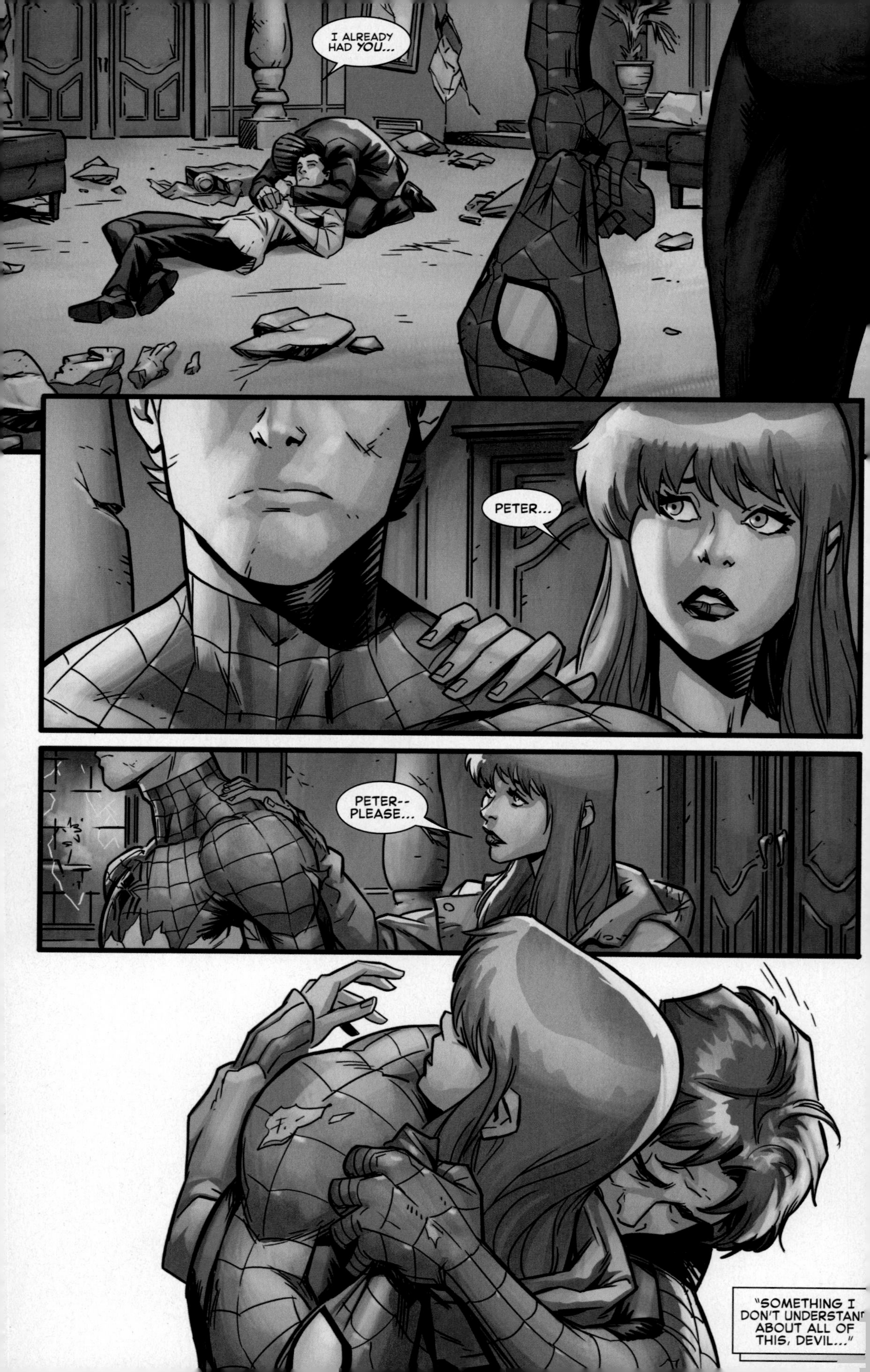
I ALREADY HAD YOU...
PETER...
PETER-- PLEASE...
"SOMETHING I DON'T UNDERSTAND ABOUT ALL OF THIS, DEVIL..."

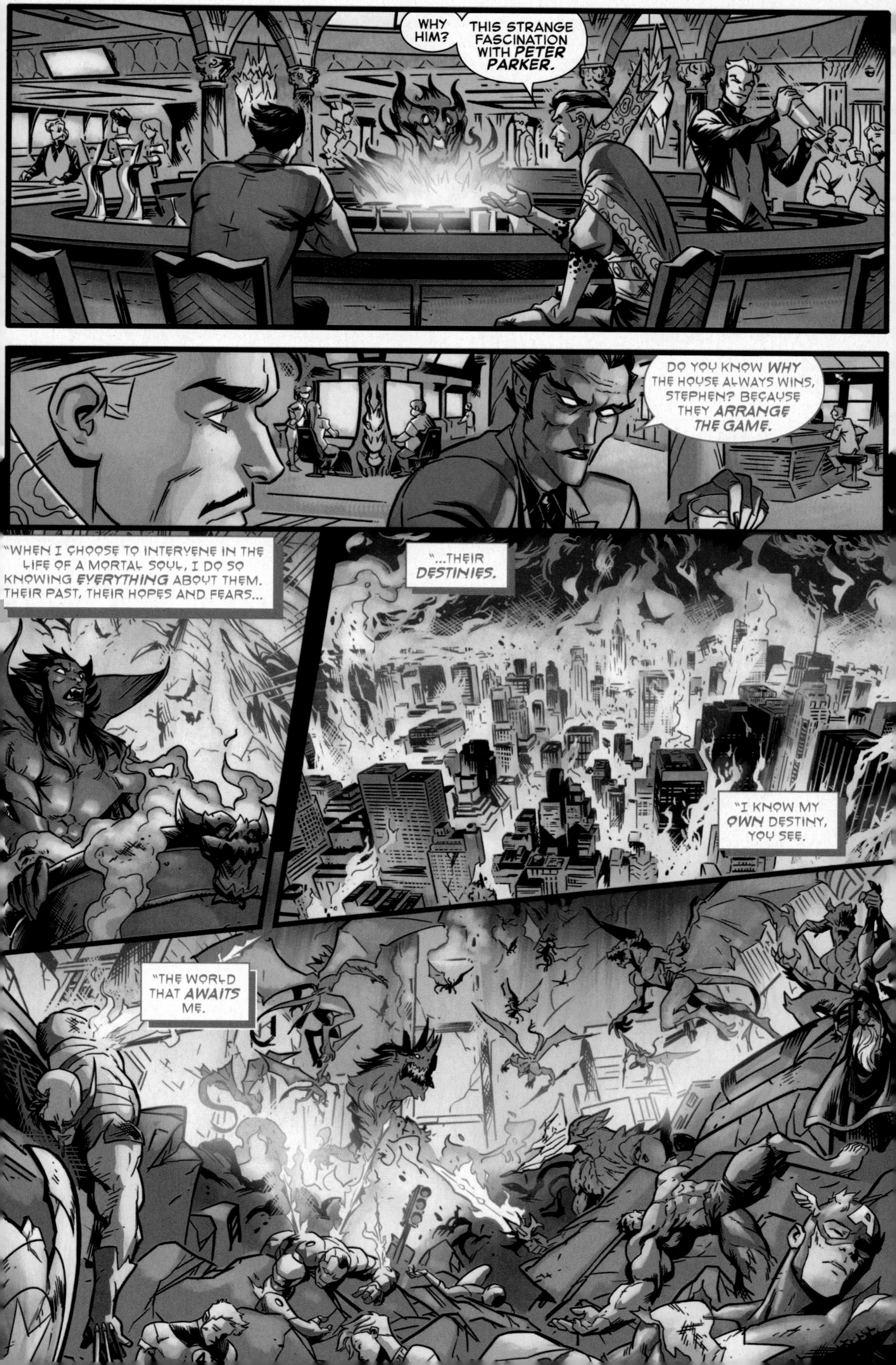
WHY HIM?
THIS STRANGE FASCINATION WITH PETER PARKER.
DO YOU KNOW WHY THE HOUSE ALWAYS WINS, STEPHEN? BECAUSE THEY ARRANGE THE GAME.
"WHEN I CHOOSE TO INTERVENE IN THE LIFE OF A MORTAL SOUL, I DO SO KNOWING EVERYTHING ABOUT THEM. THEIR PAST, THEIR HOPES AND FEARS...
"...THEIR DESTINIES.
"I KNOW MY OWN DESTINY, YOU SEE.
"THE WORLD THAT AWAITS ME.

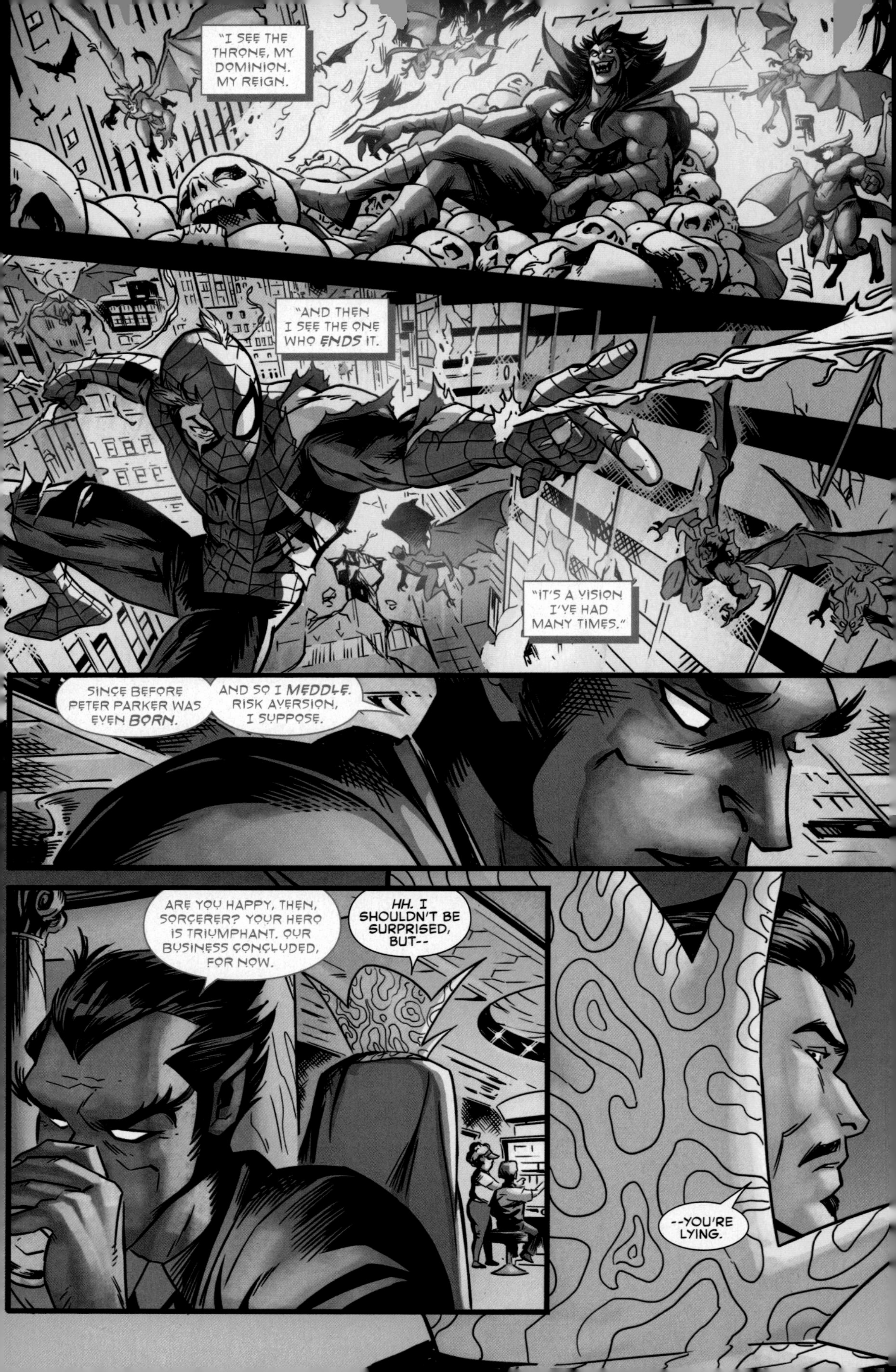
"I SEE THE THRONE, MY DOMINION. MY REIGN.
"AND THEN I SEE THE ONE WHO *ENDS* IT.
"IT'S A VISION I'VE HAD MANY TIMES."
SINCE BEFORE PETER PARKER WAS EVEN *BORN*.
AND SO I *MEDDLE*. RISK AVERSION, I SUPPOSE.
ARE YOU HAPPY, THEN, SORCERER? YOUR HERO IS TRIUMPHANT. OUR BUSINESS CONCLUDED, FOR NOW.
HH. I SHOULDN'T BE SURPRISED, BUT--
--YOU'RE LYING.

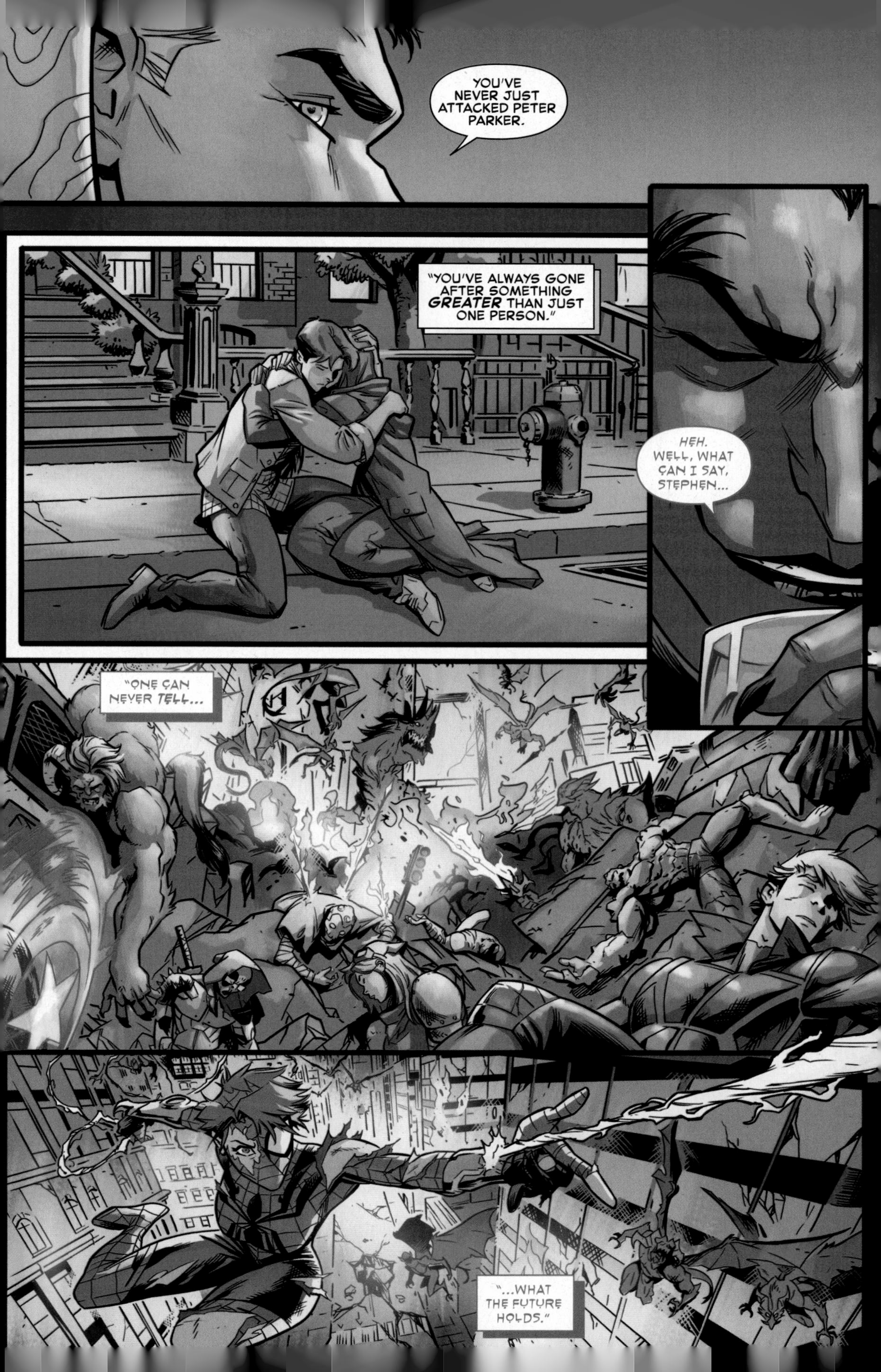
YOU'VE NEVER JUST ATTACKED PETER PARKER.
"YOU'VE ALWAYS GONE AFTER SOMETHING GREATER THAN JUST ONE PERSON."
HEH. WELL, WHAT CAN I SAY, STEPHEN...
"ONE CAN NEVER TELL...
"...WHAT THE FUTURE HOLDS."

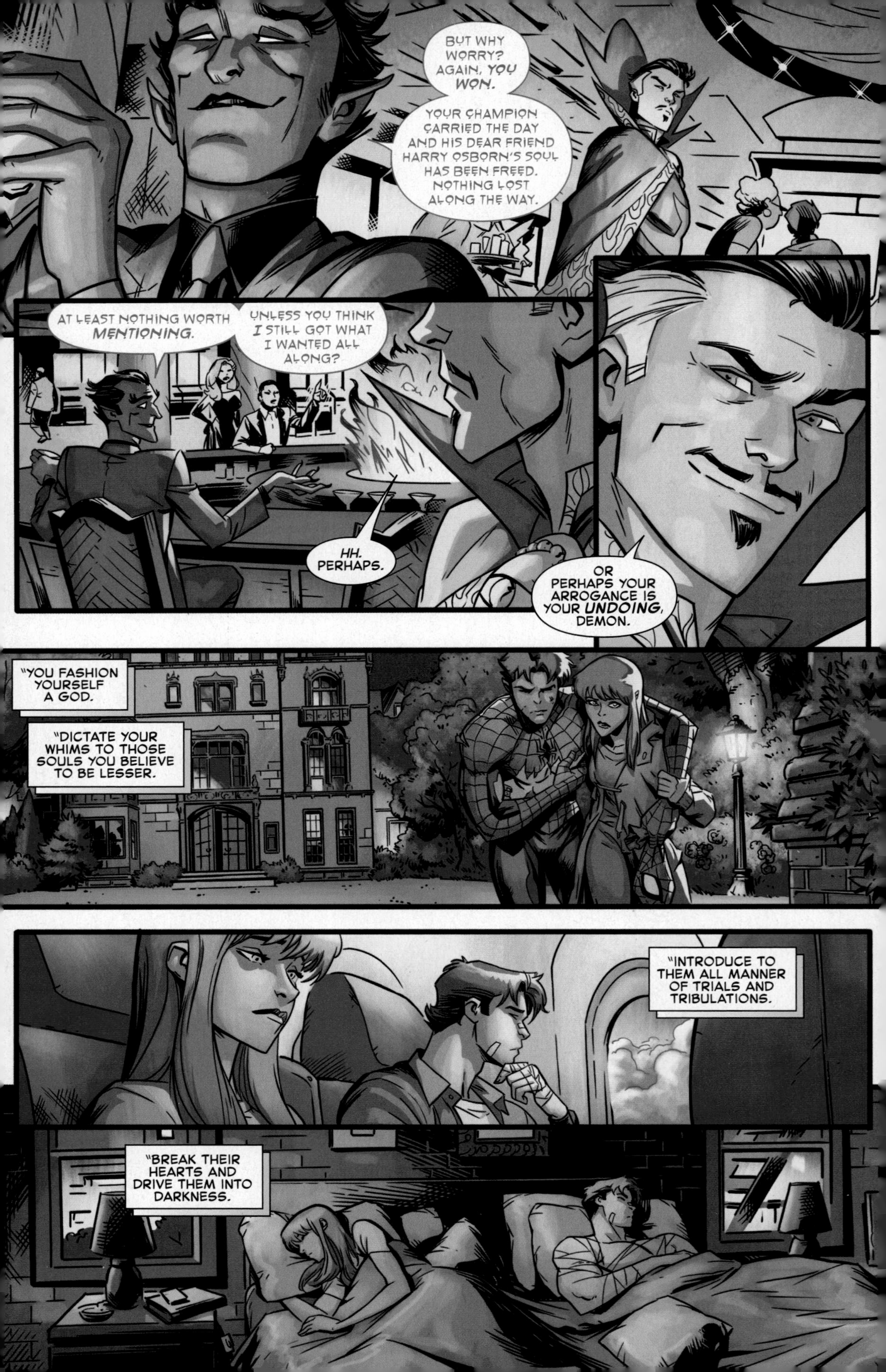
BUT WHY WORRY? AGAIN, YOU WON.
YOUR CHAMPION CARRIED THE DAY AND HIS DEAR FRIEND HARRY OSBORN'S SOUL HAS BEEN FREED. NOTHING LOST ALONG THE WAY.
AT LEAST NOTHING WORTH MENTIONING.
UNLESS YOU THINK I STILL GOT WHAT I WANTED ALL ALONG?
HH. PERHAPS.
OR PERHAPS YOUR ARROGANCE IS YOUR UNDOING, DEMON.
"YOU FASHION YOURSELF A GOD.
"DICTATE YOUR WHIMS TO THOSE SOULS YOU BELIEVE TO BE LESSER.
"INTRODUCE TO THEM ALL MANNER OF TRIALS AND TRIBULATIONS.
"BREAK THEIR HEARTS AND DRIVE THEM INTO DARKNESS.

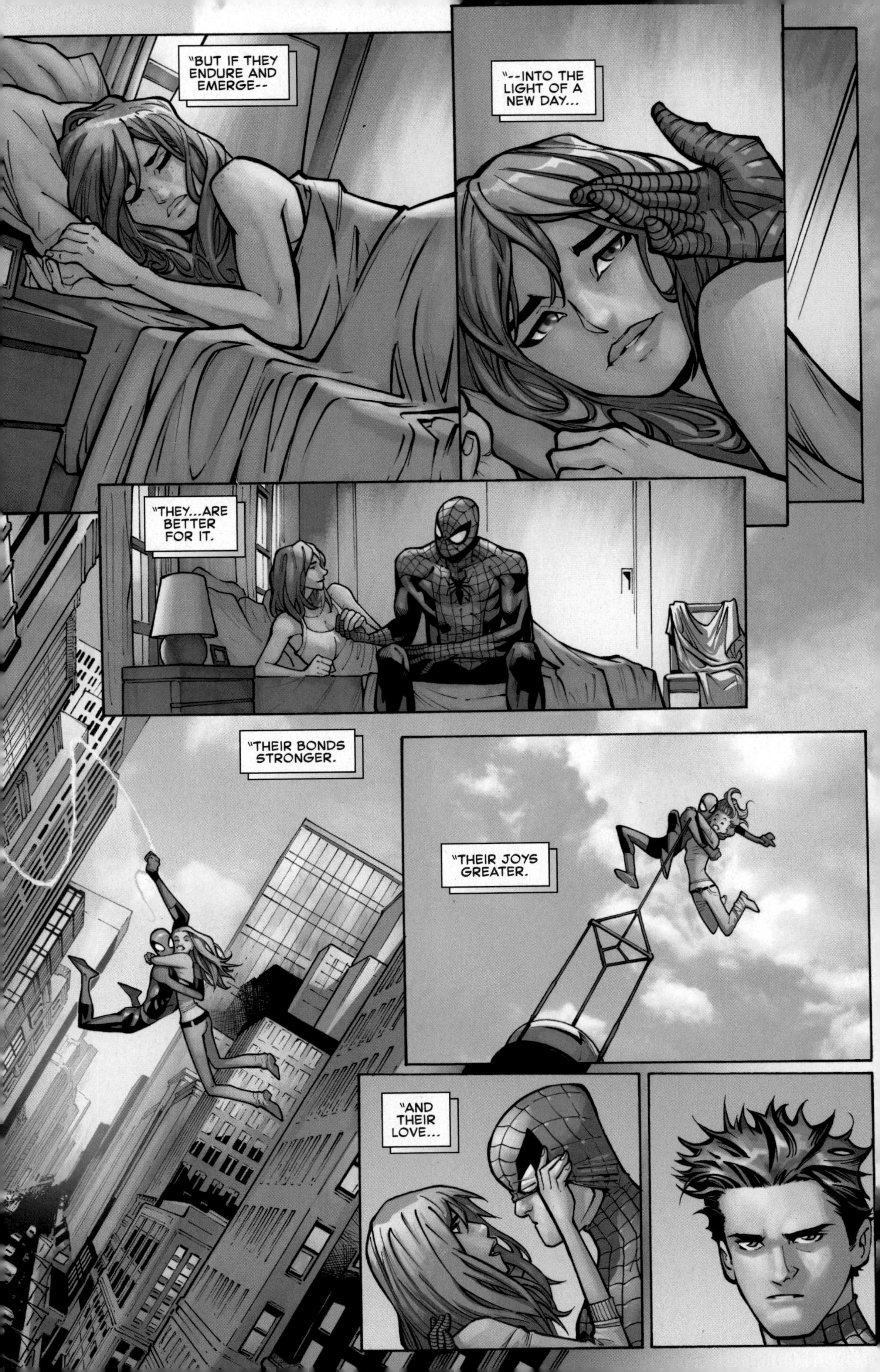
"BUT IF THEY ENDURE AND EMERGE--
"--INTO THE LIGHT OF A NEW DAY...
"THEY...ARE BETTER FOR IT.
"THEIR BONDS STRONGER.
"THEIR JOYS GREATER.
"AND THEIR LOVE...

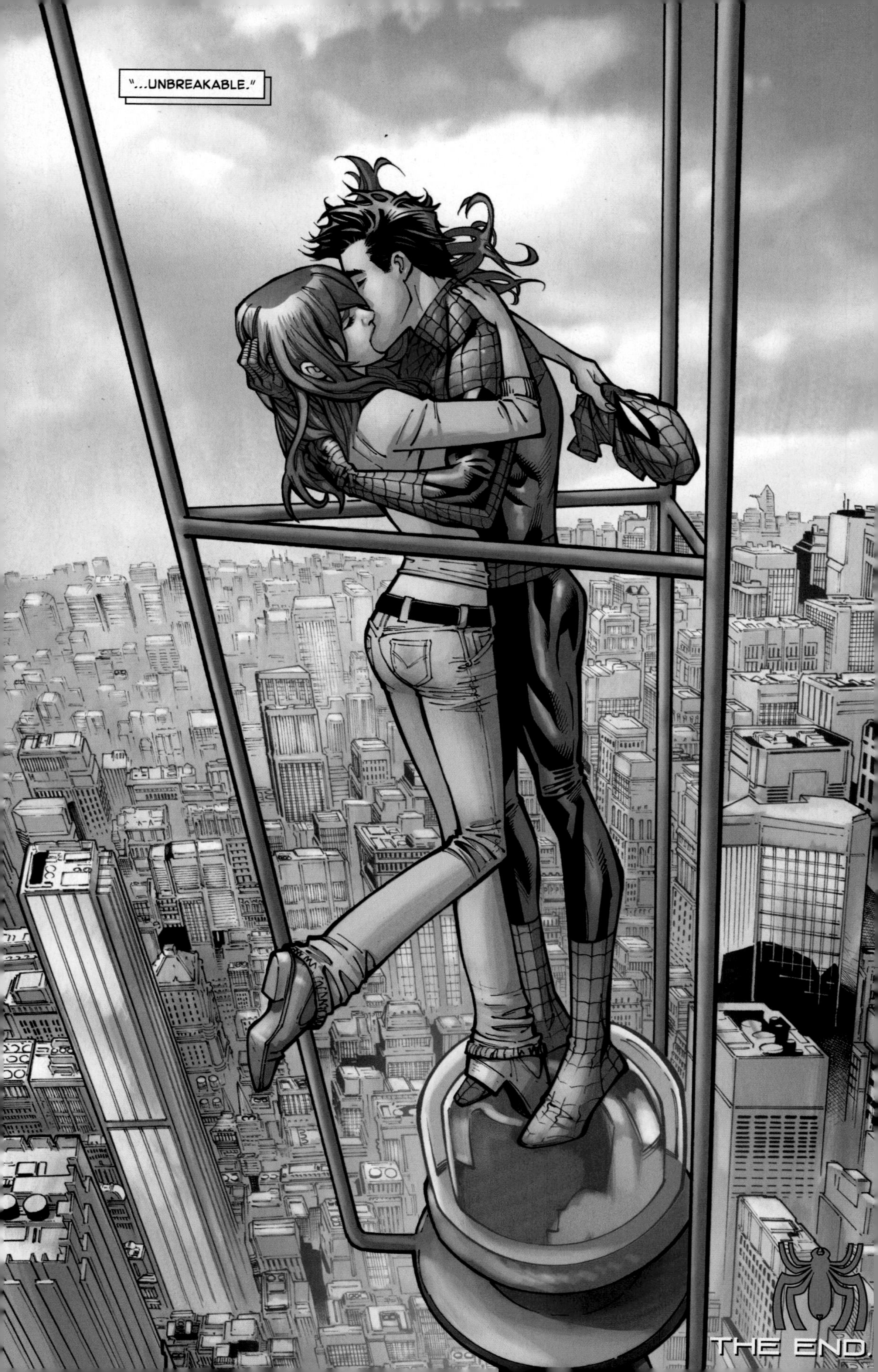
"...UNBREAKABLE."
THE END.

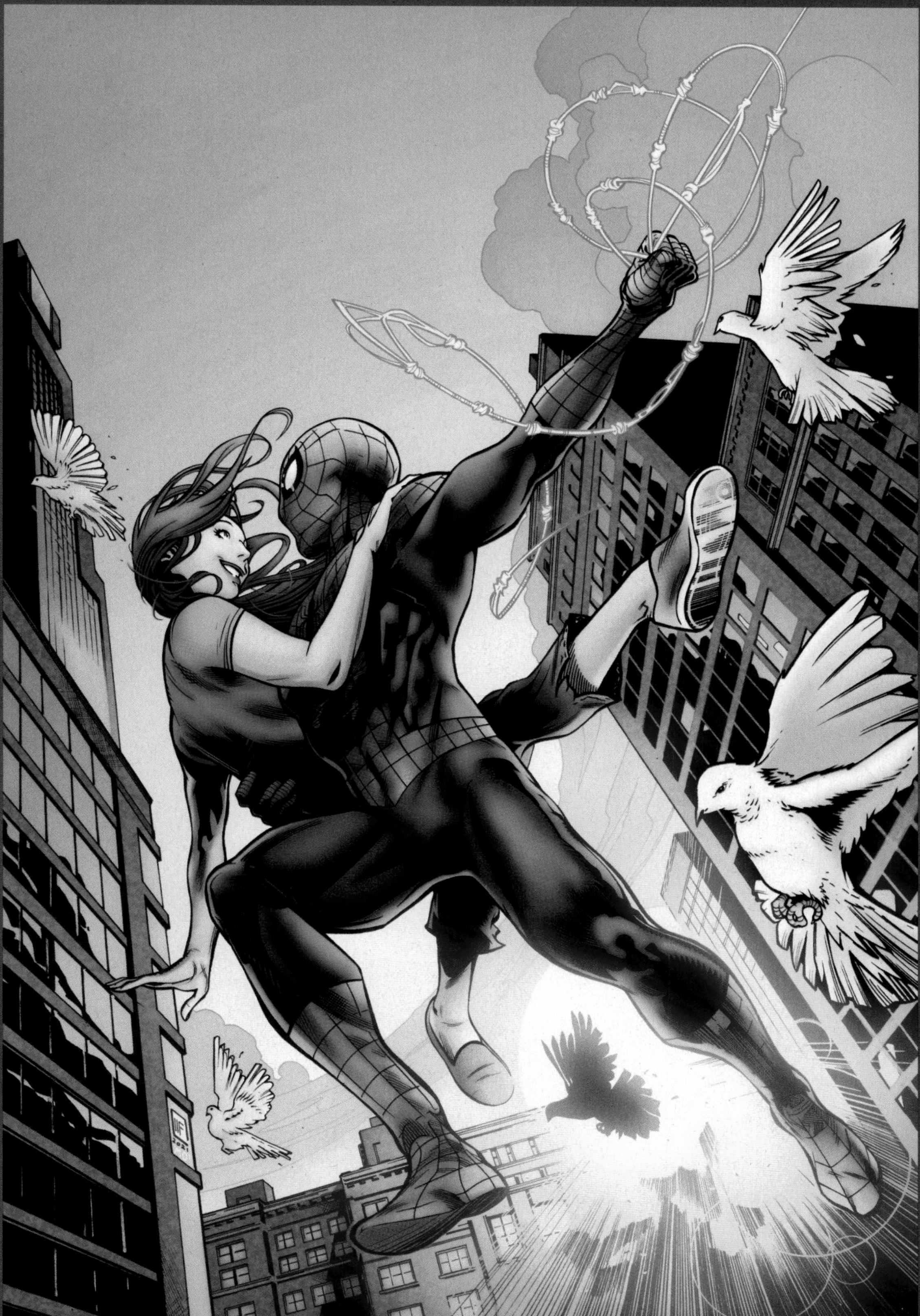

#74 VARIANT BY MARCELO FERREIRA & MORRY HOLLOWELL

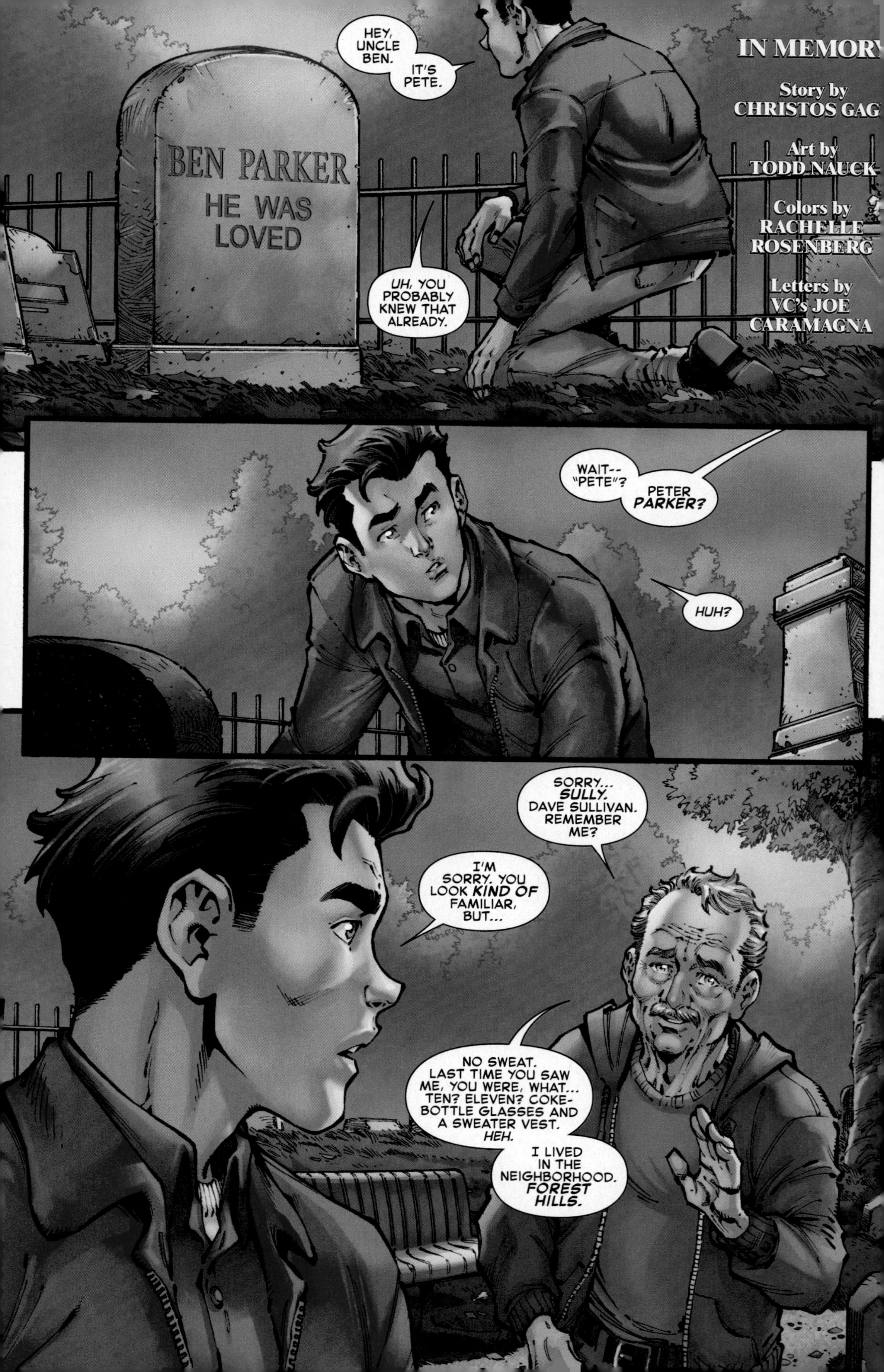
HEY, UNCLE BEN.
IT'S PETE.
IN MEMORY
Story by CHRISTOS GAGE
Art by TODD NAUCK
Colors by RACHELLE ROSENBERG
Letters by VC's JOE CARAMAGNA
BEN PARKER
HE WAS LOVED
UH, YOU PROBABLY KNEW THAT ALREADY.
WAIT-- "PETE"? PETER PARKER?
HUH?
SORRY... SULLY. DAVE SULLIVAN. REMEMBER ME?
I'M SORRY. YOU LOOK KIND OF FAMILIAR, BUT...
NO SWEAT. LAST TIME YOU SAW ME, YOU WERE, WHAT... TEN? ELEVEN? COKE-BOTTLE GLASSES AND A SWEATER VEST. HEH.
I LIVED IN THE NEIGHBORHOOD. FOREST HILLS.

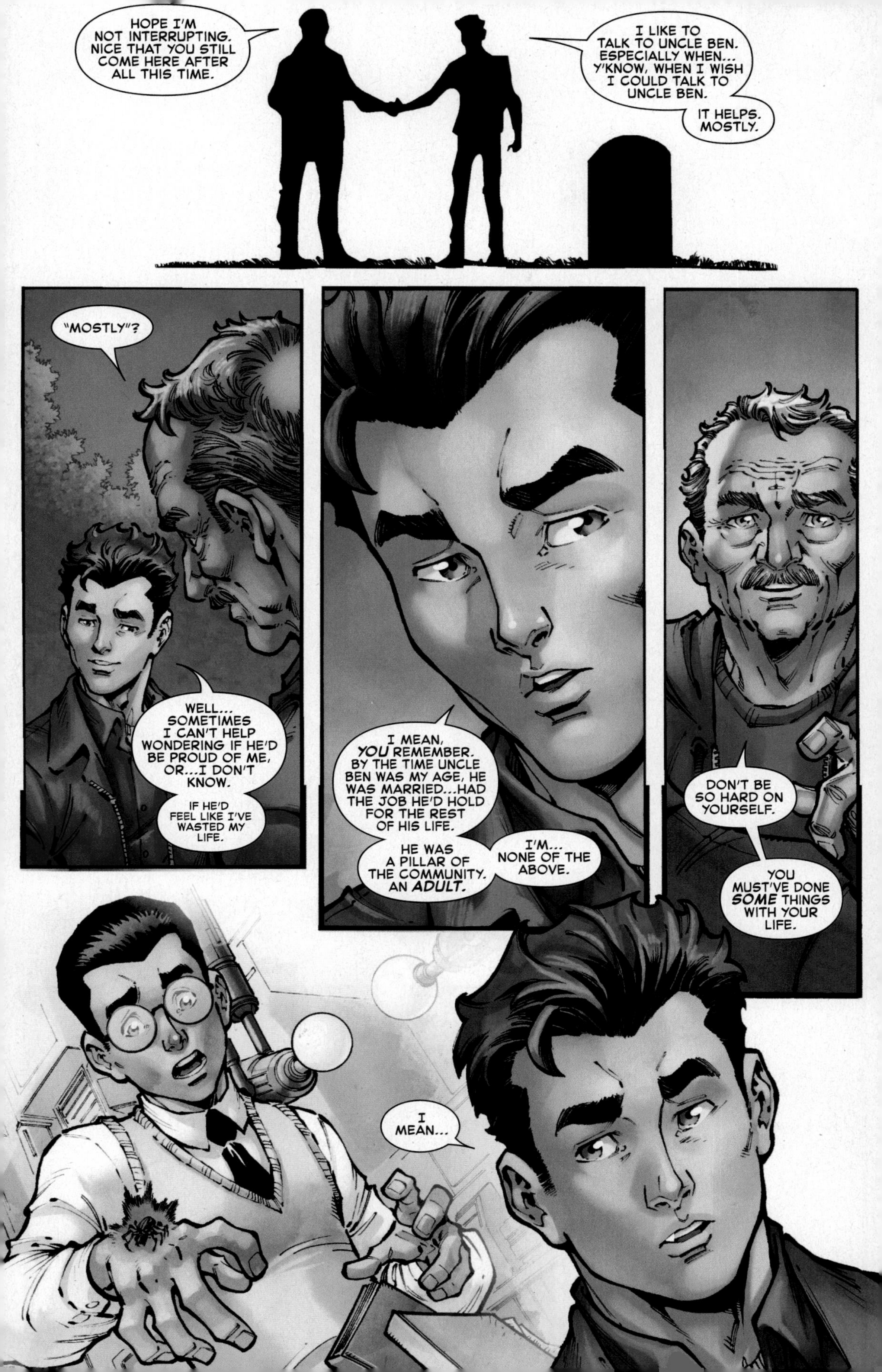
HOPE I'M NOT INTERRUPTING. NICE THAT YOU STILL COME HERE AFTER ALL THIS TIME.
I LIKE TO TALK TO UNCLE BEN. ESPECIALLY WHEN... Y'KNOW, WHEN I WISH I COULD TALK TO UNCLE BEN.
IT HELPS. MOSTLY.
"MOSTLY"?
WELL... SOMETIMES I CAN'T HELP WONDERING IF HE'D BE PROUD OF ME, OR...I DON'T KNOW.
IF HE'D FEEL LIKE I'VE WASTED MY LIFE.
I MEAN, YOU REMEMBER. BY THE TIME UNCLE BEN WAS MY AGE, HE WAS MARRIED...HAD THE JOB HE'D HOLD FOR THE REST OF HIS LIFE.
HE WAS A PILLAR OF THE COMMUNITY. AN ADULT.
I'M... NONE OF THE ABOVE.
DON'T BE SO HARD ON YOURSELF.
YOU MUST'VE DONE SOME THINGS WITH YOUR LIFE.
I MEAN...

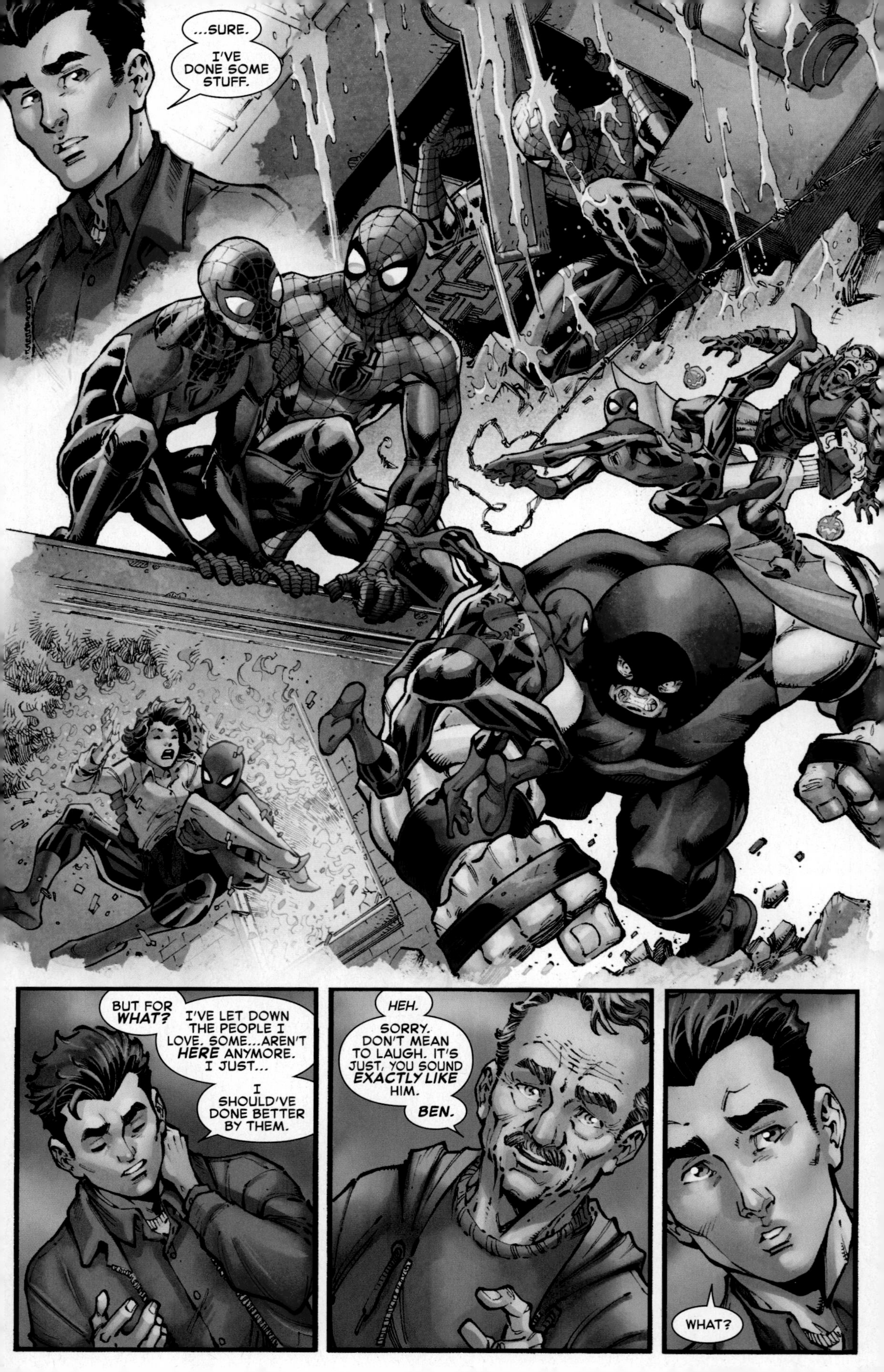
...SURE.
I'VE DONE SOME STUFF.
BUT FOR WHAT?
I'VE LET DOWN THE PEOPLE I LOVE. SOME...AREN'T HERE ANYMORE. I JUST...
I SHOULD'VE DONE BETTER BY THEM.
HEH.
SORRY. DON'T MEAN TO LAUGH. IT'S JUST, YOU SOUND EXACTLY LIKE HIM.
BEN.
WHAT?

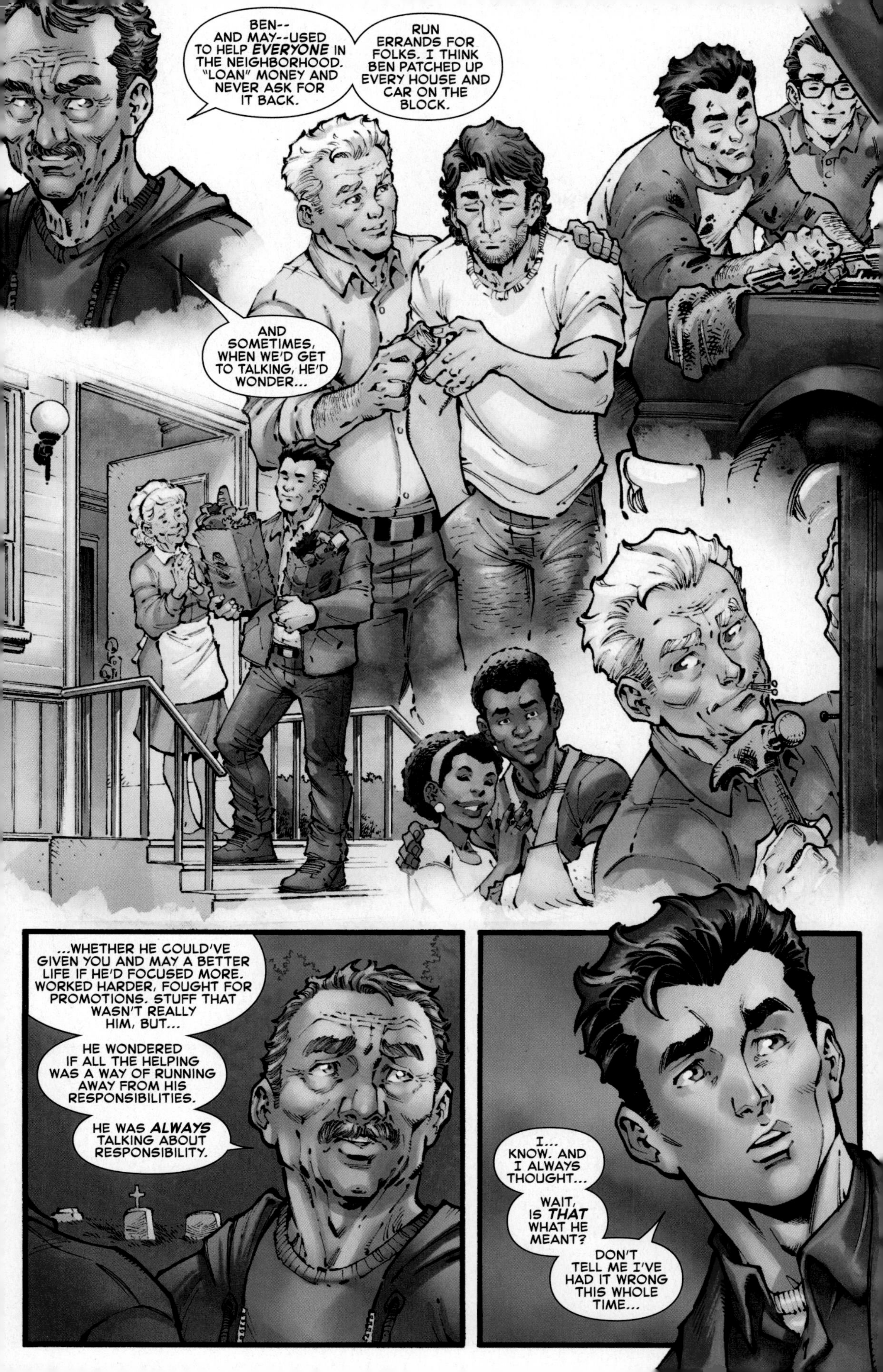

BEN-- AND MAY--USED TO HELP *EVERYONE* IN THE NEIGHBORHOOD. "LOAN" MONEY AND NEVER ASK FOR IT BACK.
RUN ERRANDS FOR FOLKS. I THINK BEN PATCHED UP EVERY HOUSE AND CAR ON THE BLOCK.
AND SOMETIMES, WHEN WE'D GET TO TALKING, HE'D WONDER...
...WHETHER HE COULD'VE GIVEN YOU AND MAY A BETTER LIFE IF HE'D FOCUSED MORE. WORKED HARDER, FOUGHT FOR PROMOTIONS. STUFF THAT WASN'T REALLY HIM, BUT...
HE WONDERED IF ALL THE HELPING WAS A WAY OF RUNNING AWAY FROM HIS RESPONSIBILITIES.
HE WAS *ALWAYS* TALKING ABOUT RESPONSIBILITY.
I... KNOW. AND I ALWAYS THOUGHT...
WAIT, IS *THAT* WHAT HE MEANT?
DON'T TELL ME I'VE HAD IT WRONG THIS WHOLE TIME...

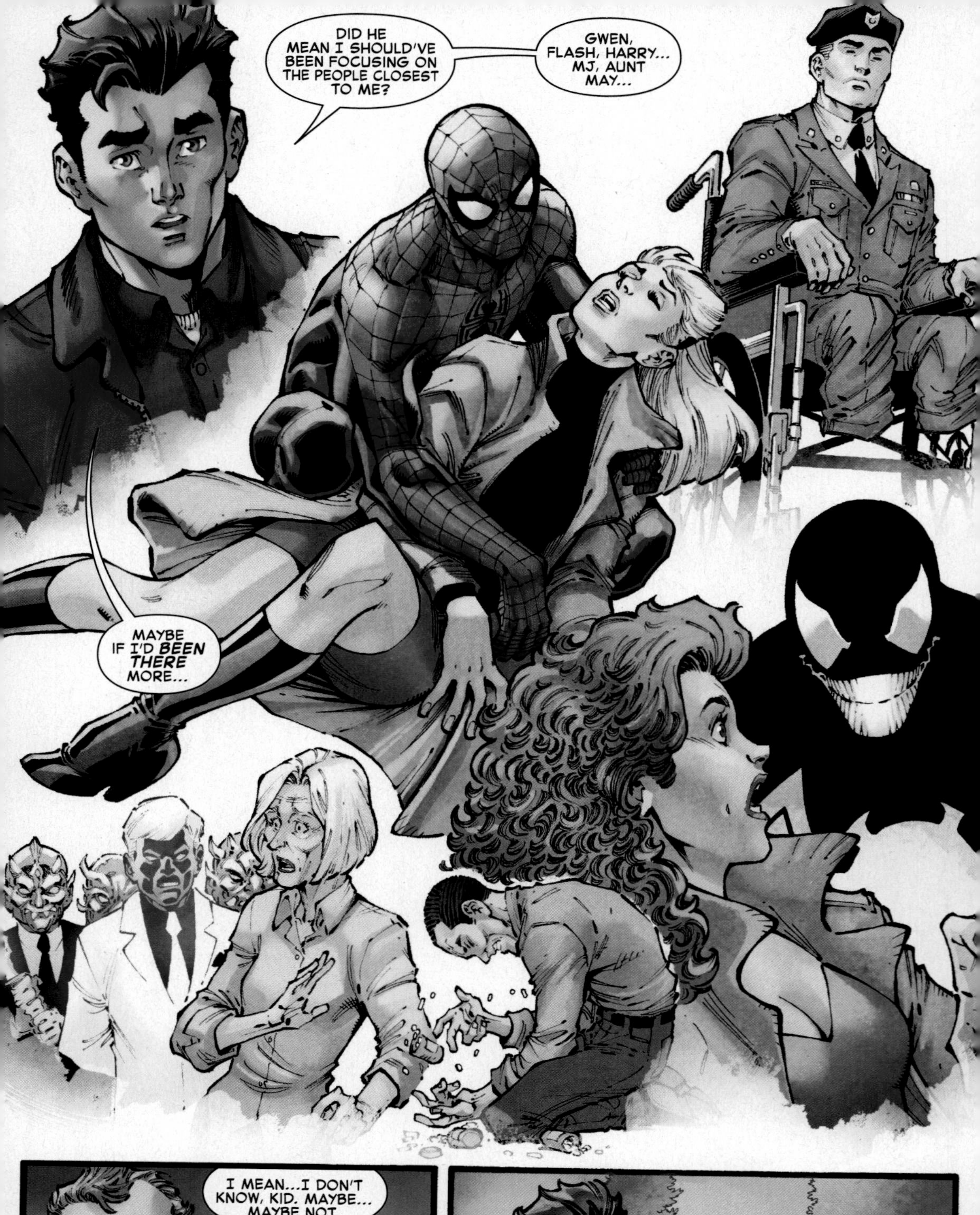

DID HE MEAN I SHOULD'VE BEEN FOCUSING ON THE PEOPLE CLOSEST TO ME?
GWEN, FLASH, HARRY... MJ, AUNT MAY...
MAYBE IF I'D BEEN THERE MORE...

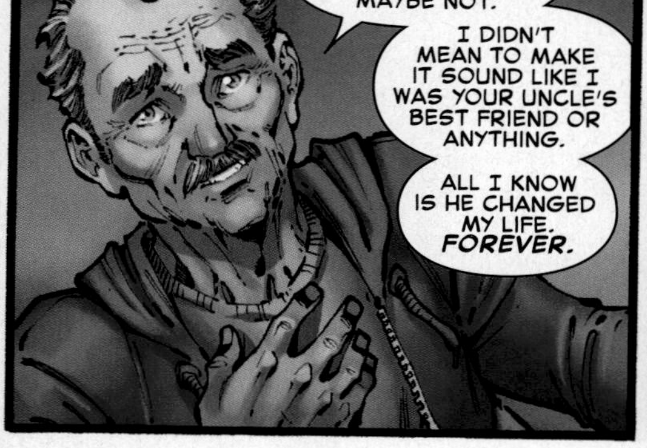

I MEAN...I DON'T KNOW, KID. MAYBE... MAYBE NOT.
I DIDN'T MEAN TO MAKE IT SOUND LIKE I WAS YOUR UNCLE'S BEST FRIEND OR ANYTHING.
ALL I KNOW IS HE CHANGED MY LIFE. FOREVER.

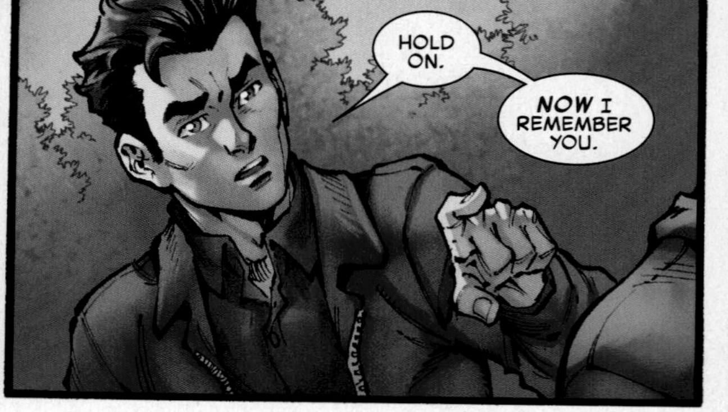

HOLD ON.
NOW I REMEMBER YOU.

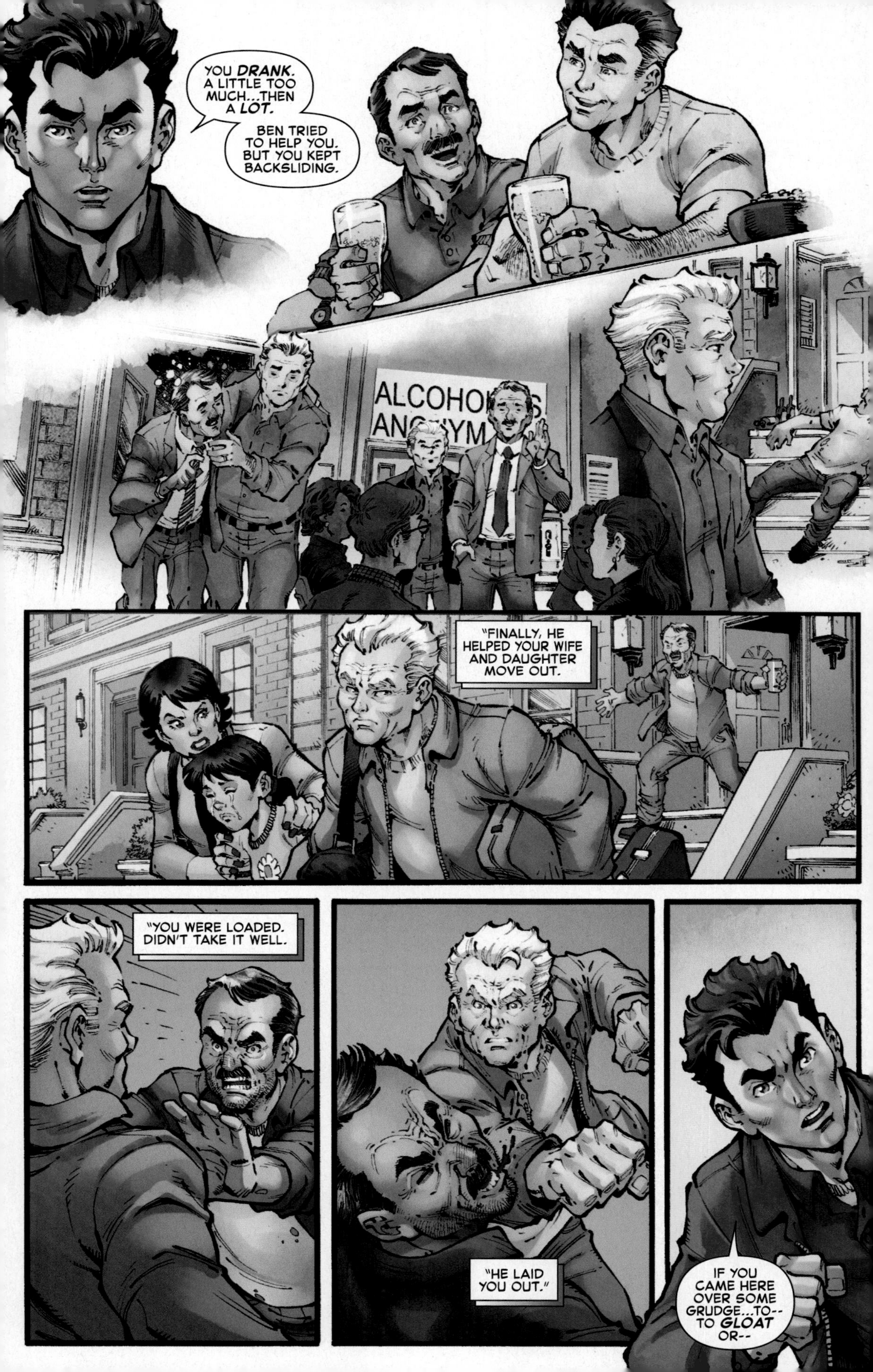

YOU DRANK. A LITTLE TOO MUCH...THEN A LOT.
BEN TRIED TO HELP YOU. BUT YOU KEPT BACKSLIDING.
ALCOHOL ANO YM
"FINALLY, HE HELPED YOUR WIFE AND DAUGHTER MOVE OUT.
"YOU WERE LOADED. DIDN'T TAKE IT WELL.
"HE LAID YOU OUT."
IF YOU CAME HERE OVER SOME GRUDGE...TO-- TO GLOAT OR--

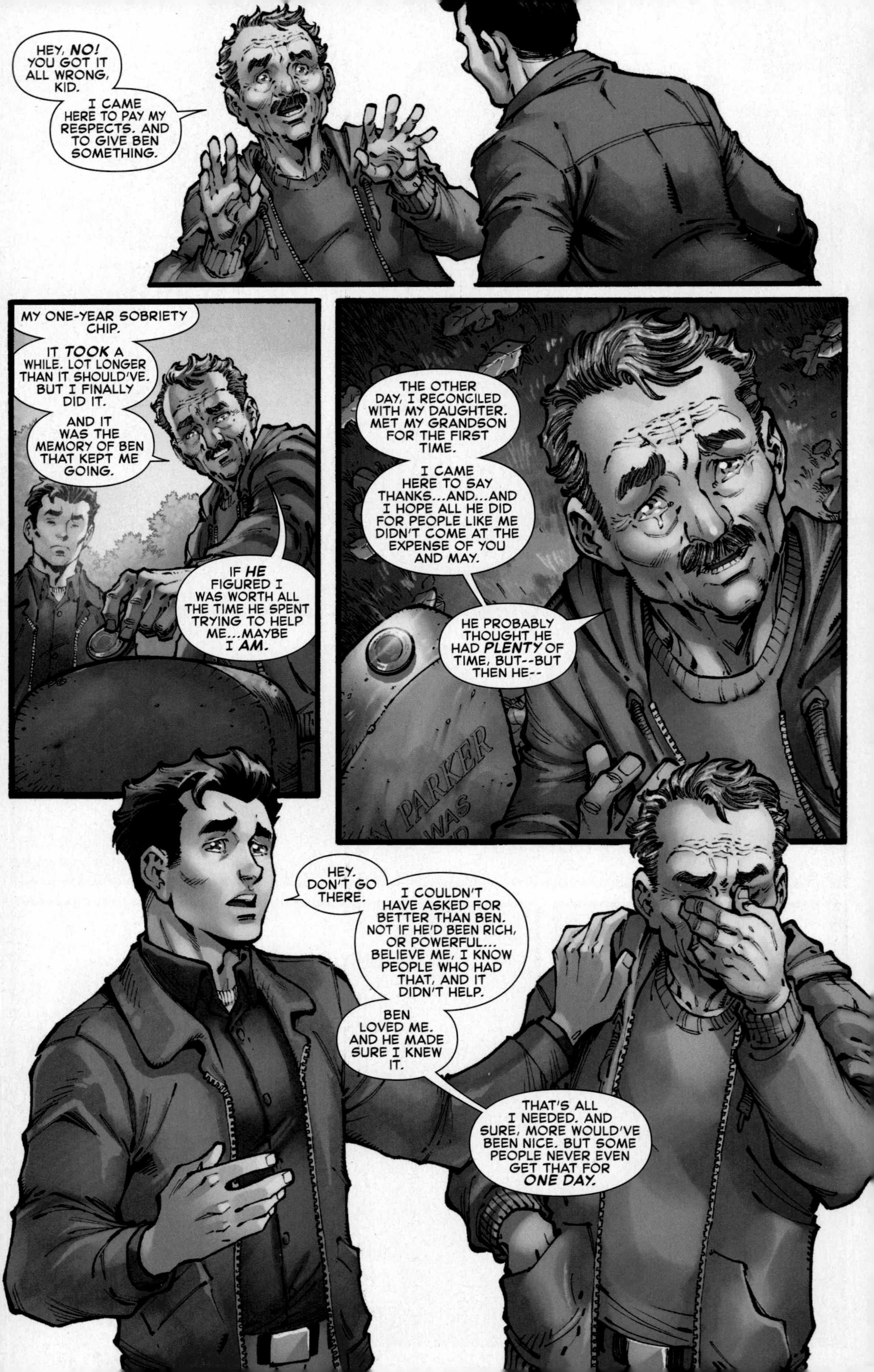
HEY, NO! YOU GOT IT ALL WRONG, KID.
I CAME HERE TO PAY MY RESPECTS. AND TO GIVE BEN SOMETHING.
MY ONE-YEAR SOBRIETY CHIP.
IT TOOK A WHILE. LOT LONGER THAN IT SHOULD'VE. BUT I FINALLY DID IT.
AND IT WAS THE MEMORY OF BEN THAT KEPT ME GOING.
IF HE FIGURED I WAS WORTH ALL THE TIME HE SPENT TRYING TO HELP ME...MAYBE I AM.
THE OTHER DAY, I RECONCILED WITH MY DAUGHTER. MET MY GRANDSON FOR THE FIRST TIME.
I CAME HERE TO SAY THANKS...AND...AND I HOPE ALL HE DID FOR PEOPLE LIKE ME DIDN'T COME AT THE EXPENSE OF YOU AND MAY.
HE PROBABLY THOUGHT HE HAD PLENTY OF TIME, BUT--BUT THEN HE--
PARKER
WAS
HEY. DON'T GO THERE.
I COULDN'T HAVE ASKED FOR BETTER THAN BEN. NOT IF HE'D BEEN RICH, OR POWERFUL... BELIEVE ME, I KNOW PEOPLE WHO HAD THAT, AND IT DIDN'T HELP.
BEN LOVED ME. AND HE MADE SURE I KNEW IT.
THAT'S ALL I NEEDED. AND SURE, MORE WOULD'VE BEEN NICE. BUT SOME PEOPLE NEVER EVEN GET THAT FOR ONE DAY.

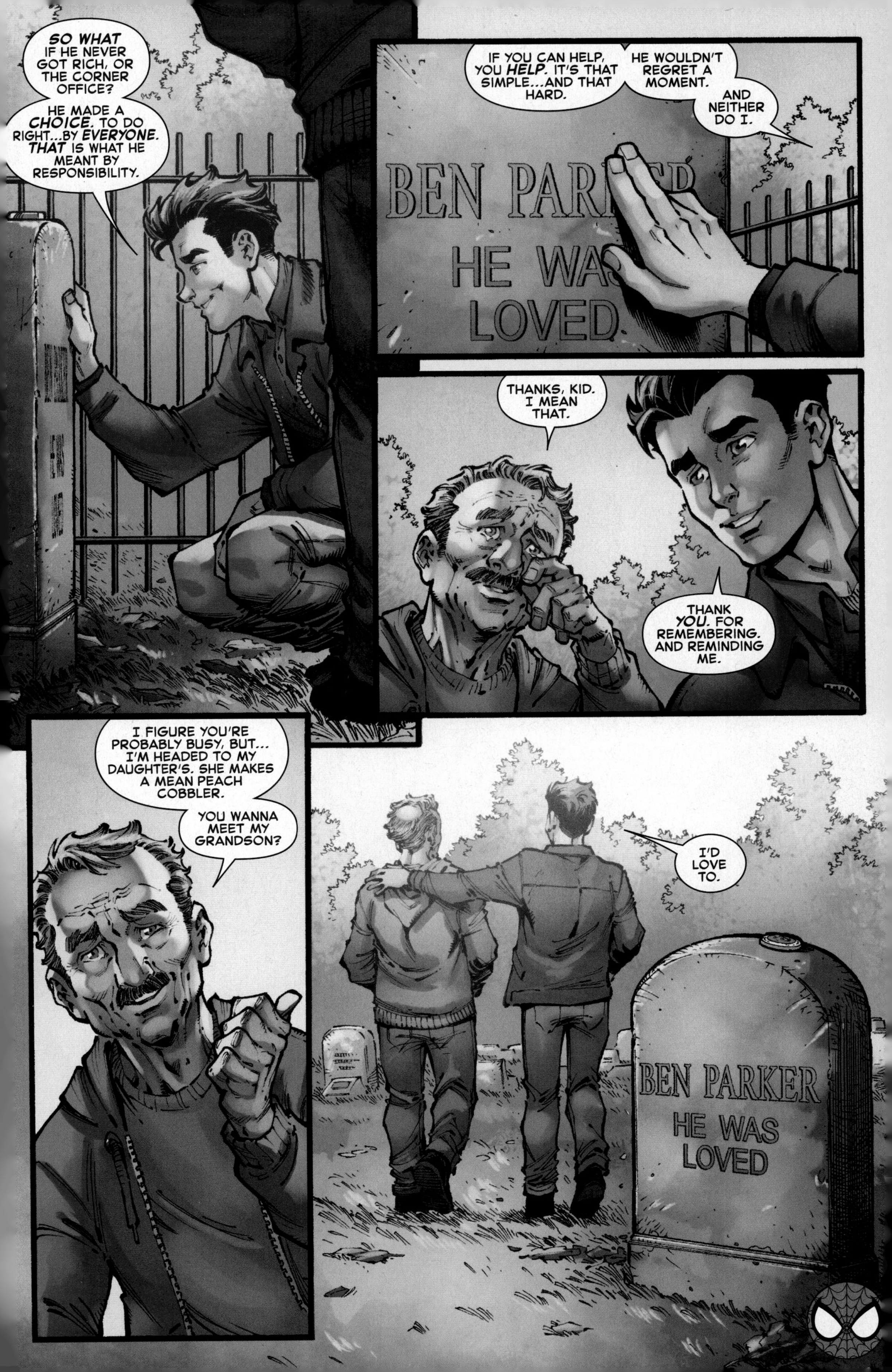
SO WHAT IF HE NEVER GOT RICH, OR THE CORNER OFFICE?
HE MADE A CHOICE. TO DO RIGHT...BY EVERYONE. THAT IS WHAT HE MEANT BY RESPONSIBILITY.
IF YOU CAN HELP, YOU HELP. IT'S THAT SIMPLE...AND THAT HARD.
HE WOULDN'T REGRET A MOMENT.
AND NEITHER DO I.
BEN PARKER
HE WAS LOVED.
THANKS, KID. I MEAN THAT.
THANK YOU. FOR REMEMBERING. AND REMINDING ME.
I FIGURE YOU'RE PROBABLY BUSY, BUT... I'M HEADED TO MY DAUGHTER'S. SHE MAKES A MEAN PEACH COBBLER.
YOU WANNA MEET MY GRANDSON?
I'D LOVE TO.
BEN PARKER
HE WAS LOVED

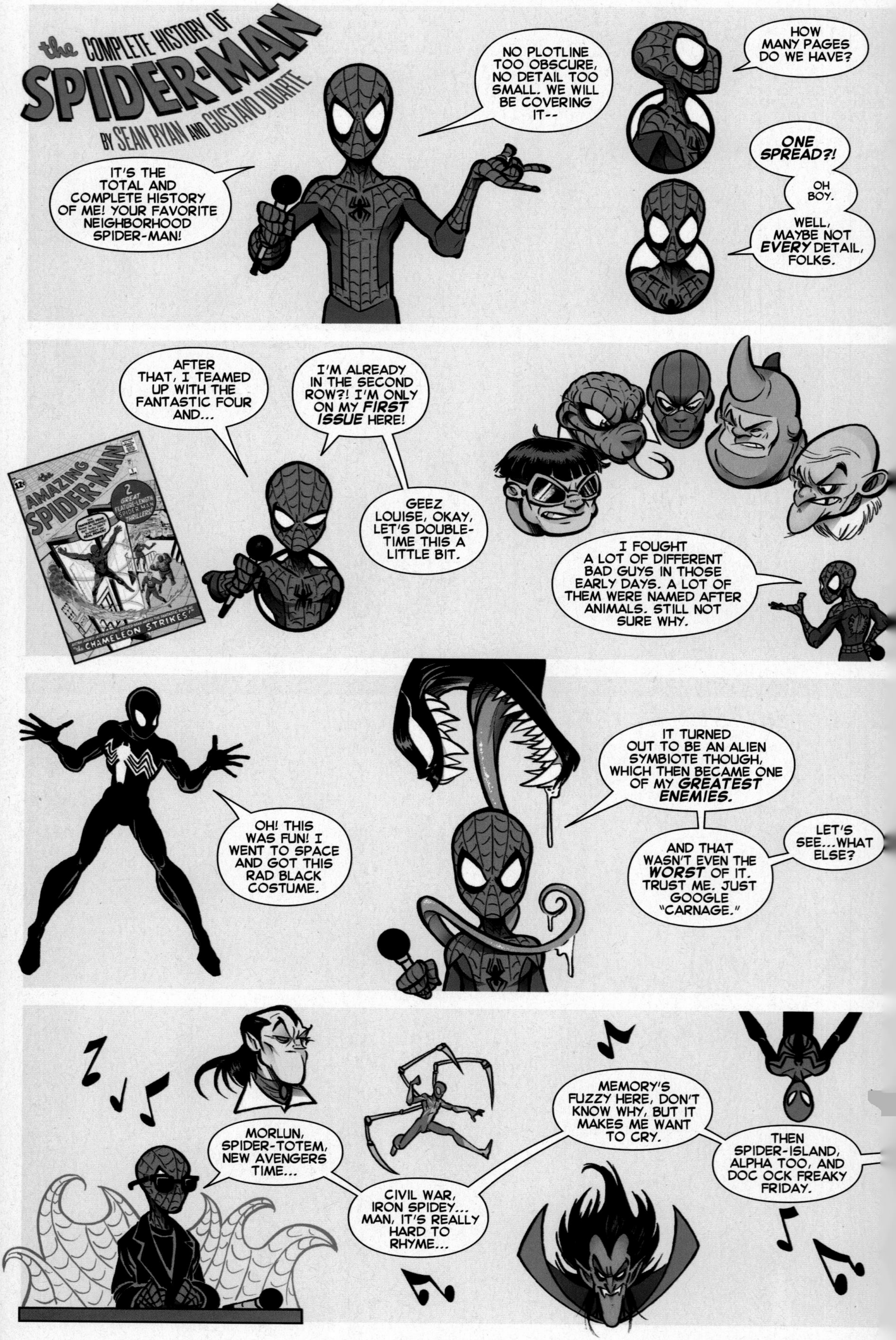

the COMPLETE HISTORY OF SPIDER-MAN
BY SEAN RYAN AND GUSTAVO DUARTE
IT'S THE TOTAL AND COMPLETE HISTORY OF ME! YOUR FAVORITE NEIGHBORHOOD SPIDER-MAN!
NO PLOTLINE TOO OBSCURE, NO DETAIL TOO SMALL. WE WILL BE COVERING IT--
HOW MANY PAGES DO WE HAVE?
ONE SPREAD?!
OH BOY.
WELL, MAYBE NOT EVERY DETAIL, FOLKS.
the AMAZING SPIDER-MAN
2 GREAT FEATURE-LENGTH SPIDER-MAN THRILLERS!
"the CHAMELEON STRIKES!"
AFTER THAT, I TEAMED UP WITH THE FANTASTIC FOUR AND...
I'M ALREADY IN THE SECOND ROW?! I'M ONLY ON MY FIRST ISSUE HERE!
GEEZ LOUISE, OKAY, LET'S DOUBLE-TIME THIS A LITTLE BIT.
I FOUGHT A LOT OF DIFFERENT BAD GUYS IN THOSE EARLY DAYS. A LOT OF THEM WERE NAMED AFTER ANIMALS. STILL NOT SURE WHY.
OH! THIS WAS FUN! I WENT TO SPACE AND GOT THIS RAD BLACK COSTUME.
IT TURNED OUT TO BE AN ALIEN SYMBIOTE THOUGH, WHICH THEN BECAME ONE OF MY GREATEST ENEMIES.
AND THAT WASN'T EVEN THE WORST OF IT. TRUST ME. JUST GOOGLE "CARNAGE."
LET'S SEE...WHAT ELSE?
MORLUN, SPIDER-TOTEM, NEW AVENGERS TIME...
CIVIL WAR, IRON SPIDEY... MAN, IT'S REALLY HARD TO RHYME...
MEMORY'S FUZZY HERE, DON'T KNOW WHY, BUT IT MAKES ME WANT TO CRY.
THEN SPIDER-ISLAND, ALPHA TOO, AND DOC OCK FREAKY FRIDAY.

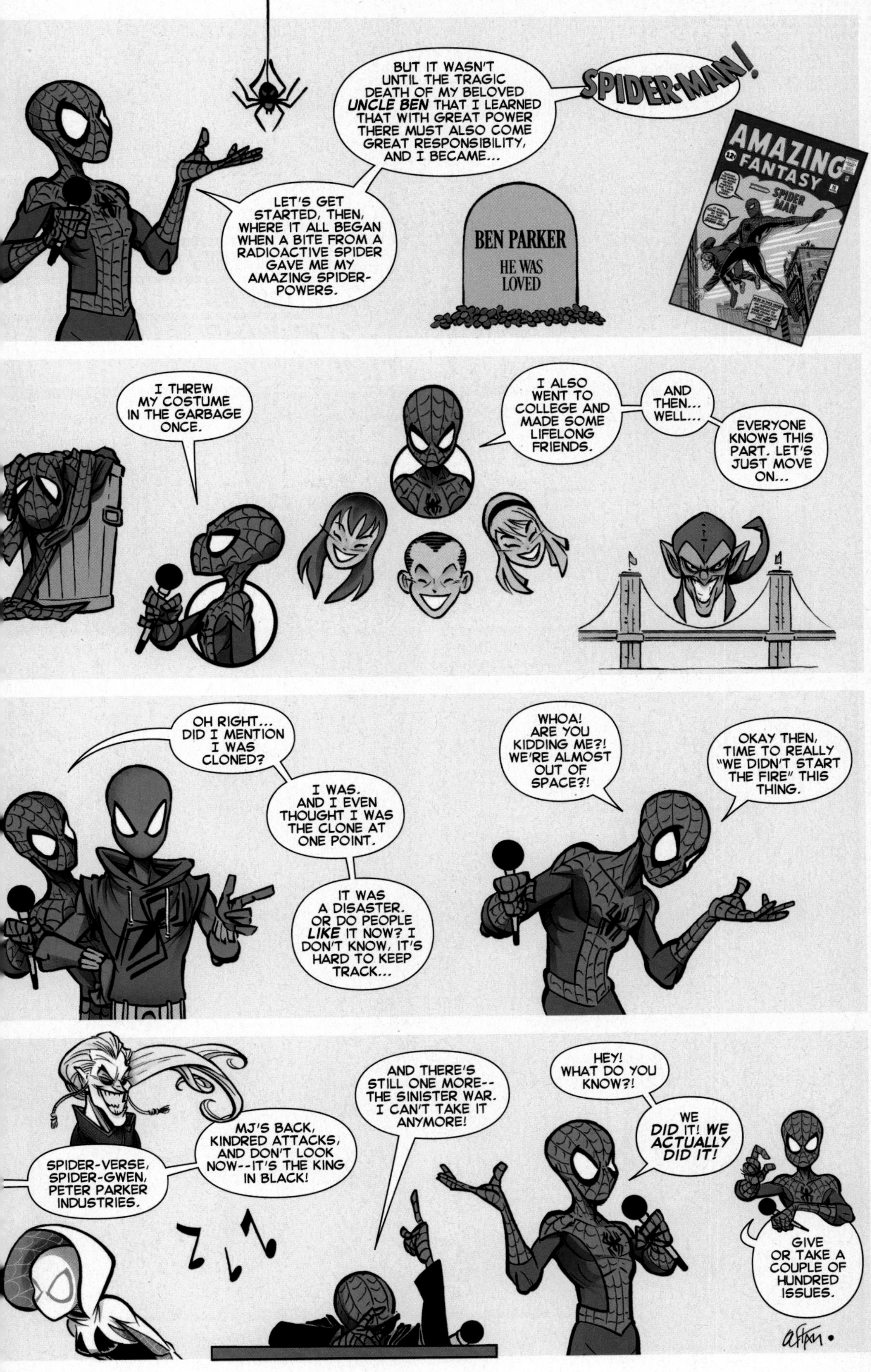
LET'S GET STARTED, THEN, WHERE IT ALL BEGAN WHEN A BITE FROM A RADIOACTIVE SPIDER GAVE ME MY AMAZING SPIDER-POWERS.
BUT IT WASN'T UNTIL THE TRAGIC DEATH OF MY BELOVED UNCLE BEN THAT I LEARNED THAT WITH GREAT POWER THERE MUST ALSO COME GREAT RESPONSIBILITY, AND I BECAME...
SPIDER-MAN!
BEN PARKER
HE WAS LOVED
AMAZING FANTASY
SPIDER MAN
I THREW MY COSTUME IN THE GARBAGE ONCE.
I ALSO WENT TO COLLEGE AND MADE SOME LIFELONG FRIENDS.
AND THEN... WELL...
EVERYONE KNOWS THIS PART. LET'S JUST MOVE ON...
OH RIGHT... DID I MENTION I WAS CLONED?
I WAS. AND I EVEN THOUGHT I WAS THE CLONE AT ONE POINT.
IT WAS A DISASTER. OR DO PEOPLE LIKE IT NOW? I DON'T KNOW, IT'S HARD TO KEEP TRACK...
WHOA! ARE YOU KIDDING ME?! WE'RE ALMOST OUT OF SPACE?!
OKAY THEN, TIME TO REALLY "WE DIDN'T START THE FIRE" THIS THING.
SPIDER-VERSE, SPIDER-GWEN, PETER PARKER INDUSTRIES.
MJ'S BACK, KINDRED ATTACKS, AND DON'T LOOK NOW--IT'S THE KING IN BLACK!
AND THERE'S STILL ONE MORE--THE SINISTER WAR. I CAN'T TAKE IT ANYMORE!
HEY! WHAT DO YOU KNOW?!
WE DID IT! WE ACTUALLY DID IT!
GIVE OR TAKE A COUPLE OF HUNDRED ISSUES.

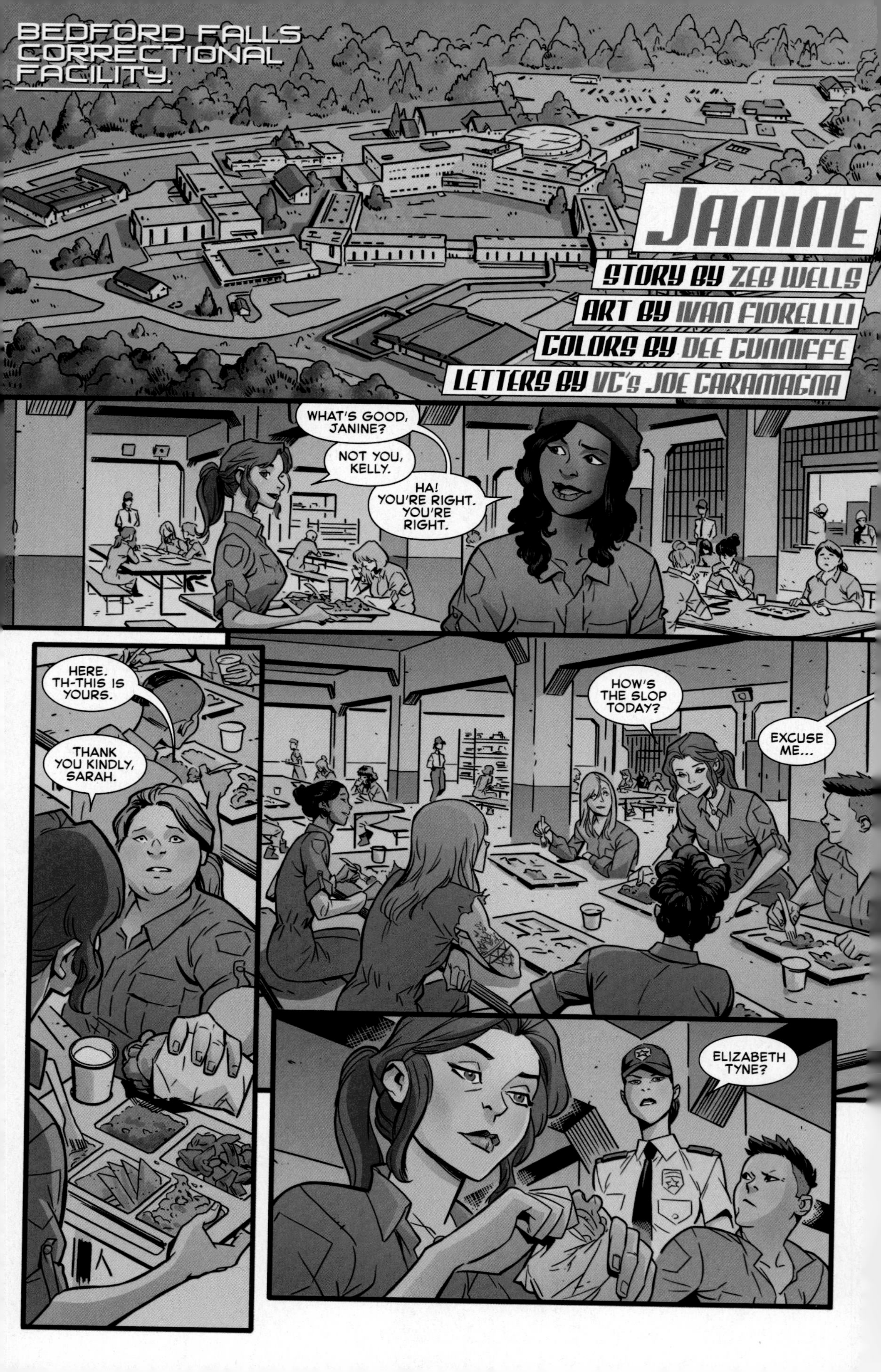

BEDFORD FALLS CORRECTIONAL FACILITY.
JANINE
STORY BY ZEB WELLS
ART BY IVAN FIORELLI
COLORS BY DEE CUNNIFFE
LETTERS BY VC's JOE CARAMAGNA
WHAT'S GOOD, JANINE?
NOT YOU, KELLY.
HA! YOU'RE RIGHT. YOU'RE RIGHT.
HERE. TH-THIS IS YOURS.
THANK YOU KINDLY, SARAH.
HOW'S THE SLOP TODAY?
EXCUSE ME...
ELIZABETH TYNE?

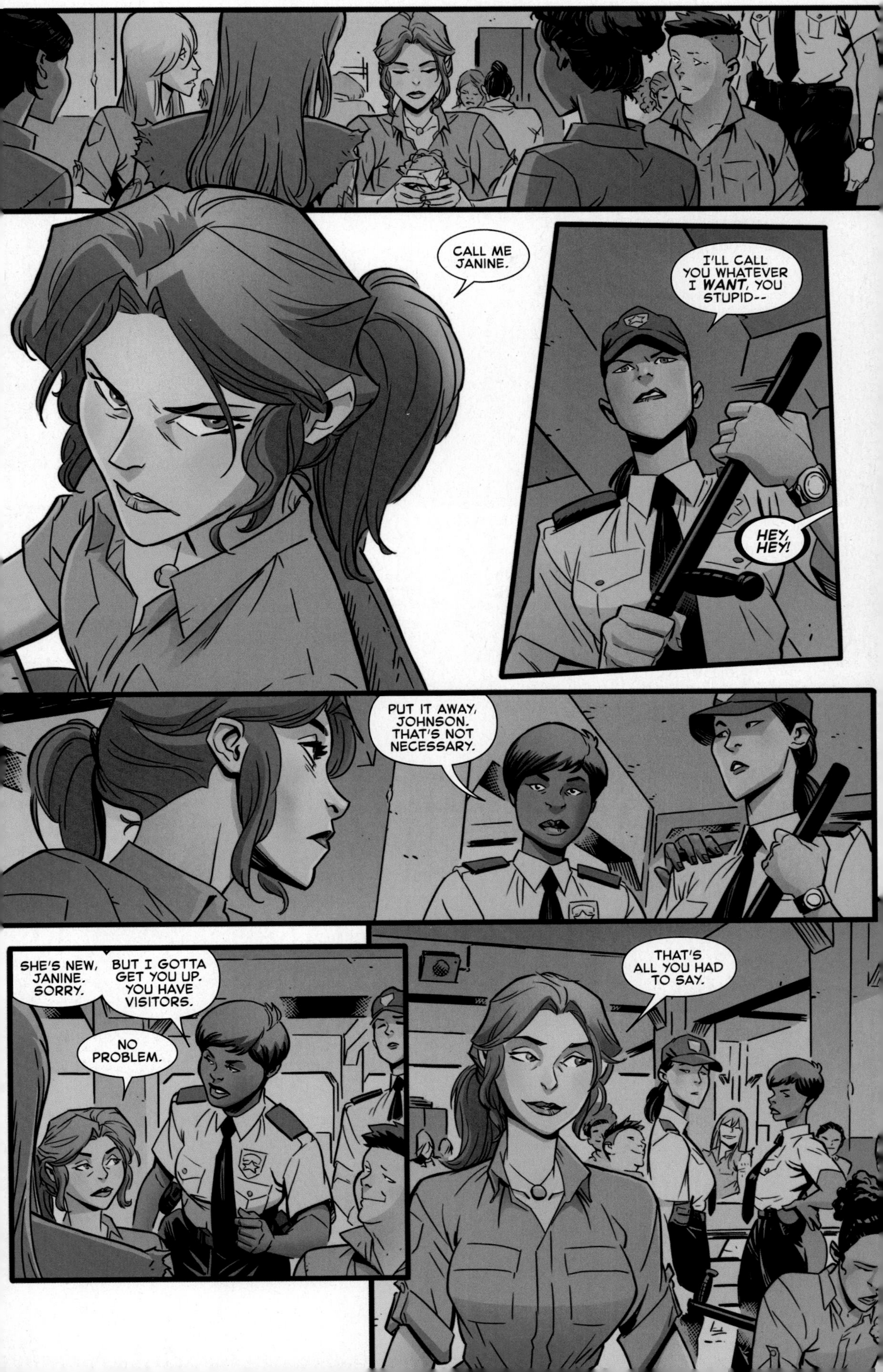
CALL ME JANINE.
I'LL CALL YOU WHATEVER I WANT, YOU STUPID--
HEY, HEY!
PUT IT AWAY, JOHNSON. THAT'S NOT NECESSARY.
SHE'S NEW, JANINE. SORRY.
BUT I GOTTA GET YOU UP. YOU HAVE VISITORS.
NO PROBLEM.
THAT'S ALL YOU HAD TO SAY.

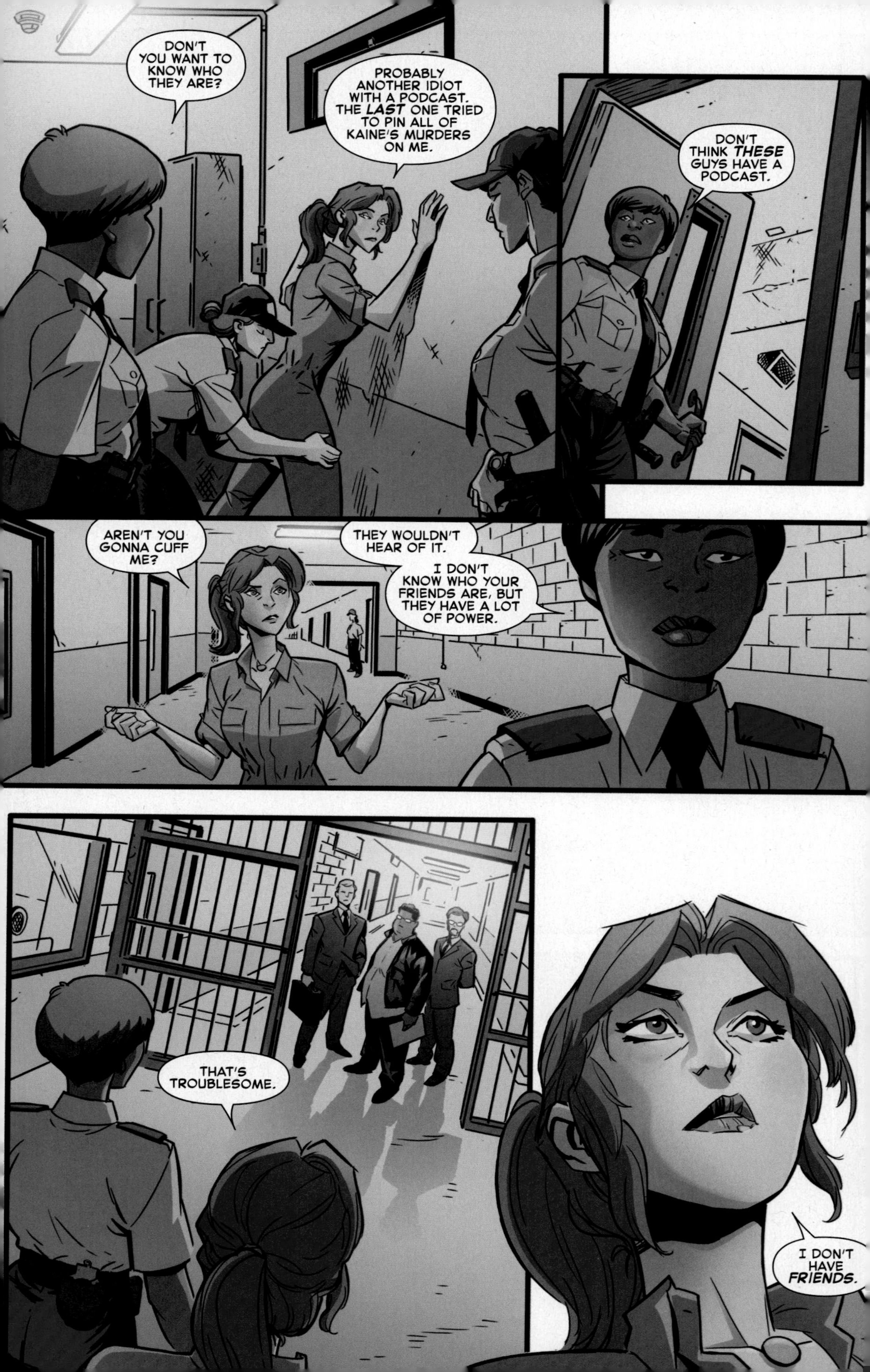
DON'T YOU WANT TO KNOW WHO THEY ARE?
PROBABLY ANOTHER IDIOT WITH A PODCAST. THE LAST ONE TRIED TO PIN ALL OF KAINE'S MURDERS ON ME.
DON'T THINK THESE GUYS HAVE A PODCAST.
AREN'T YOU GONNA CUFF ME?
THEY WOULDN'T HEAR OF IT.
I DON'T KNOW WHO YOUR FRIENDS ARE, BUT THEY HAVE A LOT OF POWER.
THAT'S TROUBLESOME.
I DON'T HAVE FRIENDS.

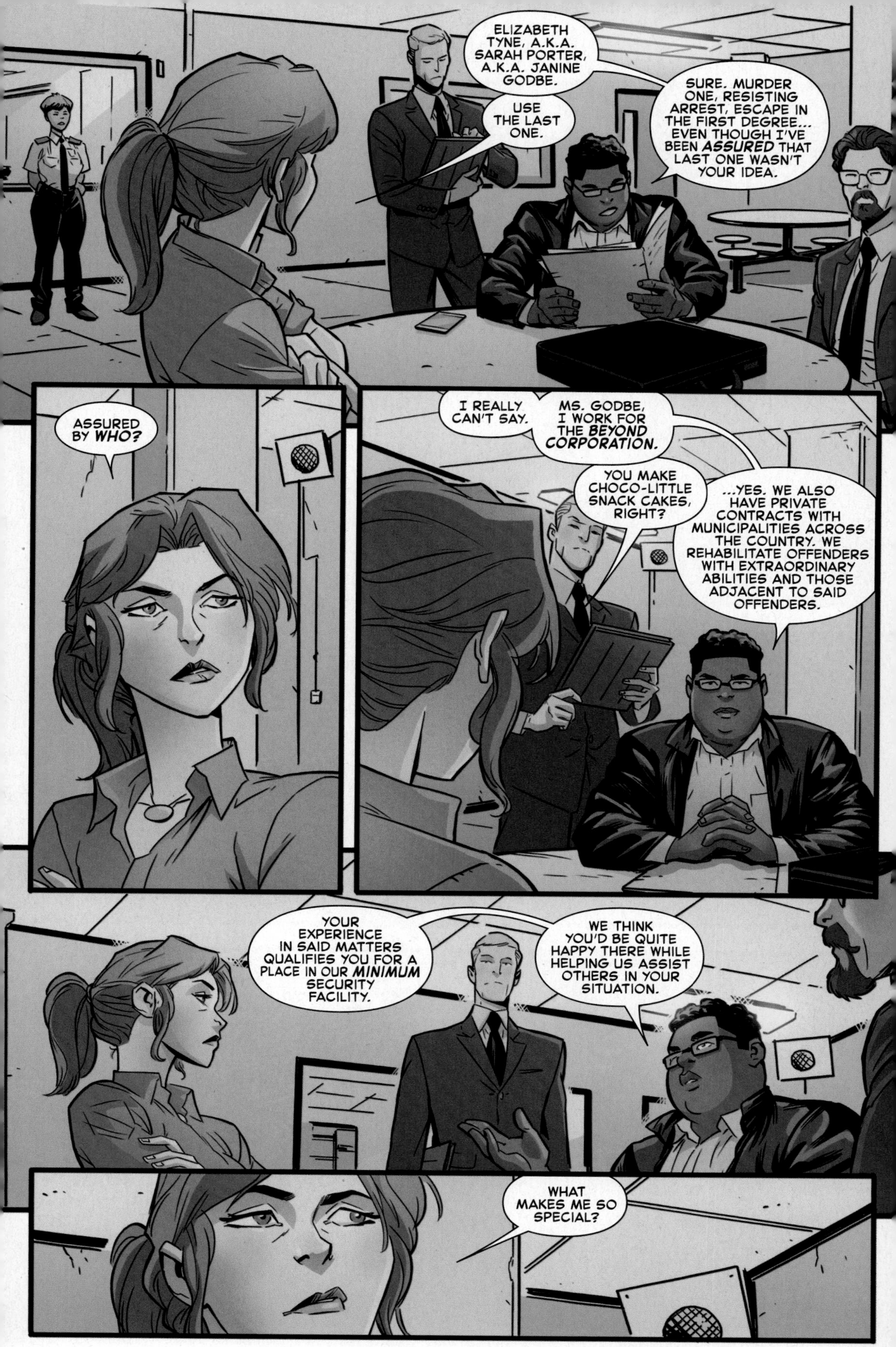
ELIZABETH TYNE, A.K.A. SARAH PORTER, A.K.A. JANINE GODBE.
USE THE LAST ONE.
SURE. MURDER ONE, RESISTING ARREST, ESCAPE IN THE FIRST DEGREE... EVEN THOUGH I'VE BEEN *ASSURED* THAT LAST ONE WASN'T YOUR IDEA.
ASSURED BY *WHO?*
I REALLY CAN'T SAY.
MS. GODBE, I WORK FOR THE *BEYOND CORPORATION.*
YOU MAKE CHOCO-LITTLE SNACK CAKES, RIGHT?
...YES. WE ALSO HAVE PRIVATE CONTRACTS WITH MUNICIPALITIES ACROSS THE COUNTRY. WE REHABILITATE OFFENDERS WITH EXTRAORDINARY ABILITIES AND THOSE ADJACENT TO SAID OFFENDERS.
YOUR EXPERIENCE IN SAID MATTERS QUALIFIES YOU FOR A PLACE IN OUR *MINIMUM* SECURITY FACILITY.
WE THINK YOU'D BE QUITE HAPPY THERE WHILE HELPING US ASSIST OTHERS IN YOUR SITUATION.
WHAT MAKES ME SO SPECIAL?

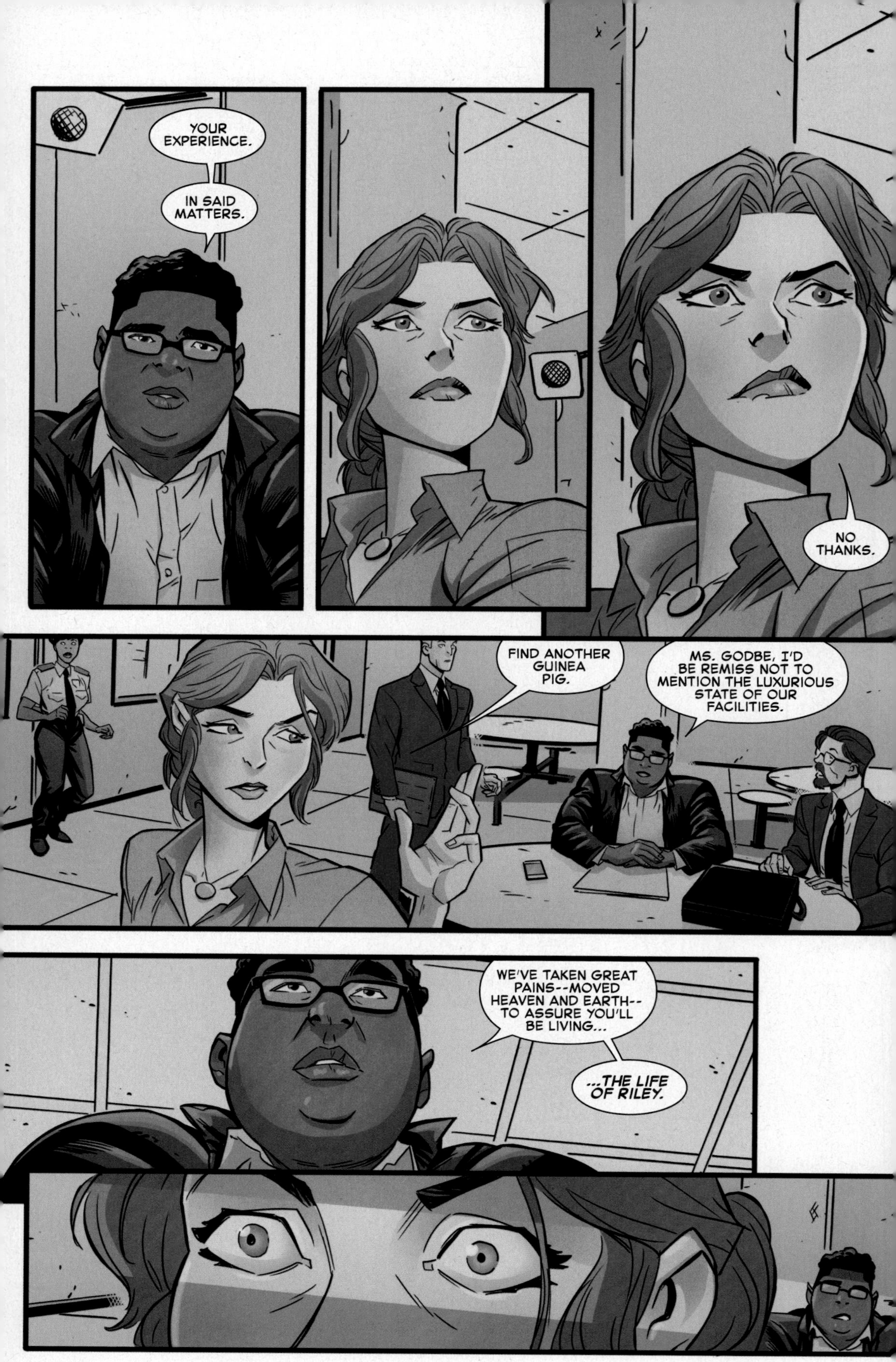
YOUR EXPERIENCE.
IN SAID MATTERS.
NO THANKS.
FIND ANOTHER GUINEA PIG.
MS. GODBE, I'D BE REMISS NOT TO MENTION THE LUXURIOUS STATE OF OUR FACILITIES.
WE'VE TAKEN GREAT PAINS--MOVED HEAVEN AND EARTH--TO ASSURE YOU'LL BE LIVING...
...THE LIFE OF RILEY.

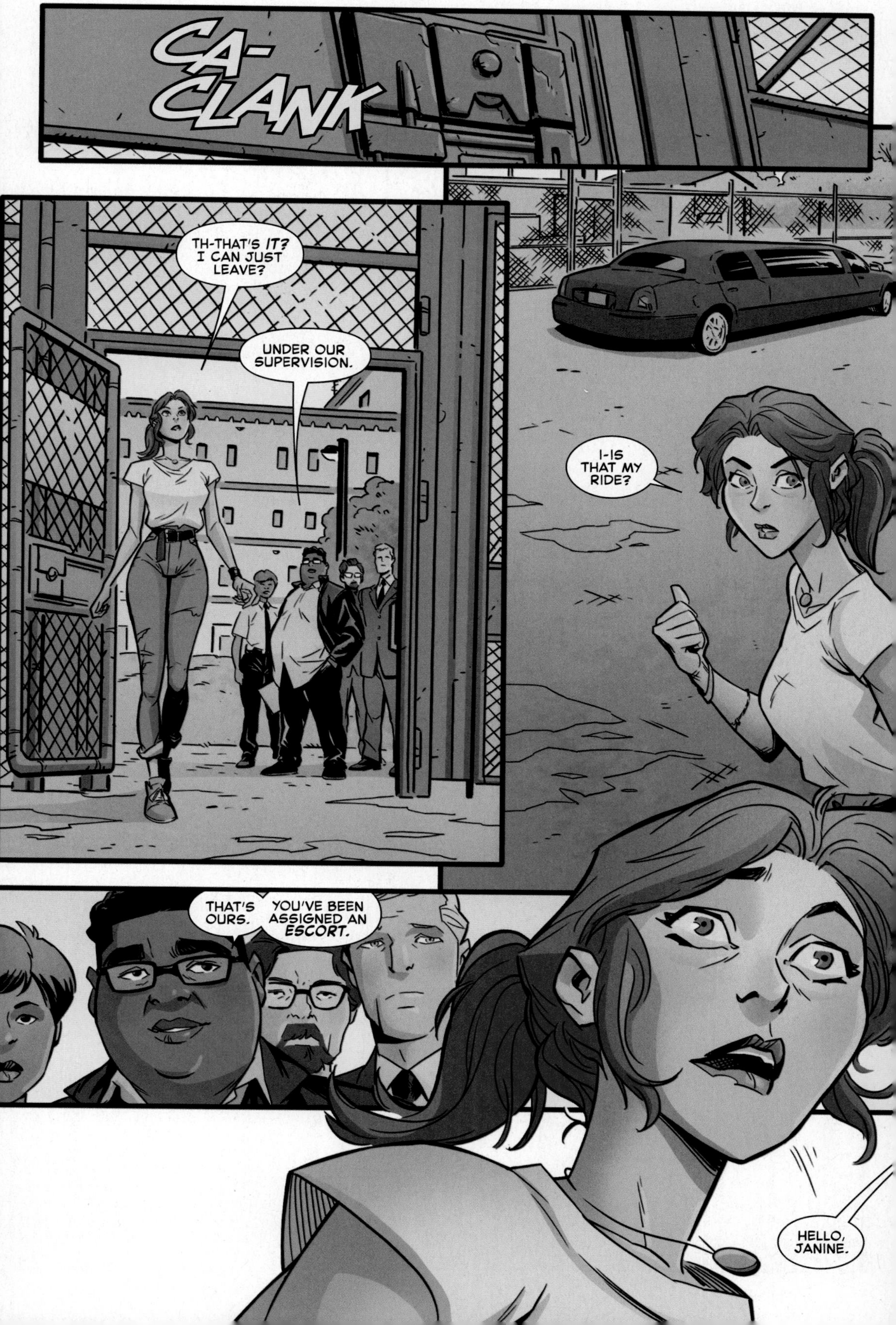
CA-CLANK
TH-THAT'S IT? I CAN JUST LEAVE?
UNDER OUR SUPERVISION.
I-IS THAT MY RIDE?
THAT'S OURS.
YOU'VE BEEN ASSIGNED AN ESCORT.
HELLO, JANINE.

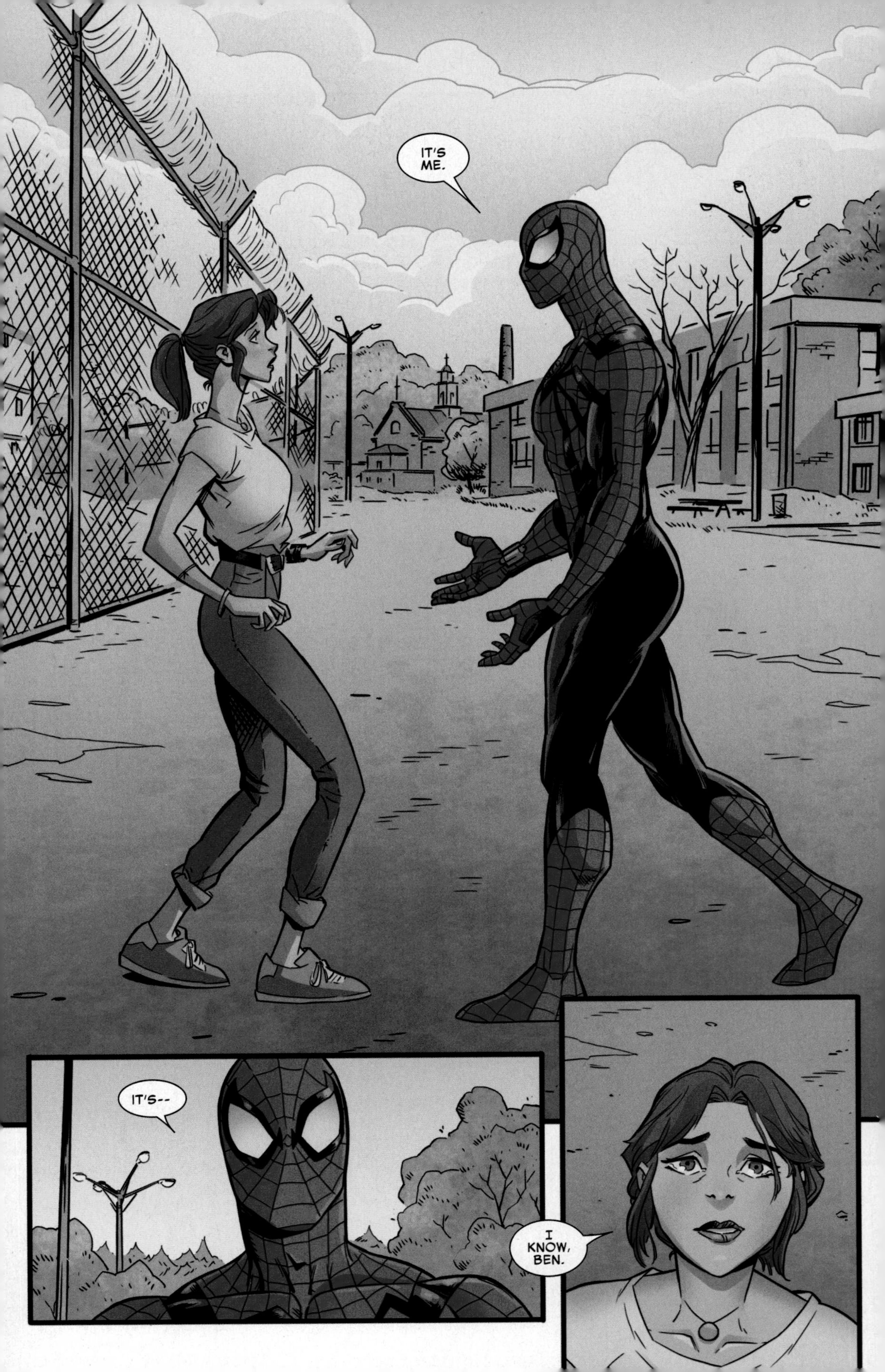
IT'S ME.
IT'S--
I KNOW, BEN.

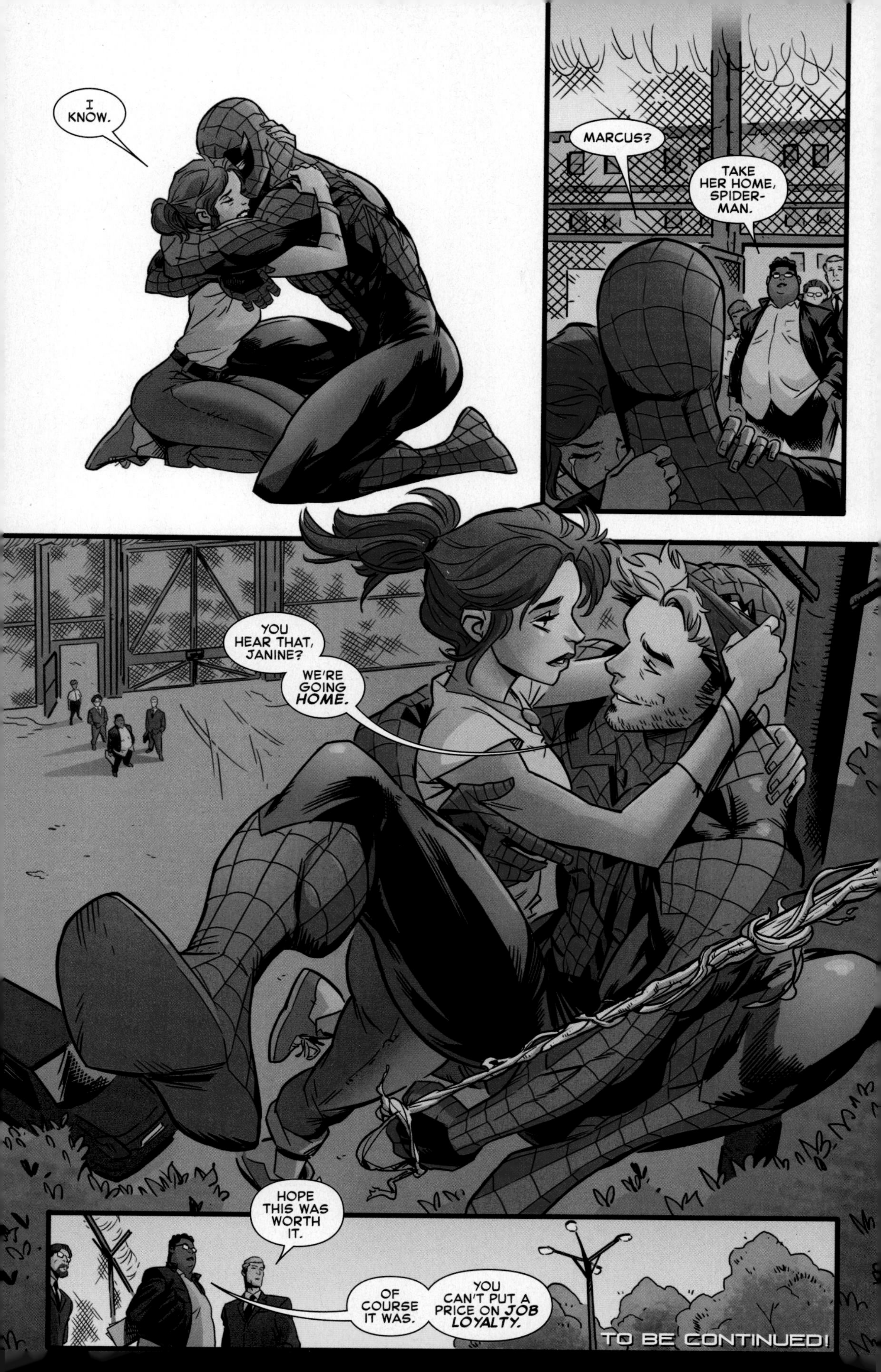

I KNOW.
MARCUS?
TAKE HER HOME, SPIDER-MAN.
YOU HEAR THAT, JANINE?
WE'RE GOING HOME.
HOPE THIS WAS WORTH IT.
OF COURSE IT WAS.
YOU CAN'T PUT A PRICE ON JOB LOYALTY.
TO BE CONTINUED!

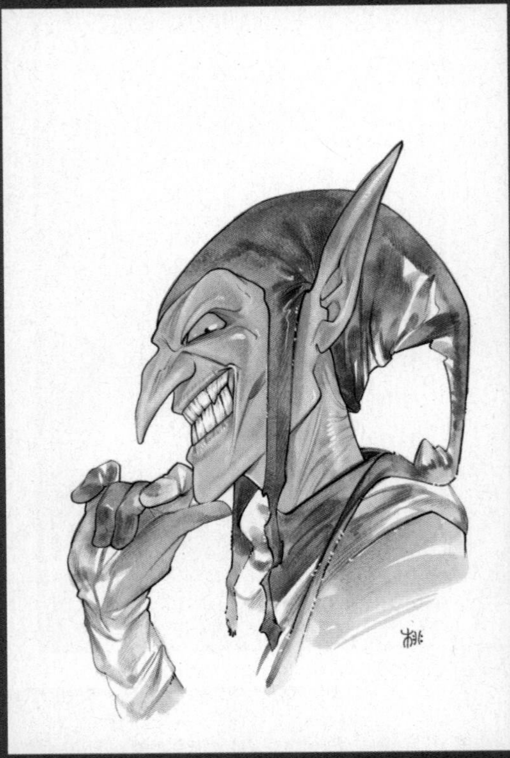

#70 ANIME VARIANT BY
PEACH MOMOKO

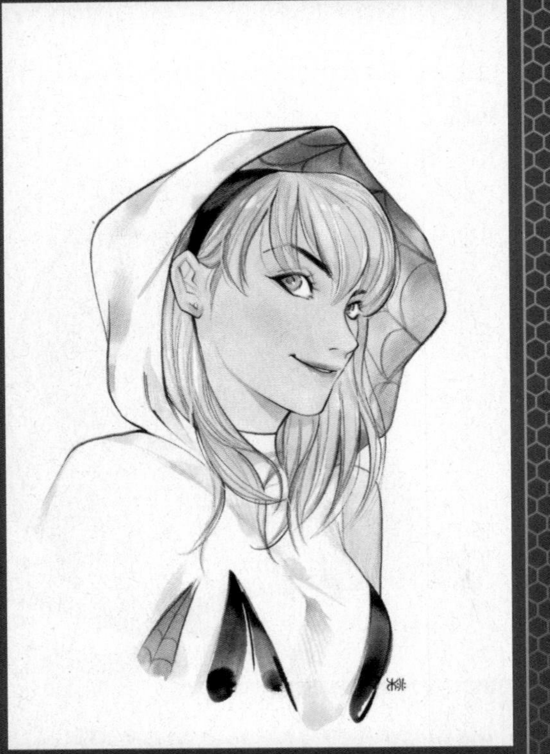

#71 ANIME VARIANT BY
PEACH MOMOKO

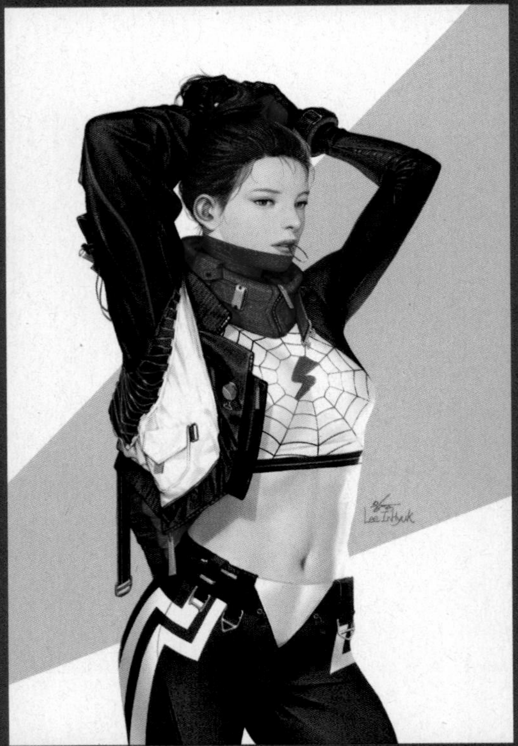

#72 SILK ASIAN VOICES VARIANT BY
INHYUK LEE

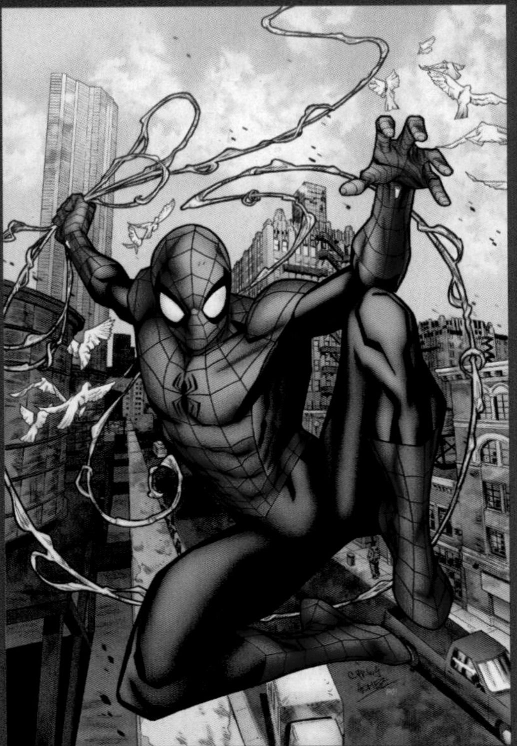

#74 VARIANT BY
CARLOS GÓMEZ & MORRY HOLLOWELL

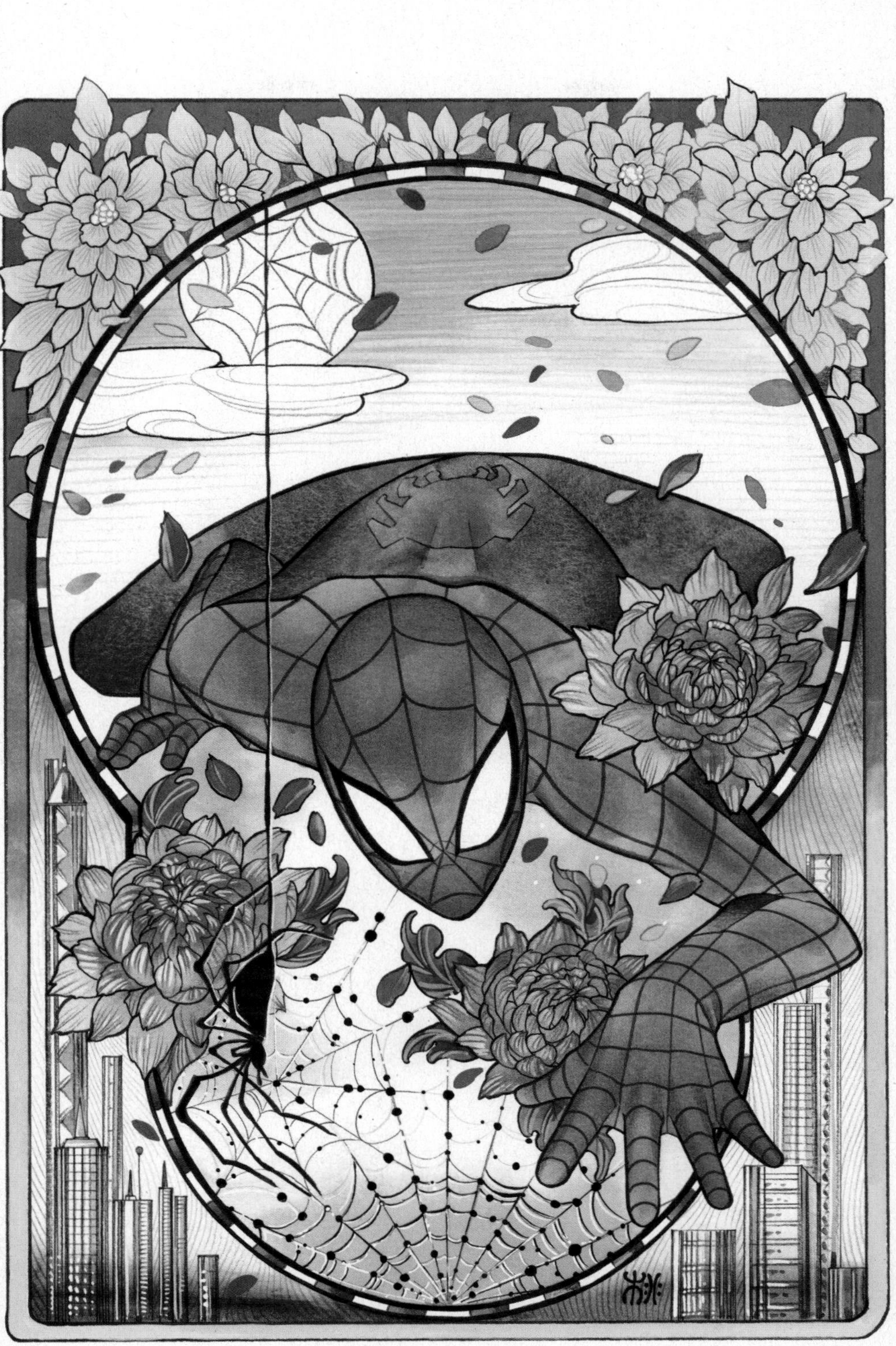

#74 VARIANT BY PEACH MOMOKO

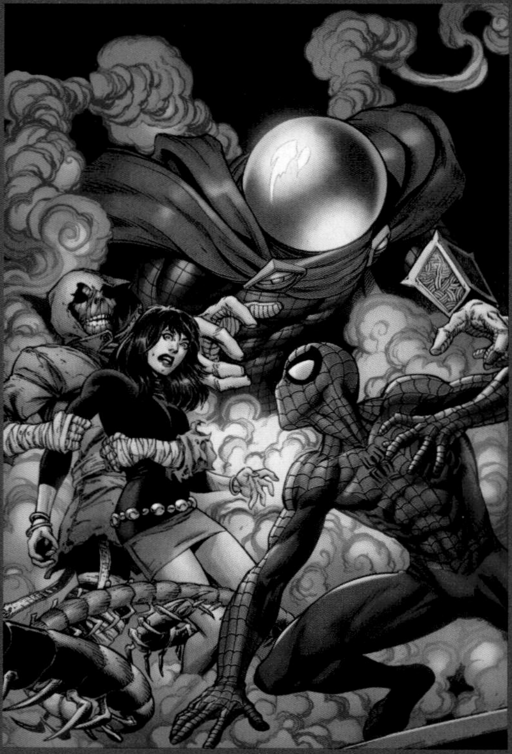

#74 VARIANT BY
MARK BAGLEY, JOHN DELL & BRIAN REBER

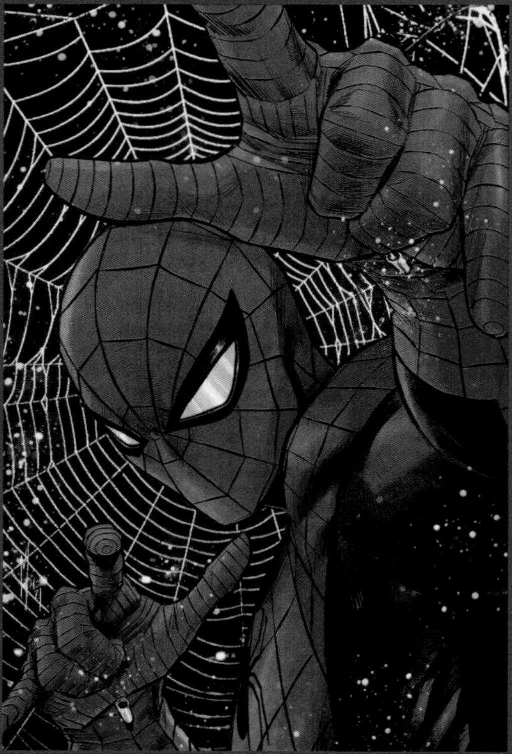

#74 VARIANT BY
MARCO CHECCHETTO

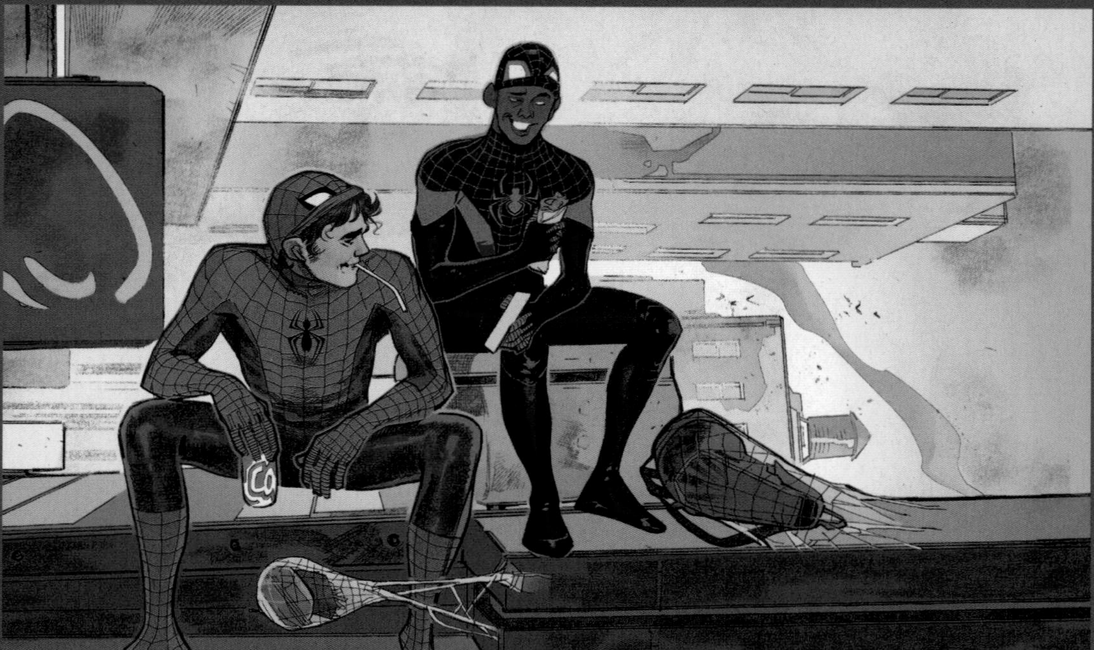

#74 VARIANT BY
SARA PICHELLI & TAMRA BONVILLAIN

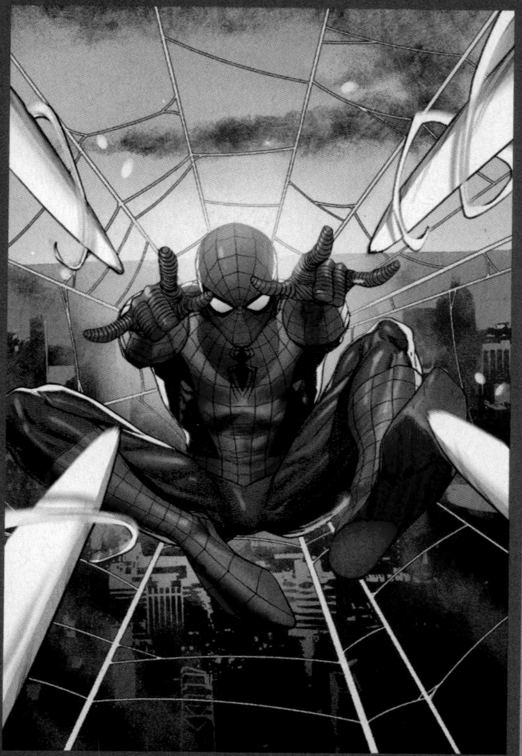

#74 VARIANT BY
LEINIL FRANCIS YU & SUNNY GHO

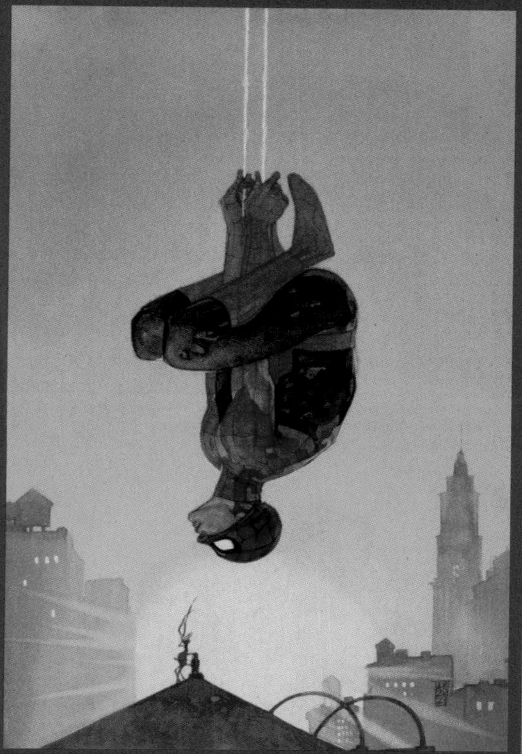

#74 VARIANT BY
ALEX MALEEV

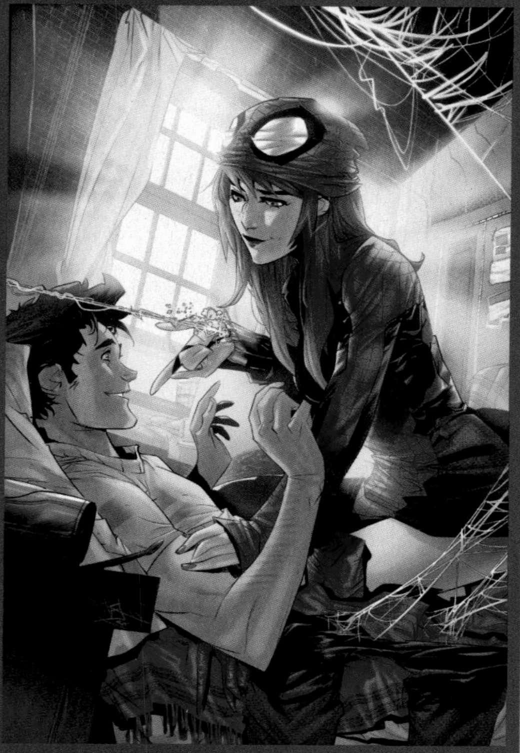

#74 VARIANT BY
FEDERICO VICENTINI & ALEX SINCLAIR

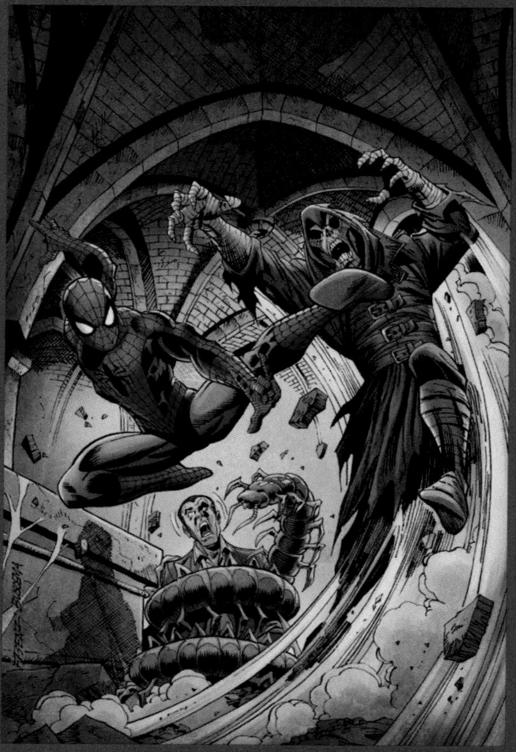

#74 VARIANT BY
RON FRENZ, SAL BUSCEMA & JIM CAMPBELL

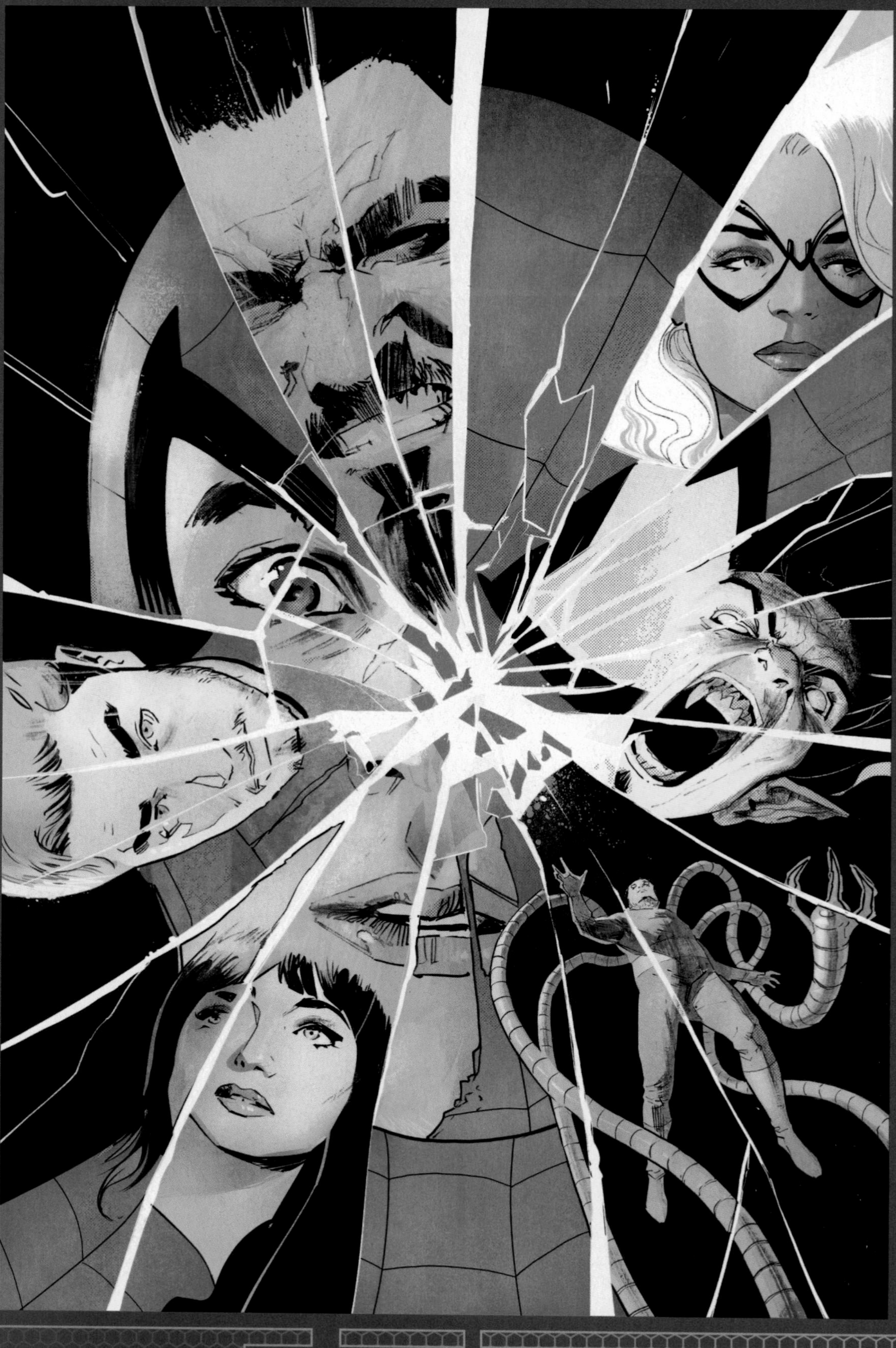

#74 FORESHADOW VARIANT BY MICHAEL DOWLING

DOCTOR OCTOPUS

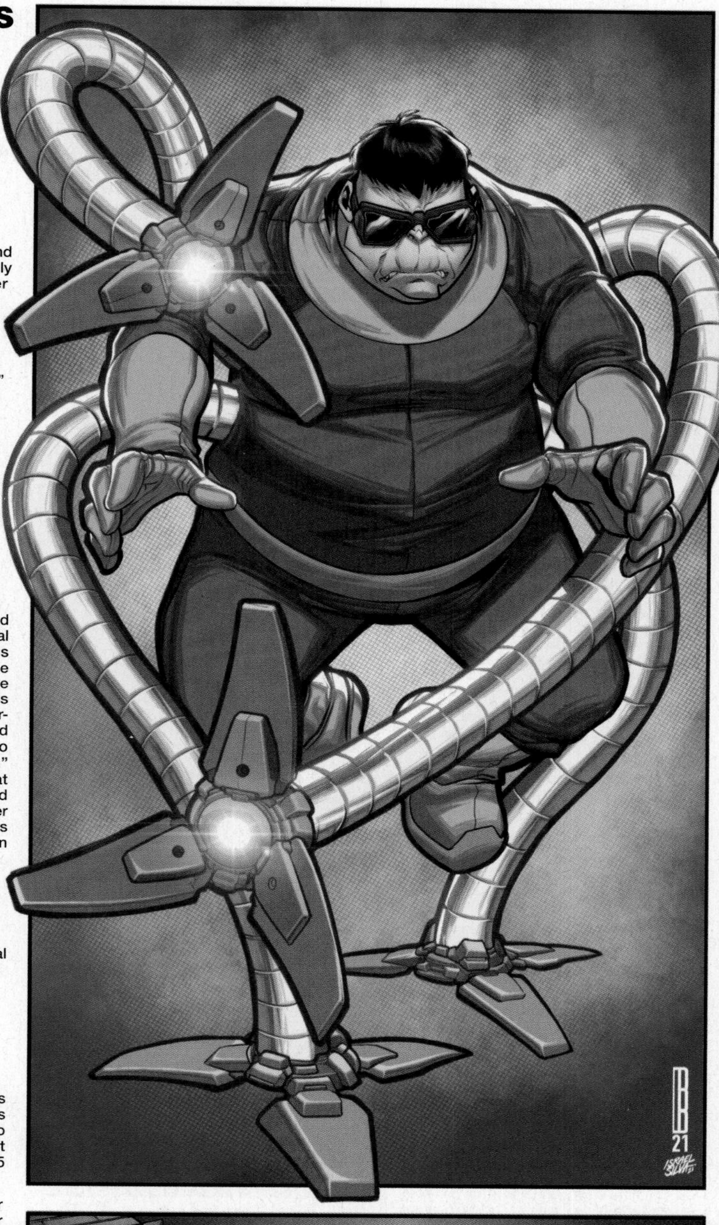

Real name: Otto Gunther Octavius

Occupation: Criminal mastermind, ex-atomic research consultant

Legal status: Citizen of the United States with a criminal record

Identity: Publicly known

Place of birth: Schenectady, New York

First appearance and origin: AMAZING SPIDER-MAN (1963) #3

History: Despite an overbearing mother and a bullying father, Otto Octavius eventually became a brilliant atomic researcher who used four mechanical tentacles to safely handle radioactive materials. When a laboratory accident left him with irreversible brain damage and the ability to mentally control the tentacles, the now-megalomaniacal "Doctor Octopus" sought to amass power and wealth through criminal means. Operating briefly as the Master Planner, Doctor Octopus battled many superhuman heroes on his own and with the Sinister Six, but Spider-Man (Peter Parker) became his predominant foe. During a later battle, bystander and NYPD Captain George Stacy (father of Parker's girlfriend, Gwen) was killed by falling debris, solidifying the animosity between Spider-Man and Octavius. When Parker's Aunt May inherited an island with a uranium mine, Octavius tried to marry May to obtain it, unaware of her relation to Spider-Man. When the island was destroyed during a battle between Octavius, his rival Hammerhead, and Spider-Man, Octavius abandoned his marital plans. Later, while dying of a neurodegenerative disease after years of combat injuries, Octavius technologically swapped minds with Spider-Man, but Parker's lingering memories and goodness ultimately inspired Octavius to fight evil as the "Superior Spider-Man." Eventually, Octavius came to realize that Parker was the better hero and relinquished control of Spider-Man's body to him. After downloading a copy of his consciousness into the robotic Living Brain, Octavius then transferred into a clone synthesis of Peter Parker and Octavius. Octavius later struck a bargain with the demonic Mephisto to return to his Doctor Octopus body and mind so he could better understand and defeat another criminal mastermind. Whether Octavius will resume his criminal endeavors remains to be seen.

Height: 5'9"

Weight: 245 lbs.

Eyes: Brown

Hair: Brown

Strength level: Doctor Octopus possesses the normal human strength of a man his age, height, and build who engages in no regular exercise. Each tentacle can lift approximately 8 tons and grip with 175 pounds per square inch.

Known superhuman powers: Doctor Octopus can psionically control his four tentacles and "feel" basic sensations with them.

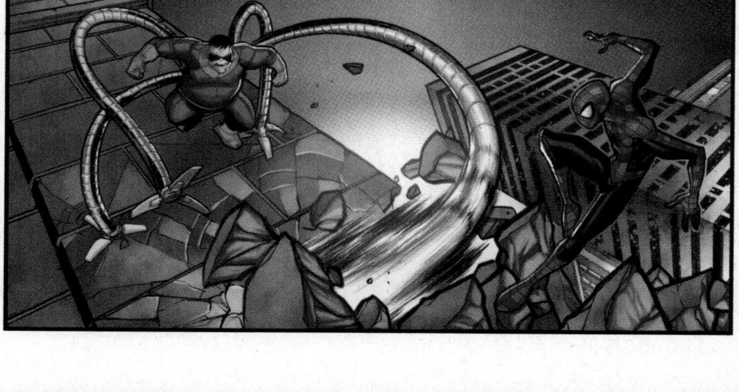

Abilities: Doctor Octopus is one of the world's leading authorities on nuclear radiation and its effects on human physiology. He is also a brilliant engineer and inventor.

Weapons: Doctor Octopus utilizes four mentally controlled, telescoping, prehensile, titanium-steel tentacles that are attached to a stainless-steel harness he wears around his torso. Each tentacle can extend to 24 feet in length, is powered by a small nuclear-powered thermoelectric generator, can move at 90 feet per second, and can strike with the force of a jackhammer. He can use his tentacles to scale walls and move up to 50 mph.

LIZARD

Real name: Curtis Connors

Occupation: Leading researcher in biogenetics, college professor

Legal status: United States citizen with a criminal record

Other current aliases: None

Identity: Known to authorities

Place of birth: Coral Gables, Florida

Marital status: Widower

Known relatives: Martha Connors (wife), William Connors (son)

Group affiliation: Formerly Sinister Twelve

Base of operations: New York City, New York, and West Palm Beach, Florida

First appearance and origin: AMAZING SPIDER-MAN #6 (1963)

History: Army surgeon Dr. Curt Connors' right arm was amputated after a war wound turned gangrenous. Unable to perform surgery any longer, Connors was inspired by a reptile's ability to regenerate lost limbs and became a leading authority in reptilian molecular biology and DNA. After creating a formula to regenerate human limbs, Connors ingested it and regrew his arm. However, the chemical mixture turned him into a bestial human lizard aiming to destroy humans with an army of cold-blooded creatures. Spider-Man (Peter Parker) used his own scientific knowledge and Connors' notes to make an antidote that he forced the Lizard to take, temporarily returning Connors to his human form. Since then, Connors has periodically transformed into the violent Lizard, often battling Spider-Man. Sometime after a maddened Lizard ate Billy, the Jackal (Ben Reilly) cloned Martha and Billy to entice Connors to help him in his failed quest to defeat death by killing all humans and transferring their minds into replaceable clone bodies. To save his family from dying again, Connors was forced to inject them with the Lizard formula, granting them Lizard transformations as well. Whether the Connors family will be able to control their Lizard personas remains to be seen.

Height: (Connors) 5'11"; (Lizard) 6'8" (variable)

Weight: (Connors) 175 lbs.; (Lizard) 550 lbs. (variable)

Eyes: (Connors) Blue; (Lizard) Red pupils

Hair: (Connors) Brown; (Lizard) None

Strength level: Curtis Connors possesses the normal human strength of a man of his age, height, and build who engages in minimal regular exercise. As the Lizard, he can lift (press) 12 tons.

Known superhuman powers: The Lizard can regenerate limbs, release pheromones to induce violence in others, and has a superior reaction time in moderate to warm climates. He can jump 12 feet in a standing high jump and 18 feet in a standing broad jump and run at speeds up to 45 miles per hour. He has an alligator-like hide capable of resisting small-caliber bullets, his 6.5-foot-long tail can be whipped at speeds up to 70 miles per hour, and scores of tiny claws on his fingers and toes enable him to adhere to most surfaces. He can quasi-telepathically communicate and command reptiles within a one-mile radius.

Limitations: When Connors transforms into the Lizard, the R-complex in his brain takes over, making him more bestial and inhuman. Due to his cold blood, exposure to low temperatures can slow his reflexes, and extremely cold temperatures can induce hibernation.

Abilities: Connors is a brilliant medical doctor and surgeon who holds twin doctorates in biology and mutagenic biochemistry and is a leading herpetologist.

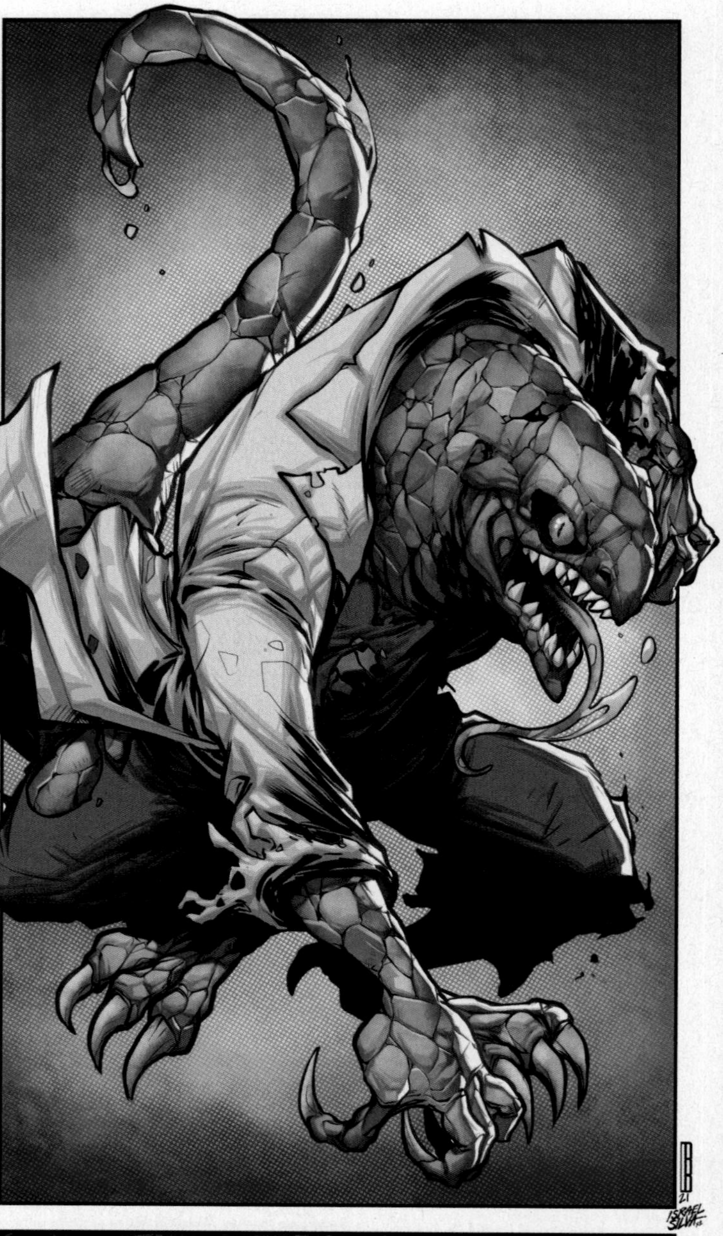

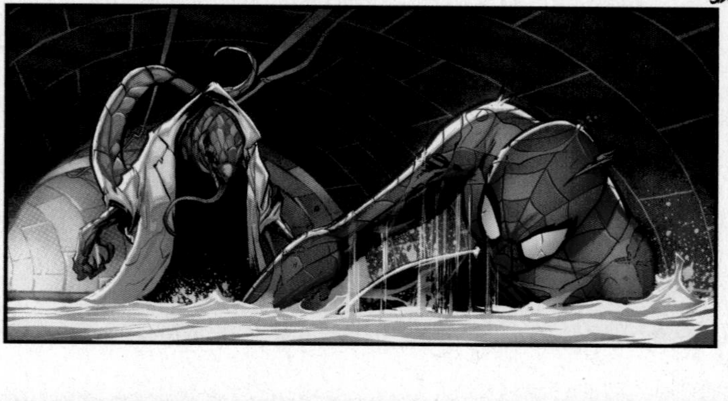

VULTURE

Real name: Adrian Toomes

Occupation: Professional criminal, former electronics engineer

Legal status: Citizen of the United States with a criminal record

Other current aliases: None

Identity: Publicly known

Place of birth: Staten Island, New York

Marital status: Widower

Known relatives: Unidentified wife (deceased), Valeria Jessup (daughter), Frankie Toomes (son), Lenora Toomes (daughter-in-law, deceased), Tiana Toomes (Starling, granddaughter), unidentified son, Ramona (last name unrevealed, daughter-in-law), two unidentified grandsons

Group affiliation: Savage Six, Sinister Six

Base of operations: New York City area

First appearance: AMAZING SPIDER-MAN #2 (1963)

Origin: AMAZING SPIDER-MAN #241 (1983)

History: While engineer Adrian Toomes' attention was focused on creating a harness that would enable the wearer to fly, his business partner, Gregory Bestman, embezzled funds from their small electronics firm and manipulated papers so that the company was only in Bestman's name. After discovering the harness also granted superhuman strength, and despite his advanced age, Toomes set out to terrorize Bestman as the Vulture, and decided to pursue superhuman crime. Vulture's activities eventually brought him into conflict with the crimefighting Spider-Man (Peter Parker), who repeatedly defeated the Vulture even when Vulture teamed with other Spider-Man villains in the Sinister Six. During a later battle with Spider-Man, Vulture grabbed May Parker as a human shield, not knowing she was Spider-Man's aunt. While trying to help her, May's companion and Toomes' friend Nathan Lubensky leaped onto Vulture but suffered a fatal heart attack when the Vulture ascended into the air. Lubensky's death exacerbated the animosity between Vulture and Spider-Man, one that continues to the present. When Vulture's daughter-in-law died during surgery, Vulture became the guardian of his granddaughter, Tiana, for whom he created a similar flight suit. Tiana used the suit to become the superhuman Starling. Vulture remains a threat to society and is at large, working closely with a group of animal-themed superhumans as the Savage Six.

Height: 5'11"

Weight: 175 lbs.

Eyes: Hazel

Hair: None (formerly Brown)

Strength level: Vulture possesses the normal human strength of a man of his age, height, and build who engages in moderate exercise. His harness somehow enhances his musculature, allowing him to lift (press) 700 lbs.

Known superhuman powers: After years of exposure to his flight harness, Vulture can levitate unaided.

Limitations: Vulture is sometimes hindered by his advanced age and poor health.

Abilities: Vulture is a brilliant electronics engineer, inventor, and chemist.

Weapons: Vulture wears an electromagnetic flying harness powered by an anti-graviton generator, which allows him to fly at 95 miles per hour for up to six hours at a maximum altitude of 11,000 feet. The harness' wings can cut concrete, and his costume is armored. Vulture has utilized conventional firearms, a lasso, oil sprayers, tractor beams, grenades, and a device that absorbed the life force of others to temporarily restore his youth.

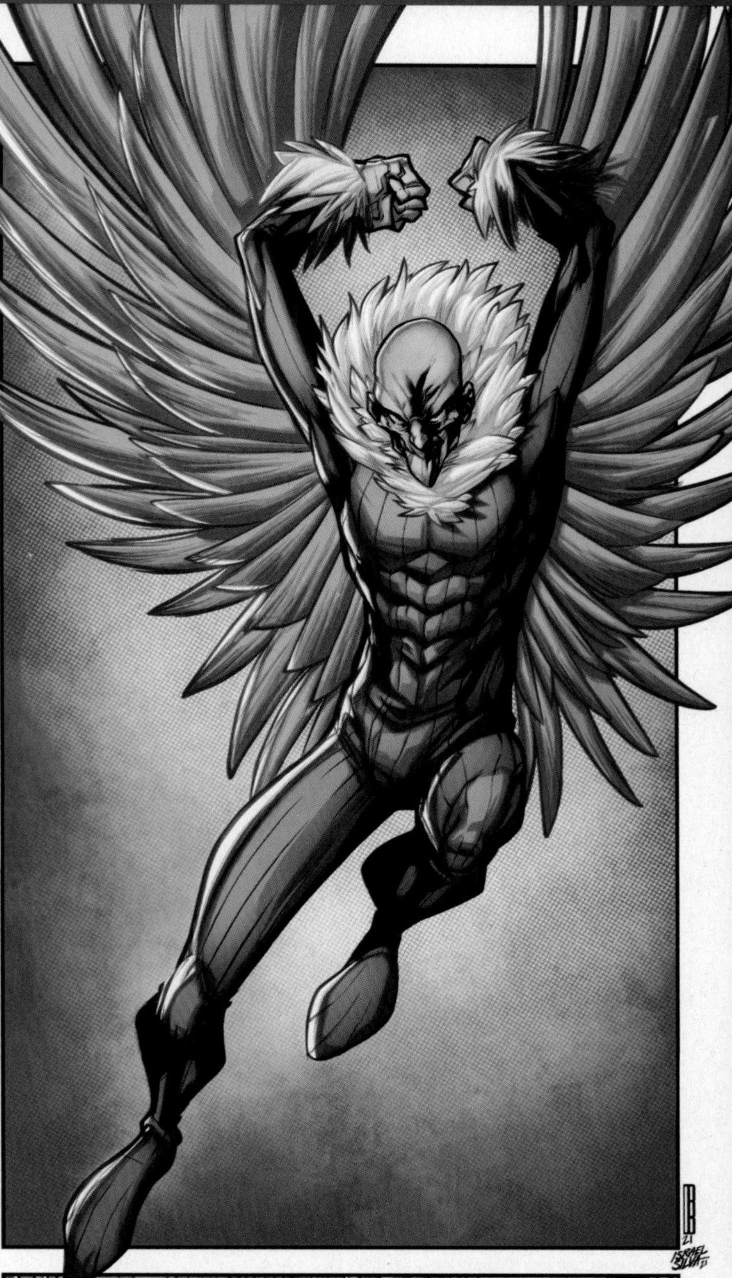
ISRAEL SILVA 21

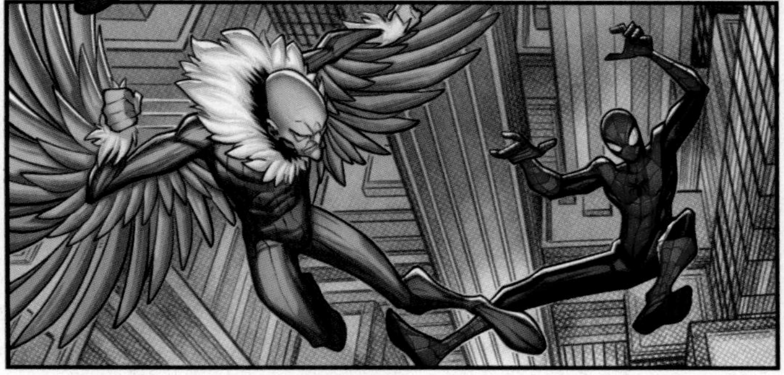

#74 HANDBOOK VARIANT BY DAVID BALDEÓN & ISRAEL SILVA; TEXT BY MIKE O'SULLIVAN

SHOCKER

Real name: Herman Schultz

Occupation: Professional criminal

Legal status: Citizen of the United States with a criminal record

Other current aliases: None

Identity: Publicly known

Place of birth: New York City, New York

Marital status: Divorced

Known relatives: Unidentified mother (deceased), unidentified father, Martin Schultz (brother, deceased), unidentified ex-wife

Group affiliation: Sinister Six

Base of operations: New York City, New York

First appearance and origin: AMAZING SPIDER-MAN #46 (1967)

History: Failed burglar Herman Schultz was serving his third prison term when he used stolen prison-workshop parts to create a device that projected powerful vibrational waves. After using it to escape, he created a special uniform that absorbed the device's shockwave feedback, mounted a projector on each wrist, and began a professional criminal career as the Shocker. However, Shocker was repeatedly defeated by Spider-Man (Peter Parker) and sent back to prison. During a time when Shocker was out of prison, the Punisher (Frank Castle) and the Scourge of the Underworld killed numerous super villains, causing Shocker to suffer panic attacks that, combined with his eroded confidence from constant defeats by costumed super heroes, resulted in his crippling incompetence as a criminal. Shocker subsequently joined forces with other B-level super villains led by Boomerang (Fred Myers) as the Sinister Six, but this group eventually broke up due to the members' self-serving, double-crossing natures. After a positive encounter with She-Hulk (Jennifer Walters), who spoke with him instead of beating him up, Shocker voiced a desire to be a hero instead of a criminal. Despite this, Shocker later tried to rob a Manhattan bank. The hero Rogue (Anna Marie LeBeau) opposed his plan until she had to divert her attention to fight invading monsters from the Darkforce dimension. Seeing the threat to innocents, Shocker aided Rogue in this battle. Because of this, Rogue later served as a character witness when Shocker stood trial for his various crimes, testifying he had potential to be redeemed.

Height: 5'9"

Weight: 175 lbs.

Eyes: Brown

Hair: Brown

Strength level: Shocker possesses the normal human strength of a man of his age, height, and build who engages in moderate exercise. When enhanced by his vibro-shock units, he can punch with the equivalent of superhuman strength.

Known superhuman powers: None

Paraphernalia: Shocker uses two wrist-mounted vibro-shock units to project high-pressure air blasts that hit with concussive force powerful enough to crumble concrete, shatter metal, or gravely damage a human body. He wears a heavily padded suit to protect himself from the effects of his weapons; the suit is bulletproof and projects a vibrational shield that deflects blows and allows him to escape any grasp. Shocker has also used high-tech firearms.

Abilities: Shocker is a gifted, self-taught inventor, a skilled safecracker, and trained in the use of firearms.

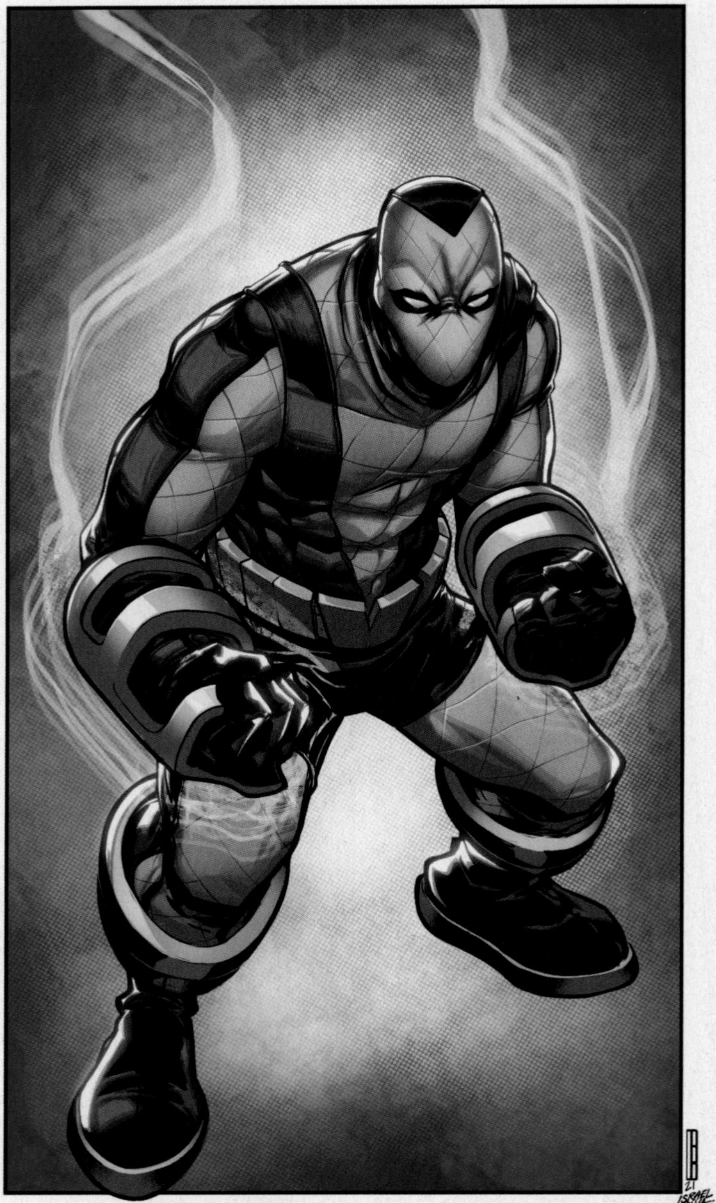
ISRAEL SILVA

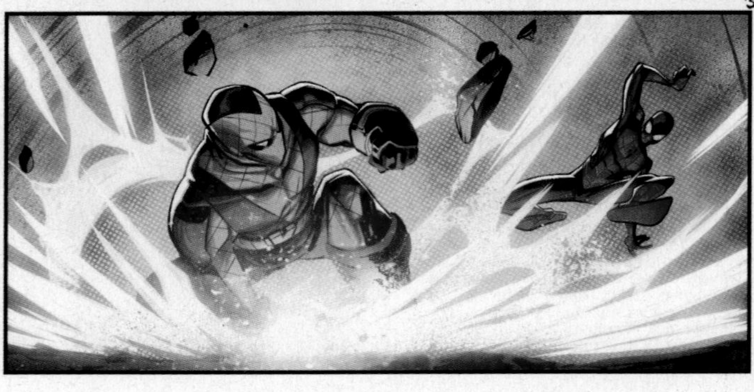

& ISRAEL SILVA; TEXT BY MIKE O'SULLIVAN